RETIRING THE STATE

Retiring the State

The Politics of Pension Privatization in Latin America and Beyond

RAÚL L. MADRID

Stanford University Press
Stanford, California
2003

Stanford University Press
Stanford, California
© 2003 by the Board of Trustees of the
Leland Stanford Junior University.
All rights reserved.

Printed in the United States of America
on acid-free, archival-quality paper.

Library of Congress Cataloging-in-Publication Data

Madrid, Raúl L.
Retiring the state : The politics of pension privatization
in Latin America and beyond / Raúl L. Madrid.
    p.   cm.
Includes bibliographical references and index.
ISBN 0-8047-4706-7 (cloth : alk. paper)
—ISBN 0-8047-4707-5 (pbk. : alk. paper)
1. Pensions—Latin America.   2. Privatization—Latin
America.   I. Title.

HD7130.5 .M33 2003
331.25'22—dc21   2002015664

Original Printing 2003
Last figure below indicates year of this printing:

12   11   10   09   08   07   06   05   04   03

Typeset by G&S Typesetters, Inc. in 10.5/12 Bembo

For Paloma, Nico, and Bela

Acknowledgments

I HAVE ACCUMULATED a great number of debts in the many years that it has taken to complete this book. This study began as a dissertation in the Department of Political Science at Stanford University and was supervised by Terry Karl. In many ways, Terry was the ideal dissertation adviser: warm and enthusiastic, but also intellectually demanding and methodical. I am grateful to her for believing in this project from the beginning and for her labors to improve it. I must also thank the other members of my dissertation committee: Larry Diamond, Geoff Garrett, and Philippe Schmitter. Each made important, and quite different, contributions to this study as well as to my intellectual development more generally. The National Science Foundation, the Department of Political Science, and the Center for Latin American Studies at Stanford helped finance my graduate studies; I hope that this book represents some return on their investment in me.

During my field research in Latin America, I benefited from the assistance of a wide variety of institutions and individuals. More than one hundred scholars, interest group leaders, policymakers, and politicians agreed to be interviewed for this study, and their observations considerably enriched my research. I am particularly grateful to George Avelino, Marcus Faro de Castro, Alvaro Sólon de França, Carlos García, Carlos Gervasoni, Laura Golbert, Luis Gutiérrez, Marcelo Viana de Moraes, Vera Paiva, Vinicius Pinheiro, and Jorge San Martino for going out of their way to make my field research a productive (and pleasant) experience. I would also like to thank Rubén LoVuolo and the Centro Interdisciplinario para el Estudio de Políticas Públicas in Buenos Aires as well as Federico Estévez and the Instituto Tecnológico Autónomo de Mexico in Mexico City for providing me with a congenial work environment during my field research. The Littlefield Fellowship of the Institute for International Studies at Stanford and the Institute for the Study of World Politics generously helped fund my field research.

In the last three years, my research has also benefited from the support and goodwill of my colleagues in the Department of Government of the

University of Texas at Austin. I am particularly indebted to Wendy Hunter and Kurt Weyland, who read an earlier version of this book manuscript and commented on it in great detail. Their comments have improved this study immeasurably; I am only sorry that I was unable to respond adequately to all of their suggestions. A number of other faculty members of the Department of Government, including Catherine Boone, Henry Dietz, and Tse-Min Lin, also provided useful comments on portions of this manuscript. Gratitude is also due to my current and former department chairs, John Higley and James Fishkin, who facilitated my research in numerous ways.

The University of Texas at Austin generously furnished financial support that made the completion of the book manuscript possible. A Dean's Fellowship and a Summer Research Assignment from the College of Liberal Arts at the University of Texas at Austin provided me with the time off from teaching necessary to complete the final revisions of this book. A University Cooperative Society Subvention Grant awarded by The University of Texas at Austin paid for the compilation of the index.

I am also indebted to a large number of colleagues around the world whose research on social security helped make this study possible. Among them, a few people merit special mention. Steve Kay, Evelyne Huber, Robert R. Kaufman, Milko Matijascic, Carmelo Mesa-Lago, Katharina Müller, and Joan M. Nelson provided data and useful comments on different versions of this manuscript or on related papers. I thank them not only for their generosity and insights but also for setting a high standard in research on social security reform. Of course, none of the people mentioned in these acknowledgments is responsible for any errors or omissions in this book.

This book also benefited a great deal from the review process at Stanford University Press. Evelyne Huber and Steven Levitsky provided detailed comments that helped me sharpen the analysis and improve the flow of the book. I am grateful for their insights and also for their enthusiasm for this study. I would also like to thank Amanda Moran, Anna Friedlander, and Kate Wahl of Stanford University Press who shepherded this book through the publication process with grace and efficiency. Alex Giardino provided expert copyediting.

Parts of Chapters 1 and 2 appeared in *Latin American Research Review*, and small sections of Chapters 3, 4, and 5 appeared in *Journal of Latin American Studies*. I am grateful to both journals for granting permission to use these selections here.

My greatest debts are to my family. I would like to thank my mother, Robin Madrid, for encouraging me to pursue a Ph.D., and my father, Arturo Madrid, for encouraging me to do it quickly. I am grateful to them not only for their love and support but also for their intellectual curiosity, which planted the seeds of this book many years ago. This book also benefited from the inspiration and assistance provided by other members of my family, including Marisa Madrid, Carlos, Sarah, and Amalia Madrid, Antonia Castañeda, Concha Madrid and Tony Silva, Ibañez Madrid, Arturo Madrid Sr., and Doria Wilstach.

My two children, Nico and Bela, arrived midway through this project, and they have brightened every day thereafter. I thank them not for their contributions to this book, but for keeping my mind on more important things. My wife, Paloma, has lived with this study as long as I have, and she has contributed to this book in more ways than I can say. My love for her, and for my two children, has seen me through the most difficult moments of the writing process, and it is to them that I dedicate this book.

Contents

Tables

Abbreviations

ABRAPP	Asociação Brasileira das Entidades Abertas de Previdência Privada (Brazilian Association of Open Private Pension Funds)
ADEBA	Asociación de Bancos Argentinos (Association of Argentine Banks)
ADN	Acción Democrática Nacionalista (Democratic Nationalist Action, Bolivia)
AFJP	Administradora de Fondos de Jubilaciones y Pensiones (Administrator of Pension Funds, Argentina)
AFORE	Administradora de Fondos para el Retiro (Administrator of Retirement Funds, Mexico)
AFP	Administradora de Fondos de Pensiones (Administrator of Pension Funds)
AIOS	Asociación Internacional de Organismos de Supervisión de Fondos de Pensiones (International Association of Supervisory Organisms of Pension Funds)
AMCB	Asociación Mexicana de Casas de Bolsa (Mexican Association of Stockbrokers)
AMIS	Asociación Mexicana de Instituciones de Seguros (Mexican Association of Insurance Institutions)
AMPO	Aporte Medio Previsional Obligatorio (Average Mandatory Pension Contribution, Argentina)
ANFIP	Asociação Nacional dos Fiscais de Contribuições Previdenciárias (National Association of Social Security Auditors, Brazil)
ARENA	Alianza Republicana Nacionalista (Nationalist Republican Alliance, El Salvador)
BNDES	Banco Nacional de Desenvolvimento Econômico e Social (National Bank for Economic and Social Development, Brazil)

CANACINTRA	Cámara Nacional de Industria de la Transformación (National Chamber of Industry of the Transformation, Mexico)
CCE	Consejo Coordinadora Empresarial (Business Coordinating Council, Mexico)
CCJ	Comissão de Constituição e Justiça (Committee on the Constitution and Justice, Brazil)
CEBRAP	Centro Brasileiro de Análise e Planejamento (Brazilian Center for Planning and Analysis)
CEDESS	Centro para el Desarrollo Estratégico de Seguro Social (Center for Strategic Development of Social Security, Mexico)
CEP	Centro de Estudios Públicos (Center for Public Studies, Chile)
CEPAL	Comisión Económica para América Latina (United Nations Economic Commission for Latin America)
CGT	Confederación General del Trabajo (General Confederation of Labor, Argentina)
CIDE	Centro de Investigación y Docencias Económicas (Center for Economic Research and Teaching, Mexico)
CIEDESS	Corporación de la Investigación, Estudio y Desarrollo de la Seguridad Social (Corporation for Research, Study, and Development of Social Security, Chile)
CIEPLAN	Corporación de Investigaciones Económicas para Latinoamérica (Corporation of Economic Research for Latin America, Chile)
CMHN	Consejo Mexicano de Hombres de Negocios (Mexican Council of Businessmen)
CNI	Confederação Nacional da Industria (National Confederation of Industry, Brazil)
COB	Central de Obreros Bolivianos (Central of Bolivian Workers)
COBAP	Confederação Brasileiro de Aposentados e Pensionistas (Brazilian Confederation of Pensioners)
CONCANACO	Confederación Nacional de Cámaras de Comercio (National Confederation of Chambers of Commerce, Mexico)
CONDEPA	Conciencia de Patria (Conscience of the Homeland, Bolivia)
CONSAR	Comisión Nacional del Sistema de Ahorro para el Retiro (National Commission of the Retirement Savings System, Mexico)
COPARMEX	Confederación Patronal de la República Mexicana (Employers' Confederation of the Mexican Republic)

CROC	Confederación Revolucionaria de Obreros y Campesinos (Revolutionary Confederation of Workers and Peasants, Mexico)
CTA	Congreso de Trabajadores Argentinos (Congress of Argentine Workers)
CTM	Confederación de Trabajadores Mexicanos (Confederation of Mexican Workers)
CUT	Central Unica dos Trabalhadores (Unique Workers' Central, Brazil)
DP	Partido Democrático Progresista (Progressive Democratic Party, Argentina)
FDN	Frente Democrática Nacional (National Democratic Front, Mexico)
FEBRABAN	Federação Brasileiro dos Bancos (Brazilian Federation of Banks)
FF.AA.	Fuerzas Armadas (Armed Forces)
FIAP	Federación Internacional de Administradoras de Fondos de Pensiones (International Federation of Pension Fund Administrators)
FIEL	Fundación de Investigaciones Economicas Latinoamericanos (Foundation for Latin American Economic Research, Argentina)
FIESP	Federação das Indústrias do Estado de São Paulo (Federation of Industries of the State of São Paulo, Brazil)
FLACSO	Facultad Latinoamericano de Ciencias Sociales (Latin American Faculty of Social Sciences)
FMI	Fondo Monetario Internacional (International Monetary Fund)
FNT	Frente Nacional de Trabajadores (National Front of Workers, Nicaragua)
FREPASO	Frente del País Solidario (Front for Country Solidarity, Argentina)
FSLN	Frente Sandinista de Liberación Nacional (Sandinista National Liberation Front, Nicaragua)
GATT	General Agreement on Tariffs and Trade
GDP	Gross domestic product
IADB	Inter-American Development Bank
IBMEC	Instituto Brasileiro dos Mercados de Capitais (Brazilian Institute of Capital Markets)

IFI	International financial institution
ILD	Instituto de Libertad y Desarrollo (Institute of Liberty and Development, Chile)
ILO	International Labor Organization
IMF	International Monetary Fund
IMSS	Instituto Mexicano de Seguridad Social (Mexican Social Security Institute)
INEGI	Instituto Nacional de Estadísticas Geográficas e Información (National Institute for Geography Statistics and Information, Mexico)
INFONAVIT	Instituto del Fondo Nacional de la Vivienda de los Trabajadores (Institute of the National Housing Fund for Workers, Mexico)
INSS	Instituto Nacional do Seguro Social (National Social Security Institute, Brazil)
IPEA	Instituto de Pesquisa Econômica Aplicada (Institute for Applied Economic Research, Brazil)
ISSA	International Social Security Association
ISSSTE	Instituto de Seguridad Social al Servicio de los Trabajadores del Estado (The Institute of Social Security at the Service of State Workers, Mexico)
ITAM	Instituto Tecnológico Autónomo de México (Autonomous Technological Institute of Mexico)
MIR	Movimiento de la Izquierda Revolucionaria (Movement of the Revolutionary Left)
MNR	Movimiento Nacionalista Revolucionario (Nationalist Revolutionary Movement, Bolivia)
MODIN	Movimiento para la Dignidad y la Independencia (Movement for Dignity and Independence, Argentina)
MPAS	Ministério da Previdência e Assistência Social (Ministry for Social Security and Social Assistance, Brazil)
MU	Movimiento de Unidad (Unity Movement, El Salvador)
MUNJP	Movimiento Unificador Nacional de Jubilados y Pensionados (National Unifying Movement of Pensioners and Retired Persons, Mexico)
NDC	Notional defined contribution
ODEPLAN	Oficina de Planificación Nacional (National Planning Office, Chile)

OECD	Organisation for Economic Cooperation and Development
OLS	Ordinary least squares
PAN	Partido de Acción Nacional (National Action Party, Mexico)
PARM	Partido Auténtico de la Revolución Mexicana (Authentic Party of the Mexican Revolution)
PAP	Prestación Adicional para Permanencia (Additional Benefit for Permanency, Argentina)
PBU	Prestación Básica Universal (Universal Basic Benefit, Argentina)
PC	Prestación Compensatoria (Compensatory Benefit, Argentina)
PCN	Partido de Conciliación Nacional (Party of National Reconciliation, El Salvador)
PDT	Partido Democrático Trabalhista (Democratic Labor Party, Brazil)
PFL	Partido da Frente Liberal (Party of the Liberal Front, Brazil)
PJ	Partido Justicialista (Justicialist Party, Argentina)
PMDB	Partido do Movimento Democrático Brasileiro (The Party of the Brazilian Democratic Movement)
PPB	Partido Brasileiro Progressista (Brazilian Progressive Party)
PRD	Partido de la Revolución Democrática (Party of the Democratic Revolution, Mexico)
PRI	Partido Revolucionario Institucional (Institutional Revolutionary Party, Mexico)
PRONATASS	Programa Nacional de Asistencia Técnica para la Administración de los Servicios Sociales (National Program for Technical Assistance for the Administration of Social Services, Argentina)
PSDB	Partido da Social Democracia Brasileira (Brazilian Social Democratic Party)
PT	Partido del Trabajo (Labor Party, Mexico)
PT	Partido dos Trabalhadores (Workers' Party, Brazil)
PTB	Partido Trabalhista Brasileiro (Brazilian Labor Party)
SAFP	Superintendencia de Administradoras de Fondos de Pensiones (Superintendency of Pension Fund Administrators, Chile)
SAR	Sistema de Ahorro para el Retiro (Retirement Savings System, Mexico)

SHCP	Secretaría de Hacienda y Crédito Público, (Secretariat of Finance and Public Credit, Mexico)
SNTSS	Sindicato Nacional de Trabajadores de Seguro Social (Social Security Workers Union, Mexico)
STF	Supremo Tribunal Federal (Federal Supreme Court, Brazil)
UCEDE	Unión del Centro Democrático (Union of the Democratic Center, Argentina)
UCR	Unión Cívica Radical (Radical Civic Union, Argentina)
UCS	Unión Cívica Solidaridad (Civic Solidarity Union, Bolivia)
UIA	Unión Industrial Argentina (Argentine Industrial Union)
UN	United Nations
UNAM	Universidad Nacional Autónoma de Mexico (National Autonomous University of Mexico)
UN–ECLAC	United Nations Economic Commission for Latin America
UNESCO	United Nations Educational, Scientific and Cultural Organisation
UOM	Unión de Obreros Metalúrgicos (Metalworkers Union, Argentina)
USEM	Unión Social de Empleadores Mexicanos (Social Union of Mexican Businessmen)

RETIRING THE STATE

CHAPTER 1

The Politics of Retiring the State

IN LATIN AMERICA and throughout much of the developing world, governments have increasingly embraced the market. During the course of the last fifteen years, Latin American governments have abandoned interventionist policies in favor of what has come to be known as the neoliberal model. They have cut government spending, privatized state-owned companies, opened up their economies to foreign trade and investment, and liberalized their tax and financial systems. Democratic governments have enacted most of these market-oriented reforms, and they have done so in spite of the vigorous opposition presented by the beneficiaries of the existing state-led development model.

The wave of market-oriented reforms has raised many intriguing questions: Why has the shift taken place so suddenly? Why has it occurred more rapidly in some countries and regions than others? How have democratic reformers implemented the changes in the face of widespread opposition from labor unions, domestic manufacturers, and other traditional beneficiaries of state protection?

A vast number of studies have explored the causes of the recent wave of market-oriented reforms.[1] These studies have generated important insights, but they have suffered from a couple of methodological shortcomings. First, much of the literature consists of individual case studies focused on explaining particular cases, rather than on developing a theory of the determinants of policy reform. A number of insightful studies have examined various countries and developed precise and general hypotheses, but even these studies have typically not tested the hypotheses statistically (Nelson 1990, 1994; Grindle 1991, 1996; Haggard and Kaufman 1992, 1995; Bates and Krueger 1993; Smith, Acuña, and Gamarra 1994; Williamson 1994; Graham 1999; Weyland 2002).[2] Because existing theories of market-oriented reform have not been subject to rigorous quantitative tests, much uncertainty persists about the validity of their claims. Indeed, even the most basic claims of the literature, such as the assertion that crisis tends to lead to reform, continue to be the subject of much debate.

Second, the existing literature tends to treat reform as a single policy, rather than as a package of many different and, at times, contradictory policies.[3] The underlying assumption has been that the causes of different types of reforms are the same (for example, the factors that lead a country to reduce its trade barriers are the same as those that cause a country to reduce its fiscal deficit or privatize its pension system). This assumption is highly suspect, however, given that different types of reforms are governed by different institutional rules and have sharply varying distributions of costs and benefits. Trade liberalization and the elimination of manufacturing subsidies tend to hurt many domestic manufacturers, but these same manufacturers often benefit from financial deregulation, the privatization of state-owned companies, and measures that combat inflation. Moreover, some reforms can be instituted by executive decree, whereas other measures require the approval of the legislature or a constitutional amendment, which makes them much more difficult to enact (Naím 1995; Nelson 1995). It also seems unlikely that the same factors determine the likelihood of all different types of reforms given that countries have often adopted sweeping reforms in some areas and not in others. For example, some countries, such as Chile and Colombia, have opened up their economies dramatically to foreign trade and have privatized numerous state-owned companies, while maintaining significant controls on the flow of capital. Other countries have enacted numerous market-oriented economic reforms, but have so far eschewed major labor and social policy reforms.

This study seeks to avoid the shortcomings of previous works in two ways. First, it focuses on a specific, but extremely important, type of reform: pension privatization. By focusing on a single policy area, this book is able to explore the politics of reform at a level of detail and over a range of cases that would not be possible if it dealt with economic reform more generally. This approach also enables this study to identify and assess the causal weight of variables that do not matter equally across all policy areas. Indeed, many of the variables that play an important role in pension privatization could easily be overlooked in studies that examine reform more generally. The aim of this study is to unravel the determinants of pension privatization rather than market-oriented reform as a whole; however, many of the findings may have relevance for other types of reforms in Latin America and beyond.

Second, this study seeks to remedy the methodological shortcomings of much of the literature on market-oriented reform by using a combination of case study and statistical methods. Many of the arguments presented in this book were developed through extensive field research on pension reform in

Argentina, Brazil, and Mexico. The field research included more than one hundred loosely structured interviews with key policymakers, legislators, interest group representatives, and academics.[4] The hypotheses derived from these case studies were then tested through statistical analyses as well as a qualitative survey of pension reform efforts in other parts of Latin America and the postcommunist world.

The Wave of Pension Privatization

Some of the most sweeping market-oriented reforms of the last decade have occurred in the area of social security.[5] The recent wave of social security reform has affected nearly all regions of the world, but it has done so unequally. In Asia, Africa, and the Middle East, social security reform has been relatively uncommon, and where it has occurred it has been largely confined to adjustments in contribution rates. Among the industrialized countries, social security reform has been widespread, but it has been mostly limited to what have become known as "parametric reforms"—that is, minor adjustments in the parameters of the existing public pension systems. Parametric reforms that reduce benefits or tighten pension eligibility requirements have been particularly common in the industrialized world. To date, the only industrialized countries that have carried out pension privatization schemes are the United Kingdom and Sweden. Beginning in the mid-1980s, a few industrialized countries, namely Australia, Denmark, the Netherlands, and Switzerland, also added compulsory or quasi-compulsory private pension systems to their existing public systems, but they did so without reducing the benefits offered by the latter systems.[6]

Latin America has witnessed the broadest changes in social security policy. Since 1992, ten Latin American countries have pared back or eliminated their existing public pension systems and replaced them with privately managed pension systems based on individual retirement accounts. In the postcommunist world, too, pension privatization has become increasingly common. Since 1996, eight postcommunist countries, including Hungary, Poland, and Kazakhstan, have enacted major pension privatization schemes. Numerous other Latin American and Eastern European nations have either proposed major pension privatization schemes in the past or are planning to do so in the near future. The significance of these reforms can hardly be overstated. The measures radically restructure pension systems that serve millions of people, many of whom will depend on social security as their principal source of income in retirement. The ultimate social and economic effects of these reforms are still unknown, but both supporters and opponents of pension privatization acknowledge that the risks involved are enormous.

The recent privatization schemes are modeled to varying degrees on the

1981 Chilean reform. They allow (or oblige) members of the existing public pension schemes to make their mandatory social security contributions to individual retirement accounts managed by private pension fund administrators instead of to the state-run pension system. Although some countries have opted for partial pension privatization (allowing workers to transfer only a portion of their total publicly mandated pension contributions to the individual retirement accounts), other countries have chosen to carry out full-scale pension privatization schemes that enable workers to transfer most or all of their publicly mandated contributions to individual retirement accounts. Even the most sweeping schemes retain an important role for the state, however, since the state typically continues to provide some guarantees, such as a minimum pension, to members of the private pension system.[7] Moreover, the full-scale privatization schemes typically allow at least some current workers to remain in the public system rather than switching to the new private system, which means that the existing state-managed pension system will only be gradually eliminated.

This book defines "pension privatization" as the partial or complete replacement of a public pension system with a privately managed pension system.[8] Pension privatization, as the term is used here, involves three major types of changes in the way that the pension system operates, although the portion of the pension system affected by these changes varies considerably from country to country. First, the pension privatization schemes involve a shift from public to private management. Whereas the existing pension systems were managed, typically entirely, by the state, the new pension systems are administered, at least partially, by private pension funds. Second, the privatization schemes entail a shift from systems based on defined benefits to systems based on defined contributions. In systems based on defined benefits, workers who contribute for a certain amount of time are guaranteed a specified pension (usually equivalent to a certain portion of their salary) upon retirement. By contrast, in systems based on defined contributions, the contribution levels of workers are fixed but their final pensions will vary depending on the amount of funds in their retirement accounts. Third, the pension privatization schemes involve a shift from a system that operates on a pay-as-you-go or a partly pay-as-you-go basis to a system based, to some degree, on individual capitalization. In pay-as-you-go systems the pension benefits of retirees are financed by the pension contributions of active workers; in systems based on individual capitalization, by contrast, the contributions of each worker go to his or her account alone and are steadily built up for use upon retirement.

This book seeks to explain why pension privatization became so widespread during the 1990s, and why some nations have embraced this new policy model and others have not. It makes three general claims. First, this study argues that pension policy has become increasingly driven by macroeconomic rather than social policy considerations. Policymakers, it suggests, have opted to privatize their pension systems largely in order to boost their domestic savings rates and reduce the long-term economic burden of public pension spending. Variance in the pension reform choices of policymakers can thus be explained in part by two economic factors: the sufficiency of domestic capital sources; and the level of existing public pension obligations.

Second, this study argues that ideational factors have played an important role in shifting the emphasis of pension reform from social to macroeconomic considerations, thereby helping bring about the trend toward privatization. Indeed, it is not possible to understand why policymakers concluded that pension privatization would bring major macroeconomic and social benefits without examining the ways in which ideas about pension privatization were formed. This analysis identifies three principal mechanisms through which belief in the efficacy of pension privatization has spread: (1) regional diffusion of the Chilean model; (2) the expanding influence of international financial institutions, especially the World Bank, in the area of pension policy; and (3) the rise of liberal economists to top social security policy-making positions. Each factor helps explain varying ideational acceptance of pension privatization across time and among countries.

Finally, this book argues that the political fate of pension privatization efforts has depended more on the executive's degree of control of the legislature than on the strength of particular interest groups or the nature of each country's political institutions. Executives whose parties have enjoyed a majority or a near-majority in the legislature have typically managed to enact pension privatization schemes, whereas executives whose parties are small or undisciplined have usually encountered serious obstacles to pension reform. Interest groups and institutions do help shape the details of pension privatization legislation, but they do not typically play a direct and decisive role in determining whether pension privatization schemes are enacted.

This study thus adopts an integrative approach to understanding pension reform. It argues that a combination of economic pressures, ideational variables, and political factors has shaped pension reform efforts in recent years, but that each type of variable has mattered more at a different stage of the reform process.[9] Economic pressures have typically put pension reform on the policy agenda, but such pressures alone cannot explain what led governments to seek to privatize their pension systems or opt for some other type of reform. Ideational factors have helped shape what reform path is taken, but they have not by themselves put pension reform on the policy agenda. Political variables, meanwhile, have helped determine whether each government's reform proposal has been enacted, modified, or blocked, but they have been less important in the initial formulation of the reform proposals.

Implications for Theory

The findings put forth in this book have significant implications for the growing literature on market-oriented reform in developing countries. To begin with, this study suggests that economic crisis does not play an equally important role with all types of reforms. Specifically, economic crisis may be much less closely linked with the so-called second-generation reforms, such as pension, health, civil service, and labor law reform, than it is with the initial structural reforms and stabilization measures. Whereas this study found little evidence that economic crisis per se caused pension reform, it did find a great deal of evidence that certain types of economic problems, namely low savings rates and high public pension spending, led to pension privatization. This suggests that the economic crisis variable needs to be reformulated to specify what kinds of economic problems are associated with which types of reforms.

This book also provides support for those scholars who argue that ideational factors have played an important role in market-oriented reform (Conaghan, Malloy, and Abugattás 1990; Kahler 1992; Stallings 1992; Centeno 1994; Biersteker 1995; Edwards 1995; Domínguez 1997; Hira 1998; Centeno and Silva 1998). Specifically, it indicates that ideas about reform are often regionally diffused—policymakers tend to be more influenced by the policies and programs of neighboring lands than those of distant polities. Thus, policy models tend to be more influential within their particular region of origin than elsewhere, at least at the outset. It also suggests that the power of ideas may be related more to the influence of their proponents than to the intrinsic persuasiveness of the ideas themselves. Proponents of ideas who have political power, technical expertise, and domestic and external linkages will tend to be more successful in promoting their ideas than ideational entrepreneurs that lack these attributes. In addition, this book suggests that ideas tend to be most influential at the middle stages of the reform process and within the executive branch of government. Government policymakers are often looking for solutions to pressing policy problems; thus they are particularly open to new ideas. Once the reform proposal enters the political arena, however, ideas frequently take a backseat to interests.

In addition, my research suggests that scholars of market-oriented reform need to pay a greater degree of attention to the role of the legislature, particularly with regard to second-generation reforms. O'Donnell (1994) and others have argued that in many of the newly democratizing Latin American countries, presidents have largely bypassed the legislature, implementing important policy reforms by decree. This study, however, finds little evidence of "delegative democracy" with regard to pension reform. Indeed, to date, only authoritarian regimes in Peru and Chile have privatized their pension systems by decree. In other countries, governments have sought legislative approval of the reforms, in part to ensure a strong legal foundation for the new pension systems. As a result, the legislature has played an important role in the policy process. Legislatures have blocked pension privatization bills in some Latin American countries and made important modifications to the pension privatization proposals in other nations. As Naím (1995) and Nelson (1995) have suggested, other second-generation reforms may require a similarly high degree of involvement by the legislature because executives have a hard time justifying the enactment of major institutional reforms by decree, particularly in a noncrisis context.

This study contributes an important new dimension to research on the welfare state as well. The welfare state literature has not suffered from the methodological shortcomings that have plagued research on market-oriented reform in developing countries. Welfare state theorists have carried out rigorous statistical analyses as well as rich historical case studies (Pierson 2000).[10] Scholars have also undertaken studies of specific social policy areas, such as housing, unemployment, and health care, as well as broader analyses of the welfare state as a whole.[11] The literature on the welfare state, however, has suffered from a curious bias. Until recently, research in this field has focused almost exclusively on the advanced industrialized countries (especially Western Europe), even though in many cases social programs in Latin America and Eastern Europe are as old and developed as they are in some parts of the industrialized world.[12] As a result of this bias, welfare state scholars may have overestimated the importance of certain variables and underestimated others. This book, for example, suggests that welfare state scholars may have exaggerated the importance of interest-group and institutional barriers to pension privatization (Pierson 1994, 1996; Myles and Pierson 2001). At the same time, they have paid insufficient attention to the macroeconomic and ideational factors that have driven pension privatization in other parts of the world.

In the last several years, a growing number of studies have sought to correct the regional bias of the welfare state literature by examining the politics of social security reform in Latin America and Eastern Europe (Huber and Berensztein 1995; Huber 1996; Mesa-Lago 1997b, 1999; Kay 1998, 1999; Cruz-Saco and Mesa-Lago 1998; Madrid 1999, 2002; Müller 1999, 2002; Orenstein 1999; Huber and Stephens 2000; James and Brooks 2001; Nelson 2001; Coelho 2001; Mesa-Lago and Müller 2002). This literature has consisted for the most part of comparative case studies, which have sought to explain reforms in particular countries or regions. These studies have therefore not demonstrated the methodological pluralism that has been the hall-mark of the welfare state literature as a whole. Nevertheless, the emerging literature on social security in developing countries has generated some important insights, and this study builds on these insights in developing a comprehensive explanation for the pension privatization schemes that took place at the close of the twentieth century.

As noted above, the principal aim of this book is to explain why some countries have privatized their pension systems in recent years, and others have not. The arguments made in this book are supported by a good deal of evidence from Latin America as well as the postcommunist world. In addition, the statistical tests presented in the study suggest that the findings are generalizable to middle- and upper-income countries worldwide. However, the economic, ideational, and political variables discussed here may not be equally important in all regions of the globe. It is particularly unlikely, for example, that these findings apply to low-income countries in Africa and elsewhere, and they may not apply equally well to developing and industrialized countries alike.

The findings of this study have some temporal limitations as well. Many of the variables that shaped the likelihood of pension privatization during the 1990s did not play the same role in the past. As Chapter 2 discusses, the Chilean pension model did not exist prior to 1981, and its true influence was not felt until the end of the 1980s when it had time to accumulate positive results in a number of areas. Before the late 1980s, few people argued that pension privatization would increase a country's savings rate, and some of the most important proponents of pension privatization, such as the World Bank, only began to advocate it in the 1990s. Thus, we would not expect domestic savings rates, World Bank influence, and the local salience of the Chilean model to be correlated with pension privatization in the 1970s or 1980s. The Chilean government's decision to privatize its pension system in 1980 had nothing to do with regional diffusion or World Bank influence and relatively little to do with domestic capital shortages, although the rise of market-oriented economists to positions of policy-making power certainly played an important role in Chile (Borzutzky 1983; Piñera 1991; interviews with Piñera 1997, with Larraín 1997, and with Gazmuri 1997).

As Chapter 8 discusses, it is also uncertain whether the variables high-lighted in this study will be as important in the future as they were in the 1990s. Regional diffusion of the Chilean model, for example, will probably become less significant over time as pension privatization schemes in other countries become better known and studied. The relationship between domestic capital shortages and pension privatization may also become weaker over time unless more substantial evidence emerges that pension privatization will, in fact, increase a country's domestic saving rate. Nevertheless, other variables, such as the economic burden of public pension spending and the executive's degree of control of the legislature, may well continue to be important determinants of the likelihood of pension privatization in the future.

The Evolution of Social Security in Latin America

The first major social security programs in Latin America were established at the beginning of this century, although some minor pension programs for members of the military and state employees date to the early part of the nineteenth century.[13] Argentina, Brazil, Chile, Cuba, and Uruguay were pioneers in the establishment of major social security programs, but other South American countries, along with Costa Rica, Panama, and Mexico, followed suit toward the middle of the twentieth century. The last Latin American countries to create social security programs were rural and relatively undeveloped Central American and Caribbean nations, most of which established their first significant pension programs in the 1960s (Mesa-Lago 1989, 1994).

Throughout the region, social security coverage was initially extended to only a small sector of the population ("Gradual Extension" 1958; Mallet 1970; Mesa-Lago 1978). The first groups to receive pension coverage were typically military officers and state employees, followed by members of the labor aristocracy such as railroad employees, the merchant marines, and workers in other key sectors of the economy (Mesa-Lago 1978). Agricultural and domestic workers and the self-employed have usually been the last groups to be included in pension schemes. Indeed, workers in these occupational categories are still not covered in most of the region, and even in the most developed Latin American countries their rate of coverage is typically low (Mesa-Lago 1991b, 1994). In most cases, governments first extended old-age, disability, and survivors' pensions to the eligible population, followed by health care and family allowances (Mesa-Lago 1978).

The emergence of social security programs in Latin America, as elsewhere, was partly a product of increasing economic development and industrialization, which created a surplus that permitted the financing of large-scale social programs for the first time (Cutright 1965; Collier and Messick 1975; Wilensky 1975). Indeed, the more economically developed countries in the region were typically the first to establish social security programs. Economic development also increased life expectancy and undermined the extended family structures that had been the traditional means of social protection. This created a greater need for social security programs throughout much of Latin America. Growing awareness of social security programs in other countries, facilitated by contacts with the International Labor Organization, clearly played some role in the spread of social security programs as well (Collier and Messick 1975; Usui 1987; Strang and Chang 1993).

Most studies of the origins of social security in Latin America, however, stress the critical role played by domestic political leaders in the formation of the systems (Malloy 1979; Spalding 1980; Rosenberg 1979; Isuani 1985; Papadópulos 1992).[14] In many countries, national political leaders took the initiative in creating social security programs with little pressure from either workers or employers. Politicians established social security programs to woo political support and to co-opt and control emerging labor movements, particularly those composed of workers in key areas of the economy. Indeed, governments often launched social security programs during periods or rising union activity, hoping to calm waves of strikes and demonstrations (Mesa-Lago 1978; Spalding 1980; Isuani 1985; Arellano 1985; Horowitz 1995). Some unions initially opposed the social security programs because they distrusted the state and were reluctant to pay the taxes necessary to fund the systems (Mesa-Lago 1978; Rosenberg 1979; Spalding 1980; Isuani 1985; Papadópulos 1992; Horowitz 1995). Labor unions, however, subsequently gained control of many of the social security funds and became staunch defenders of social security benefits.

From the outset, the pension systems of Latin American countries suffered from a number of deficiencies. First, the social security systems were profoundly inequitable in that coverage was limited to the relatively privileged sectors of the population. Although the level of coverage increased steadily as time passed, only four Latin American countries—Argentina, Cuba, Chile, and Uruguay—had social security programs that covered more than 25 percent of the economically active population in 1960 (Mesa-Lago 1991b: 50). Moreover, even in those four countries, the poorest sectors of the population, such as rural and domestic workers, typically lacked coverage

The social security systems were also inequitable internally, offering more generous pension programs to some groups. The most privileged categories were typically groups with relatively high incomes, such as congressmen, military officers, teachers, and the judiciary (Mesa-Lago 1978, 1989). The social security systems of the pioneer countries—Argentina, Brazil, Chile, Cuba, and Uruguay—were the most stratified. They typically had dozens of different social security programs, and each had different pension benefits, contribution levels, and eligibility requirements. By the 1960s, Chile had eighty different pension schemes, and Cuba had forty different social security institutions (Mallet 1970: 54–55). Most of the countries that established social security programs in the latter part of the twentieth century had more unified systems, but they still usually had special programs for the military and for state employees.

The administration of the Latin American social security systems was highly inefficient, particularly in comparison to the industrialized countries. Administrative costs were typically high and service was often slow. In Chile, administrative costs were estimated to account for 13.9 percent of social security income in 1959 (UN-ECLAC 1968: 37). In many countries, pensioners had to wait months or even years to receive initial pension benefits, and they often needed to pay bribes to intermediaries in order to expedite the process. Some of the administrative inefficiencies were caused by the plethora of different pension schemes, many of which were too small to benefit from economies of scale. However, even the countries with relatively unified systems had substantial administrative problems (UN-ECLAC 1968; Mallet 1970; Mesa-Lago 1978).

To make matters worse, many countries carried out very little actuarial planning. Pension eligibility requirements and benefit and contribution levels were established according to political decisions rather than actuarial calculations. As a result, many pension schemes, particularly those for privileged groups, offered benefits that were unsustainable in the long run. Moreover, because of political pressures, benefits tended to increase at a much faster rate than did contributions. These administrative problems were aggravated by the widespread evasion of payments, which most social security systems were powerless to prevent. In 1960 and 1961, the Argentine social security administration, for example, collected only 53 percent of the social security payments that were due during that period (UN-ECLAC 1968: 36). Evasion was encouraged by the relatively low requirements—in terms of years of contributions—needed to gain access to a pension in many Latin American countries (Mesa-Lago 1991b).

All of these problems were financially manageable while the Latin American social security systems were young, but as they aged, many of them began to encounter financial difficulties. When the Latin American pension systems were first established, they typically had very favorable dependency ratios (that is, the ratio of contributors to pensioners). As the systems matured, however, a larger percentage of the population qualified for pensions, which worsened the dependency ratios. Demographic shifts also hurt the dependency ratios of many Latin American countries by increasing the relative size of the elderly population. Increases in life expectancy, for example, meant that pensioners were living longer, whereas declining birth rates in some countries slowed the growth of the number of contributors to the pension system. In many countries, the maturation of the pension systems was accelerated by the relatively loose requirements for gaining access to pensions. Although average life expectancy in the region increased from fifty-two years of age in the 1950s to sixty-eight years in the 1990s (UN 1995: 118), most Latin American countries failed to increase the minimum age of retirement. Indeed, a few countries, such as Costa Rica, Panama, and Uruguay, actually lowered the minimum retirement age (Mesa-Lago 1991b: 73).

To compound matters, Latin American governments jeopardized the long-term financial health of their pension systems by failing to invest their initial revenue surpluses in financial instruments that would generate dependable interest income for the pension systems (Thullen 1985; Mesa-Lago 1991a, 1991b). The surplus revenue was typically invested in government bonds, which were not indexed against inflation, or it was diverted to fund infrastructure projects, which often had beneficial effects for the countries as a whole but undermined the financial position of the pension systems. Latin American social security systems were initially intended to operate on the basis of full capitalization, meaning that the contributions to the social security system were supposed to generate reserves that would be sufficient to cover the future obligations of the pension system as the system aged. However, most Latin American countries failed to maintain these reserves at adequate levels from the outset. In practice if not by law, Latin American systems shifted from full capitalization to partial capitalization or to a pay-as-you-go basis. The systems that used the pay-as-you-go method took care of pension obligations on an annual basis, maintaining only a small amount of reserves for short-term contingencies.

Beginning in the 1950s, Latin American governments undertook numerous efforts to reform these systems. The reforms, which were promoted by a coalition of domestic social security technocrats and international pension experts associated with the International Labor Organization, consisted principally of parametric changes to the existing public pension systems. The reforms sought to improve the financial health of the systems and make them more efficient and equitable (UN-ECLAC 1968; Mallet 1970; Rosenberg and Malloy 1978). Some of the reforms aimed at extending benefits to other sectors of the population or increasing the level of benefits available to existing members of the systems. Other reforms sought to expand revenues by increasing the level of contributions that workers or their employers were obliged to make to the systems. Still other reforms hoped to improve the financial position of the pension systems by cutting back on benefits or tightening pension eligibility requirements. Finally, in some countries, policy-makers sought to unify the pension schemes on the grounds that the plethora of different schemes was the source of much inefficiency and inequity. These latter measures typically involved cutbacks in benefits for some privileged groups.

Many of these reform efforts foundered in the face of staunch opposition from the beneficiaries of the existing pension systems. The beneficiaries of social security included some of the most powerful interest groups in Latin American society, such as the military, congressmen, state employees, and unions covering workers in key areas of the economy. These groups vigorously opposed any effort to scale back their social security benefits, which made reform difficult to enact. Former Chilean president Eduardo Frei Montalva anticipated this opposition when he announced his intention to reform the Chilean system in 1966: "I am conscious that a project of such importance is going to call forth opposition even stronger than in the case of the agrarian reform project. In social security questions, all sectors agree that the present norms are unsatisfactory and unjust; but when the moment of losing privileges is at hand, violent rebellions arise and all sorts of pressures come into play" (UN-ECLAC 1968: 35).

Efforts to unify fragmented pension systems also provoked resistance from powerful interest groups. Members of privileged pension schemes opposed the unification of the pension system because such measures typically sought to eliminate or reduce their traditional pension privileges. Employees of the smaller pension funds also feared that the consolidation of the funds would eliminate many of their jobs. The leadership of labor unions, meanwhile, often opposed proposals to unify the system because such measures would do away with a major institutional source of patronage for them. In many countries, the unions administered the smaller pension funds, which allowed them to reward allies, punish opponents, and, in some cases, finance union activities.

In the face of such opposition, numerous social security reform proposals foundered, including that undertaken by the Frei Montalva administration in Chile in 1966. In some cases, the interest groups lobbied their allies in the legislature to vote down the reform proposals. In other instances, the interest groups used their control of key social security policy-making posts within the government to torpedo reform proposals at their inception. Often the reform proposals never even left the drawing board because politicians feared antagonizing powerful interest groups, or because they had insufficient incentives to carry out the reforms.

It was not until the 1990s that widespread changes in the social security systems of Latin America took place, although the 1981 Chilean reform presaged the reforms of the ensuing decade. Between 1992 and 2002, ten Latin American nations—namely, Peru, Argentina, Colombia, Uruguay, Mexico, Bolivia, El Salvador, Costa Rica, Nicaragua, and the Dominican Republic—partially or fully privatized their public pension systems, and a number of other Latin American nations placed similar reforms on the agenda.[15] These reforms not only allowed (or in some cases obliged) workers to move from the public pension to new private pension systems, but also they typically slashed the benefits available in what remained of the public pension systems. Minimum retirement ages were increased, privileged pension schemes were eliminated, and state guarantees were scaled back. Never in the history of social security had so much change taken place in such a short period of time.

Degrees of Pension Privatization

The scope of pension privatization has varied substantially from country to country. Mesa-Lago (1996a, 1996b) has developed a useful typology of the reforms. The first type of reform, which creates what Mesa-Lago terms "private substitutive" systems, was carried out in Chile and, subsequently, in Mexico, Bolivia, El Salvador, Kazakhstan, Nicaragua, and the Dominican Republic.[16] This type of reform involves the complete replacement of the existing public pension system with a new private pension system. In some countries, such as Chile, El Salvador, Nicaragua, and the Dominican Republic, the phasing out of the existing public pension system is gradual. Current workers are given the option of joining the new private pension system or remaining in the existing public pension system, whereas future entrants to the labor force are required to join the new private pension system. In other countries, such as Mexico, Bolivia, and Kazakhstan, current as well as future workers are required to join the new private pension system from the beginning and the existing public pension system is shut down immediately. In both cases, however, existing pensioners continue to receive their pensions from the state, and the state continues to offer some guarantees, such as a minimum pension, to members of the private system.

The second type of reform creates what Mesa-Lago calls a "parallel" system. Under this type of reform, the existing public pension system remains open, albeit typically with some modifications, and competes with a new private pension system for members. Thus, future entrants to the labor force as well as current workers are given the option of choosing between the two systems. Both Peru and Colombia have implemented this type of reform. In Colombia, however, only workers who were under the age of forty (thirty-five for women) at the time of the reform could switch to the private system, whereas in Peru workers of any age were allowed to join the private system. Currently, Colombian workers can switch between the public and private systems every three years, whereas Peruvian workers who opt for the public system can switch to the private system at any time, but once they opt for the private system, they cannot switch back to the public system.

The third type of reform establishes what Mesa-Lago characterizes as a "mixed" system. To date, mixed systems have been created in Argentina, Uruguay, Costa Rica, Hungary, Poland, Croatia, Latvia, Bulgaria, Estonia, and a few industrialized countries. In mixed systems, workers typically contribute to the public system as well as the new private system and receive a pension from both systems. In some cases, however, they may choose (or be obliged) to join only one of the two systems. In Argentina, the employer's social security contribution continues to go to the (reformed) public system and workers receive a flat public benefit based on it. Workers must choose, however, where they want their individual contribution to go. If they choose to contribute to the public system, they receive an additional public pension benefit, whereas if they choose to contribute to the new private system, they receive a private pension that supplements their flat public benefit. In Uruguay, the employer's contribution continues to go to the public system, as does the pension contributions that employees make on the first 5,000 Uruguay pesos that they earn each month.[17] The contributions made on any salary exceeding 5,000 Uruguayan pesos per month, however, go to the private system, earning the workers a private pension to supplement their public benefit.

All three types of pension privatization schemes have excluded categories of workers based on their age at the time of the reform. The reforms in El Salvador, Nicaragua, Uruguay, and Colombia, for example, allowed or obliged workers above a certain age to continue to contribute to the public system and to retire under the rules prevailing prior to the reforms.[18] The recent reforms have also exempted certain occupational categories. The armed forces, for example, were excluded from the pension privatization schemes in every country save Bolivia, enabling members of the military to retain their traditional pension privileges. In Colombia, the reform also exempted legislators, public-school teachers, and oil workers, as well as members of various provincial and municipal pension funds. The Dominican and Mexican reforms, meanwhile, excluded most state employees, whereas the Uruguayan reform exempted notaries and university and bank employees.

Some of the pension reforms have called for the state to establish public pension fund administrators that will compete with privately owned pension fund administrators in the new private pension system.[19] Under the Argentine and Uruguayan reforms, state-owned banks established pension fund administrators that operate in the private system, and in Mexico, the state agency that had traditionally run the public social security system—the Mexican Social Security Institute (IMSS)—cofounded a pension fund administrator. The Costa Rican reform authorized a state-owned bank as well as the state agency in charge of the public social security system to establish pension fund administrators that will compete in the private system. The Dominican reform also called for the creation of at least one state-owned pension fund administrator. Many of the reforms have also permitted nonprofit institutions, such as cooperatives and labor unions, to establish pension funds, but these institutions have typically only gained a small share of the market.

One way to compare the different reforms on a single scale is by the degree of pension privatization in each country. Table 1.1 presents an index of pension privatization.[20] The index was derived by calculating the percent-

TABLE I.I

Index of Degree of Pension Privatization

Country	Contributions to private pillar/total contributions* (1)	Members of private system/ total members (2)	Score on privatization index (1 × 2)
Argentina	.41	.67	.27
Bolivia	1.00	1.00	1.00
Chile	1.00	.95	.95
Colombia	.93	.38	.35
Costa Rica	.36	1.00	.36
Dominican Republic	1.00	.90**	.90
El Salvador	1.00	.91	.91
Mexico	.82	1.00	.82
Nicaragua	1.00	1.00**	1.00
Peru	1.00	.58	.58
Uruguay	.375***	.39	.15

SOURCES: Mesa-Lago 1997, personal communication; Queisser 1998; Palacios and Pallarès-Miralles 2000; legislation from individual countries.
*For those people belonging to the private system.
**Estimates.
***This figure assumes that the members of the private pension system earn the equivalent of 10,000 May 1995 pesos on average.

age of all state-mandated pension contributions (from both employees and employers) that members of the private system contribute to the private system, multiplied by the percentage of total members who choose, or are obliged, to join the private system. The index provides a way to rank mixed, parallel, and fully private systems on a single continuum. It takes into account not only the extent to which workers contribute to the private system, but also whether membership in the private system is voluntary or obligatory, and what sorts of incentives, if any, are provided for workers to join the private system.[21] This index can also capture whether there are certain groups that are left out of the privatization scheme (for example, the armed forces or state employees) and whether workers can and do opt to join pension funds that are managed by state agencies that compete in the private system. I did not take the latter two factors into consideration in assigning scores to each reform here because I lacked comprehensive data on these issues. The scores provided in the table are therefore based on membership and contributions in the *main* private and public pension systems and are derived largely from data provided in Mesa-Lago (1997a). Not surprisingly, the reforms that establish private substitutive systems involve the greatest degree of privatization, and the reforms that create mixed systems involve the least amount of privatization.

The reforms have also varied in a number of other ways that have little or nothing to do with the degree of privatization, as Table 1.2 makes evident. Different countries have decided to compensate workers in different ways for past contributions to the public pension system, and some countries have opted not to compensate them at all. Chile, Peru, Colombia, Argentina, Bolivia, El Salvador, Nicaragua, and the Dominican Republic all offer recognition bonds or special pensions to compensate workers who switch to the private pension system for their past contributions to the public system. These bonds and pensions vary considerably in terms of how they are calculated and who is eligible to receive them. Mexico does not compensate workers for past payments to the public system, but, upon retirement, workers who contributed to the previous system are allowed to choose between a private pension and a public pension that is calculated according to the rules prevailing prior to the reform.

In many countries, the reforms significantly changed the level of contributions workers and their employers make to the pension systems. Many of the countries reduced or eliminated the employer's contribution and increased the worker's contributions. Chile, Peru, and Bolivia, for example, eliminated the employer's contribution to the private pension system, whereas Argentina and Uruguay reduced it.[22] The Salvadoran, Nicaraguan, and Colombian reforms, however, increased the employers' contributions, whereas Mexico maintained it at the same level. Workers' contributions to the pension systems were increased in Colombia, El Salvador, Nicaragua, Argentina, Uruguay, Bolivia, Chile, and Peru. The latter four countries, however, offset these changes by obliging employers to raise their employee's salaries. Thus, the take-home pay of workers in Uruguay, Bolivia, Chile, and Peru increased or remained the same as a result of the reforms. In Argentina and Uruguay, the employer's contributions go entirely to the public pension system, whereas in the other countries, the employers' contributions go to whichever system the worker belongs. In all of the countries, the worker's contributions are paid into the system of which he or she is a member, except in the case of Uruguay, where the worker's contribution is divided between the two systems according to the worker's salary level.

Many of the reforms tightened the eligibility requirements for pensions. The minimum retirement age for both men and women was increased in Argentina, Bolivia, Colombia, Chile, Peru, and Uruguay. In Costa Rica, Nicaragua, Mexico, and El Salvador the minimum retirement age remained the same, although in the latter two countries the government had initially proposed increasing it. Argentina, Colombia, Mexico, Uruguay, and Nicaragua

TABLE 1.2

Pension Privatization Schemes in Latin America

	Argentina	Bolivia	Colombia	Chile	El Salvador	Mexico	Peru	Uruguay
Date enacted (implemented)	Sept. 1993 (July 1994)	Nov. 1996 (May 1997)	Dec. 1993 (Apr. 1994)	Nov. 1980 (May 1981)	Dec. 1996 (Apr. 1998)	Dec. 1995 (July 1997)	Dec. 1992 (June 1993)	Sept. 1995 (Apr. 1996)
Type of system created	Mixed	Private (substitutive)	Parallel	Private (substitutive)	Private (substitutive)	Private (substitutive)	Parallel	Mixed
Which system covers people in the workforce at the time of reform?	Both systems (private system is optional)	Private system	Either system (workers over 40 remain in public system)	Either system	Either system for workers 36–55; workers <36 go to the private system and >55 to the public system.	Private system	Either system	Both systems (private system is optional for low-income workers or workers >40)
Which system covers future entrants to the labor force?	Both systems (private system is optional)	Private system	Either system	Private system	Private system	Private system	Either system	Both systems (private system is optional for low-income workers)
What happens to the existing public system?	Reformed	Closed	Reformed	Reformed and phased out	Reformed and phased out	Closed	Reformed (1995)	Reformed
Groups exempted from the reform	Armed forces; provincial and municipal employees	None (Armed forces are incorporated under special rules)	Armed forces; congressmen; schoolteachers; oilworkers; provincial and municipal employees	Armed forces	Armed forces	Armed forces; most public-sector employees; oil workers	Armed forces	Armed forces; bank and university employees; notaries

Who operates pension fund administrators?	Domestic and foreign firms, public entities, cooperatives, and labor unions	Domestic and foreign firms	Domestic and foreign firms, public entities, cooperatives, and nonprofits	Domestic and foreign firms, labor unions	Domestic and foreign firms	Domestic and foreign firms and public entities	Domestic and foreign firms	Domestic and foreign firms and public entities
Are past contributions to the public system compensated?	Yes, through a compensatory pension	Yes, through a compensatory pension	Yes, through a recognition bond that pays interest	Yes, through a recognition bond that pays interest	Yes, through a recognition bond that pays interest	No, but workers can elect to retire under the pre-reform rules	Yes, through a recognition bond that doesn't pay interest	No
Any changes to worker's contributions under reform?	Increased to 11% of salary	Increased to 12.5% of salary, but salaries were increased to compensate	Increased to 3.375–4.375% of salary	Increased to 13.1% in the private system and 18.8–20.7% in the public system	Gradually increased to 6.75% in the private system and 7% in the public system	Remained at 2.125% of salary	Increased to 11% in private system (1995); increased to 13% in public system (1996)	Increased 1% to 15%, but offset by salary increase
Any changes to employer's contributions under reform?	Remained at 16% of salary (subsequently reduced)	Eliminated, but employers had to increase salaries by a corresponding amount	Increased to 10.125% of salary	Eliminated, but employers had to increase salaries by a corresponding amount	Gradually increased to 6.75% in the private system and 7% in the public system	Remained at 7.95% of salary	Eliminated, but employers had to increase salaries by a corresponding amount	Decreased 1% to 12.5%, but employers had to increase salaries by 1%
Total pension contribution levels?	27%	12.5%	14.5%	13.1% in private system, 18.8–20.7% in public system	13.5% in private system; 14% in public system	10.075% plus a contribution from the state of about 2.0%	11.8% in private and 13% in public (since 1996)	27.5%

(continued)

TABLE 1.2
(continued)

	Argentina	Bolivia	Colombia	Chile	El Salvador	Mexico	Peru	Uruguay
Any changes to the minimum retirement age under reform?	Gradually increased to 65 for men and 60 for women	Increased to 65 for both sexes	Gradually increased to 62 for men and 57 for women in public system; no minimum in private system	Increased to 65 for men and 60 for women (in 1979 prior to reform)	Remained at 60 for men and 55 for women	Remained at 65 for both sexes	Increased to 65 for both sexes	Increased to 60 for both sexes
Any changes to the years of contributions required?	Increased to 30 years of contributions	No minimum	Increased from 10 to 20 years in the public system; no minimum in private system	No minimum in private system	25 years of contributions required to retire at the minimum age	Increased to 24 years of contributions	Increased to 20 years of contributions	Increased from 30 to 35 years
Is there a minimum pension?	Yes (requires 30 years of contributions)	No, but all people over 65 receive a flat pension	Yes (requires 23 years of contributions)	Yes (requires 20 years of contributions)	Yes (requires 25 years of contributions)	Yes (requires 24 years of contributions)	Yes, but not yet implemented in the private system	Yes (requires 35 years of contributions)

SOURCES: Mesa-Lago 1997, 2001; Mesa-Lago and Bertranou 1998; Cerda and Grandolini 1997; Lora and Pagés 2000, Devesa-Carpio and Vidal-Melía 2001.

also increased the minimum years of contributions required to be eligible for a pension.

Research Design

Pension reform in Latin America and beyond has thus varied considerably from country to country. It has varied not only in terms of the degree of privatization, but also in terms of what kinds of changes have been made to contribution rates, eligibility requirements for benefits, and many other issues. This study seeks to explain not only why countries opted (or declined) to privatize their pension systems, but also why their privatization schemes took certain forms.[23]

The following chapters examine the politics of pension privatization using three complementary research methods: (1) a focused comparison of three cases; (2) a broad qualitative survey of other pension reform efforts in Latin America and Eastern Europe; and (3) statistical analyses of the determinants of pension privatization throughout the world. This study uses different methods to attack the same basic research question—a process known as "triangulation" (Tarrow 1995)—because a combination of these methods yields greater insights and provides more rigorous hypothesis testing than does the use of any one of these methods alone. Each of these methods has distinct advantages. The statistical method, for example, provides the most rigorous test of the hypotheses. By making use of a large number of cases, it guards against the bias that would result from the selection of a few unrepresentative cases to test a given theory. Statistical techniques also provide an effective way to measure the individual impact of each variable by controlling for the effect of other variables.

The comparative case study method, by contrast, is particularly useful for the development of hypotheses (Lipjhart 1971; Eckstein 1975). In case studies, scholars can use process tracing to identify the causal mechanisms that connect certain variables to policy outcomes (George 1982). Case studies often permit researchers to see how different variables interact to produce outcomes in ways that are not readily apparent. The case study method also enables scholars to examine a vast number of potential causal variables—and not just those variables for which a large-n data set is available or can be readily assembled. Moreover, the use of the comparative case study method allows scholars to examine the causes and significance of subtle variations in the values of the variables that may be obscured by quantitative data or coding.

Although case studies cannot by themselves rigorously test hypotheses (especially if the hypotheses have been developed on these same cases), they can serve as a useful complement to other methods of testing. Crucial case studies can serve as preliminary tests of hypotheses, and deviant case studies can be used to explore the limits of existing theories (Lipjhart 1971; Eckstein 1975). Process tracing, meanwhile, can be used to guard against purely spurious correlations. Case studies can also be used to test the observable implications of the hypotheses under study—a form of within-case testing (Campbell 1975; King, Keohane, and Verba 1994). Finally, case study methods can be used to test for measurement error, such as conceptual stretching (Sartori 1970), since they allow the researcher to gain a greater familiarity with the data for those cases that are the subject of intensive study.

The broad survey approach takes an intermediary position between these two methods. This method will often provide a more rigorous test of hypotheses than do case study methods, since it uses a larger set of observations to test hypotheses. Although this approach cannot test hypotheses at the same level of rigor as the statistical method, it can be quite useful where data limitations prevent some or all of the hypotheses from being tested using quantitative techniques. This method may also help scholars develop and refine hypotheses since it permits researchers to trace the processes through which the independent variables influence outcomes in a variety of contexts. However, the number of cases involved necessarily limits the amount of process tracing that can be implemented.

This study employs a comparable case methodology (Lipjhart 1975). The goal of this methodology is to control for the large number of presumably irrelevant independent variables that might otherwise be assumed to play a role in explaining the different outcomes on the dependent variable. The cases that were chosen for intensive analysis—Argentina, Brazil, and Mexico—are roughly similar in a large number of cultural and socioeconomic characteristics, but they have different outcomes on the dependent variable under study. Whereas Mexico has fully privatized its social security system, Argentina has adopted a mixed public/private system, and Brazil has yet to implement any significant social security reform whatsoever. The inclusion of an intermediate case, Argentina, not only allows greater variation on the dependent variable but also helps to avoid another methodological pitfall: the selection of cases with extreme values on the dependent variable (Collier and Mahoney 1996; Geddes 1990).

The cases chosen differ in terms of the type of reforms the executives initially proposed, as well as in the degree of success that the executives have had in getting these proposals enacted. Whereas the government of Mexico enacted a reform that closely resembled its initial proposal, the Argentine government was obliged to alter its proposed reform substantially, and the government of Brazil had its reform proposal largely eviscerated. This mix of cases enables two important questions to be addressed: What leads a government to propose certain kinds of social security reforms? And what determines whether a government is able to enact its preferred reform proposals?

The book unfolds as follows. Chapter 2 lays out the theoretical argument in more detail, discussing the economic, ideational, and political factors behind pension privatization. Chapters 3–5 explore the fate of pension reform efforts in Mexico, Argentina, and Brazil, respectively. Chapter 6 examines how well the arguments made in this book can explain the fate of other pension reform efforts in Latin America, Eastern Europe, and the former Soviet Union. This chapter also tests these arguments statistically through analyses of the determinants of pension privatization worldwide. Chapter 7 discusses how interest groups and institutions have shaped the content of the recent reforms. Chapter 8 discusses the significance of these findings for existing theories of the welfare state and market-oriented reform and examines the policy implications of Latin America's experience with pension privatization.

CHAPTER 2

Explaining Pension
Privatization in the 1990s

THE RECENT WAVE of pension privatization is puzzling given the well-known political costs of social security reform. In the United States, social security is commonly referred to as the "third rail" of politics because of its tendency to "electrocute" those politicians who attempt to tamper with it. In Latin America, social security reform is equally controversial. Indeed, until recently, no major social security reform in Latin America took place under democratic rule (Malloy 1985). Not surprisingly, then, the recent pension privatization proposals have generated a great deal of resistance in Latin America and beyond. Opposition political parties, labor unions, pensioners' associations, and the beneficiaries of privileged pension schemes have typically led the charge against social security privatization, but the population as a whole has also greeted pension privatization proposals with skepticism. In a 1995 poll of ten Latin American countries by Latin Barometer, only 27 percent of the respondents stated that private enterprises should be in charge of pensions, whereas 73 percent of the interviewees responded that such pensions should be the responsibility of the government (Basáñez 1997: 15). Where social security privatization schemes have come before the electorate, as in Ecuador and New Zealand, they have been soundly defeated.

Pension privatization has met staunch opposition in large part because it imposes considerable financial risks on workers since they will bear the costs if the funds in their retirement accounts do not reap sufficient returns.[1] Many of the pension privatization schemes have also reduced, at times dramatically, the benefits offered by the public pension systems. Countries that have privatized their pension systems have not only eliminated some state pension guarantees, but also they have abolished many of the pension privileges available to members of certain occupational categories. In addition, they have frequently tightened pension eligibility requirements by raising the minimum age of retirement or the minimum years of contributions. In some cases, they have even boosted the size of the contributions that workers must pay into the pension systems. These changes have been undertaken not only to cut expenditures in the public systems, which reduces the cost of the transition from a public to a private system, but also to ensure that contribution rates and pension entitlements in the private and public schemes are roughly comparable.

What then explains the recent wave of pension privatization measures in Latin America and elsewhere? Why have so many political leaders sought to enact reforms in spite of the political opposition to such measures? And what accounts for the variance in the recent trend? Why have some governments opted to privatize fully their pension systems, while other governments have opted to privatize partially or have eschewed privatization altogether?

This chapter offers an explanation for the recent pension privatization schemes in Latin America and beyond. First, the chapter discusses some of the shortcomings of the academic literatures on market-oriented reform and the welfare state and why they cannot account for the recent wave of pension privatization. It then sets forth a new explanation for patterns of pension privatization in the 1990s, which integrates economic, ideational, and political factors. The chapter examines both the economic considerations that placed pension reform on the agenda in the last decade and the ideational influences that led numerous governments to seek to privatize their pension systems rather than carry out some other type of pension reform. Finally, it analyzes the political factors that have helped determine the ultimate fate of the pension privatization proposals.

A Power Resources Explanation

One potential explanation for the recent wave of pension privatization in Latin America stems from the dominant paradigm in the welfare state literature, the so-called power resources approach. The power resources approach attributes temporal and cross-national differences in the size and nature of social policy programs principally to the distribution of political resources between business and labor (Huber and Stephens 2001; Esping-Andersen 1985; Korpi 1983; Stephens 1979).[2] From this perspective, the recent wave of social security reforms might be viewed as the product of the rising clout of business and conservative political parties and of the decline of labor movements and their political allies.[3]

An explanation for the recent wave of pension privatization based primarily on the changing balance of political power between business and labor is inadequate for several reasons. Pension reform has been pushed not only by conservative business-allied parties but also by traditionally populist parties, some of which have close ties to the labor movement.[4] For example, political parties with close ties to the labor movement have pushed for pension privatization in Argentina and Mexico as well as in Hungary and Poland. Indeed, many of the political parties that have carried out pension privatization in Latin America were responsible for the development of the public pension systems in the first place. Moreover, neither business nor labor has played a decisive role in determining whether pension privatization has been implemented. Other factors, particularly the ruling party's legislative strength and discipline, have proven to be far more crucial to the fate of pension privatization proposals. Finally, neither business nor labor strength appears to be able to explain the variance in pension privatization. Indeed, countries with well-organized business communities or weak labor movements are not any more likely to privatize their pension systems than countries with poorly organized business sectors or strong labor movements.

A power resources approach does yield some important insights into the politics of pension privatization, however. In recent years, growing capital mobility has clearly increased the political power of business by providing it with a credible exit option. As the power resources perspective would expect, the business community has supported pension privatization, and it has used its increased political influence to press governments to enact privatization schemes. In a number of instances, members of the business community have persuaded the government to expand the scope of the privatization schemes, to loosen the proposed regulations governing the operation of the private pension system, or otherwise to alter the reform legislation to suit the interests of the private sector. The labor movement, meanwhile, has typically resisted pension privatization, but declining unionization levels as well as the rise in capital mobility have undermined the ability of organized labor to block the privatization measures. Although the labor movement has not typically been strong enough to block pension privatization outright, it has, at times, managed to alter the reform proposals to benefit the unions. Labor unions with close ties to the ruling party have been particularly successful at modifying proposed pension privatization proposals.

The Role of Crisis

Another explanation for the recent wave of pension reforms, which emanates from the theoretical literature on market-oriented reform in developing countries, would focus on the role of economic crisis. Much of the existing literature on market-oriented reform in developing countries identifies economic crisis as one of the principal causes of reform (Weyland 2002; Haggard and Kaufman 1995; Rodrik 1996; Drazen and Grilli 1993).[5] Bates and

Krueger (1993: 452) argue that "crisis is perhaps the more frequent stimulus to reform." In all of the country studies included in their volume, "reforms have been undertaken in circumstances in which economic conditions were deteriorating" (Bates and Krueger 1993: 454). In a recent survey of the literature on economic reform, Tommasi and Velasco (1995: 13–14) conclude "that economic crises seem either to facilitate or outright cause economic reforms is part of the new conventional wisdom on reform."

What constitutes a crisis has not always been made clear, but where scholars have been specific they have usually focused on inflation. Bruno and Easterly (1996: 214), for example, argue that "broader reforms [are] the children of high-inflation crises." Weyland (1998: 650) similarly contends that hyperinflation is likely to lead to economic reform because it "is the economic problem that most severely threatens to disorganize a country's economy; that imposes high costs on the largest number of people." Remmer (1998: 10), meanwhile, argues that high inflation may undermine price controls and "a broad array of other politically protected benefits, including agricultural price supports, minimum wages, unemployment benefits, and public sector salaries."

Neither inflation nor economic recession can explain the recent efforts of Latin American countries to privatize their pension systems, however. Most of the Latin American countries that have privatized their pension systems were not facing an economic crisis at the time. Bolivia, Chile, Colombia, Costa Rica, El Salvador, and Nicaragua had all enjoyed relatively strong economic growth and low inflation for several years before they enacted their privatization schemes, and Argentina and Peru were in the midst of economic recoveries. Only Mexico and Uruguay were truly in an economic recession when they privatized their pension systems, and neither of these countries suffered from hyperinflation. Moreover, as the statistical analyses presented in Chapter 6 show, countries that have experienced hyperinflation or economic recession at some point during the 1980s and 1990s are not significantly more likely to privatize their pension systems.

Another problem with attributing pension privatization to hyperinflation is that pension privatization does nothing to combat runaway price rises. On the contrary, pension privatization may worsen hyperinflation by dramatically increasing the size of a government's fiscal deficit. Thus, it is not clear why a government would respond to hyperinflation by privatizing its pension system. We might, in fact, reasonably expect governments facing hyperinflation and economic crises to be quite reluctant to privatize their pension systems, at least in the short run. Hyperinflation and economic crisis in general may discourage pension privatization by undermining public confidence in the ability of the private sector to manage effectively the retirement funds. Workers and policymakers alike may fear that declining stock prices and high inflation will erode the real value of their retirement funds. Under situations of crisis, policymakers thus may become less likely to propose pension privatization schemes, and workers may become more apt to resist such schemes if they are proposed.

Nevertheless, economic crises may facilitate pension privatization in a number of indirect ways over the long run. First, economic crises may undermine support for the existing development model, which in Latin America and many other regions was associated with state management of the economy. In the wake of the crises of the 1980s, market-oriented reforms, such as pension privatization, became increasingly popular among Latin American policymakers, many of whom blamed government mismanagement for the crises. Second, economic crises may gradually weaken those groups that oppose pension privatization and strengthen those groups that support it. Certainly, the economic crises of the 1980s increased the influence of the World Bank and neoliberal economists in Latin America, both of which played an important role in promoting pension privatization. Third, economic crisis may undermine the financial position of the public pension system, which creates pressure for reform. Economic crises, for example, cut into the revenues of the public pension systems in many Latin American countries and wiped out the reserves that some public pension systems in the region had built up over many decades. Finally, economic crises may undermine a country's domestic savings rate and increase its vulnerability to capital flight, both of which will increase the attractiveness of pension privatization.

Thus, in the long run, economic crisis may set the stage for pension privatization through its effect on a number of other variables, such as the domestic savings rate, the financial position of the pension system, and the influence of neoliberal economists and the World Bank. Economic crisis is only one of the many factors that affect these variables, however. In many cases, it is not even the important influence. As a result, the relationship between economic crisis and pension privatization is a relatively weak one, as the statistical analyses demonstrate. This study argues that two other economic factors—rising public pension spending and low domestic savings rates—played a much more important role than economic crisis did in bringing pension privatization to the top of the policy agenda. Policymakers have sought to privatize their pension systems, not in response to hyperinflation, but rather because of concerns about local capital shortages and the economic burden of public pension spending. Many policymakers have believed, rightly or wrongly, that privatizing their public pension systems would boost their domestic savings rate and cut their public pension expenditures, thereby reducing their dependence on unstable foreign capital and freeing up resources for other, more productive, uses. As a result, public pension spending and domestic savings rates have had a stronger, more direct, and more immediate impact on the likelihood of pension privatization than has economic crisis.

Rising Public Pension Spending

Public pension systems have become an increasing economic burden for many countries across the globe, especially in Latin America, Eastern Europe, and the industrialized world. During the last several decades, public pension expenditures have increased rapidly. Between 1960 and 1995, public pension expenditures in the OECD countries rose from approximately 4.6 percent of GDP to approximately 9.7 percent of GDP (Pierson 2001: 88–89; Palacios and Pallarès-Miralles 2000: 31–32). Pension expenditures rose even more quickly in Eastern Europe, jumping from approximately 6 percent of GDP in 1980 to approximately 11 percent in 1995 (Holzmann 1997: 9). Social security expenditures in Latin America and the Caribbean, meanwhile, remained much lower than those in Europe, but they nevertheless increased dramatically, climbing from 3.3 percent of GDP in 1980 to 5.8 percent of GDP in the early 1990s (Mesa-Lago and Bertranou 1998: 105). Barring some kind of reform, public pension expenditures are projected to rise even more quickly in many of these countries during the years ahead.

The increased expenditures stem from a number of factors. Demographic trends, such as rising life expectancies and declining birth rates, have contributed to the financial problems by causing the world's population to age. The aging of the population has been particularly noticeable in Europe and the former Soviet Union, but it is also quite apparent in the Southern Cone of Latin America. The demographic trends have meant that the percentage of the population eligible for pension benefits has increased, which has pushed pension expenditures upward. Demographic shifts have also meant that the proportion of the population (that is, active workers) that must support the pensioners has declined. To make matters worse, these demographic trends are supposed to worsen in many countries in the decades ahead. In Latin America, the ratio of the population of working age (twenty–fifty-nine) to those of retirement age (over sixty) is projected to decline from 6.75 to 1 in 1995 to 3.23 to 1 in 2040 (Palacios and Pallarès-Miralles 2000: 86–87). In Eastern Europe and the former Soviet Union, this ratio is supposed to decline from 3.99 to 1 in 1995 to 2.10 to 1 in 2040, and among the OECD countries, it is projected to drop from 2.95 to 1 in 1995 to 1.41 to 1 in 2040 (Palacios and Pallarès-Miralles 2000: 86–88).

The maturation of the pension systems in many countries has also contributed to rising pension expenditures. In the years immediately following the establishment of a pension system, few people will have contributed to the system long enough to qualify for a pension. As pension systems age, however, an increasing number of people become eligible for pension benefits. In most countries, the maturation process has been accelerated by loose requirements for obtaining access to pensions. Many Latin American countries, for example, have set low minimum ages for retirement and have allowed people to retire with relatively few years of contributions. Some European governments have also allowed workers to retire early in order to provide jobs to the young.

The economic problems that many countries have experienced in recent years have also contributed to the financial problems of the pension systems. Growing unemployment and stagnating wages cut into the revenues of the public pension systems in many areas of the world. In Latin America, the economic crises of the 1980s hit the pension systems particularly hard. Rising unemployment and underemployment and the growth of the informal sector reduced the number of contributors to the systems, while falling wages cut into the systems' revenues in many countries. In addition, hyperinflation wiped out the reserves that some public pension systems in Latin America had built up throughout many decades. Inflation, along with the generalized economic crisis, also increased the incentives for companies to delay their social security payments, which exacerbated the systems' financial imbalances (Mesa-Lago 1991b, 1994). Some Latin American governments tried to cope with the financial difficulties by allowing inflation to erode the real value of pension benefits, but this created widespread dissent among pensioners.

The growth in public pension expenditures has put pressure on countries to reform their systems. This pressure has been the strongest where public pension expenditures (as a percentage of GDP) have been the highest, namely in the industrialized countries, formerly communist nations, and a few Latin American countries. Governments with large and growing public pension expenditures have feared that their public pension programs would hinder economic growth and absorb scarce resources that would be better used on other programs. They have become increasingly reluctant to pay for the growing pension expenditures by boosting payroll taxes because they have feared that such measures would increase unemployment and reduce their ability to compete in the world economy.

Some policymakers have advocated privatization as a means to solve the financial problems of the public pension systems. According to its advocates, pension privatization will help resolve the financial problems of Latin American social security systems in a number of different ways. By shifting the social security system from a pay-as-you-go (or partly pay-as-you-go) to a fully funded basis, privatization may reduce the vulnerability of the pension system to future demographic changes. In pay-as-you-go systems, the pension benefits of retirees are financed by the social security contributions of current workers. Thus, pay-as-you-go systems encounter growing financial problems as the population ages and the ratio of active workers to pensioners declines. Under the Chilean model, however, retirement pensions are funded by each individual's savings, which means that the financial health of the system does not depend as much on the ratio of active workers to pensioners.

Proponents of privatization also argue that private fully funded pension systems can generate better rates of return than public pay-as-you-go systems, which means that they can make do with lower payroll taxes. The assumption underlying this contention is that the long-term rate of return to capital, on which funded schemes depend, will be higher than the annual percentage growth in total real wages, on which pay-as-you-go systems depend. Moreover, advocates of privatization maintain that privatizing the pension system will improve the financial health of the pension systems by reducing payment evasion. They point out that workers will have greater incentives to contribute to a system based on individual capitalization since their final pension is tied more closely to their contributions.

Finally, proponents of privatization contend that it insulates the social security system from political interference. Privatization, they maintain, reduces the likelihood that political authorities will be able to divert pension revenues for their own purposes or grant financially unsustainable benefits to powerful interest groups—a practice that was common in most Latin American countries. In the private systems, the pension contributions that each individual makes are channeled directly to his or her retirement account. This increases the transparency of the pension system and prevents politicians from spending pension revenues as they see fit.

Domestic Savings and Capital Shortages

Concern about the insufficiency of domestic capital has also placed pension privatization on the policy agenda of many nations throughout the world. In recent years, countries have become increasingly vulnerable to sudden capital outflows. The growing vulnerability of countries to capital outflows is largely a result of the increased mobility of international capital. Capital has become increasingly mobile partly because of technological innovations that have reduced transportation costs and improved global communications, making it easier for individuals and firms to transfer and manage their assets overseas (Goodman and Pauly 1993; Cohen 1996). The decisions of numerous governments to reduce barriers to capital flows have also contributed to capital's increasing mobility.[6]

The rise in capital mobility has made countries more vulnerable to sudden cutoffs of foreign capital by increasing their dependence on foreign investors. Reduced barriers to capital flows have led the amount of cross-border finance to mushroom, as firms, countries, and individuals have sought attractive opportunities to borrow, lend, and invest abroad. The amount of funds raised by OECD nations on the international capital markets grew from less than $4.3 billion in 1970 to $77.6 billion in 1980, $316.6 billion in 1990, and $732.2 billion in 1995 (OECD 1996). Private capital flows to developing countries, meanwhile, soared in the 1970s, dropped off sharply in the 1980s, then skyrocketed again in the 1990s. In 1995 net private capital flows to developing countries equaled $184 billion, up from $43 billion in 1990 and approximately $25 billion in 1985 (World Bank 1997: 238–39).

The growing mobility of international capital has also increased the vulnerability of countries to capital outflows by making it easier for both domestic and foreign investors to transfer quickly their assets overseas. In the last two decades, numerous countries have experienced massive capital outflows when investors suddenly lost confidence in their economies. Latin American countries, for example, suffered from massive capital flight in the 1980s, which worsened the capital shortages that were brought on by the cutoff of foreign lending. Eastern European countries have also seen foreign capital come and go like swallows. Even advanced industrial countries, such as France, Sweden, and the United Kingdom, have at times suffered from major capital outflows, which have wreaked havoc on their economies.

Governments have sought to boost their domestic savings rates as a means to reduce their dependence on skittish foreign sources of capital.[7] Some countries have been particularly eager to boost domestic savings because they have seen their domestic savings rates deteriorate sharply in recent years. In Latin America and the Caribbean, for example, domestic savings fell sharply in the early 1990s, dropping from 25 percent in 1989 to 19 percent in 1998 (World Bank 2000). In Europe and Central Asia, meanwhile, the domestic savings rate fell from 31 percent in 1989 to 20 percent in 1998 (World Bank 2000).

Many policymakers have favored pension privatization in part because they believe that it will raise their domestic savings rates. Countries with low domestic savings rates have found pension privatization particularly attractive because of its potential to boost domestic capital formation. One of the architects of Mexican pension privatization plan, former finance minister Guillermo Ortiz, remarked, "The key for Mexico's future development is to induce a much higher savings rate. This is why we attach particular importance to the pension fund initiative" (Sheridan 1996: D1). Indeed in Mexico, the aim of boosting domestic savings was clearly stated in the legislation that privatized the Mexican public pension system (Cámara de Diputados de los Estados Unidos Mexicanos 1996a: 202). In Argentina, too, policymakers endorsed pension privatization partly because they believed that it would boost the country's domestic savings rate. As the former secretary for social security in Argentina put it: "The incentive behind the [Argentine] social security reform was not so much the issue of social security, but rather the need to reconstruct savings, and behind savings, investment" (interview with de Estrada 1996).

Advocates of pension privatization have argued that it will boost domestic savings for a variety of reasons. Some economists have long argued that pay-as-you-go systems reduce national savings by discouraging private savings since individuals know that the government will provide them with a pension in their old age.[8] Privatizing the pension system, they argue, would reverse this negative effect. Feldstein (1999: 30), for example, maintains that "an unfunded pay-as-you-go system . . . reduces national saving by discouraging private saving without doing any public saving. In contrast, the substitution of a funded program for an unfunded program can eventually raise national saving by nearly the full amount of the mandatory saving." According to advocates of pension privatization, mandatory private pension schemes boost private savings by requiring people to save above a level that they would do voluntarily. The authors of an important World Bank study of pension reform, for example, acknowledge that a mandatory private pension system would probably reduce voluntary savings to some degree, but they suggest that "this crowd-out effect may be only partial because people are shortsighted and would not have saved as much voluntarily for old age" (World Bank 1994b: 209). Some economists also suggest that the creation of individual retirement accounts may raise awareness of the need to save, leading workers to set aside funds in addition to their mandatory pension saving (World Bank 1994b: 308–9; Corsetti and Schmidt-Hebbel 1995: 21).

Advocates of pension privatization also argue that the privatized pension systems will promote savings by reducing "the probability that governments will have to borrow to cover escalating pension costs as populations age" (James 1997a: 20). Furthermore, they maintain that pension privatization will reduce payroll taxes and other labor market distortions that impede growth. Higher growth will boost savings, which, in turn, will promote further growth. Proponents of pension privatization also maintain that it will improve the depth, liquidity, and efficiency of the local capital markets, which will similarly boost growth and productivity, thereby increasing savings (James 1997b; CIEDESS 1995). They point to the case of Chile where the domestic savings rate, along with the stock market and the economy in general, soared in the wake of the privatization of the pension system. Domestic savings in Chile rose from approximately 18 percent in the late 1970s to 30 percent in 1989, which gave Chile the highest savings rate in the region and helped fuel a decade of growth (World Bank 1995c: 64–65). Some analysts have also argued that the high savings rates in Switzerland, Singapore, and Malaysia are partly the result of the existence of fully funded pension plans in those countries (James 1997b; World Bank 1994b).

Domestic Savings, Pension Spending, and Reform

Two types of economic pressures—growing public pension spending and insufficient domestic savings—thus place pension reform on the policy agenda. How these two variables interact also shapes what types of pension reforms countries will tend to consider. Nations that have high public pension expenditures and low domestic savings rates are the most likely to privatize their pension systems, but, as the upper-right-hand quadrant of Table 2.1 indicates, they will typically favor partial rather than full pension privatization. Most of the countries of the former Soviet bloc fit into this category, as do the nations of the Southern Cone of Latin America, and a significant number of them have already opted to partially privatize their pension systems.

The leaders of countries with low domestic savings rates and high public pension expenditures will be tempted to privatize their social security systems in order to try to boost their domestic savings rates and to reduce the long-term economic burdens of the pension system. They will find the transition costs of full-scale privatization quite daunting, however. Full-scale pension privatization is costly because it allows (or obliges) members of the social security system to transfer their social security contributions to private pension funds instead of paying them to the state.[9] The transition costs of social security privatization are especially large for countries that have high pension expenditures because they tend to have greater numbers of retirees whose pensions must continue to be provided by the state after the pension system is privatized.[10] They also tend to have more elderly workers that must be compensated for past contributions to the public pension system.

Partial privatization, or the creation of mixed public/private systems, represents an intermediary solution for countries with high levels of public pension commitments and low domestic savings. In mixed public/private systems, the government continues to collect a portion of the contributions that were traditionally paid to the public social security system. (Under full privatization, the government typically forgoes these revenues entirely.) The payroll taxes that the state collects in mixed systems can be used to partially finance the pensions of current retirees, which makes the fiscal burden of such reforms more manageable. Governments with high public pension expenditures may also seek to reduce the costs of pension privatization by reneging on some of their public pension commitments, particularly those to active workers. Governments, for example, may increase the minimum retirement age or decline to compensate workers for past contributions to the public pension systems, both of which will reduce the transition costs of reform.

In contrast, nations that have low domestic savings rates and low public

TABLE 2.1

Economic Determinants of Pension Reform Preferences

Public pension spending	Domestic savings rates	
	High	Low
High	Cutbacks in public benefits *(Most OECD countries)*	Partial privatization *(Most Eastern European countries, Uruguay, and Argentina)*
Low	No reform *(Most Asian and Middle Eastern countries)*	Full privatization *(Most Latin American countries)*

pension expenditures will tend to favor full pension privatization, as the lower-right-hand quadrant of Table 2.1 indicates. Most Latin American countries fit into this category, and a significant number of them have opted to carry out sweeping pension privatization schemes. The leaders of these countries will typically be tempted to privatize their pension systems because of their desire to increase their savings rates, and they will find full privatization schemes more affordable than do nations with high pension expenditures. In this sense, countries with low pension expenditures enjoy what Pei (1995) has termed an "advantage of backwardness": reform is easier in these countries because their pension systems are still relatively undeveloped. These nations are somewhat less likely to privatize their pension systems than the countries in the previous category, however, since their low level of pension expenditures means that they have fewer economic incentives to privatize. Indeed, the low level of public pension expenditures in these countries may mean that pension reform is not on the agenda at all. If these countries do opt to privatize their pension systems, however, they are likely to do it in a sweeping manner in an effort to maximize the potential effects on their savings rates.

As the lower-left-hand cell of Table 2.1 suggests, nations that have high domestic savings rates and low levels of public pension expenditures are unlikely to privatize their pension systems. East Asian countries typically fit into this category, as do some of the oil-exporting developing nations. These countries have so far eschewed pension privatization. Nations that have plentiful domestic sources of capital lack strong economic incentives to privatize their social security systems. Although they may believe privatizing their pension systems would boost their domestic savings rates and reduce their long-term public pension expenditures, the leaders of these countries are likely to decide that these benefits do not warrant the political and fiscal costs of privatization. Nor are these countries likely to undertake politically controversial cutbacks in public pension benefits since their pension expenditures are still relatively low. These countries may, however, opt for other types of reforms, including measures designed to increase benefits or improve the administrative efficiency of the pension system.

As the upper-left-hand quadrant of Table 2.1 indicates, nations that have high public pension expenditures and ample domestic sources of capital will also typically eschew pension privatization in favor of parametric reforms that cut pension benefits or tighten eligibility requirements. Most OECD nations fit into this category; indeed, the majority of these countries have scaled back public pension benefits or tightened benefit eligibility in recent years. These countries have fewer economic incentives to privatize their social security systems than the countries in the right-hand cells since they already have high domestic savings rates. Moreover, privatization would be extremely costly for these countries to undertake because they have accumulated substantial public pension commitments. These countries do have substantial incentives to undertake some type of pension reform, however, since their large pension expenditures absorb state resources and require high payroll taxes, which hinder growth and employment. Since they are typically reluctant to increase their already high payroll taxes, they will usually opt to reduce their pension expenditures through benefit cutbacks. These cutbacks may involve tightening their pension eligibility requirements, changing their pension benefit formulas, or altering the procedures they use to grant cost-of-living increases in pensions over time.

Ideas and Pension Privatization

An explanation for pension reform choices that focuses on economic factors alone is insufficient. Economic factors cannot explain reform choices or even the decision to reform. In the words of Adler (1991: 53), the "environment does not 'instruct' policymakers, it challenges them." How policymakers respond to those challenges depends in part on what sorts of beliefs the policymakers and other influential actors have. Economic problems may make an existing institutional or policy equilibrium unstable, but ideas will frequently help policymakers find a new equilibrium.

Investigating the beliefs that framed the choices of policymakers is particularly important in this case because of the controversy surrounding the effects of pension privatization. It is not clear that pension privatization will resolve the difficulties associated with rising public pension spending and serious domestic capital shortages, which many nations confronted in the 1990s. To begin with, privatization worsens, rather than improves, the financial situation of pension systems in the medium term. Pension privatization involves transition costs because it allows (or obliges) workers to make their social security payments to private pension funds. The state, however, continues to pay the pensions of existing retirees. In most cases, the state also compensates members who transfer to the private system for the contributions that they had previously made to the public system.[11] The state therefore loses a substantial portion of its social security revenue with no corresponding drop in expenditures in the short to medium term.

Pension privatization may not even resolve the financial problems of public pension systems in the long term. As critics of pension privatization point out, private fully funded pension systems, like public pay-as-you-go systems, may be affected by demographic transitions since the return on their investments may decline once large cohorts of workers retire and begin to sell their assets.[12] Political interference may also occur with private pension systems, just as with public pension systems, since the government decides who may operate private pension funds and in what they can invest. This interference can jeopardize the financial health of the private pension systems by leading to the mismanagement of the funds under investment. As the Latin American experience demonstrates, private pension systems may also be prone to high administrative costs and high rates of evasion, both of which reduce the amount of funds flowing into workers' individual retirement accounts. Should large numbers of workers fail to have enough funds in their accounts upon retirement, the state would almost certainly be required to carry out a massive bailout of the system, which could prove extremely costly in the long run.

It is also far from certain that pension privatization will boost a country's saving rate. Some strong theoretical arguments have been made as to why pension privatization should generate increased domestic savings. Nevertheless, as proponents of privatization acknowledge, privatizing the pension system is unlikely to generate any increase in savings if the costs of the transition are financed by borrowing rather than through taxation or fiscal cutbacks (Corsetti and Schmidt-Hebbel 1995; James 1997b; Orszag and Stiglitz 2001).[13] Where the transition is debt-financed, the increase in private savings generated by the pension privatization plan will be offset by an increase in public dissaving. Skeptics also point out that the empirical evidence linking pension privatization to higher savings is tenuous (Mesa-Lago 2001; Barrientos 1998). Most of the studies of the macroeconomic effects of pension privatization have examined a single country—Chile—and these studies have yielded contradictory results. The sizable literature on the macroeconomic effects of pay-as-you-go systems, meanwhile, has yet to find conclusive evidence that the pay-as-you-go systems lower domestic savings (Aaron 1982; World Bank 1994b; Thompson 1998). This ambiguity is to some extent the result of the thorny nature of the problem. It is difficult to isolate the impact of pension systems on savings rates in part because savings rates depend on numerous factors.

These controversies raise several key questions: Why have so many policy-makers concluded that privatizing their pension systems would boost their savings rates and solve the long-term financial problems of their pension systems? Why have policymakers in some countries reached this conclusion more readily than in others? Where do ideas about pension privatization come from, and what determines whether they take hold?

Theories of ideas and policy offer some insights into these questions. To begin with, they draw attention to the importance of regional diffusion of ideas. As the large literature on diffusion has shown, policymakers often enact reforms that they believe have proven beneficial in a neighboring polity (Mooney 2001; Berry and Berry 1992; Rogers 1995; Walker 1969). The experience of neighboring polities with particular policy reforms thus plays an important role in the formation of beliefs about the efficacy of those reforms. Regional diffusion was clearly crucial to the spread of pension privatization. The 1981 Chilean reform persuaded many policymakers that pension privatization would not only solve the growing financial problems of their public pension systems but also boost their countries' savings rates. Policymakers in Latin America were particularly receptive to the Chilean pension privatization model both because they knew more about it and because they viewed it as more relevant to their own countries than did policymakers in other regions.

In addition, theories of ideas suggest that the acceptance of policy ideas is often shaped more by the influence wielded by the bearers of the ideas than by the persuasiveness of the ideas per se (Hall 1989; Sikkink 1991; Goldstein and Keohane 1993; McNamara 1998; Marcussen 2000). Influential actors do not necessarily have the power to impose ideas or policy solutions, but their influence typically gives their ideas a special hearing. They may even be able to dominate the discourse on a particular topic. According to theories of ideas, two types of actors frequently help diffuse policy ideas cross-nationally: international institutions and networks of knowledge-based experts with similar interests and principled beliefs (Haas 1992; Adler and Haas 1992; Meyer 1994; Finnemore and Sikkink 1998). Both of these types of actors have played an important role in the spread of pension privatization. Internally, the main proponents of pension privatization were typically neoliberal economists. These economists came to dominate the key social security policy-making positions in many countries in Latin America and elsewhere during the 1990s. Externally, the most important advocate of pension privatization was the World Bank, which also gained a great deal of influence over social security policy in many countries during the 1990s. Both the World Bank and the neoliberal economists used their influence to lobby tirelessly for pension privatization.

The influence of the World Bank and market-oriented economists is not purely ideational. The World Bank's influence stems in part from the financial resources it commands, which it can use to pressure countries to enact reforms. The clout of market-oriented economists, meanwhile, derives in part from the positions of authority that they sometimes occupy as well as from their political connections. Nevertheless, neither the World Bank nor the neoliberal economists are typically able to compel political leaders to privatize their pension systems or adopt other policy reforms. Instead, they must rely on persuasion—that is, they must convince political leaders that such reforms will bring benefits—and such persuasion takes place largely in the realm of ideas. The power of persuasion that World Bank officials and market-oriented economists enjoy in many countries is partly a result of the technical expertise that these actors command. It is also, however, a product of the political access that they enjoy and the material resources that they control, which grant their ideas a special hearing.

The influence of World Bank officials and market-oriented economists are also ideational variables in the sense that these actors' support for pension privatization is shaped more by their beliefs than by their immediate interests.[14] The World Bank gradually came to advocate pension privatization, not because of the intervention of groups or institutions that stood to benefit from the reform, but rather because key World Bank staff members became convinced that countries would benefit from privatizing their pension systems. In the late 1980s and early 1990s, World Bank staff members closely studied the Chilean model as well as the problems afflicting public pension systems in developing countries and concluded that pension privatization would bring numerous economic and social benefits (interviews with James 1998, with Schwarz 1998, and with Schmidt-Hebbel 1997). The increasing involvement of macroeconomists in setting the World Bank's policies on pension reform also contributed to the policy shift since these staff members were better disposed toward pension privatization than the traditional social welfare specialists within the World Bank (interview with Vittas 1998). Many economists both inside and outside the World Bank have tended to be predisposed toward pension privatization because of their training in orthodox economic theory. In addition, economists, more than the traditional social security specialists, have tended to be concerned with the effects of pension policy on the economy as a whole, which has also led them frequently to favor pension privatization.

As Table 2.2 suggests, changing ideas about the purposes and benefits of pension reform thus led to a dramatic shift in the logic underlying such reforms during the 1990s. Social security reforms, which had previously fo-

TABLE 2.2

The New Economic Logic of Social Security Reform

	Traditional logic (1950s–1980s)	Current logic (1990s – Present)
Model for the reforms	European countries	Chile
Main types of reform promoted	Unification and parametric reforms of public systems	Privatization of the public pension systems
Main stimulus to the reforms	Inequities and inefficiencies of pension systems	Rising pension spending and capital shortages
Main goals of the reforms	Social	Economic
Main domestic agencies promoting the reforms	Social security institutes; ministries of labor	Ministries of finance or economy; central banks
Typical background of reform promoters	Lawyers (social security specialists)	Economists (generalists)
Main international agency promoting the reforms	International Labour Organisation	World Bank

cused on improving the efficiency and equity of the pension systems, came to incorporate larger macroeconomic aims, such as reducing the financial burden of public pensions, boosting the domestic savings rate, and bolstering the local capital markets. The World Bank, which in previous decades had played little role in pension reform, became the single most important international actor in pension reform, displacing the International Labor Organization, which continued to defend the traditional European public pension model. Economists and economic ministries, such as the Ministry of Finance and the Central Bank, became more involved in pension reform and sought to impose their own views on political leaders. These views often clashed dramatically with those of the social security specialists in the ministries of labor and the social security institutes who had traditionally made pension policy in Latin America. In many instances, the economists succeeded in taking over the key policy-making positions in the social security institutes and ministries, and they used these new positions of authority to lobby, often successfully, in favor of pension privatization. The Chilean private pension system thus gradually became the new policy model that many countries in Latin America and beyond sought to emulate.

Regional Diffusion of the Chilean Model

Scholars have long noted that emulation plays an important role in the spread of policies and programs across polities (Dolowitz and Marsh 2000;

Rogers 1995; Bennett 1991; Siegel and Weinberg 1977; C. Anderson 1971).[15] Policymakers emulate the policies and programs they find elsewhere partly in order to reap the perceived benefits that such policies have brought. This does not mean that policy emulation is necessarily a rational and efficient process that maximizes the interests of the policy borrower, however. Although policymakers will often try to adapt borrowed policies to suit local needs and characteristics, a policy that functions well in one country may not work in another. Moreover, policymakers sometimes undertake only a limited amount of analysis before copying a policy model, relying instead on guesswork and cognitive shortcuts (Weyland 2001). Indeed, according to a variety of scholars, policymakers are particularly likely to copy the programs and policies found in other areas when they have limited time, knowledge, and resources (Dolowitz and Marsh 2000; Dimaggio and Powell 1983).

The literature on policy innovation within the United States (Walker 1969; Berry and Berry 1992; Mintrom and Vergari 1998; Mooney 2001) has shown that the diffusion of policy innovations is partly determined by regional location. The likelihood that a state will adopt a new policy or program increases as the percentage of neighboring states that have already adopted the program rises. Scholars offer a number of explanations for why this occurs. First, policymakers tend to have greater access to information about neighboring states. Neighboring states typically receive greater media coverage than do distant states, and policymakers in neighboring states are more likely to participate in the same policy networks. This means not only that they are more likely to know about innovative policies that their neighbors implement, but also that they find it easier to gather additional information about such policies from a neighboring state when they need to do so. Both policymakers and citizens are also more likely to think that the policies adopted by a neighboring state are relevant to their own state. People in neighboring states are more likely to share common values and to have similar cultural, political, and economic institutions and characteristics. These similarities make it more likely that borrowed policies will be technically appropriate and politically acceptable. Finally, neighboring states are more likely to compete with each other socially, politically, and economically. Thus, a state may feel competitive pressure to emulate the policies and programs of its neighbor. Walker, for example, suggests that state policymakers adopt new programs "when they become convinced that their state is relatively deprived, or that some need exists to which other states in their 'league' have already responded" (Walker 1969: 897).

Although less often discussed, regional location may be equally important in the international diffusion of policy innovations. This is true because national policymakers, like state policymakers, are more likely to be aware of innovations that take place in neighboring areas. National decision makers, like state decision makers, tend to view policy innovations adopted by a neighboring polity as more relevant to their own situation. Furthermore, nations, like states, are more likely to compete with neighboring polities for economic resources and political and social legitimacy.

A number of scholars have argued that the recent wave of economic and social reforms in Latin America have been inspired in large part by the Chilean model (Hojman 1994; Edwards 1995). During the military regime of General Augusto Pinochet (1973–90), the government of Chile carried out an unprecedented number of market-oriented reforms. These reforms eventually succeeded in generating impressive economic growth. Indeed, between 1985 and 1998 the Chilean economy grew an average of 7.3 percent annually, easily the fastest rate in Latin America. This success prompted other Latin American nations to emulate the Chilean model.

Chile's pension privatization scheme was particularly influential because it was pathbreaking and widely viewed as a success. Although the possibility of pension privatization had long been discussed in academic circles, prior to the 1980s it was an untested idea with unclear implementation guidelines and unknown consequences. As a result, it was rarely considered as a serious policy option. The 1981 Chilean social security reform changed all that, providing a model that policymakers from other countries could use to craft similar reforms and, more importantly, demonstrating the potential economic benefits of pension privatization. Many of these benefits were not readily apparent at the time that the reform was implemented, but by the end of the 1980s they were being widely discussed.

The Chilean reform convinced many observers that pension privatization could benefit the economy in a number of ways. First, it persuaded some policymakers that pension privatization could boost a country's domestic savings rate. As noted earlier, analysts commonly attributed the rapid rise of the Chilean savings rate in the 1980s and 1990s to the privatization of the country's pension system. Second, it led many people to conclude that pension privatization would stimulate the local capital markets. The Chilean privatization scheme channeled vast sums of money into the country's capital markets, leading to the dramatic expansion and diversification of the domestic insurance industry, the growth of the Chilean stock market, and the emergence of new financial instruments and intermediaries (Diamond and Valdés-Prieto 1994; Holzmann 1996; Santamaría 1992).[16] Third, it convinced many people that a private pension system would function more efficiently than a public pension system, which would reduce the amount of resources that would need to be devoted to pensions. From the outset, the Chilean private pension system generated very high returns on the funds that workers deposited in their individual retirement accounts. Between 1982 and

2000, the Chilean pension funds generated returns that averaged approximately 11 percent annually above inflation (Devesa-Carpio and Vidal-Meliá 2001: 11). As a result of these strong returns, pensions have so far been substantially higher in the Chilean private system than in the public system in spite of the lower level of contributions (and the relatively high administrative costs) in the private system.

The lessons that policymakers drew from the Chilean reform were based on meager and preliminary evidence, however. Although some studies have linked the Chilean reform to the increase in the country's savings rate (Haindl 1997; Morandé 1996; Corsetti and Schmidt-Hebbel 1995), other studies have found no relationship or even a negative relationship between the two variables (Holzmann 1996; Agosín, Crespi, and Letelier 1996; Mesa-Lago and Arenas de Mesa 1998).[17] There is also some debate about how important a role the Chilean pension privatization scheme played in the expansion of the country's capital markets, although most analysts suggest that it at least contributed to the boom (Mesa-Lago and Arenas de Mesa 1998; Holzmann 1996; Arrau 1994; Diamond and Valdés-Prieto 1994; Santamaría 1992). Finally, the long-term impact of the privatization scheme on the pension system remains uncertain. It is not clear, for example, that the high returns of the Chilean private pension system will hold up over the long run, nor is it clear whether those returns will be able to offset the high administrative costs and widespread evasion that have afflicted the system.

Proponents of pension privatization nevertheless managed to persuade many observers that the Chilean pension reform was an unquestionable success that brought manifold economic benefits to the country. Throughout the 1990s, mainstream media reports on the Chilean pension privatization were overwhelmingly positive. A 1994 *New York Times* article was typically effusive, arguing that "private pension funds have almost doubled [Chile's] savings rate in a decade. . . . These institutional investors have fueled corporate growth and added stability to a once flighty [stock] exchange. . . . At the same time, Chilean account holders have benefited so handsomely that some may retire with pensions larger than their salaries" (Brooke 1994: 37).

The Chilean pension privatization model has been especially influential within Latin America because of the cultural, economic, and institutional ties that bind these countries to Chile. In spite of the ongoing processes of globalization, the diffusion of information is still hindered by institutional, geographic, cultural, and language barriers. Policymakers as well as interest groups in Latin America became acquainted with the Chilean reform before their counterparts outside of the region, and they continue to be much more familiar with it than are political actors in other regions.

In Latin America the diffusion process has been aided by policy networks that lead policymakers within the region to be in frequent contact with one another. Regional institutions, such as the Inter-American Development Bank, the United Nations' Economic Commission for Latin America, and the Inter-American Conference on Social Security, have served as forums in which the Chilean model has been widely discussed. Moreover, a variety of policy entrepreneurs have actively promoted social security privatization in the region. Beginning in the early 1990s, the architect of the Chilean reform, José Piñera, became a self-described missionary for the Chilean model, journeying throughout the region to champion social security privatization (interview with Piñera 1997). In recent years, a number of other Latin American-based institutions, including consulting firms, think tanks, governmental agencies, and international organizations, have also actively promoted social security privatization throughout Latin America by providing technical assistance to countries considering such measures.

Latin American policymakers not only have been more familiar with the Chilean model than their counterparts outside the region, but also they have been more inclined to view the Chilean experience with social security privatization as relevant to their own countries. Because of their countries' numerous similarities to Chile, many Latin American policymakers have assumed that if Chile could benefit from social security privatization, their countries could do so as well. Chile has represented an especially compelling model for many Latin American policymakers because it is the only country in the region that has enjoyed strong and sustained economic growth since the mid-1980s. Policymakers from other regions, in contrast, have typically held up other countries as models. They have questioned the relevance of the Chilean experiment to their own countries, arguing that even if the Chilean model worked in Chile, it would not necessarily work in their own countries, which have little in common with the South American nation. In Hungary and Poland, for example, many participants in the reform debate criticized social security privatization as a Latin American import, arguing that the country should opt for the European model of reform (Palacios and Rocha 1998; Inglot 1995; Müller 1999).

In recent years, a number of countries outside of Latin America, especially in Eastern Europe, have also privatized their pension systems, which has created new loci for diffusion. These new loci, along with the growing worldwide familiarity with this new policy model, may eventually lead pension privatization to become equally common outside of Latin America as inside it. Nevertheless, throughout the 1990s the Chilean model was the main locus for diffusion of pension privatization. Partly as a result, Latin American countries were much more likely than countries in other regions to opt to privatize their pension systems.

Ideas and International Institutions

Theorists of ideas have identified international organizations as key promoters of policy ideas. A number of studies, for example, have argued that the International Labor Organization has contributed to the spread of social security programs throughout the world (Collier and Messick 1975; Strang and Chang 1993; Usui 1994). Other studies have made the case that UNESCO has shaped science and educational policies, programs, and institutions worldwide (Finnemore 1990; Meyer, Ramírez, and Soysal 1992). International institutions are influential promoters of ideas for a number of reasons. To begin with, they often constitute the core of global policy networks, which places them in regular contact with policymakers in numerous countries around the world. International institutions issue publications, hold conferences, and dispatch technical missions, all of which are used as forums to propagate their ideas. Many national policymakers also work for periods at international institutions, which provides the agencies with further opportunities to promote their policy ideas and approaches. Furthermore, international institutions tend to have a high degree of international standing and prestige, giving credence to the ideas that they promote. International institutions not only are presumed to have a great deal of policy expertise, but also are commonly deemed to embody world opinion as to what is morally, culturally, and politically appropriate (Meyer 1994). Thus, the views of international institutions tend to carry extra weight. Finally, international institutions typically control material resources that they can use to help persuade countries to do their bidding. International development banks, for example, can offer financial inducements to countries to adopt certain policies.[18] Foreign governments, private firms, and nongovernmental organizations often provide further material support to those projects that are backed by international institutions, which reduces the costs of reform.

Much of the theoretical literature on market-oriented reform in developing countries argues that the international financial institutions (IFIs) have played an important role in the spread of neoliberal ideas in these countries (Stallings 1992; Kahler 1992; Biersteker 1995; Edwards 1995; Teichman 2001). As these scholars and others point out, the influence of the international financial institutions increased markedly after the outbreak of the debt crisis in 1982 because many developing countries badly needed the financing that the IFIs controlled. The international financial institutions took advantage of this increased leverage to press developing countries to implement market-oriented reforms. The International Monetary Fund and the World Bank, for example, made their increasing loans to the debt-troubled developing countries contingent on the enactment of certain reforms. Foreign governments and commercial banks, meanwhile, typically refused to make new loans or reschedule their existing loans to developing countries unless they reached an agreement with the International Monetary Fund to carry out certain reforms.

Most scholars, however, maintain that the international financial institutions persuaded developing countries to implement reforms not so much through economic pressure, but rather by convincing the countries that such reforms were in their best interests (Kahler 1992; Biersteker 1995; Edwards 1995; Teichman 2001). Williamson and Haggard (1994: 595), for example, argue "that the most useful intellectual help [from the IFIs] came not in the form of hard conditionality ('leverage') but rather by changing the intellectual climate ('linkage')." By publishing countless studies that trumpeted the merits of market-oriented reforms and by promoting the reforms in their numerous contacts with policymakers of the developing countries, the international financial institutions managed to convince many policymakers that such policies would benefit their countries.[19] In contrast, efforts by the IFIs to oblige governments to adopt reforms that their leaders opposed largely failed. The governments would typically either refuse to sign an agreement with the IMF or would quickly fall out of compliance with an agreement after they had signed one (Kahler 1992; Mosley, Harrigan, and Toye 1991; Remmer 1986).

The international financial institutions, especially the World Bank, have played a particularly important role in promoting pension privatization; as a result, pension privatization has been more common in those countries where the World Bank has more influence (Lacey 1996; Mesa-Lago 1996b; Müller 1999; Brooks 2000; Holzmann 2000; Queisser 2000; Huber and Stephens 2000). Before the 1990s, the World Bank only occasionally promoted pension reform, and when it did, it typically advocated parametric changes to the existing public pension systems. In the 1990s, however, the World Bank became a strong advocate of pension privatization and began to devote large amounts of resources to promoting it. The shift to a policy favoring pension privatization was pushed mostly by the macroeconomists and public finance experts at the World Bank who believed that privatization would benefit the macroeconomy as well as the pension system itself. It was opposed by most of the World Bank's traditional social security specialists, however, on the grounds that pension privatization might undermine the developing countries' meager social safety nets (interview with Vittas 1998).

The World Bank has gradually displaced the International Labor Organization (ILO) as the main international actor involved in pension reform. The two institutions were at loggerheads for most of the 1990s, engaging in a highly public debate about the merits of pension privatization and offering conflicting advice to member countries (Beattie and McGillivray 1995; James 1996). Recently, however, the two institutions have created a forum to exchange views in an attempt to build a consensus on social security reform, and the differences between the two institutions have narrowed (Holzmann 1998; ISSA 1998; Scherman 2000; Queisser 2000). The World Bank has gone on record as supporting partial rather than full-scale privatization and, in practice, has shown a fair amount of pragmatism and flexibility, providing assistance for parametric reforms of public pension systems as well as privatization efforts (Holzmann 2000; Queisser 2000; Ross 2000).[20] The ILO, meanwhile, has recommended the establishment of fully funded, defined contribution pension schemes to supplement the existing pay-as-you-go systems, but it is ambivalent with regard to whether the defined contribution schemes should be privately or publicly managed (Gillion 2000; Queisser 2000).

Other international financial institutions have also helped promote pension privatization, although not with the same level of intensity as the World Bank. The Inter-American Development Bank (IADB) expanded its involvement in pension reform in the 1990s, but it has shown more flexibility on this issue than the World Bank (Mesa-Lago 1996b; interview with Márquez 1998). Indeed, the IADB became involved in some countries, such as Uruguay and Venezuela, when the World Bank pulled out because of disagreements about the nature of the reform plans (interview with Palacios 1998 and with Márquez 1998). The International Monetary Fund (IMF) has been less involved in pension reform, although it has done some research and consulting in this area. The IMF has had some concerns about the fiscal implications of pension privatization (Chand and Jaeger 1996), but it recently changed the way in which it views reform-induced deficits in order to facilitate pension privatization (Holzmann 1998; Queisser 2000).

The international financial institutions have provided some financial incentives to countries to privatize their pension systems. The World Bank and the Inter-American Development Bank have made loans to countries to pay for the design and implementation of the reforms as well as to cover some of the transition costs of pension privatization.[21] World Bank and IADB loans have financed the considerable start-up costs associated with planning and implementing the pension privatization schemes, and, in some instances, they have even eased the large transition costs of pension privatization. During the past fifteen years, the World Bank has granted a total of $3.4 billion in loans to thirty-six countries to finance pension reform, including loans to cover the transition costs of pension privatization in Argentina, Mexico, Uruguay, Hungary, and Kazakhstan (Holzmann 2000; Queisser 2000: 39). Nevertheless, the financial incentives that the international financial institutions have provided to countries to persuade them to privatize their pension systems are tiny compared to the costs of pension privatization, typically amounting to less than 1 percent of the total transition costs.

International financial institutions have been able to persuade developing countries to privatize their pension systems not so much by offering them financial incentives to do so, but rather by persuading them that the privatization schemes would bring significant benefits. The influence of the international financial institutions thus has been more ideational than material in nature. Since 1990, the World Bank has carried out a vast amount of research, held numerous courses, workshops, and conferences, and disseminated a wide variety of publications detailing the problems with the existing public pension systems and extolling the benefits of pension privatization. The World Bank has played a particularly important role in persuading policymakers that pension privatization would bring major macroeconomic benefits, including an increase in the domestic savings rate.[22] Indeed, Estelle James (1997a: 16), one of the principal architects of the new World Bank pension reform strategy, wrote, "The chief theoretical argument for the recommended multi-pillar system is that it will have a positive effect on efficiency and growth." The focus on the macroeconomic benefits of pension privatization was particularly evident in the World Bank's 1994 publication, *Averting the Old Age Crisis*, which had the subtitle: "Policies to Protect the Old and Promote Growth." This publication, which set out a blueprint for reform, has been highly influential in Latin America and elsewhere. Indeed, the *World Bank Policy and Research Bulletin* ("World Bank Research" 1996: 2) has claimed that "partly as a result of this report, the Bank has witnessed an upsurge in pension reform efforts among client countries, and its support to such efforts has increased dramatically."

The World Bank and the Inter-American Development Bank have also promoted pension privatization by providing technical assistance to nations considering pension reforms. In the last decade, the World Bank has carried out pension reform consulting missions in most of Latin America, Eastern Europe, and the former Soviet Union (Schwarz and Demirgüç-Kunt 1999). The World Bank's technical assistance has helped countries model the consequences of different types of reforms and come up with creative solutions to their problems. The technical assistance has also strengthened domestic advocates of pension privatization in their battles against its opponents. Opponents of pension privatization typically have not had the technical resources that have been available to advocates of privatization; as a result, they have been at a distinct disadvantage. The reform missions have also put World Bank staff members in close contact with key social security policymakers in developing countries, which has enabled the World Bank officials to influence the host countries' views with regard to pension privatization.

As one World Bank economist told me, "Some countries initially have said that they don't want to [privatize their pension systems], but we have sometimes been able to convince them to do so" (interview with Schwarz 1998).

The Rise of the Economists

Another branch of the literature on ideas and policy has focused on the role played in the spread of policy ideas by knowledge-based experts or what are sometimes called "epistemic communities" (Haas 1992; Adler and Haas 1992). According to Haas (1992: 3), epistemic communities are composed of networks of professionals that have a shared set of principled or normative beliefs, similar causal beliefs and notions of validity, and a common policy enterprise. The epistemic-communities literature suggests these experts tend to wield influence for a number of different reasons. First, the knowledge and training that they possess provide them with a distinct advantage over policymakers who lack such expertise. Such knowledge not only confers special legitimacy to their views but also enables them to present sophisticated analyses that support their positions. Epistemic communities tend to be particularly influential where a great deal of uncertainty exists, such as during periods of crisis or with regard to issues that are viewed as technically complex. Under these circumstances, political leaders are likely to turn to groups of experts, such as epistemic communities, to find policy solutions that resolve their confusion.

The influence of epistemic communities also flows from their links to international firms and institutions. Members of epistemic communities often develop ties to international firms and institutions through their research, studies, or consulting activities. These links help members of epistemic communities acquire influence because the international agencies frequently encourage countries to appoint the experts to key policy-making positions. The agencies may also facilitate the policy-making agenda of members of epistemic communities by providing them with access to information and resources. Finally, members of epistemic communities have gained influence by cooperating extensively with each other. Members of epistemic communities have at times sought to have like-minded experts appointed to key policy-making positions because they typically prefer to deal with colleagues with similar interests and training. Once in these positions, the shared knowledge and interests of the members of epistemic communities often provide them with a degree of unity that helps advance their common policy enterprise.

Many studies have argued that the spread of neoliberal ideas has been fueled by the rise of policy experts—dubbed "technocrats"—to key policy-making positions throughout Latin America and in many other regions

(Conaghan, Malloy, and Abugattás 1990; Waterbury 1992; Markoff and Montecinos 1993; Harberger 1993; Centeno 1994; Williamson and Haggard 1994; Valdés 1995; Domínguez 1997; Centeno and Silva 1998; Hira 1998). The technocratic takeover has been particularly noticeable in Mexico and Chile, but it has occurred on a lesser scale in most Latin American countries (Centeno 1994; Grindle 1996; Camp 1996; Golob 1997; V. Montecinos 1988; Silva 1991; Valdés 1995; Hira 1998). According to Centeno and Silva (1998: 1): "From the Rio Grande to Tierra del Fuego, technocrats are triumphant. Despite differences in the economic and political evolution of the Latin American countries during the last decades, they share one trend: an increasing number of economic and financial experts taking key positions at the highest level of the decision-making process." Hojman (1994: 197), meanwhile, suggests, "The presence of these specialists may have been decisive for the design and implementation of free market open economy policies."

Taken as a whole, technocrats, who have traditionally been defined as individuals with specialized academic training who occupied decision-making posts in either the public or private sector, would not constitute an epistemic community (O'Donnell 1973; Collier 1979).[23] Much of the recent literature on technocrats, however, focuses on a subgroup of technocrats, the neoliberal economists who have gained increasing policy influence. Neoliberal economists resemble an epistemic community in that they share many principled beliefs—for example, they tend to value economic freedom and individual responsibility—as well as many causal beliefs and notions of scientific validity.[24] Neoliberal economists also tend to share a common policy enterprise: they tend to advocate market-oriented reforms, although their preferences often differ with respect to the exact content, timing, and mode of implementation of these measures.

The rise of neoliberal economists has been particularly noticeable in the field of social security (Madrid 1999; Müller 1999). Until recently, social security policy making in Latin America and elsewhere was dominated by lawyers and, to a lesser extent, doctors, sociologists, and actuaries. These individuals usually specialized in social security and typically spent their entire careers in the field. In the 1990s, however, economists assumed an increasing portion of the key decision-making posts in many Latin American countries. These economists, unlike their predecessors, were typically not social security specialists; indeed, in many cases, they had no prior experience in the field. Nevertheless, they quickly succeeded in making their presence felt by aggressively promoting pension privatization.

Economists have increasingly assumed leading social security policy-making roles for a number of reasons. First, the economic crises that plagued Latin American countries and some other nations in the 1980s helped propel economists into key positions in a variety of policy areas, including social security. According to Biersteker (1995: 186), "Although their factions were present in some form before the early 1980s, the magnitude of the economic crisis, along with the failure of past policies, provided these technocratic groups with an opportunity to articulate an alternative set of ideas." Schneider (1998a: 78) argues that governments appointed technocrats in order to "signal government commitment to economic reform and thereby restore investor confidence." Increased awareness of the link between pension systems and the macroeconomy has also contributed to the recruitment of economists into top social security policy-making positions. As the macroeconomic implications of social security policy have become better known, policymakers have felt it necessary to bring more economists into the field since only they are believed to have the requisite training to understand complex problems and formulate technical solutions (Malloy 1989; Markoff and Montecinos 1993).[25] In many countries, the number of people with degrees in economics, particularly from U.S. universities, has increased dramatically in recent decades, which has meant that there has been a larger pool to draw on in staffing policy-making positions in social security and other areas (Hojman 1994; Centeno 1994; Coats 1997; Harberger 1997; Biglaiser 1998). Many of these economists had close links to policy networks centered in the international financial institutions, and they have used these networks to advance their careers. Neoliberal economists themselves have helped increase their penetration of social security policy making by showing a distinct preference for similarly trained colleagues in the staffing of positions (Centeno 1994; Camp 1996; Schneider 1998a).

In some countries, the economists influenced social security policy from positions within the central bank, the Ministry of Finance, or other economics ministries. These ministries have taken on an increasingly important role in pension policy, often at the expense of the Ministries of Labor or Social Security. The efforts of economists in the financial ministries to promote pension privatization, however, has typically met serious opposition where traditional social security specialists have continued to control the key social security policy-making institutions, such as the Ministries of Labor or Social Security. These specialists have often used their political influence and technical expertise to block pension privatization initiatives. Pension privatization has been much more likely to take place where liberal economists have taken over the key positions in the main social security policy-making institutions. In these cases, the government has typically been unified in its support of pension privatization, which has facilitated the enactment of the reforms.

Neoliberal economists have tended to support pension privatization much more frequently than their counterparts from other disciplines or professions, in part because of their training. Most of the economists have been

trained in liberal economic theory (frequently in the United States), which
came to dominate the discipline of economics throughout much of the
world during the latter half of the twentieth century (Colander and Brenner
1992; Ascher 1997; Coats 1997; Harberger 1997). As a result, they show a
decided preference for market-oriented solutions.[26] The economists also
tend to support pension privatization because they typically believe that the
pension system should serve the aims of macroeconomic policy as well as social policy, unlike the traditional social security experts who tend to focus
narrowly on the social goals of the pension systems. In addition, the economists, unlike the traditional social security experts, do not have any stake
in the existing public pension system since they tend to be new to the field
and therefore have no association with previous policies. This tends to make
them more willing to advocate privatization, which involves a major break
with the established order. Finally, the economists also tend to be more favorably disposed to pension privatization because they have much closer
links than the traditional social security experts to the international financial
institutions and the private sector, both of which have commonly supported
pension privatization. Indeed, many of the economists have worked previously for the IFIs or in the private sector, and they may hope to do so in the
future. Thus, they may well stand to benefit personally from the privatization of the pension systems.

Political Determinants of Pension Privatization

Ideational factors, namely, the increasing influence of the World Bank,
neoliberal economists, and the Chilean model, shaped how policymakers
chose to respond to the economic problems that they faced during the 1990s.
Once economic difficulties placed pension reform on the policy agenda, neoliberal economists, the World Bank, and the Chilean model played an important role in defining the policy options and their consequences. Numerous governments sought to privatize their pension systems, in part because
neoliberal economists, the World Bank, and the Chilean example all suggested that pension privatization would bring a host of benefits, including
increases in domestic saving rates and reductions in pension spending. The
governments most likely to privatize their pension systems proved to be
those governments where neoliberal economists, the World Bank, and the
Chilean model had the most influence.

Economic and ideational factors have shaped the pension reform choices
of leaders worldwide, but political factors have determined whether and
how these choices have been translated into actual reforms. The reform preferences of presidents or prime ministers are not necessarily shared by other

political actors. Legislators, for example, are typically less concerned about domestic capital shortages or high public pension spending than the executive since they are less likely to be held politically accountable for the health of the economy as a whole. Individual legislators tend to be focused on attending to their particular base of political support, which is typically not the entire nation. Interest groups are also typically more concerned about the effect of a given reform on their particular constituency than on its impact on the economy as a whole. Both social and political actors may try to block reforms that harm the constituency that they represent.

The degree of opposition that political leaders encounter depends partly on the nature of the pension reforms. Reforms that expand pension benefits are not likely to encounter great political opposition, although the private sector and some other groups may be concerned about how such benefits will be financed. Cutbacks in benefits, by contrast, are likely to provoke more vigorous dissent. Where public pension expenditures are very high, however, a broad consensus may emerge that some cutbacks are inevitable. Such a consensus has emerged in a number of European countries in recent years, enabling reforms to be approved through concert with a diverse set of political parties and interest groups (Myles and Pierson 2001; Hinrichs 2001). No such consensus has emerged regarding the necessity of privatization, however, in part because the benefits of pension privatization are still under debate. To enact privatization schemes, political leaders must therefore overcome opposition from a variety of quarters.

The labor movement, pensioners' associations, and the beneficiaries of privileged pension schemes have typically been at the forefront of the resistance to pension privatization. These interest groups have succeeded in altering the pension privatization proposals to suit their own interests. The beneficiaries of privileged pension schemes, such as the military, the judiciary, and state employees, have sometimes managed to have themselves excluded from the reforms. Organized labor, meanwhile, has at times managed to water down the reforms as a whole or to obtain concessions that benefit the unions and their leaders, particularly when the unions have enjoyed close ties to the ruling political party.

Interest groups have usually been too weak or too self-interested to block the pension privatization proposals, however. In most countries, pensioners' organizations lack the financial resources and political clout necessary to present a serious obstacle to pension privatization. The beneficiaries of privileged pension schemes, meanwhile, are often more interested in preserving their own pension programs than in blocking pension privatization as a whole. Organized labor has posed a more serious threat to pension privatization, but in most cases the unions have been too poorly organized or dependent on the state to block the reforms on their own. The most effective opposition to pension privatization has come not from interest groups, but from political parties, including members of the executive's own party.

Institutions and Pension Privatization

Numerous scholars have argued that the opposition to pension reform and other policy measures is mediated by political institutions. One influential approach that has been used to understand the impact of political institutions on social policy reform focuses on the number of opportunities (or veto points) that political institutions provide to opponents of reform to block the policy measures (Immergut 1992: Huber, Ragin, and Stephens 1993; Tsebelis 1995; Kay 1998, 1999; Orenstein 1999; Bonoli 2000). As this literature shows, some political institutions grant more opportunities to veto policy measures than do others. Parliamentary systems, for example, typically offer fewer veto points than presidential systems since the prime minister is usually elected by a parliamentary majority, which eliminates the potential for divided government (Tsebelis 1995; Bonoli 2000). Unicameral parliaments also obviously offer fewer chances to block reforms than bicameral parliaments, and unitary systems typically have fewer veto points than federal systems (Huber, Ragin, and Stephens 1993; Tsebelis 1995; Bonoli 2000). Countries that permit citizen referendums, meanwhile, have more veto points, since opponents of reform may use these referendums to block the measures that they oppose (Immergut 1992; Kay 1999; Bonoli 2000). The type of electoral system also influences the number of veto points available. Electoral systems that use single-member districts, for example, tend to produce fewer parties and thus fewer veto players than systems that use proportional representation.

None of these institutional variables can explain pension privatization within Latin America, although they may well be important in other areas of the world.[27] Numerous Latin American countries have been able to enact pension privatization schemes in spite of the fact that they all have presidential systems and use proportional representation to elect the lower chambers of their legislatures.[28] Some Latin American countries have unicameral systems, which should make it easier for them to enact policy reforms, but these countries do not appear to be any more likely to approve the pension privatization schemes. Indeed, less than half of the Latin American countries that have unicameral legislatures have privatized their pension systems, whereas more than half of the Latin American countries that have bicameral legislatures have done so.[29] Nor do Latin American countries with unitary systems appear to be any more likely to enact pension privatization schemes than Latin American countries with federal systems. Half of the Latin American countries with unitary systems have privatized their pension systems, but so have half of the countries with federal systems.[30] Finally, the existence of a citizen's referendum has not played a significant role in determining the fate of pension privatization in Latin America. Only one Latin American country, Uruguay, permits citizen's referendums and this country managed to privatize its pension system, although with some difficulty.[31]

Other political institutions have shaped efforts to privatize the pension system in important ways, however. The constitutional rules governing social security have placed constraints on what sorts of reforms are politically feasible. Based on what they say or do not say about social security, constitutions determine what sorts of reforms can be enacted through ordinary legislation and which reforms require a constitutional amendment. Not surprisingly, executives that must amend the constitution in order to enact a given social security reform will have a difficult time doing so, since amending the constitution typically requires supermajority votes in the legislature. Constitutions vary considerably in terms of what they say about social security, from those that say nothing at all to those that spell out very detailed rights.[32] Although many constitutions specify that social security is the responsibility of the state, in most instances they do not explicitly prohibit the private provision of social security benefits. Thus, most governments that have proposed pension privatization have not felt obliged to seek a constitutional amendment. Constitutional restrictions have nevertheless shaped some social security privatization proposals by proscribing certain reform possibilities, such as closing the public pension system or eliminating the social security contributions made by employers.

Regime type has also influenced the outcome of efforts to privatize the pension systems. Many of the early studies of market-oriented reform maintained that authoritarian regimes were more likely to carry out harsh neoliberal reforms since they had the strength and autonomy necessary to repress labor or other opponents of such measures (Sheahan 1980; Díaz-Alejandro 1983; Kaufman 1986). A few scholars made similar arguments with regard to social security reform, suggesting that only authoritarian regimes were likely to overcome the opposition to pension privatization or other sweeping pension reforms (Rosenberg and Malloy 1978; Malloy 1985). There is no evidence that authoritarian regimes are more likely to privatize their pension systems than democratic regimes, however. Indeed, the vast majority of pension privatization schemes have taken place under democratic rather than authoritarian rule. Authoritarian regimes may actually be less likely than democratic regimes to support pension privatization because many authoritarian regimes are reliant on the military, which tends to be skeptical of the merits of pension privatization. This may partly explain why to date only one military regime—the Pinochet government in Chile—has privatized its pension system.[33]

If authoritarian regimes do opt to privatize their pension systems, however, they are more likely to be able to carry out a sweeping pension privatization scheme (Mesa-Lago 1997b; Madrid 1997; Mesa-Lago and Müller 2002). As Mesa-Lago (1999: 133) has argued, there is "an inverse relationship between the degree of democratization and [pension] privatization: the regimes that are the least democratic at the time of the reform introduce the most privatized systems (least public) and the most democratic regimes maintain the most public systems (least privatized)." Whereas democratic governments have frequently been obliged to grant concessions to the opponents of pension privatization schemes, authoritarian regimes have typically ignored or suppressed the opposition, enabling them to enact relatively sweeping privatization schemes quite quickly.

Executive Control of the Legislature

The most important political determinant of pension privatization is the executive's degree of control of the legislature. The fate of social security reform proposals is determined to a large extent by partisan political battles within the legislature, which makes it crucial that the executive control the legislature. Unlike economic stabilization measures and some of the first-stage structural reforms, major social security reforms usually require congressional approval (Naím 1995; Nelson 1995). Although some executives have decree powers, the scope of these powers is typically the subject of a great deal of controversy (Carey and Shugart 1998). In most countries, the enactment of a major social security reform by decree would provoke legal and parliamentary challenges. In order to provide the reforms with a solid legal foundation, democratic leaders will therefore typically prefer to seek legislative approval for the reform measures.[34] Without this legal security, the private sector might be reluctant to make the substantial up-front investments required to establish private pension funds.

Some scholars have argued that market reform is easier to carry out in consolidated party systems than in fragmented party systems. (Packenham 1992; Haggard and Kaufman 1995). The degree of party system fragmentation only matters, however, because the ruling party's share of seats in the legislature tends to be lower in fragmented party systems. It is not clear that it would be more difficult for an executive to implement market-oriented reform in a fragmented party system than in a cohesive party system if the ruling party's share of seats were the same in both systems. Indeed, an executive that controls a majority or a near majority of the seats in the legislature might prefer to face numerous small opposition parties rather than a single large opposition party.

The composition of the legislature is particularly important with regard to pension reform. The unpopularity of pension privatization means that executives frequently have a difficult time obtaining votes for pension reform legislation. Even legislators who are ideologically sympathetic to the social security reform proposals may be loath to assume the political costs of voting for the unpopular reforms. In order to gain approval for social security reform bills, executives therefore typically need to have a good deal of control over their legislatures. Indeed, executives need to have some degree of control over their legislatures even if they choose to enact a major social security reform by decree, since they will need to ensure that legislators do not veto the decree. The degree of control that the executive has over the legislature depends in large part on the percentage of seats that the executive's party holds in the legislature, which in turn depends partly on institutional variables such as electoral rules and the degree of party system fragmentation. The ruling party's share of seats in the legislature is important because the executive typically has much more influence over the votes of members of his or her own party than other parties, particularly when it comes to unpopular measures like social security reform.[35]

Executives can typically obtain the votes of members of their own parties more easily, in part because the policy positions of executives are more likely to resemble the positions of legislators from their own party than other parties. Even where this is not the case, the logic of political competition often leads legislators from the executive's party to support his or her initiatives more often than do legislators from opposition parties. Legislators are inclined to support an executive from their own party, because they tend to benefit electorally from sharing the party label of a popular and successful national leader. A major legislative defeat will not only hurt the executive but also other members of his or her party. Legislators from the ruling party thus have personal electoral incentives to help the executive get legislation passed. Legislators from parties in the opposition have the opposite incentive, since they will tend to benefit if the executive's popularity declines. Thus, they may seek to block legislation, even if they agree with the basic principles behind it, in order to damage the executive's reputation as an effective leader.

Executives have a number of tools at their disposal that they can use to obtain the support of legislators who are members of their own party, but they have considerably fewer means of eliciting votes from legislators of other parties. As leaders of their parties, executives usually have at least some control over a variety of party resources. These resources may be used to punish or reward legislators in accordance with how they vote. Executives may have some influence over committee assignments or positions in the party leadership. More importantly, executives may help decide the position of candidates on the party's electoral lists and they may have some control over who receives party financing as well. Thus, executives frequently have a great deal of influence over the electoral possibilities of legislators running for reelection or seeking new posts.

Legislators from allied parties are less likely than members of the ruling party to support the executive on unpopular issues such as social security reform, but they are considerably more likely to do so than are members of opposition parties. First, members of allied parties are more likely to agree with the president's policy positions than are members of opposition parties. Indeed, ideological similarities are often what lead political alliances to be forged between parties. In addition, the political fortunes of legislators from allied parties tend to be linked to the political success of the government, which provides them with incentives to back the executive's initiatives. This is particularly true in parliamentary systems where the defeat of key legislation can lead to the dissolution of the government.

Although executives typically do not control the financing or electoral lists of allied parties, they nevertheless have some means of pressuring legislators of allied parties to vote for their bills. Some members of allied parties are typically placed in charge of government ministries, and the executive can pressure these ministers to use their influence within their parties to obtain votes for the president's legislation. Executives can even go so far as to promise positions in government to allied party legislators who agree to support the president. Moreover, as the heads of government, presidents control tremendous amounts of state patronage resources such as jobs and state contracts, which may be offered to the family, friends, or districts of legislators in order to secure their votes. Although these patronage resources are often used to buy the votes of members of the executive's own party or allied parties, it is much more politically controversial to use them to win the votes of legislators from opposition parties.

The executive's degree of control of the legislature will also depend on the degree of internal party discipline. Although executives will almost always have greater influence over members of their own parties than they do over legislators from other parties, the amount of internal discipline varies considerably between parties. Party discipline depends to a certain extent on the degree of control that party leaders have over the ballot since party leaders may use their control over the ballot to oblige party members to toe the line (Carey and Shugart 1995; Ames 1995; Mainwaring and Shugart 1997). Conjunctural factors, such as personality or ideological differences among party members and their leaders, also play an important role in party discipline since they may lead to internal splits.

Conclusion

A combination of economic pressures, ideational mechanisms, and political factors has shaped pension reform efforts in recent years. Each of these different types of variables has played a crucial role at a particular stage of the reform process. As Table 2.3 indicates, economic factors, especially rising

TABLE 2.3

The Determinants of Pension Reform Outcomes at Different Stages of the Policy Process

	Stage 1: Agenda setting	Stage 2: Policy choice	Stage 3: Proposal enactment
Potential outcome at each stage	Pension reform does (not) enter the policy agenda	Executive opts for privatization (or other reform type)	Reform is enacted (or modified or blocked)
Main arena of debate	Executive branch of government	Executive branch of government	Legislature
Main actors involved	Economics and social ministries	Economics and social ministries; World Bank	Political parties and members of the legislature
Which type of factors are key	Economic	Ideational	Political
Primary determinants of outcome at each stage	1) Economic burden of public pension spending 2) Domestic capital shortages	1) Salience of Chilean model 2) Influence of World Bank 3) Influence of economists	1) Ruling-party strength 2) Ruling-party discipline

public pension spending and recurrent capital shortages, have placed pension reform on the policy agenda in many countries throughout the world. Nations facing chronic domestic capital shortages have considered pension privatization as a means to boost their sagging domestic savings rates and to reduce their dependence on volatile foreign capital. Some countries with high public pension expenditures have also contemplated pension privatization in the hope that it would reduce their public pension spending in the long run. The large existing public pension commitments of these latter countries have placed limits on the degree of privatization that is financially feasible, however.

Economic factors alone cannot explain why numerous governments opted to privatize their pension system, particularly considering that many of the economic benefits of pension privatization are debateable. To explain policy choice, this chapter explored the channels through which ideas about the efficacy of pension privatization have flowed. It identified three main factors that shaped beliefs about pension privatization during the 1990s: regional diffusion of the Chilean model; the growing influence of the World Bank; and the ascent of neoliberal economists. Each of these variables helps explain why some countries have sought to privatize their pension systems, whereas others did not. The Chilean experiment with pension privatization helped persuade many Latin American policymakers that pension privatization would boost their domestic savings rates, bolster their capital markets, and bring higher pensions at a lower cost. The World Bank and neoliberal economists, meanwhile, used their growing policy-making influence in some countries to promote aggressively the benefits of pension privatization. As a result, pension privatization has been more common where the Chilean model has been more salient and where neoliberal economists and the international financial institutions have had more policy-making influence.

Whereas economic and ideational factors have shaped what sorts of social security reforms governments have proposed in recent years, political factors have determined when and how they have been able to enact the reform proposals. In order to enact pension privatization schemes, the executive has typically needed to hold a majority or a near majority of seats in the legislature since legislators from other parties have typically opposed the reforms. At the same time, the executive has needed to maintain a high degree of control over his or her own party to prevent disgruntled party members from voting against the reforms. Other political factors, such as regime type, the constitutional rules governing social security, and the strength of affected interest groups, have shaped the details of the pension privatization proposals, but they have not typically played a crucial role in determining whether the pension privatization schemes were enacted.

CHAPTER 3

The Politics of Sweeping Privatization: Pension Policy in Mexico in the 1990s

IN DECEMBER 1995, the administration of President Ernesto Zedillo (1994–2000) enacted the most sweeping pension reform that had been carried out anywhere since Chile privatized its pension system in 1981. The Mexican reform established a new private pension system and required all current (as well as future) members of the main public pension system—the Mexican Social Security Institute (IMSS)—to transfer to the new system. As in Chile, the new system is based on individual retirement accounts, which will be managed mostly by private pension fund administrators. In the future, the size of the pensions that most Mexican workers receive will depend largely on the amount of funds that they have accumulated in their private retirement accounts.

This chapter seeks to explain why the Mexican government chose to implement such a sweeping privatization plan, and how it was able to do so in spite of the widespread opposition it faced in various quarters of Mexican society. The reform was largely a response to the capital shortages that plagued Mexico beginning in the 1980s. These capital shortages destabilized the Mexican economy, undermining the ruling party's base of popular support. By privatizing its pension system, the Mexican government hoped to boost its savings rates and financial markets to Chilean levels, thereby reducing the country's dependence on unstable foreign capital. The Zedillo administration also hoped that pension privatization would resolve the long-term financial problems of the main public pension system, but these problems were still relatively minor compared to those faced by most European countries and some Latin American countries, such as Argentina and Brazil.

The successes of the Chilean model played an important role in persuading the Mexican government of the benefits of pension privatization.

Throughout the early 1990s, Mexican policymakers had a substantial amount of contact with Chilean pension experts who lobbied them to follow the Chilean path. The World Bank also promoted pension privatization in Mexico in its contacts with Mexican policymakers, even going so far as to bring some Chilean consultants to the country to help formulate a privatization plan. The main proponents of pension privatization in Mexico, however, were the neoliberal economists who took over the key policy-making roles in the Mexican government in the late 1980s and early 1990s. The economists used their expertise and considerable influence to persuade the top political leaders that pension privatization would bring a host of economic and social benefits to the country.

The Mexican government was able to carry out such a sweeping privatization in part because its existing public pension obligations were still relatively low, particularly in comparison to Argentina and Brazil. This reduced the transition costs of reform. Perhaps more importantly, President Ernesto Zedillo's dominance of the Mexican political system meant that he could push through the privatization plan in spite of its widespread unpopularity. In the mid-1990s, Mexico still had a semiauthoritarian political system, dominated by a single party, the Partido Revolucionario Institucional (PRI). At the time of the reform, the ruling PRI held a solid majority of seats in the legislature and maintained a high level of party discipline, which enabled the Zedillo administration, unlike its counterparts in Argentina and Brazil, to enact its proposed reform with only relatively minor changes. Mexican labor unions were able to obtain some concessions from the government thanks in large part to their close ties to the ruling party, but labor leaders were ultimately too dependent on the ruling party to press for more substantial modifications.

The Origins of Social Security in Mexico

The Mexican Social Security Institute was established in 1943 during the presidency of Manuel Avila Camacho. The IMSS constituted the first major Mexican social security program, although minor social security programs serving relatively privileged sectors of the Mexican workforce such as the military and civil servants date from the 1920s and 1930s (Mesa-Lago 1978; IMSS 1952; Sánchez Vargas 1963). Mexico was not one of the social security pioneers in Latin America, but it gradually became one of the leaders of the second generation of social security innovators in the region. From the beginning, the IMSS, which was funded by contributions from workers, their employers, and the state, provided workers and their families with medical care as well as old-age, invalidity, and survivors' pensions.

The impetus for the creation of the IMSS came largely from the state itself (Spalding 1980; Zertuche Muñoz 1980). Under the direction of Avila Camacho, a small team of government bureaucrats, with the assistance of social security experts from the ILO, drew up a plan based on proposals that had been formulated by previous administrations (Sánchez Vargas 1963; Pozas Horcasitas 1990; Zertuche Muñoz 1980). Social security policymakers in the 1940, like in the 1990s, were motivated in large part by economic concerns. According to Spalding (1980), the bureaucrats pushed for the creation of the Mexican Social Security Institute in order to facilitate the country's drive toward industrialization.[1] Social security programs, the policymakers believed, would help ensure labor quiescence and would generate revenue that could be used to develop the country's infrastructure.

The Avila Camacho administration used its ties to business and to labor leaders and its domination of Congress to obtain support for the proposed legislation. The government first submitted a draft of the initial proposal to a tripartite commission composed of representatives from business, labor, and the state. Although business and labor had shown some reluctance in the past to finance the costs of a national social security system, they ultimately signed off on the proposed legislation without making any major modifications (Spalding 1980; Zertuche Muñoz 1980). The bill was then submitted to the ruling party-dominated legislature, which approved it immediately.

Opposition to the legislation soon surfaced, however. Some employers' associations, including the National Confederations of Chambers of Commerce and Industry, the Association of Bankers, and some insurance companies campaigned to annul or postpone the new social security law (Pozas Horcasitas 1990; López Villegas 1990). Some labor unions also organized demonstrations against the reform, although the main labor federations continued to support it (Dion 2000; Pozas Horcasitas 1990). The Avila Camacho administration managed to overcome this resistance through a combination of appeasement and repression, however. The government first slowed down the implementation of the program and agreed to exempt railroad and petroleum workers from the new law, enabling these unions to maintain their separate, privileged programs (Spalding 1980). When some opposition persisted, the government responded by arresting the leaders of the opposition, a move that quickly broke the back of the resistance movement (Spalding 1980; Pozas Horcasitas 1990; Dion 2000).

Although the new social security system was intended to ultimately serve the population as a whole, only a very small portion of the labor force (almost exclusively urban workers) was incorporated into the system at the outset. At the end of 1946, the Mexican Social Security Institute covered only 2 percent of the population and six years later, the IMSS still only covered 4 percent of the population (Mesa-Lago 1978: 216–17). Throughout the next several decades, however, social security coverage increased steadily as

TABLE 3.1

The Evolution of Social Security Coverage in Mexico

(in thousands of persons)

	1960	1970	1980	1990	1994
Pensioners	72	287	634	1,378★	1,700★
Insured workers	1,521	3,845	8,158	12,776★	13,631★
Family members of the insured	2,969	8,201	22,028	32,723★	30,248★
Total insured population	4,562	12,333	30,820	48,256	47,850
Pensioners/Insured workers	4.7%	7.5%	7.8%	10.8%★	12.5%★
Insured workers/Total labor force	15.6%	28.1%	42.0%	56.7%★	58.1%★
Insured population/ total population	12.3%	24.1%	45.2%	59.4%	54.1%

SOURCE: Mesa-Lago 1989; Ulloa Padilla 1996b; López Angel 1996; INEGI 1996; Nacional Financiera 1995.
★Includes IMSS and ISSSTE only.

benefits were extended, albeit unevenly, to most occupational categories. As Table 3.1 shows, the percentage of the population covered by the various social security systems rose steadily until 1990, when it reached 59.4 percent (Mesa-Lago 1989: 150–51; Ulloa Padilla 1996a: 38). During this period, the government also extended new benefits, such as day care services and family allowances, to members of the system.

The social security system remained somewhat fragmented throughout this period in spite of intermittent government efforts to unify it (Mesa-Lago 1989). State employees, oil workers, military personnel, and railroad and electrical workers all maintained separate social security programs, although the latter two categories of workers were finally incorporated into the IMSS in the 1980s. The Institute of Social Security at the Service of State Workers (ISSSTE) was the most important of these separate systems, covering 8.3 million people in 1990, which represented 17.2 percent of the total population covered by social security programs in Mexico (López Angel 1996: 65; Ulloa Padilla 1996a: 38). This system, however, was dwarfed by the IMSS, which covered 38.5 million people in 1990, or approximately 80 percent of the insured population (Ulloa Padilla 1996a: 38).

The fragmentation of the system created inequalities since the smaller systems typically provided better services and benefits than did the IMSS. In 1990, for example, the average pension extended by the ISSSTE represented 62.8 percent of the average salary of contributors to this system, whereas the average pension doled out by the IMSS constituted 34.4 percent of the average salary of IMSS contributors (Soto 1992: 221). The smaller systems also typically had looser requirements to gain access to benefits (Mesa-Lago 1978,

1989). The ISSSTE, for example, granted pension benefits to state employees who had worked for thirty years (twenty-eight years for female employees) regardless of their age, whereas the IMSS only granted pensions to workers over sixty-five years of age, or over sixty years of age in the case of the unemployed (Soto 1992: 224).

Emerging Financial Problems

In the 1980s, the Mexican social security system began to encounter financial problems for the first time. These problems were caused in large part by the decline of the system's dependency ratio (that is, the ratio of contributing workers to pension recipients), which fell from sixty-seven to one in 1950 to around eight to one in 1994 (Sales, Solís, and Villagómez 1998: 138). The decline of the dependency ratio stemmed in part from demographic changes. Whereas in 1960 a 65-year-old man could expect to live for 12.9 more years, by 1994 life expectancies at age 65 had increased to 18.6 years for men (IMSS 1995: 60). The main factor behind the falling ratio of workers to pension recipients was the aging of the pension system itself, however. In the 1950s, the pension system had not been around a long enough time to have accumulated many pensioners since individuals needed to have contributed for at least ten years to be eligible for a pension. By the 1980s, however, a much larger proportion of people over the age of sixty-five met the pension eligibility requirements. The slowdown in the expansion of pension coverage that occurred in the 1980s and 1990s also caused the dependency ratio to fall by reducing the growth in the number of active workers joining the system.

The financial health of the IMSS was also undermined by the Mexican government's failure to increase mandatory pension contributions during the first five decades of the system's operation. Although the life expectancy of pensioners increased and the IMSS added a variety of pension benefits, the total pension contribution rate remained at 6 percent of a worker's salary until the 1990s when it was gradually increased to 8 percent (Soto 1992: 240–41). In addition, certain administrative policies contributed to the IMSS's financial difficulties by enabling workers and their employers to strategically manipulate the system. For example, the Mexican Social Security Institute only required workers to have contributed to the pension system for 500 weeks in order to qualify for a pension, which led many workers to contribute no more than that. Indeed, 15 percent of pensions authorized in 1994 were to workers who had contributed for exactly 500 weeks (Cámara de Diputados de los Estados Unidos Mexicanos 1995a: 2367). The Mexican Social Security Institute also facilitated payment evasion by basing pension benefits on the worker's salaries during the last five years rather than over the course of the worker's lifetime. As a result, some workers would contribute only in the years immediately before their retirement.

To make matters worse, the IMSS failed to invest profitably the large surpluses that were generated in the first decades of the system's operation when the dependency ratio was quite favorable. Although a portion of the pension surpluses were invested in financial assets, most of the pension surpluses were plowed into the construction of office buildings, hospitals, and other fixed assets, which typically did not produce an investment yield. The pension surpluses also subsidized current expenditures for the IMSS's health care programs, which consistently ran large deficits (IMSS 1995; Mesa-Lago 1989: 159). Thus, although the IMSS pension system was nominally a fully funded system, in practice it functioned basically like a pay-as-you-go system. According to one government study, by 1966, the IMSS's pension fund already had an *actuarial* deficit of 8 billion pesos (Mesa-Lago 1978: 243).

The economic crisis that erupted in the early 1980s accelerated the decline in the financial health of the IMSS. First, the inflation that broke out in the early 1980s wiped out the pension system's financial reserves since these assets typically bore fixed interest rates. Between 1981 and 1983, the IMSS's financial assets had a negative annual yield of 20.8 percent, which quickly eroded the real value of these assets (Mesa-Lago 1991a: 33). Second, the economic crisis caused wages and formal sector employment to decline, which cut into the IMSS's revenues. Between 1981 and 1987, the IMSS's total revenues fell 45 percent in real terms, before beginning a recovery in 1988 (McGreevey 1990: 89). The ratio of revenue to expenditures in the IMSS's pension system, meanwhile, dropped from 2 to 1 in 1980 to 1.15 to 1 in 1987 (Bertranou 1994: 85). The only reason that this ratio did not decline further was that the government slowed down pension expenditures by allowing inflation to erode the real value of pensions. As Table 3.2 shows, by 1988, the average pension was approximately half of its 1980 level in real terms (Soto 1992: 230).

The emerging financial problems of the Mexican social security system, coupled with the increasing protests from pensioners upset about their declining benefit levels, put pressure on the Mexican government to undertake reform. Some policymakers and interest groups promoted pension privatization as a means to solve these problems. They argued that shifting from a pay-as-you-go to a fully funded operating method would reduce the system's vulnerability to future demographic changes. A private system, they suggested, would also produce higher pension benefits in the long run. Proponents of pension privatization in Mexico pointed to the 1981 Chilean reform, which had stabilized the long-term financial position of that country's pension system while increasing its average pension levels.

Financial problems alone cannot explain why the Mexican government

TABLE 3.2

Financial Problems of the Mexican Social Security Institute

	1982	1983	1984	1985	1986	1987	1988	1989	1990
Pension spending/GDP	0.20%	0.19%	0.19%	0.21%	0.24%	0.21%	0.22%	0.40%	0.37%
Real pension★	0.91	0.69	0.63	0.65	0.64	0.55	0.53	0.98	0.89
Growth in pensioners	11.1%	7.1%	20.0%	10.7%	7.3%	7.2%	10.3%	6.2%	4.0%
Growth in insured workers	−1.1%	0.3%	8.1%	6.6%	−1.8%	9.7%	1.8%	11.3%	8.4%
Pensioners/insured workers	8.4%	8.9%	9.9%	10.3%	11.3%	11.0%	11.9%	11.4%	10.9%

★ 1980 equals 1.0.

SOURCES: Soto 1990; Ulloa Padilla 1996a.

chose to privatize the IMSS's pension system, however. First, the financial problems do not indicate why the Mexican government opted for privatization rather than some other type of reform. Privatization was not only politically controversial, but also it had substantial fiscal costs. The Mexican government could easily have opted for a different kind of reform with fewer political and economic costs. Indeed, when Carlos Salinas assumed the presidency in 1988, he initially took this route. During the first years of his tenure, Salinas passed legislation that substantially increased the real value of the minimum pension, boosted health care and pension contributions, prohibited the Mexican Social Security Institute from using pension revenues to finance its other social programs, and obliged the IMSS to invest at least 50 percent of its pension reserves in financial assets (Soto 1992).

Second, the financial problems facing the Mexican Social Security Institute were relatively mild in comparison to those facing some other Latin American countries, not to mention the industrialized countries. The pension system of the Mexican Social Security Institute continued to run an annual surplus through the early 1990s, although deficits were projected for future decades (IMSS 1995). Moreover, both the dependency ratio of the IMSS and its annual pension spending were still well within sustainable levels. In 1990, Mexico's total pension spending represented roughly 0.57 percent of the country's GDP (Soto 1992: 221), whereas the OECD countries were spending approximately 9.2 percent of their gross domestic product on pensions by the late 1980s (World Bank 1994b: 358).

Economic Crisis and Neoliberal Reform

To understand why the Mexican government chose to privatize its pension system, we must examine the severe capital shortages that plagued Mexico beginning in the 1980s. The move toward pension privatization responded not so much to the long-term problems of the Mexican social security system as it did to the more immediate and serious macroeconomic problems that the country faced. Policymakers advocated pension privatization in large part because they believed that it would boost the country's domestic savings rate, thereby reducing the country's vulnerability to cutoffs of foreign capital. The leading proponents of pension privatization were neoliberal economists who came to dominate the Mexican government in the late 1980s and early 1990s. The international financial institutions and some domestic business organizations also strongly advocated the privatization of the pension system, however.

The severe economic crisis that struck Mexico in the 1980s was brought on by the sudden cutoff of foreign capital inflows. In the 1970s, Mexico had borrowed heavily on the international markets, taking advantage of the plentiful credit available in a highly liquid international financial system. Most of these loans had floating interest rates, however, which meant that the cost of servicing the credits increased substantially as a result of the sharp rise in international interest rates that began in 1979. Mexico's interest payments on long-term loans rose from $1.1 billion in 1975 to $4.6 billion in 1980 and $7.8 billion in 1982 (World Bank 1989: 262). To make matters worse, the price of oil, which was Mexico's principal source of export revenue, began to decline in mid-1981, leaving the country starved of foreign currency. Concerned about Mexico's deteriorating financial situation, some commercial banks began to cut back on their loans to the country or provided only expensive short-term credits. Both domestic and foreign investors also transferred large sums of money out of the country because of their concerns about Mexico's economic stability. According to one estimate, Mexican capital flight totaled $11.6 billion in 1981 and $6.5 billion in 1982 (Lustig 1992: 40).

The sudden withdrawal of capital plunged Mexico into a serious economic crisis. Gross domestic product fell 0.6 percent in 1982 and 4.2 percent in 1983, causing unemployment to surge. Inflation, meanwhile, rose from 27.9 percent in 1981 to 58.9 percent in 1982 and 101.9 percent in 1983. The economic crisis had devastating effects on the population as a whole, creating widespread discontent. Real wages per worker dropped 5.1 percent in 1982 and 22.9 in 1983, while private consumption dropped by 2.5 percent in 1982 and 5.4 percent in 1983 (Lustig 1992). The economic crisis caused disenchantment with the existing state-led development model and increased the influence of advocates of market-oriented reform.

In the wake of the debt crisis, the international financial institutions (IFIs), such as the International Monetary Fund (IMF), the World Bank, and the Inter-American Development Bank (IDB), began to play a much more important role in Mexican policy making. These institutions provided financing to Mexico that helped keep the country afloat. More importantly, the IFIs effectively controlled the fate of Mexico's efforts to refinance its privately contracted debt, since commercial banks refused to reschedule their loans or grant new credits to Mexico unless the country signed a lending agreement with the IMF. In order to obtain credits from the international financial institutions, the Mexican government had to agree to undertake certain policy reforms. At the outbreak of the crisis, the required reforms consisted principally of stabilization measures such as cuts in government expenditures and the devaluation of the peso. As time wore on, however, the international financial institutions increasingly pressed the Mexican government to adopt more far-reaching structural reforms, such as reducing its barriers to foreign trade and investment and cutting back on the role of the state in the economy.

The political clout of the business community also increased in the 1980s;

it, too, used its influence to lobby for market-oriented reforms. The outbreak of the debt crisis in 1982 and the ensuing nationalization of the banks caused the business community to mobilize in defense of its economic interests (Maxfield and Anzaldúa 1987; Valdés Ugalde 1994). The two years following the economic crisis were the most confrontational in the history of business-state relations in Mexico, because business leaders began to press the government to allow more participation of the private sector in policy making and to reduce state intervention in the economy (Millán 1988; Valdés Ugalde 1994; Tirado and Luna 1995). Although not all members of the private sector favored neoliberal reform, most of the principal business associations did. Indeed, the main division within the business community was not between opponents and advocates of neoliberal reform, but rather was between the moderate business organizations such as the Mexican Council of Businessmen (CMHN), the Mexican Association of Stockbrokers (AMCB), and the Mexican Association of Insurance Institutions (AMIS) that loyally supported the government's gradualist approach to reform, and the more confrontational business organizations such the Employers' Federation of the Mexican Republic (COPARMEX) and the National Confederation of Chambers of Commerce (CONCANACO), which demanded more radical measures (Millán 1988; Puga 1993).[2]

The business community's influence was enhanced by its willingness to use "exit" as well as "voice" to demonstrate its unhappiness with government policies (Thacker 2000). During the 1980s, a growing number of businessmen, particularly those from the northern states, switched their allegiances from the governing PRI to the Partido de Acción Nacional (PAN). Indeed, several prominent businessmen ran for governorships under the aegis of the PAN, and in 1988, Manuel Clouthier, a former head of a business peak association, became the PAN's presidential candidate (Montesinos 1992: 111; Puga 1993). Even more threatening to the ruling party, however, was the propensity of Mexican businessmen to show their displeasure with the government's economic policies by transferring much of their assets abroad. During the 1970s when foreign capital was relatively plentiful, the Mexican government did not feel especially threatened by capital flight, but in the wake of the debt crisis, such flight became a major concern. To convince Mexican businessmen to maintain their investments in the country as well as to retain their political support, the Mexican government was obliged to pay increasing heed to the business community's economic and political demands.

The Rise of the Technocrats

The main push for market-oriented reform came from within the government itself, however. In the 1980s and 1990s, the main policy-making posts in the Mexican government were gradually taken over by a new breed of policymaker. The newly dominant policymakers, who were commonly referred to as "technocrats," typically had advanced degrees in economics or administration from prestigious universities in the United States. The technocrats had been trained in classical economic thought, which stressed the superior allocative efficiency of the market. Partly for this reason, they typically recommended market-oriented solutions to the economic and social problems that afflicted Mexico (Centeno 1994; Grindle 1996; Golob 1997; Babb 2001). Most of the technocrats had little, if any electoral or political experience, which might have led them to adopt a more cautious or even populist approach to public policy. Instead, their careers usually were rooted in the economics ministries, such as the Ministry of Finance, the Ministry of the Budget and Planning, or the Central Bank, although they subsequently branched out into other agencies.

The increasingly technocratic background of Mexican policymakers was apparent from the president on down. Whereas Mexican presidents prior to 1982 typically had no graduate-level training, President Miguel de la Madrid had obtained a master's degree in public administration from Harvard, President Carlos Salinas had a doctorate in political economy from Harvard, and President Ernesto Zedillo had a doctorate in economics from Yale. All three of these presidents had spent most of their careers in the Ministry of Finance and the Ministry of Budget and Planning, where they had developed large networks of like-minded colleagues. They drew heavily on these networks for their main advisers, and, as a result, the cabinets that these presidents appointed had a strong technocratic bent. The percentage of cabinet members with graduate degrees rose from less than 30 percent during the administration of José López Portillo to more than 40 percent during the presidency of de la Madrid, more than 50 percent under the Salinas administration, and more than 70 percent during the tenure of Ernesto Zedillo (Centeno 1994: 121; Camp 1996: 121). Most of these cabinet members had obtained their graduate degrees in economics or administration and had typically studied in the United States. The vast majority of them had no electoral experience (Centeno 1994; Camp 1996). The increasing dominance of technocrats was also noticeable, although to a lesser degree, in the upper reaches of the Mexican bureaucracy (Centeno 1994).

The rise of the Mexican technocrats is at least partly attributable to the economic crisis, which made expertise in economics particularly desirable (Maxfield 1990; Centeno 1994; Teichman 1995; Grindle 1996). In the wake of the crisis, the economics ministries and the technocrats who worked in them were granted a greater policy-making role. The technocrats flourished during this period in part because they, unlike the traditional politicos, offered a rigorous diagnosis of Mexico's most pressing problems as well as a credible way to address them. The technocrats also benefited from their close links with members of the international financial institutions and the private sector, which took on increasing political influence. In addition, the authoritarian nature of the Mexican political system facilitated the rise of the technocrats since political advancement was based not on electoral experience and popular appeal, which most of the technocrats lacked, but rather on insider influence (Golob 1997). Many of the technocrats showed themselves to be highly effective at insider politics, building networks of alliances, called "*camarillas*," which helped advance their careers. Moreover, the most successful technocrats typically contributed to the rise of their colleagues by favoring people with similar outlooks and educational backgrounds (Camp 1990).

The process of neoliberal reform in Mexico began slowly, but gathered speed as the decade wore on. The administration of José López Portillo initially responded to the outbreak of the crisis with statist policies, imposing currency controls and nationalizing Mexico's private banks. When de la Madrid assumed the presidency in late 1982, he quickly moved to carry out IMF-backed stabilization measures, cutting public sector spending and borrowing, but he did not undertake major structural reforms until the mid-1980s. Beginning in 1986, when Mexico joined the General Agreement on Tariffs and Trade (GATT), the de la Madrid administration also opened the Mexican economy to foreign trade. The proportion of domestically manufactured products that were protected by import licenses fell from 92.2 percent in 1985 to 46.9 percent in 1986 and 23.2 percent in 1988 (Lustig 1992: 120). Average tariff levels, meanwhile, dropped from 23.5 percent to 11.0 percent during this period (Lustig 1992: 120). During this period, the de la Madrid administration also substantially reduced the role of the state in the economy, privatizing a large number of state-owned or partially state-owned enterprises. The number of firms with at least partial state-ownership dropped from 1,155 in 1982 to 941 in 1985 and 412 in 1988 (Valdés Ugalde 1994: 226). Most of the privatized firms were relatively small, however, and were located in nonstrategic sectors.

These reforms met resistance within certain sectors of the ruling party who wanted to maintain the PRI's long tradition of statist policies. In 1986, some left-wing members of the PRI, led by Cuauhtémoc Cárdenas and Porfirio Muñoz Ledo, formed a dissident faction within the PRI called the Democratic Current, which advocated reversing the party's rightward drift and increasing popular participation in the selection of the party's candidates. Months of growing conflict between the Democratic Current and the leadership of the PRI culminated with the selection of Carlos Salinas to be the party's presidential candidate in the elections of 1988. As head of the Ministry for Planning and the Budget during the de la Madrid administration, Salinas had been one of the principal architects of the neoliberal policies implemented during this period, and he was therefore viewed with antipathy by the members of the Democratic Current. In the wake of Salinas's nomination, Cárdenas decided to run as the presidential candidate of a small left-of-center party, the Partido Auténtico de la Revolución Mexicana (PARM), and a number of his supporters left the PRI alongside him (Bruhn 1997; Garrido 1993). Cárdenas and his supporters subsequently created the Frente Democrática Nacional (FDN), which eventually comprised a wide variety of left-wing parties, including both the independent left as well as those left-leaning parties such as the PARM that had traditionally supported the PRI. In spite of the enormous disadvantages they faced in terms of resources and the control of the media, Cárdenas and the FDN did surprisingly well at the polls. According to the official returns, Cárdenas received 31 percent of the vote to Salinas's 51 percent, but most observers agree that the PRI inflated its vote totals through widespread electoral fraud.

Salinas, who took office in late 1988, deepened the reform process considerably. The Salinas administration accelerated the privatization of state enterprises in Mexico, reprivatizing the banks that had been nationalized in 1982 and selling some or all of the government's shares of many other major companies for the first time (Teichman 1995). Between 1990 and 1994, the Mexican government earned almost $24.3 billion in revenues from the sale of state-owned firms, substantially more than any other Latin American country earned during this period (IADB 1996a: 171). The Salinas administration also took steps to further deregulate the economy and open it up to foreign trade and investment, negotiating the North American Free Trade Agreement with the United States and Canada as well as bilateral agreements with a number of Latin American countries.

The Economic Rationale for Pension Privatization

Pension privatization came onto the policy agenda in Mexico for the first time during the Salinas administration.[3] The Salinas administration viewed pension privatization not only as a means to resolve the long-term financial problems of its pension system, but more importantly as a means to boost Mexico's domestic savings rate, which was becoming an increasingly important issue (Bertranou 1994). The debt crisis of the 1980s had taught Mexican policymakers a painful lesson about the risks of excessive dependence on foreign capital. The Salinas administration was therefore determined to boost the country's domestic savings rate to balance the renewed inflows of foreign capital. As Salinas noted in introducing the pension reform to Congress, Mexico needed "to increase its savings rates to finance investment. . . . In particular, it needed long-term savings to make possible long term financing" (Cámara de Diputados de los Estados Unidos Mexicanos 1992: 255). The private pension system, he argued, "would increase considerably the mass of lendable funds in the country, facilitating investment" (Cámara de Diputados de los Estados Unidos Mexicanos 1992: 255). A study commissioned by the Ministry of Finance and carried out by economists associated with a private university, the Autonomous Technological Institute of Mexico (ITAM), suggested that the pension reform would boost the country's domestic savings rate from approximately 22 percent in 1990 to around 28 percent in 1998 (Rivera Ríos 1992; Bertranou 1994: 101–2).

Salinas's initial pension privatization plan met strong internal opposition, and he ultimately decided to implement a scaled-back version of the reform, which was dubbed the Retirement Savings System. Many Mexican policymakers continued to be quite preoccupied with increasing domestic savings. This concern increased during the early 1990s, as the country's domestic savings rate fell. In the early 1990s, Mexico's domestic savings rate declined steadily in spite of the implementation of the SAR. Domestic savings dropped from 22 percent of gross domestic product in 1988 to 15.8 percent in 1994, obliging Mexico to depend heavily on foreign capital for its investment needs. Moreover, the risks of sudden capital outflows had grown. To attract foreign investment, the Mexican government had loosened up restrictions on the outflow of capital during the late 1980s, which made it easier for both foreign and domestic investors to quickly transfer money out of the country. In addition, most of the capital that entered Mexico in the early 1990s, unlike during previous periods, was in the form of highly liquid portfolio investment, such as stocks and bonds, which could be sold off relatively quickly by nervous investors. Between 1990 and 1993, portfolio investment constituted 53.7 percent of net capital flows to Mexico (Gurría 1995: 199).

The outbreak of the peso crisis in late 1994 confirmed the worst fears of many policymakers. In 1994, foreign investors, concerned about Mexico's increasing political instability, growing current account deficit, and deteriorating reserves, balked at renewing their investments in the country. Investors, fearing a devaluation of the peso, also began to spirit millions of dollars out of the country. When the devaluation finally came in December 1994, it provoked further panic, which was only calmed by the extension of mammoth loans from the IMF and the U.S. government. The foreign loans were unable to prevent a severe economic crisis, however. In 1995, Mexico's economy shrank by 6.2 percent, real wages dropped by 14.8 percent, and inflation rose to 34.4 percent (IADB 1997: 285).

Many policymakers placed the blame for the peso crisis on the country's low savings rates, which had obliged it to depend heavily on foreign capital. Carlos Noriega, a top official in the Ministry of Finance and one of the key planners of the reform observed, "There is a consensus that there has been a lack of domestic savings in the Mexican economy that makes it vulnerable to capital flows" (Noriega 1997: 2). Zedillo himself noted that he was "absolutely convinced that the most delicate point that our economy has had for many years has been the insufficiency of internal savings to finance our development" ("Peligro" 1996: 4). Boosting the country's savings rate thus became one of the Zedillo administration's main policy goals, featuring prominently in the government's National Development Plan. The private sector was largely in agreement with this diagnosis. On the day that the pension privatization plan was announced, Héctor Larios Santillán, the head of the Business Coordinating Council, stressed "the necessity that the country has to increase considerably domestic savings so as not to depend on external resources. It is well known that without savings there is no investment and without this, development is not possible" (Alemán Alemán 1995b: 12).

Supporters of pension privatization argued that it was the most effective means to boost domestic savings. As one of the architects of the reform and a colleague wrote in 1995: "If retirement saving is, for the moment, the most important single source to increase private saving, then it is crucial to have an adequate and efficient pension scheme that facilitates the achievement of this goal" (Solís and Villagómez 1996: 10). Another one of the planners of the reform, along with a World Bank colleague, meanwhile, argued that "the pension reform offers the most important opportunity for the government to foment savings and the growth of the financial markets" (Cerda and Grandolini 1997: 93). According to one estimate, the proposed pension privatization scheme would account for almost one-quarter of the Zedillo administration's planned increase in the domestic savings rate, which was set out by the National Development Plan for 1995–2000 (Sales, Solís, and Villagómez 1998: 167).[4]

Government policymakers argued that the Mexican reform was likely to have a particularly strong effect on savings for a number of reasons. First, the transition costs of the privatization scheme would be financed through taxes rather than debt, thereby reducing the possibility that increases in private saving would be entirely offset by public dissaving (Noriega 1997: 11; Cerda and Grandolini 1997: 92). Second, the low dependency ratio of the Mexican pension system ensured that the transition costs of privatization would be small relative to many other countries (Cerda and Grandolini 1997: 92). Third, because the Mexican economy was plagued with high rates of social security payment evasion and a large informal sector, it would be in a strong position to benefit from the reduction in evasion and expansion of coverage that a privatized pension system would bring about. This would, in turn, help boost savings since it would add to the mass of funds being saved through the social security system (Noriega 1997: 10; Cerda and Grandolini 1997: 92). Fourth, the mandatory contributions to private pension funds would not simply replace voluntary savings, since voluntary savings were quite low in Mexico. On the contrary, advocates of privatization maintained that the private pension system might increase voluntary savings by fostering a "culture of savings" (Cerda and Rivera Cabello 1996: 15).

Policymakers in the Mexican government argued that pension privatization would also bring important economic benefits by contributing to the development of the country's capital markets. In introducing the reform, the Zedillo administration pointed out that it would "deepen and diversify financial intermediation, leading to the appearance of new financial instruments. The increase in the availability of resources in the financial markets will result in the decrease in interest rates for business loans, the development of new debt instruments and the growth of the capital markets" (Cámara de Diputados de los Estados Unidos Mexicanos 1996a: 202). Pension privatization, the government maintained, would create a particularly strong demand for long-term financial instruments since the pension funds would need to make extensive long-term investments. Sales, Solís, and Villagómez (1998: 166) estimated that the Mexican reform would lead long-term instruments to grow from 11.9 percent of gross domestic product in 1994 to 21.9 percent in 2000 and approximately 45 percent in 2010.

Advocates of pension privatization also believed that it would bolster the Mexican stock market since private pension funds would probably invest a substantial portion of the funds under their management in the local stock market. One estimate predicted that the stock market would receive investments equal to approximately 11 percent of Mexico's gross domestic product within fifteen years after the implementation of the reform (Sales, Solís, and Villagómez 1998: 166). According to government policymakers, the Mexican insurance industry would similarly benefit from pension privatization since retirees in the new private pension system would use the funds in their retirement accounts to purchase annuities from private insurance companies. By contributing to the development of Mexico's capital markets, pension privatization would reduce the country's dependence on foreign companies for certain types of financial services. Deeper and more sophisticated capital markets would also foster economic growth by allowing resources to be allocated more efficiently than they had been in the past.

Ideational Influences

Only meager empirical evidence existed to support the claim of some Mexican policymakers that pension privatization would boost the country's domestic savings rate. Nor was it clear that the reform would definitively reduce the long-term economic burden of pension spending or bring as many benefits to the capital markets as was often argued. Nevertheless, proponents of pension privatization managed to press their claims quite effectively, dominating the discourse on this topic. The Mexican media routinely reported that pension privatization plan would provide a major boost to the country's economy, and Mexican opponents of pension privatization rarely disputed these facts. Rather, their criticism of the reform proposals focused almost exclusively on the effects of the reform on the workers and pensioners themselves.

The Chilean model played an important role in shaping beliefs about the economic benefits of pension privatization in Mexico. Proponents of pension privatization repeatedly justified their assertions about the benefits of pension privatization with references to the Chilean experience. In 1991, for example, Rolando Vega, who was then president of the Mexican Business Coordinating Council, argued, "The experience of [Chile] is particularly interesting for Mexico because in scarcely 11 years the magnitude of their pension funds has gone from being as small as ours—2.6 per cent of GDP—to 23 per cent of GDP. In Chile, pension funds have become the most important source of capital" (Holt 1991). Vega estimated that the privatization scheme had raised the Chilean savings rate by 5 percent. During this period, Luis Manuel Guaida, director of the Advisory Commission on Labor of the National Chambers of Commerce, similarly extolled the benefits of the pension privatization, which he argued operated with "magnificent results" in Chile ("Qué se dijo" 1992: 56).

The World Bank and liberal Mexican economists played a particularly important role in promoting the Chilean model. The influence of both of these actors rose considerably during the late 1980s and early 1990s, and they used this influence to champion the merits of pension privatization. The impressive academic training and credentials wielded by the neoliberal economists and the intellectual and material resources of the World Bank gave them a decided advantage in policy debates. Opponents of pension privatization typically did not have the expertise to contest the assertions of the reform proponents, nor did they have the capability to carry out their own economic analyses of the reform.

In the wake of the debt crisis, Mexico became heavily dependent on the international financial institutions for funds as the commercial banks ceased to lend to the country. World Bank loans to Mexico skyrocketed from a mere $2.7 billion in 1982 to $11.0 billion in 1990, and continued to rise, albeit at a slower pace, thereafter. During the 1980s and early 1990s, the World Bank also initiated a large number of technical assistance programs to Mexico that helped the government plan the vast number of reforms it began to implement during this period. The financial and technical assistance programs brought World Bank representatives into the policy-making apparatus in Mexico and allowed them to influence the course of the reforms. Many

Mexican policymakers also performed stints at the Bank or worked on World Bank contracts, which further exposed them to World Bank views.

The World Bank gradually became involved in Mexican pension policy and played an important role in building domestic support for pension privatization. At the end of the 1980s, the World Bank carried out a major study of contractual savings institutions in Mexico; as part of this study, it recommended the gradual privatization of the Mexican pension system (interview with Vittas 1998). Shortly thereafter, the Mexican government attempted to carry out a pension privatization plan similar to that recommended by the World Bank, but this effort, which culminated in 1992 with the creation of the small private Retirement Savings System (SAR), was largely aborted. In the years that followed, World Bank officials continued to lobby Mexican policymakers to undertake a more far-reaching privatization of the pension system. The push for pension privatization gathered more steam in 1994 with the publication of *Averting the Old-Age Crisis*, the widely acclaimed World Bank study that highlighted the shortcomings of existing public pension systems. This study heightened awareness of and interest in pension privatization among Mexican policymakers and led World Bank officials to redouble their efforts to promote pension privatization in Mexico and abroad.

When Mexican policymakers began to formulate a new pension privatization plan in early 1995, however, they maintained their distance from the World Bank and other international financial institutions (interviews with Cajiga 1997; with Cerda 1997; and with Vittas 1998). The Zedillo administration kept the IFIs out of the process in part because the government believed that their participation would be politically controversial—"the kiss of death," in the words of one key policymaker (interview with Dávila 1997). Once the government had enacted the privatization plan, however, it sought funds from the international financial institutions, which helped it carry out the reform. In 1996, the World Bank put forward $400 million and the IADB coughed up an additional $300 million to "facilitate the adequate implementation of the new pension scheme and ensure that maximum benefits are obtained from the reform" (IADB 1996b).

The most important proponents of pension privatization in Mexico were internal rather than external actors, however. In the 1980s and 1990s, economists came to occupy many of the key policy-making positions in the Mexican government, including some posts that had direct or indirect responsibility for social security policy. The economists, many of whom had been trained in the United States, shared a strong commitment to liberal economic ideas, and they used their influence to lobby for market-oriented reforms, including pension privatization. The neoliberal economists not only persuaded the key political leaders that pension privatization would bring substantial economic benefits, but also they devised the actual reform proposals. Thus, they shaped the overall direction as well as the details of pension reform in Mexico.[5]

The first effort to privatize the pension system began in early 1990, when the Ministry of Finance and the Central Bank established the Project on the Stabilization of Pensions. Two liberal economists, Alejandro Reinoso of the Ministry of Finance and Augustín Carstens of the Central Bank, headed the project (Bertranou 1994; Holt 1991). The reform team carefully studied the social security systems of a large number of countries, making visits to Chile, Argentina, Brazil, Denmark, France, Spain, Singapore, and the United States among other countries. Chile was the object of particular fascination by the Mexican policymakers, however, and they dedicated long hours to studying the Chilean model (Holt 1991; Bertranou 1994). The members of the reform team also had contacts with Chilean pension reform experts in a variety of forums both inside and outside Mexico. Indeed, Chilean consultants had participated in the World Bank-funded study of Mexico's contractual savings institutions, which had recommended the privatization of the pension system (interview with Iglesias 1996). The Chilean experts both championed the benefits of pension privatization and made concrete suggestions about how such a reform might be implemented in Mexico.

The reform team devised a proposal that was based in large part on the Chilean model, although they concluded that it would not be appropriate to completely copy any other country's system because Mexico was facing substantially different problems than the other countries (Bertranou 1994). The proposal, which had been formulated in very general terms by the end of 1990, called for the immediate creation of a private social security system based on individual retirement accounts. The private system would initially be complementary to the existing public system, but the social security contributions of workers would be gradually transferred from the public to the private system during a period of ten years (Bertranou 1994, 1995; Rivera Ríos 1992; Holt 1991).

The reform team initially worked largely on their own, although the director of the Mexican Social Security Institute was kept informed of the project (González Rossetti and Mogollon 2000: 50). In late 1990, however, the reform team shared a draft of the proposal with a minor business association, the Social Union of Mexican Businessmen (USEM), and with the staff of the IMSS (Bertranou 1994, 1995). Other business associations as well as labor unions subsequently received copies of the reform proposal. The business associations generally supported the proposal, although they opposed the increase in employers' social security contributions that it entailed.

Different financial institutions, including banks, insurance companies, and stockbrokers, also lobbied the government to entrust them with the responsibility of managing the private retirement accounts (Bertranou 1994, 1995).

The privatization proposal met substantial opposition from the labor unions as well as from the staff of the Mexican Social Security Institute, which was run mostly by doctors and lawyers rather than economists. After extended negotiations with the unions, the Salinas administration agreed to reduce substantially the scope of the reform in return for labor's support for the initiative. The Salinas administration backed down in large part because it did not want to antagonize the labor movement when it was trying to gain approval for the North American Free Trade Agreement, which was the government's principal policy priority at the time. The government had received the support of the main union confederation for NAFTA and did not want to jeopardize this support by pushing through a sweeping pension privatization plan that the unions strongly opposed.

The main concession by the government was to eliminate the gradual phasing out of the IMSS. The final reform therefore did not actually involve privatization, nor did it address any of the financial problems of the IMSS, which was left untouched. The revised proposal, enacted in early 1992, simply created a small private pension system that functioned alongside the existing public system. The new private system, which was dubbed the Retirement Savings System (SAR), consisted of individual retirement accounts managed by banks. The accounts were funded by an additional employer's contribution equal to 2 percent of each worker's salary and guaranteed an interest income of at least 2 percent above inflation. The funds accumulated in these accounts were to be paid out to workers upon retirement and would supplement the pensions that the workers received from the public pension system. All current and future members of the social security systems were required to participate in the new private pension system, including both private-sector workers who were members of the IMSS and public-sector workers who were members of ISSSTE.

The enactment of the SAR did not end efforts to privatize the Mexican pension system, however, since many policymakers continued to lobby for a more sweeping reform.[6] These efforts initially came from neoliberal economists within the Ministry of Finance and the Ministry of Commerce. The leader of the new reform effort was Guillermo Ortíz, who was then undersecretary in the Ministry of Finance (González Rossetti and Mogollon 2000: 50). Ortíz, who had a Ph.D. in economics from Stanford University, would later preside over the pension privatization plan as the minister of finance during the Zedillo administration.

In 1993, some of the top leadership of the Mexican Social Security Institute also began to advocate pension privatization. In that year, Genaro Borrego was named head of the IMSS; although he was not a technocrat, he brought in a number of liberal economists to important policy-making positions at the IMSS.[7] He did this in order to build up the prestige of the IMSS within the technocratic-oriented government and win back control of pension policy from the economics ministries (González Rossetti and Mogollon 2000). Borrego created a new think tank called the Center for Strategic Development of Social Security (CEDESS) within IMSS to formulate reform proposals. He appointed Enrique Dávila, a professor of economics at the Autonomous Technological Institute who had a Ph.D. from the University of Chicago, as head of CEDESS's pension reform team (interview with Dávila 1997). Dávila's team gradually put together a sweeping reform proposal, which came to be known as Project Eagle (*Proyecto Aguila* 1995). Supporters of pension privatization gained another ally in the Mexican Social Security Institute shortly thereafter when Gabriel Martínez, another Ph.D. in economics from the University of Chicago, was appointed the director of planning at the IMSS. Martínez was named to this position by the minister of finance, who traditionally had controlled this appointment (González Rossetti and Mogollon 2000: 51). Martínez quickly assembled a team of economists and accountants, most of whom had no previous experience with social security reform, and began to work on a pension privatization plan. This team met resistance from many of the directors and staff of the IMSS, however (González Rossetti and Mogollon 2000).

The formulation process accelerated after Zedillo became president in December 1994. On taking office, Zedillo instructed the Mexican Social Security Institute to carry out a study of the IMSS's existing health care, child care, and pension programs. This study, released in March 1995, set forth the main problems facing the IMSS based on the work carried out by Project Eagle (IMSS 1995). A second part of this study, which consisted of the broad outlines of a reform proposal, was presented to the Economics Cabinet at this time, but it was not made public (interview with Dávila 1997; *Proyecto Aguila* 1995). The proposal envisioned a sweeping privatization of the pension system along with major changes to the health and day care programs managed by the IMSS (*Proyecto Aguila* 1995). The Economics Cabinet then established a committee, called the Technical Group, in order to work on this proposal further. The Technical Group was composed of representatives from the various ministries that were interested in the reform, including the IMSS, and the Ministries of Finance, Health, and Labor. The key members of the committee—Carlos Noriega, Enrique Dávila, Fernando Solís, and Gabriel Martínez—were all liberal economists, however, who strongly supported pension privatization.

In the months that followed, the Technical Group tinkered considerably with the details of this proposal, although the general orientation of the reform did not change. The various members of the Technical Group did not always see eye to eye. Economists from the Ministry of Finance often took a more neoliberal position than did the representatives of the IMSS (interviews with Martínez 1997; and with Dávila 1997). Officials from the Ministry of Finance, for example, favored allowing private insurance companies to provide life and disability insurance in the social security system as had been done in Chile, whereas the IMSS preferred to continue providing the insurance itself. Similarly, the Ministry of Finance wanted to permit each member to choose his or her own pension fund, whereas representatives of the IMSS preferred to allow employers or unions to select the pension funds for their workers in order to reduce administrative costs. Throughout 1995, most of these differences were ironed out, however, with the IMSS prevailing on some issues (for example, regarding the first dispute mentioned) and the Ministry of Finance having its way on others (such as the second point). Overall, the Ministry of Finance had the most important role in the design of the reform, but the IMSS took the lead in the political negotiation of the reform (González Rossetti and Mogollon 2000).

The reform proposal that was finally presented to Congress in November 1995 was quite similar to the Chilean model in that it aimed to transform the existing public pay-as-you-go pension system into a fully capitalized privately managed system based on individual retirement accounts.[8] The proposed legislation also sought to overhaul the financing method used to run the IMSS's health and day care programs as well as its occupational risk insurance (Cámara de Diputados de los Estados Unidos Mexicanos 1995a). The pension reform plan called for all current IMSS members to begin depositing their social security contributions in individual retirement accounts managed by newly established private pension fund administrators, called AFOREs. (Individuals who were already receiving a pension from the IMSS at the time of the reform were unaffected by the measure.) The AFOREs were to receive each worker's personal contributions, which had formerly gone to the IMSS, as well as the contributions that employers made on each worker's behalf (including the contributions that employers made to the SAR). In addition, the government pledged to make a new supplementary contribution (worth 5.5 percent of the minimum wage as of January 1997) to each member's account. Upon retirement, workers would use the funds in their account (that is, the total contributions plus interest earned) to purchase an annuity from a private insurance company or take programmed withdrawals from their AFORE. Workers who had previously contributed to the IMSS would not receive any compensation for these contributions, but they would have the option of foregoing their private pension in favor of a state pension that would be paid out under the rules that were in force prior to the reform. The state also promised to subsidize the pensions of those members of the system who met the requirements for retirement (in terms of age and years of contributions) but whose account was not large enough to yield a minimum monthly pension.

The Zedillo administration could afford to privatize fully its pension system in large part because the country's existing public pension obligations were relatively small. The Mexican pension system was still fairly immature, which meant that there were fewer pensioners who needed to be supported during the transition from a pay-as-you-go public system to a fully capitalized private one. According to one estimate, the total transition costs of the Mexican reform will equal 82.6 percent of the country's gross domestic product (Sales, Solís, and Villagómez 1998: 160). The cumulative transition costs of the Chilean reform, in contrast, were expected to equal 126 percent of GDP, owing to the greater maturity of the Chilean system (Schmidt-Hebbel 1995; Sales, Solís, and Villagómez 1998: 160).

To reduce the cost of the privatization plan and to allow workers more time to accumulate funds in their retirement accounts, the proposed reform tightened up some of the requirements for retirement. Under the reform plan, the minimum age of retirement was to increase gradually from sixty-five to sixty-seven years of age. The number of weeks of contributions required to qualify for an old-age pension was to be raised from 500 to 1,250, and the weeks of contributions required to qualify for an invalidity pension was to be increased from 150 to 500.

The Response to the Reform

When the reform was introduced to the legislature, it received a mixed reaction from societal and political actors. The business community, which had long supported pension privatization, by and large applauded the reform proposal (Bertranou 1994: 95–98; Laurell 1995: 24–35; Hazas 1995; Arias Jiménez 1995). The political opposition, particularly members of left-wing parties, denounced the proposed reforms, however, as did some members of the ruling party. Pensioners' associations and some labor unions organized marches and demonstrations to try to build opposition to pension privatization. The public at large was also skeptical of the pension privatization plan. According to a survey carried out by the newspaper *Reforma* in March 1995, more than three-quarters of the population opposed social security privatization.[9]

Opponents of pension privatization were ultimately unable to block the Zedillo administration's plans. Pensioners' associations in Mexico, as elsewhere in Latin America, lacked the organizational strength necessary to present an effective resistance to social security reform. Although the labor movement was better organized, it was too dependent on the state to risk a

serious rupture by calling a major strike over this issue. The political opposition, meanwhile, held too few seats in Congress to block the privatization
proposal, and the iron control that the Mexican president exercised over
members of his own party (the PRI) ensured that almost all of the ruling
party's legislators voted in favor of the proposed reform regardless of their
personal views. Nevertheless, labor leaders and other critics of the reform
within the ruling party were able to obtain some minor concessions from the
government in exchange for lending their support to the reform.

The main association of retired people, the National Unifying Movement
of Pensioners (MUNJP), vigorously opposed the Zedillo administration's
privatization plan from the outset, even though current pensioners were not
directly affected by it.[10] As the leader of the MUNJP explained, the organization opposed pension privatization "not only out of concern for our children and grandchildren, but also because it broke the principle of solidarity on which social security had been based for 50 years" (interview with
Alonso 1997). The MUNJP, which was led principally by former union officials, also rejected privatization on the following grounds:

The Social Security regime, and therefore its instrument, the IMSS, are the patri-
mony of the workers and consequently no one has the right to dispose of them and
take them away, much less by applying unilateral measures defined under imported
models that have fully demonstrated their ineffectiveness as social benefits, but which
satisfy the rapacious economic policies of the International Monetary Fund. (MUNJP
1995: 432)

The pensioner's association instead wanted the government to focus on improving pension benefits and restoring the financial health of the IMSS. To
this end, it recommended that the funds that had been accumulated in the
SAR be transferred to the IMSS (MUNJP 1995: 432).

The MUNJP, however, lacked the political clout necessary to derail the
government's privatization plans. The number of pensioners in Mexico is
relatively small because of limited social security coverage and the relative
youth of the country's population—in 1994, the Mexican Social Security
Institute had approximately 1.4 million pensioners, which represented about
1.6 percent of Mexico's total population (Ulloa Padilla 1996a: 42). Although
the MUNJP claimed to have some 850,000 members, few of these members
were active and an even smaller portion of that total contributed financially
to the organization (interview with Alonso 1997). The organization had
no paid lobbyists and few financial resources. In 1996, its annual budget
amounted to less than $50,000 (interview with Alonso 1997). Although the
marches and demonstrations that the pensioners' movement organized may
have had some symbolic effect, they were clearly insufficient to turn the tide
against the privatization measures.

Defusing Labor Opposition

Organized labor was also, by and large, critical of pension privatization, and the labor unions initially tried to resist the government's proposed reform. Labor leaders, for example, tried to obtain a commitment from the government not to privatize the social security system during the negotiations between the government and the labor unions over what measures to take to deal with the economic crisis that broke out in late 1994 (Correa 1995: 14–19). In mid-1995, the secretary of social security of the CTM released a study that called for the IMSS to take over the management of the funds in the small private system that had been set up in 1992, a measure that would have taken Mexico further away from privatization (Laurell 1995: 61–62). When the government announced its proposed reform, some unions went so far as to carry out strikes and demonstrations against the privatization plans. Ultimately, however, the vast majority of the unions caved in to government pressure, agreeing to support the reforms in exchange for only minor concessions.

In early 1995, the Zedillo administration initiated an intense lobbying campaign to gain the support of the top union leaders for its pension reform plans. Throughout the year, government representatives held numerous meetings with business and labor leaders to seek their approval for the planned reform. These meetings culminated in the fall of 1995, when the government established a commission composed of representatives from the main labor confederations and the Business Coordinating Council as well as the IMSS to analyze the reform in more detail. In this commission, the government managed to obtain the backing of both business and labor for its reform proposal without making any significant concessions (interview with Martínez 1997; Acosta Córdova 1995). Business and labor then issued a joint declaration on the general principles that should govern the reform, which was consistent with the government's own reform proposal ("Propuesta obrero-empresarial" 1995). In early November, the government presented the reform to Congress as the product of the demands of the two sectors.

When the reform was officially announced, however, a sector of the labor movement rebelled.[11] The rebellion was led by the union of IMSS employees, the National Social Security Workers Union (SNTSS), which had 300,000 members, making it one of the largest unions in the country. More than a dozen other unions, including many unions that, like the SNTSS, traditionally had close ties to the ruling party, also participated in the rebellion. Together, these unions constituted the Front in Defense of Social Security, and in the weeks that followed the presentation of the reform to Congress they carried out a large number of marches and demonstrations against the reform.[12]

The leaders of the rebellious unions complained that the Zedillo administration had not sought their opinion when it formulated the reform. They argued that the government had only consulted with the main labor federations, which did not represent the labor movement as a whole. Although a representative from the SNTSS had participated along with other labor leaders in the tripartite commission that discussed the proposed social security reform, the SNTSS representative had been assigned to the committee that discussed the reform of programs of lesser importance, such as the day care centers and funeral benefits. The SNTSS was excluded from the discussion of the most controversial aspects of the reform, namely the modification of the pension and health care programs (Comisión Tripartita 1995; interview with Audry 1997).

The rebellious labor unions maintained that the pension privatization plan was too risky and that it subordinated the social aims of social security to economic objectives. The leader of the SNTSS, Antonio Rosado, contended, "The project of the government is to take these resources to direct them at the economic project of the country, which would decapitalize the IMSS and would imply in addition a major risk, since this consists of resources for pensions, which could be lost if the wrong financial decision is taken" (Becerril 1995b: 19). The unions also pointed out that the reform stripped some of the workers' existing pension privileges since it tightened the requirements for obtaining old-age and invalidity pensions and limited the benefits available to widows. The SNTSS, moreover, feared that the privatization plan would inevitably lead some of its members to lose their jobs.

The Zedillo administration, however, put a great deal of pressure on the rebellious unions to end their opposition to the reform. After extended negotiations with the leadership of the PRI, the rebellious unions reached a settlement with the government, agreeing to support the reform in exchange for a number of concessions, most of them minor, from the government. Although the leaders of the rebellious labor unions were not pleased with the final reform, they viewed it as the best deal they could achieve under the circumstances. In the face of a great deal of criticism from more militant members of his union, the head of the SNTSS could only say, "Sincerely I believe that it was not possible to extract anything more from the government" (Becerril 1995c: 10).

The main concession by the Zedillo administration was to excise from the reform the provision that allowed employers to withhold their health-care contributions to the IMSS if they contracted their own health insurance for their employees. The government also agreed to eliminate some, but not all, of the provisions that involved losses of pension privileges, including the gradual increase in the minimum retirement age. And the government agreed to allow the IMSS to establish a pension fund that would compete with the private pension funds in the new system. The Zedillo administration, however, refused the request of the rebellious unions and the CTM to eliminate the role of private pension fund administrators in the new pension system, which would have allowed the Mexican Social Security Institute to manage all of the individual retirement accounts. Thus, the main thrust of the pension privatization plan remained unchanged.

The labor unions agreed to support the reform largely because they were too dependent on the state to risk a rupture in their relationship with the ruling party. The main Mexican labor federations, the Confederation of Mexican Workers (CTM) and the Revolutionary Confederation of Workers and Peasants (CROC), long had close ties to the PRI, which had used its control of the state to channel resources to the unions and their leaders. The unions relied on the government for financial subsidies—only 10 percent of union dues came from their members (Coppedge 1993: 255; Story 1986: 87–88)—as well as for preferential access to a variety of government services, ranging from health care to housing. Indeed, the government housing fund, INFONAVIT, was run by the unions, which provided them with a tremendous source of patronage (Middlebrook 1995). The leadership of the labor movement was particularly dependent on the PRI, since labor leaders directly benefited from political appointments and a variety of other perks. Labor leaders also relied on the governing party to help maintain themselves in power, by barring challenges from independent labor unions or dissident leaders as well as by aiding in the efforts of allied unions to organize new workers (La Botz 1992; Greenway and Tuman 1996). The government also had the power to determine when strikes were permissible and helped set wages and settle labor conflicts with employers, which gave it additional leverage over the unions (Zapata 1995; Samstad 1995).

The dependence of the labor unions on the state meant that the costs of a rupture with the ruling party were extremely high, which placed the unions in a very weak bargaining position. The bargaining position of the labor movement was further weakened by the decline of its organizational strength in the 1980s. Negative economic trends such as falling wages, rising unemployment, and the increasing informalization of the labor market cut into union revenues and membership. Although data on union membership in Mexico is notoriously scarce and unreliable, most analysts suggest that the unionization rate has dropped considerably in recent years (ILO 1997; de la Garza 1994; Zapata 1995; Middlebrook 1991). A recent estimate by the Ministry of Labor and Social Welfare and the Mexican Social Security Institute estimated that union members represented roughly 12 percent of the total workforce in 1993, down from approximately 16.3 percent in 1978 (Greenway and Tuman 1996: 8; Zazueta and de la Peña 1984).[13]

Although the unions had traditionally exercised some political influence through their relationship with the ruling party, the leaders of the PRI took steps to weaken that influence in the 1980s and 1990s. The Salinas administration, for example, cut the number of positions in the state bureaucracy reserved for labor leaders (Aziz Nassif 1994: 136). The leadership of the PRI also reduced the presence of labor in the party's sectoral associations and national executive councils (Greenway and Tuman 1996: 8). Finally, the PRI began to reduce the number of labor leaders who were nominated as candidates for state and federal offices. Whereas the workers' sector accounted for 24 percent of the party's candidates for the Chamber of Deputies between 1979 and 1985, this sector only represented 21 percent of the party's candidates in 1988 and 15 percent in 1991 (Reyes del Campillo 1990; Langston 1996: 4).

The labor movement's declining strength and its heavy dependence on the ruling party made it difficult for the unions to oppose aggressively pension privatization or the other market-oriented reforms that the government undertook in the 1980s and 1990s. The deteriorating organizational strength of the labor movement cast doubt on whether the unions could seriously hurt the government by either carrying out a general strike or endorsing the political opposition. More importantly, it was highly unlikely that the main labor federations would choose to take either of these actions given the level of their dependence on the ruling party. The main labor federations, unlike their counterparts in Argentina and Brazil, did not have a recent history of militancy. Moreover, as the Zedillo administration knew, the top labor leaders were too attached to their perks and privileges to risk a rupture with the PRI. Nor were the compliant labor leaders, likely to be dislodged by more confrontational leaders, given the lack of union democracy. Thus, the Zedillo administration could afford to take a relatively hard line with the unions, insisting that they support the reforms, while refusing to grant them major concessions.

This is not to say that the Zedillo administration could completely ignore the demands of the unions and their leaders. Zedillo needed labor leaders to maintain labor quiescence and to generate votes for the ruling party, even if the ruling party did not depend on the labor unions nearly as much as the unions relied on the PRI. The government also needed the political support of labor-affiliated deputies in the Mexican legislature in order to pass legislation. Thus, the government was obliged to make some concessions, most of them minor, to the labor movement in order to quell dissent and ensure that the reform was passed.

One of the most important concessions to organized labor was made before the reform was even introduced when the government opted to exclude the state housing fund, INFONAVIT, from the privatization plan. The government's failure to include INFONAVIT in the privatization scheme meant that the private pension funds did not gain access to the 5 percent of worker's wages that traditionally were paid to this institution. Proponents of pension privatization argued that without this additional contribution, many workers would not have sufficient funds in their individual accounts upon retirement.[14] They also complained that INFONAVIT had been mismanaged, often generating negative returns on the funds that it managed. INFONAVIT had traditionally been a major source of patronage for the unions, however, and they would not have given up control of this institution without a battle.

The Zedillo administration was also careful to avoid a battle with the powerful public sector unions, preferring to exempt them, as well as the military, from the reforms. Indeed, while the reform of IMSS was being debated, the government made a number of announcements to calm speculation that it was also planning a major reform of ISSSTE, the social security system serving state employees. Although policymakers acknowledged that the privileged pension systems, such as ISSSTE, were in worse financial shape than the IMSS, they feared that attempting to reform these systems would jeopardize the survival of the reform project as a whole (interviews with Cerda 1997; with Cajiga 1997; and with Dávila 1997). Several years earlier an attempt by the government of the state of Nuevo León to privatize the pension system covering public employees in that state had met with violent protest by the public sector unions, leading the government to repeal the reform. National social security policymakers therefore preferred to exempt these workers rather than risk a repeat of this experience (James and Brooks 2001: 159–60). Some policymakers still hope to enact reforms of the privileged systems, but to do so they will have to overcome the strident opposition of some of the strongest and most militant unions in Mexico.

Presidential Control of Congress

The key to the enactment of the Zedillo administration's sweeping pension privatization plan was the government's control of the legislature. At the time of the pension reform, the ruling party controlled a large majority of the seats in the legislature and this majority proved crucial to the passage of the pension reform legislation since the reform bill failed to garner any votes from members of opposition parties. The Mexican president's substantial influence over the political careers of members of his own party also proved useful to maintaining party discipline on the reform bill since many of the ruling party's legislators were known to have personally opposed pension privatization.

The Mexican legislature has traditionally been subservient to the president, serving principally as a rubber-stamp institution. Most legislation is proposed by the president, and, until recently, bills submitted by the president were routinely enacted by the legislature, although it was not uncommon for Congress to make some, usually minor, modifications to them (Weldon 1997). The president's dominance of the legislature, however, cannot be explained by the president's constitutional powers. Although the Mexican constitution provides the president with substantial agenda-setting powers, it does not, for example, allow him to legislate by decree. The president's dominance of the legislature was instead a result of the PRI's consistent congressional majorities and the high degree of discipline within the ruling party.

Before 1988, the PRI invariably controlled more than 70 percent of the seats in the Chamber of Deputies and all or nearly all of the seats in the Senate. The PRI's traditional control of the legislature was partly a product of the party's genuine popularity and organizational strength, but it was also due to undemocratic practices that the ruling party used to inflate its vote totals. The PRI's dominance of the legislature began to wane in the late 1980s, however, owing to changes in electoral rules and growing discontent with the ruling party. Nevertheless, when the Zedillo administration proposed its social security reform bill in 1995, the PRI still controlled 74 percent of the seats in the Senate and 60 percent of the seats in the Chamber of Deputies.

The unusually high level of party discipline that prevailed within the PRI reinforced the ruling party's control of the legislature (Weldon 1997; Craig and Cornelius 1995). The strong party discipline was the result of a number of institutional rules that made legislators highly dependent on the national leadership of the PRI and, in particular, on the president who served as the acknowledged leader of the party. First, the ruling party's candidates for the legislature were typically selected by the national leadership of the PRI rather than by primaries, which meant that legislators were indebted to the national party leadership instead of local constituencies. The seats allocated through proportional representation were done via a closed list, which was also drawn up by the leadership of the PRI and therefore tended to encourage a high level of party discipline. In addition, the ban on immediate reelection of congressmen meant that the future careers of legislators depended heavily on the leadership of the PRI, rather than on local voters, since future job prospects in the administration and nominations for higher political offices were controlled by the ruling party (Nacif 1996; Langston 1996). The perennial dominance of the PRI also meant that career options with other parties were limited, which further increased the dependence of the legislators on the ruling party. As a result, legislators from the PRI almost invariably supported legislation introduced by the president, regardless of their personal feelings about the bills or the opinions of their local constituents.

When the pension privatization bill was introduced to Congress, it met with substantial opposition. The two principal left-wing parties in Congress, the Partido de la Revolución Democrática (PRD) and the Partido del Trabajo (PT), opposed the reform largely on ideological grounds (interviews with López Angel 1997 and with Guzmán 1997). In announcing her party's vote against the reform, the PRD deputy Rosa María Márquez argued that the proposed legislation "undermines the fundamental principles of Mexican social security, its public, solidaristic, redistributive, obligatory and integral character . . . the IMSS is being subordinated to economic objectives that are foreign to its substantive goals" (Cámara de Diputados de los Estados Unidos Mexicanos 1995b: 5264). Deputy Eduardo Guzmán of the PT, meanwhile, declared that his party would vote against the reform "by virtue that it is not true that the practical and financial advantages of the proposal have been demonstrated; by virtue that [the proposed reform] has withdrawn or damaged the rights won by the workers" (Cámara de Diputados de los Estados Unidos Mexicanos 1995b: 5273). The left-wing parties also objected to the ruling party's efforts to approve the reform quickly and sought to delay a vote on the reform to allow for more discussion.

The position of the PAN toward the reform was more ambivalent. On the one hand, the privatization of the pension system was generally in line with the free-market principles of the PAN, and the party had by and large voted in favor of the government's market-oriented reforms in the past. The head of the PAN, Carlos Castillo Peraza, supported the reform and lobbied the party's deputies to vote in favor of the proposal. On the other hand, many PAN legislators objected to the speed with which the PRI tried to approve the reform, complaining that they had insufficient time to analyze the proposal in detail. Jorge Urdapilleta, who was a leader of the PAN in the Chamber of Deputies, explained that the PAN favored a "system of individual capitalization for its certainty, guarantees and transparent management. Thus, we were in agreement with those proposals [of the PRI], but we didn't accept the form. That is, we wanted things to be done well and not done half-cocked" (interview with Urdapilleta 1997). The PAN's legislative contingent was also concerned about the political costs of the reform. Deputies from the PAN reasoned that since "the struggle is between the PRI [legislators] and the government; let's let them pay the political costs" (Albarrán de Alba 1995: 32). To determine the party's position, the PAN's legislative contingent ended up taking an internal vote in which those who favored supporting the reform lost handily. In spite of the aggressive lobbying of Castillo Peraza, only eighteen PAN deputies recommended voting for the reform, whereas fifty-four PAN legislators preferred to vote against it and nineteen legislators abstained (Albarrán de Alba 1995: 32).[15]

The pension reform also engendered a great deal of dissent within the PRI's congressional delegation. Opposition to the reform came from left-wing members of the PRI associated with Grupo Exhorto as well as from labor-affiliated deputies who accounted for almost 20 percent of the PRI's total delegation and an even larger proportion of the members of the joint commission that evaluated the reform. The most outspoken opponent of the reform within the PRI was Alejandro Audry, who was a member of the National Social Security Workers Union. Audry presided over the Commission on Social Security, which, along with the Commission on Labor, was responsible for analyzing the proposed reform. He was therefore in a good position to build opposition to the proposed reform.

Opponents of the reform, however, came under intense pressure to approve the initiative. The business community lobbied vigorously on behalf of the privatization initiative, organizing a letter-writing campaign and holding numerous meetings with members of the legislature. The leadership of the principal labor confederations also pressed the congressmen to vote in favor of the reform. The head of the CTM, Fidel Velásquez, for example, warned labor-affiliated congressmen that he had already promised Zedillo that they would vote in favor of the reform, although he also told them that he would look favorably on certain modifications to the reform bill (Romero and Gallegos 1995: 3). The strongest pressure, however, came from the leadership of the PRI. According to Miguel Angel Sáenz Garza, the technical secretary for the Commission on Social Security, "There was a specific meeting of the PRI deputies to tell them: '[the reform] must be approved.' Of course, it's enough to say that—appealing to their sense of party loyalty—for everyone to understand what will happen if they don't vote accordingly" (interview with Sáenz Garza 1997).

In the face of this pressure, the PRI deputies caved in, receiving only relatively minor concessions for their acquiescence. The last holdout was Congressmen Audry, who, unlike the other PRI deputies, voted against the first version of the reform that was approved in the joint commission. Shortly after the first version of the reform was approved, however, the SNTSS and most of the other rebellious unions reached an agreement with the leadership of the PRI, agreeing to support the reform legislation in exchange for a few more concessions. Under pressure from his union, Audry then switched his vote in favor of the reform, although he was far from happy with the final bill (interview with Audry 1997). Like many of the PRI congressmen, Audry justified his vote, by arguing, "Frankly, I did what I could" (interview with Audry 1997).

The final bill contained more than sixty modifications to the original proposal (not including grammatical corrections or clarifications), but most of these changes were relatively minor. The majority of the changes were proposed by Audry acting on behalf of the SNTSS, although other deputies within the PRI and the opposition political parties also managed to implement a number of changes (Sáenz Garza 1996; interviews with Sáenz Garza 1997; with Audry 1997; and with Urdapilleta 1997). The most significant change, obtained at the last minute by the rebellious unions, was the elimination of the provision that would have allowed employers to recoup their health care contributions to the IMSS if they provided their own health care for their employees. The final bill also restored some of the pension benefits that had been eliminated in the original proposal. The final legislation, for example, omitted the proposed increase in the minimum retirement age as well as the proposed increase in the number of weeks of contributions that workers needed in order to qualify for an invalidity pension. Congress also excised the provisions of the new law that eliminated survivors' pensions for widowers unless they were completely invalid and limited pension benefits to five years for widows under thirty years old who did not have children.

The general orientation of the reform of the pension system remained unchanged, however. The rebellious unions and congressmen were unable to revise the proposed reform in a way that would enable the IMSS, rather than the private pension funds, to manage the individual retirement accounts. Nor were they able to block the proposed increase in the minimum weeks of contributions required by workers to gain access to an old-age pension, which rose from 500 to 1,250. As a result of the reform, workers' pensions in the future are going to depend to a much greater extent on their contributions to the system. They are also going to depend on the ability of the private pension fund administrators to generate solid returns on the monies that workers deposit in their individual retirement accounts.[16]

The final social security reform bill was approved in the plenary of the Chamber of Deputies on December 7, 1995, only one month after it was introduced (see Table 3.3). It received 289 votes in favor and 160 votes against, with only the deputies from the PRI supporting the legislation (Cámara de Diputados de los Estados Unidos Mexicanos 1995b: 5379). The legislation then passed to the Senate where it was approved on December 12, 1995. The vote in the Senate also followed party lines with 92 votes in favor and 25 votes opposed (Senado 1995: 53). No changes were made to the bill in the Senate, which meant that it did not have to return to the Chamber of Deputies for further evaluation.

The Zedillo administration still needed to pass supplementary legislation setting forth the rules governing the private pension fund administrators (AFOREs). In the months that followed, the government hurried to put together this legislation, which was finally submitted to the Chamber of Deputies on March 20, 1996. The legislation immediately encountered a great deal of criticism from labor unions and the political opposition as well as from members of the PRI itself. As a result, the Zedillo administration was again obliged to use its congressional majority and strong party discipline to push through its proposed reform. To obtain the passage of the legislation, the Zedillo administration was also obliged to allow a large number of changes

TABLE 3.3

The 1995 Mexican Pension Reform

	Former system	New system
Operating basis	Public pay-as-you-go/partial collective capitalization	Private fully funded, based on individual retirement accounts
Employer contribution for old age, invalidity, and survivor's pensions	5.95% of each worker's salary plus another 2% for the SAR	5.95% of each worker's salary plus another 2% for the SAR
Worker contribution for old age, invalidity, and survivor's pensions	2.125% of each worker's salary	2.125% of each worker's salary
State contribution for old age, invalidity, and survivor's pensions	0.625% of each worker's salary	0.625% of each worker's salary plus 5.5% of the minimum wage★
Recipient of contributions and manager of pensions	IMSS	AFOREs (old age) and IMSS (invalidity and survivor's pensions)
Minimum retirement age	65 years of age (60 in case of unemployment)	65 years of age (60 in case of unemployment)
Minimum weeks of contributions	500 weeks (for old-age pensions)	1,250 weeks (for old-age pensions)
Pension benefit levels	Based on the average salary during the last five years of work (plus the SAR)	Based on the funds accumulated in the individual retirement accounts
Value of the minimum pension	Equals the minimum wage prevailing at the time in the Federal District	Equals the minimum wage in the Federal District at July 1, 1997, adjusted for inflation

SOURCES: Cerda and Grandolini 1997; Ulloa Padilla 1996b; IMSS 1996.
★The additional state contribution equalled approximately 2 percent of the average worker's salary at the time of the reform.

to be made to the reform bill—approximately 90 of the 114 articles of the original bill were modified—but most of the modifications were relatively minor in character.

One of the most important modifications made in the Chamber of Deputies was the inclusion of a clause stipulating that no AFORE could control more than 17 percent of the market during the first four years of the system's operation (and no more than 20 percent after the first four years). This modification, which had broad support in the legislature, was made because many deputies feared that the Mexican system might end up like the Chilean system, where three private pension funds controlled 70 percent of the market. The legislation, however, did allow for the Comisión Nacional del Sistema de Ahorro para el Retiro (CONSAR), the agency that regulated the private system, to make exceptions to this limit "as long as this did not prejudice the interests of the workers" (Cámara de Diputados de los Estados Unidos Mexicanos 1996b: 1492).

Another change, made at the behest of the unions and union-affiliated deputies, specified that two labor representatives, along with one representative of the private sector, would sit on the governing board of CONSAR. The Zedillo administration's original proposal had not called for any labor representation on the board, which was to be composed of eleven government officials. The unions protested, arguing that workers should have a role in supervising the system since it would "resolve the destiny and security of their resources in addition to their protection at the moment of retirement" (Cámara de Diputados de los Estados Unidos Mexicanos 1996b: 1458). The CTM had originally proposed that three labor representatives (and two employer representatives) be seated on this commission, but after negotiations with the administration, it settled for two members. The business and labor members were to be chosen by the secretary of finance who was to preside over the governing board.

Perhaps, the most widely debated modification concerned the role of the IMSS in the new system. The Zedillo administration had suggested on numerous occasions that it had no objections to allowing the IMSS to create an AFORE and compete on the same terms as the private AFOREs in the new system.[17] The unions, the PRD, and many of the PRI's own deputies wanted this role for the IMSS to be spelled out in the legislation, which the government had declined to do. The PAN and the private sector, in contrast, did not want the IMSS to be able to manage an AFORE at all, arguing that it would present unfair competition to the privately managed AFOREs (interviews with Urdapilleta 1997; and with Fable 1997). After extended negotiations, the Zedillo administration gave into the pressure from its allies and agreed to add language to the legislation, explicitly stating that the IMSS was allowed to create its own AFORE as long as it fulfilled all of the same requirements as the private AFOREs (Cámara de Diputados de los Estados Unidos Mexicanos 1996b: 1491; Suárez Dávila 1996).

The Zedillo administration refused to consider any modification that would alter the general orientation of its pension reform, however. Thus, it rejected out of hand the proposal made by the PRD and the SNTSS that the new system be composed of a single AFORE run by the IMSS. The government also blocked efforts by the unions to guarantee that the AFOREs provided a minimum return on the funds deposited in the individual retirement accounts. The Chamber of Deputies did, however, add a clause to the original legislation, stating that each AFORE would be obliged to maintain at least one low-risk investment vehicle composed of financial instruments that tended to "preserve the worth of the savings of the workers" (Cámara de Diputados de los Estados Unidos Mexicanos 1996b: 1473).

The Zedillo administration also blocked a couple of efforts to restrict the ownership of AFOREs. Congressmen from the PRD and the PRI as well as some labor leaders initially tried to prevent banks from owning AFOREs because of concerns about the stability of the banking system. At the time that the reform was being debated, the Mexican banking system was in the throes of a serious crisis that had led a number of Mexican banks to seek financial assistance from the government. The efforts of both PRI and PRD deputies to ban the banks from the system ran aground in the face of staunch resistance from the Zedillo administration, however. The lower chamber did, nevertheless, add language that made it clear that banks or other financial entities were ineligible to participate in AFOREs if they had benefited from programs that the Mexican government had established to aid financial institutions that had been hurt by the economic crisis (Cámara de Diputados de los Estados Unidos Mexicanos 1996b: 1466).

An even more contentious debate took place over whether some foreign companies would be allowed to create AFOREs. The proposed legislation stated that foreign companies were not allowed to own more than 49 percent of an AFORE, but it made an exception for those countries with which Mexico had free-trade agreements including Canada, Chile, and the United States (Cámara de Diputados de los Estados Unidos Mexicanos 1996a: 203). This exception provoked harsh criticisms from all ends of the political spectrum as well as from the labor unions. Critics maintained that foreign companies would inevitably come to dominate the Mexican pension system and that they would use their control of the AFOREs to transfer the pension assets out of the country, even though the law forbade the AFOREs from making foreign investments. The Zedillo administration refused to budge, however, arguing that "to try to treat companies [of its treaty partners] in a distinct manner than Mexican companies would violate the principle of national treatment" (Romero and Gallegos 1996: 47).

Although labor leaders and many PRI deputies were unhappy about many aspects of the reform, under pressure from the Zedillo administration they ultimately agreed to support the reform legislation. The PRD, the PT, and the PAN again voted against the reform, although the PAN did so after some debate. Legislators from the PAN cited their opposition to allowing the IMSS to create an AFORE as the main reason for their vote against the legislation, but deputies from the other parties contended that the PAN opposed the reform for purely political reasons (Cámara de Diputados de los Estados Unidos Mexicanos 1996b).

The solid majority that the ruling party held in both chambers of the legislature, along with its strong party discipline, enabled the Zedillo administration to enact the law without the votes of the opposition legislators. In the Chamber of Deputies, the final vote on the Law of the Retirement Savings Systems, like the earlier vote on the Law of Social Security, followed strict party lines, with 280 votes in favor and 100 votes against (Cámara de Diputados de los Estados Unidos Mexicanos 1996b: 1624). The measure then passed to the Senate where it was approved with no changes on April 25, 1996. After some delays, the new system began operation on July 1, 1997.

Conclusion

Economic problems, particularly concerns about the low domestic savings rate, brought pension privatization onto Mexico's policy agenda in the 1990s. Mexican policymakers believed that pension privatization would not only reduce the long-term financial burden of the public pension system, but also would expand the domestic savings rate and stimulate the local capital markets, thereby reducing Mexico's dependence on foreign capital. Mexican policymakers drew their conclusions about the economic benefits of pension privatization in large part from their study of the 1981 Chilean reform. Indeed, policymakers and nonpolicymakers alike constantly made references to Chile to support their arguments about the merits of pension privatization.

Of the various proponents of pension privatization in Mexico, neoliberal economists, who took over the key social security policy-making positions in Mexico during the 1990s, were clearly the most influential. Neoliberal economists used their power to convince the leading political actors that pension privatization would bring substantial economic and social benefits. The World Bank played a secondary, but nevertheless important, role in promoting pension privatization in Mexico. The Bank encouraged Mexico to consider privatizing its pension system by trumpeting the benefits of pension privatization and by financing an early study of Mexico's contractual savings institutions, which recommended privatization. The World Bank, along with the Inter-American Development Bank, also helped finance the implementation of the reform.

The Zedillo administration, unlike its counterparts in Argentina and Brazil, was able to implement a sweeping privatization scheme in part because its existing public pension obligations were relatively low. This reduced the transition costs of the reform. Political factors also facilitated pension privatization in Mexico. The semiauthoritarian ruling party in Mexico dominated the legislature and controlled the trade unions to a much greater extent than did ruling parties in either Argentina or Brazil, which helped stifle resistance to the proposed reform. As a result, the Zedillo administration was able to enact quickly its privatization plan, without making any significant concessions to the opposition.

CHAPTER 4

The Politics of Partial Privatization:
Pension Policy in Argentina in the 1990s

ARGENTINA, LIKE MEXICO, enacted a major pension privatization scheme in the 1990s. The process of reform was considerably more arduous in Argentina than it was in Mexico, however. The reform bill suffered a number of important defeats in the legislature, and it was approved only after experiencing numerous modifications. Partly as a result, the final reform was relatively mild by Mexican or Chilean standards; nevertheless, it constituted the most significant reform in the history of Argentine social security.

This chapter will explain why the Argentine government of President Carlos Menem sought to partially privatize its pension system and why it was obliged to make numerous concessions to critics of the privatization plan. Two types of economic problems motivated pension privatization in Argentina. First, the serious financial problems that the Argentine public pension system experienced in the late 1980s created a major drain on the treasury and provoked recurrent protests from pensioners, thereby putting pressure on the Argentine government to reform the system. Second, the equally serious capital shortages that the country experienced beginning in the 1980s placed pension privatization squarely on the policy agenda. The Menem administration, like its counterpart in Mexico, viewed pension privatization as a way not only to shore up the long-term financial health of the public pension system but also to build up its domestic sources of capital, thereby reducing the country's vulnerability to cutoffs of foreign capital.

As in Mexico, neoliberal economists, the World Bank, and the Chilean model all played an important role in persuading the top political leaders and other influential actors that pension privatization would bring myriad economic benefits. The experience of neighboring Chile with pension privatization loomed particularly large, given the rapid expansion of the Chilean savings rate that occurred in the wake of its pension reform. In the early 1990s, the Argentine media was full of articles extolling the economic contributions of the Chilean private pension system and numerous Chilean individuals and institutions encouraged the Argentine government to copy the Chilean model. The World Bank also helped convince the Argentine government of the wisdom of following the Chilean path of reform. World Bank representatives relentlessly championed the benefits of pension privatization in their contacts with Argentine policymakers and financed the early diagnostic studies of the Argentine pension system by covering some of the costs of the implementation of the privatization plan. The most important proponents of pension privatization in Argentina, however, were the neoliberal economists who came to occupy most of the key social security policy-making positions in the early 1990s. These economists designed the pension privatization plan and sold it to the top political leaders and the public at large partly based on the plan's predicted economic benefits.

The Argentine reform nevertheless ended up being much more limited than the Mexican reform for several reasons. First, the maturity of the Argentine pension system meant that full-scale privatization along the lines of the Mexican scheme was prohibitively expensive. By partially privatizing its pension system, the Argentine government considerably reduced the transition costs that it would have to pay. Second, and equally importantly, the political conditions were less favorable to reform in Argentina than in Mexico. The ruling party in Argentina, unlike in Mexico, did not control a majority of seats in the Chamber of Deputies, which obliged it to seek support from legislators from allied parties. Party discipline in Argentina was also significantly lower than in Mexico, where it was nearly absolute. Finally, the Argentine unions were much stronger and were traditionally more militant than their Mexican counterparts, which placed them in a better position to demand modifications to the reform bill.

Nevertheless, the political conditions in Argentina were more favorable to reform than in many countries. The ruling party in Argentina controlled a majority of seats in the Senate and a near majority in the Chamber of Deputies. The ruling party also had close ties to the main labor confederation, which helped the government secure the grudging support of the unions. As a result, the Menem administration was able to gain approval for its proposed reform, but only after making a large number of concessions to the unions and to legislators who were critical of the reform proposal.

The Origins of Social Security in Argentina

Argentina was one of the first Latin American countries to provide social security benefits to its citizens and it continues to have one of the most developed social security systems in the region. The first pension programs for private-sector workers in Argentina were established in the early part of this century, although retirement pensions for members of the military, teachers, and civil servants date from the 1800s. It was not until the middle of the twentieth century, however, that social security programs were expanded to cover the bulk of the labor force.

The impetus behind the creation of the pension programs came from the Argentine state since neither the workers nor their employers had actively lobbied for such programs. The Argentine government established the programs in an effort to co-opt and control the increasingly restless labor movement (Isuani 1985; Horowitz 1995; Mesa-Lago 1978; Feldman, Golbert, and Isuani 1988).[1] Railroad employees, who had the power to bring the Argentine economy to a halt, were the beneficiaries of the first pension program for private-sector employees. They were followed by workers who operated other essential public services, such as gas, electricity, telephone and telegraphs, and the trolleys. The proponents of social security legislation argued that the reforms would bring about labor peace by eliminating some of the causes of worker grievances and by increasing the dependence of workers on the state. The legislation creating a pension program for railroad workers went so far as to stipulate that workers who went on strike would lose the right to their pensions.[2]

Argentine unions as well as employers, however, typically opposed the initial social security legislation in large part because they objected to making contributions to the pension funds (Isuani 1985; Horowitz 1995). Partly as a result of this opposition, the Argentine pension system grew slowly and in a fragmented manner during the first half of the century. Social security coverage was gradually extended to workers in the financial system, journalism and printing, the merchant marine, and commercial airlines, but most workers had no coverage whatsoever (Mesa-Lago 1978; Feldman, Golbert, and Isuani 1988). In 1944, the entire Argentine social security system still had only 428,000 members, which represented scarcely 7 percent of the country's economically active population (Feldman, Golbert, and Isuani 1988: 30). The members of the system were grouped in six separate National Pension Funds according to their occupational categories (civil service, railroad, public utilities, banking and insurance, journalist and printing, and merchant marine). Many of these funds were poorly managed and had serious financial problems even at that early date.

The rise of Colonel Juan Domingo Perón led to the rapid expansion of the Argentine social security system in the 1940s and 1950s. Perón, who became minister of labor and social security in 1943 and president in 1946, used social security programs to help build a base of political support among the labor unions, which grew dramatically during his tenure.[3] By this time, most labor unions had shed their qualms about the social security programs and were lobbying for benefits, which Perón quickly provided to them. During Perón's tenure, old-age pension benefits were extended for the first time to commercial employees, police and penitentiary personnel, industrial workers, and, finally, rural workers, the self-employed, professionals, and entrepreneurs.[4] By 1955, the national pension system had almost 4.9 million members, although less than 2.5 million of them were making contributions (Feldman, Golbert, and Isuani 1988: 101).[5]

After Perón's removal from office in 1955, the Argentine social security system continued to grow but at a much slower pace. In 1956, the military government granted pension benefits to domestic workers, the final major occupational category that was not covered by the existing scheme. Meanwhile, other types of social security benefits, such as health coverage, life insurance, and family allowances, were extended to most workers. According to Mesa-Lago (1991b: 50), pension system coverage grew from 55 percent of the economically active population in 1960 to 68 percent in 1970, but stagnated thereafter. Nevertheless, Argentina continued to have one of the highest rates of coverage in the region.

Throughout this period, the Argentine pension system suffered from numerous financial and administrative problems, which various governments attempted to fix. Although democratic governments had little success in enacting these reforms, the military governments that ruled Argentina for most of the 1960s and 1970s successfully carried out several reforms. The highly authoritarian government of Juan Carlos Onganía, for example, carried out a major reform in 1967, which unified the fragmented Argentine pension system into three semiautonomous funds, standardized contribution rates, and eliminated the unions' control of the pension funds. In the 1970s, the military government undertook other major reforms, raising employee's pension contribution rates from 5 to 11 percent and, subsequently, replacing the employers' contributions to the pension system with a value-added tax in order to reduce labor costs.

Growing Financial Problems

In spite of these changes (or, in some cases, because of them), the financial difficulties facing the Argentine pension system grew considerably in the 1980s, putting pressure on Argentine governments to carry out deeper reforms. The financial problems had a variety of causes. First, the requirements for gaining access to pensions were relatively lax. Disability and survivorship pensions were relatively easy to obtain, and the pension system allowed workers to retire at a relatively young age. Until the recent reforms, the standard retirement age in Argentina was fifty-five years of age for women and sixty

years of age for men—minimum retirement ages that are considerably below those in the advanced industrialized countries. Moreover, some members of the system were allowed to retire even earlier if they had contributed
to the system for the requisite number of years.[6] As a result, most pensioners were collecting their pensions for a very long time; in 1980, average life
expectancy upon retirement was 24 years for women and 16.7 years for men
(Schulthess 1990: 36).

Second, the promised benefits were relatively high, particularly in comparison to those prevailing in the industrialized countries. The standard replacement rate was 70 percent of a worker's salary, and this rose to 82 percent for workers with a long history of contributions. Moreover, it was
based on the three years in which the worker's salary was the highest. In addition, a number of privileged groups, such as the military and some civil
servants, received costly additional benefits, which far exceeded what they
contributed to the system. In early 1992, the average monthly benefit in
the main pension system was $231, whereas the average pension of provin-
cial employees was $503 and the average military pension was $831 (Isuani
and San Martino 1993: 34).

Third, evasion of social security payments was widespread and growing,
which undermined the pension system's revenue base. In most years in the
1980s, approximately one-half of the eligible population failed to contribute to the pension system, and rates of evasion were even higher among the
self-employed (Cottani and Demarco 1998; Schulthess and Demarco 1993:
79; Durán 1993). Problems of evasion worsened in the 1980s because the
economic crisis made it increasingly difficult for workers and their employers to make their social security payments. The sharp increase in the size of
the informal sector that occurred during this period also contributed to the
growth in evasion rates, since independent workers were much less likely to
contribute to the social security system.

These problems were aggravated by the gradual aging of the Argentine
population and pension system. Increases in average life expectancy and declines in the birth rate meant that the Argentine population was growing
steadily older. In 1950, the ratio of the population between twenty and sixty
years of age to the population over sixty years old was more than 7.5 to 1,
but by 1990, this ratio had fallen to less than 3.7 to 1 (Schulthess 1990: 28).
The changing demographics along with growing evasion rates, loose pension eligibility requirements, and the maturation of the Argentine pension
system meant that the ratio between the workers who contributed to the
pension system and the pensioners who received benefits from it was steadily
declining. By 1990, the contributor to pensioner ratio had fallen to 1.8 to 1,
a level substantially below that prevailing in all other Latin American countries and most European countries as well (Jáuregui 1994: 50; World Bank

TABLE 4.1

Financial Problems of the Argentine Pension System

	1980	1985	1988	1989	1990
Level of self-financing of the pension system	85.1%	74.3%	67.9%	65.3%	65.8%
Average pension as a percent of average wage	65.0	52.9	74.5	30.1	39.9
Ratio of contributors to beneficiaries	2.5	1.9	1.9	1.8	1.8
Pension spending as a percent of total government spending	24.0	22.0	23.0	30.5	31.3

SOURCES: Schulthess and Demarco 1993; Jáuregui 1994.

1994b: 356–57). Table 4.1 depicts the financial problems faced by the Argentine pension system in the 1980s.

The pension system fell severely into deficit in the early 1980s when the employers' contributions were eliminated, and it remained in deficit even after these contributions were restored. In 1990, only 65.8 percent of the system's expenditures were covered by social security contributions (Schulthess and Demarco 1993: 47). To make matters worse, the Argentine government had failed to invest the surpluses that the pension system had generated when it was first established. Although the system was initially intended to be fully funded, it was quickly converted to a pay-as-you-go system as a succession of Argentine governments used the pension surpluses for their own spending needs. As a result, the pension system did not have any reserves to draw on when it fell into deficit. Instead, it had to rely on a combination of general treasury revenues as well as special taxes that were earmarked for the pension system, such as a value-added tax that was imposed in 1980 and a telephone and gasoline tax that was established in 1988.

The Argentine government relieved some of the financial pressure facing the pension system in the 1980s by allowing inflation to erode the real value of pensions. By 1988, the average pension in the main pension system was worth only 64 percent of its 1980 value in real terms (Schulthess 1990: 26). This represented approximately 40 percent of the average salary, as opposed to the 70–82 percent replacement rate promised by law (Schulthess and Demarco 1993: 37).[7] Allowing the real value of pensions to deteriorate did not eliminate the funding shortfalls, however, and it provoked a wave of protests and lawsuits from individuals who sought to obtain the pensions that they had been promised under law. In many instances, the judiciary ruled in favor of the pensioners; as a result, the state's pension debts mounted.

The growing financial problems of the pension system put intense pressure on the Argentine government to undertake a major reform of the system. The large pension deficit diverted revenues from other government programs and exacerbated the overall fiscal deficits that the Argentine government consistently ran. Policymakers as well as the public as a whole routinely cited the situation of the pensioners as one of the most important problems facing the country. Politicians feared that the rising discontent had the potential to damage their electoral chances.

Although all sides agreed that a major overhaul of the pension system was needed, a great deal of disagreement existed over what sort of reform should be undertaken. Some policymakers lobbied for the partial or complete privatization of the system. Proponents of privatization argued that it would solve the long-term financial problems of the pension system for several reasons. To begin with, privatization would shift the system from a pay-as-you-go to a fully funded system, thereby reducing the system's vulnerability to future demographic changes. Privatization would also reduce the ability of the state to manipulate the system for political purposes, which proponents of privatization argued was one of the principal causes of the system's problems. Proponents of privatization further argued that a private system would be managed more efficiently than the public one, which would enable it to generate higher pensions with the same or fewer resources.

Nevertheless, privatization had a number of drawbacks as well. First of all, the medium-term fiscal costs of pension privatization were enormous. The privatization plan enacted in Argentina was initially projected to cause the system to run deficits until the year 2005, accumulating debts of more than $6.4 billion (Posadas 1994). These projections proved to be overly optimistic, however. A more recent estimate by government economists projects the system to run deficits until 2013, with a total accumulated deficit of $42.5 billion, although the projected increase in the transition costs is partly a result of Menem's decision to reduce the level of employers' contributions to the system, rather than the privatization scheme per se (Cottani and Demarco 1998). Other estimates project even larger transition costs (FIEL 1995; Rofman and Bertín 1996).

The other major drawback of pension privatization was its political unpopularity. The Menem administration's privatization proposal met considerable resistance from the pensioners' associations and from sectors of the labor movement. The population as a whole was also decidedly unenthusiastic about the reform. In one poll, taken on the eve of the implementation of the privatization plan, only 37 percent of the respondents said they supported the reform, whereas 47 percent stated that they were opposed to the measure (Mora y Araujo et al. 1994: 24).[8]

The country's traditional social security experts, including the career employees of the Secretariat of Social Security, were also by and large opposed to the privatization scheme. The director of economic planning for the Secretariat of Social Security, Amancio López, went so far as to resign his position at the agency after the privatization plan was proposed; he subsequently became one of the principal advisers to the opponents of the reform (interview with López 1996). The social security experts recognized that a major reform of the pension system was necessary, but they typically favored tightening the eligibility requirements for benefits and cutting back benefits in the existing public pension system, rather than privatizing the system. Indeed, in the 1980s, the Secretariat for Social Security formulated reform plans along these lines, but the proposals did not prosper politically (interviews with Capuccio 1996 and with de Estrada 1996).

Economic Crisis and Neoliberal Reform

To understand why the Menem administration decided to implement a major pension privatization scheme in spite of the fiscal and political costs of such measures, we must examine not only the financial problems facing the Argentine pension system, but also the severe economic crisis that buffeted Argentina at the end of the 1980s. This crisis led to the ruling Radical Party's defeat in the 1989 elections and to the ascent of a new Peronist government that was determined to escape the fate of its predecessor. In an effort to eliminate inflation and restore investor confidence in the Argentine economy, the new government quickly moved to implement dramatic stabilization measures along with a wide array of market-oriented structural reforms. Pension privatization was one of the most important of these latter measures. By privatizing its pension system, the Menem administration hoped not only to place the pension system on more stable long-term financial footing, but also to boost the country's domestic savings rate and to bolster the country's emerging capital markets, thereby reducing its vulnerability to future capital shortages. As the Argentine Ministry of Economy declared in its 1993 report, *Argentina: A Growing Nation*:

> The reform of the social security system, in addition to the principal objective of providing a structural solution to the crisis in the system, will be another key instrument in increasing savings levels in Argentina by approximately $3 billion annually, and will increase the efficiency of its investment through the development of capital markets which will be at the disposal of the productive sector. (Ministerio de Economía 1993: 67)

Capital shortages in Argentina began with the outbreak of the debt crisis in 1982. Argentina, like most Latin American countries, had borrowed heavily from foreign banks in the 1970s and early 1980s. In late 1982, however, foreign loans to the country were suddenly cut off in the wake of a sharp rise in international interest rates and the debt-servicing problems encountered by other countries in the region. To worsen matters, numerous domestic as well as foreign investors shifted massive amounts of funds out of the country in the years immediately preceding and following the outbreak of the crisis. According to various estimates, Argentine capital flight totaled between $16.5 and $19.2 billion during the period 1980–84 (UN-ECLAC 1995: 275).

The widespread capital shortages pushed Argentina into a deep economic crisis. The Argentine economy shrank by 4.9 percent in 1982 and inflation soared to 163 percent. The administration of Raúl Alfonsín, which came to power in 1983, tried to restore economic growth through a combination of heterodox and orthodox economic policies, but these measures largely failed to restore business confidence (Smith 1990, 1991; Canitrot 1994). Foreign financial interests and internationally oriented domestic concerns were particularly skeptical of the erratic economic policies of the Alfonsín administration, which frequently fell out of compliance with its International Monetary Fund programs. As a result, flight capital remained abroad and new loans and investment failed to materialize. Brief economic recoveries were quickly followed by much more serious collapses. The deepest collapse came shortly before the presidential elections when hyperinflation struck the country with unprecedented force, averaging 87 percent per month between February and August 1989 (Canitrot 1994: 86). The economic instability set off a new wave of capital flight exceeding $4.3 billion in 1989 (Ministerio de Economía 1994: 45). According to an estimate by Morgan Guaranty Trust, by 1990, Argentines had approximately $46 billion in flight capital invested outside of the country ("Fuga de capitales" 1990: 38).

The economic instability contributed heavily to the resounding victory of Carlos Menem over Eduardo Angeloz, the candidate of Alfonsín's Radical Party, in the 1989 presidential elections.[9] President Alfonsín's popularity declined dramatically as the economic crisis intensified, falling from a 64 percent approval rating in May 1987 to a 29 percent approval rating in April 1989. Angeloz tried to distance himself from the unpopular president, but to little avail (Mora y Araujo 1991). In the May 1989 elections, Menem received 47.4 percent of the presidential vote, compared to 36.4 percent for Angeloz. The Peronist party won an even more resounding victory in the legislative races, earning 44.7 percent of the vote, as opposed to 28.7 percent for the Radical Party. With the economy in ruins, Alfonsín handed power over to the Menem administration five months before he was scheduled to leave office.

What policies the Menem administration would enact were not immediately clear. During his presidential campaign, Menem had avoided spelling out what type of economic policies he would pursue in office, but the widespread assumption was that these policies would be in the populist tradition of the Peronist party. Indeed, Menem had practiced populist policies as governor of a small Argentine province.[10] The economic crisis, however, had undermined support for the existing state-led development model and strengthened those actors who advocated sweeping market-oriented reforms. The Argentine economy was badly in need of capital, but the international financial institutions, such as the International Monetary Fund and the World Bank, refused to lend to Argentina unless it committed itself to carrying out market-oriented reforms. Private investors were also reluctant to invest in Argentina until the government took concrete steps to address their concerns.

Menem, who took office in July 1989, recognized that his political future depended in large part on his ability to stabilize the Argentine economy and to restore economic growth. Upon taking office, he immediately undertook a number of measures designed to please the financial community and to restore confidence in the Argentine economy. Menem first announced a new political alliance with a small center-right party, the Unión del Centro Democrático (UCEDE), whose leader, Alvaro Alsogaray, had run for president against Menem on a platform of strong neoliberal reform. Alsogaray was appointed as Menem's personal adviser and intermediary with the international financial community and two other leaders of the UCEDE, including Alsogaray's daughter, were given top economic policy-making posts (Gibson 1990). Even more importantly, Menem appointed as his minister of economy a top executive of Bunge & Born, a huge multinational agricultural conglomerate that was one of Argentina's leading exporters. Unlike many Argentine companies, Bunge & Born was not dependent on state subsidies or contracts and thus was more inclined to press for a strict neoliberal program (Acuña 1994; Erro 1993).[11] Although Menem's initial minister, Miguel Roig, died shortly after taking office, he was immediately replaced with Nestor Rapanelli, another vice president of Bunge & Born. These appointments gave advocates of neoliberal ideas a great deal of influence over policy making within the Menem administration.

The Menem administration immediately launched a stabilization plan to bring down hyperinflation. The currency was sharply devalued, government spending was cut, and government-controlled prices were allowed to rise. The government also negotiated an agreement with 350 leading companies to slow future price rises. After slowing inflation initially, this plan foundered, leading to the resignation of Rapanelli in December 1989. He was replaced by Antonio Erman González, an accountant who had served as minister of economy for the province of La Rioja during Menem's term of governor. Under González, the government opted to deepen the stabilization and liberalization process, but his efforts to eliminate inflation also encountered problems. It was not until Domingo Cavallo, a Harvard-trained economist, took over as the minister of economy in early 1991 that inflation finally subsided. Under Cavallo, the Argentine government passed the Convertibility Law, which made the Argentine currency freely convertible into dollars. By prohibiting the Central Bank from issuing money unless it was backed by gold or foreign currency, the law effectively conquered the inflationary expectations that had driven price rises in the past.

Cavallo brought with him a large team of neoliberal economists who set to work designing a comprehensive reform program. Cavallo had been the director of a neoliberal think tank that was set up by a private foundation, the Fundación Mediterránea, in the city of Córdoba, Argentina. Cavallo used his contacts from this think tank to staff many of the key policy-making posts in the Menem administration. Indeed, Carlos Sánchez, a Cavallo ally and the former secretary of commerce and investment, estimated that approximately eighty economists from the Fundación Mediterránea took policy-making posts during the Menem administration (Huneeus 1997: 190). Many of these economists, like Roque Fernández, who was appointed president of the Central Bank during Cavallo's tenure, had Ph.D.s in economics from prestigious U.S. universities. Regardless of their academic credentials, however, the economists shared a commitment to economic liberalism.

From the outset of its tenure, the Menem administration embarked on a sweeping program of structural economic reform, but this reform program was accelerated once Cavallo became minister of the economy. A host of companies, including the state-owned telephone and oil companies, electrical utilities, and airlines were privatized and subsidies to already privately owned firms were reduced or eliminated.[12] The nominal value of the privatizations that took place between 1990 and 1993 totaled $15.5 million (Azpiazu and Vispo 1994: 134). Import tariffs and other barriers to foreign trade were substantially reduced. By the end of 1990, almost all quantitative restrictions on trade had been eliminated, and the average tariff had fallen to 17 percent (Gerchunoff and Torre 1996: 741). The Menem administration also carried out a major tax reform and substantially liberalized the financial sector.

After a rocky start, the Menem administration's efforts began to reap some positive results, although the unemployment rate remained high. Inflation fell from 4,923 percent in 1989 to 84 percent in 1991 and just 17.5 percent in 1992 (UN-ECLAC 1994: 757). The Menem administration's success in reducing inflation and meeting other economic targets was rewarded with the extension of an Extended Fund Facility credit—the first time in decades that Argentina had gained access to these funds. The IMF credit in turn helped lead to an agreement with Argentina's foreign creditors to reduce the country's foreign debt under the auspices of the Brady Plan. Buoyed by the increase in Argentina's country risk ratings, domestic and foreign investors began to bring capital back into the country. Net private capital flows to Argentina, which had been overwhelmingly negative in 1989 and 1990, exceeded $2.3 billion in 1991 and $7.8 billion in 1992 (Ministerio de Economía 1994: 45). The capital flows helped fuel strong economic growth. Gross domestic product, which had declined by 6.2 percent in 1989 and registered no growth in 1990, grew by an astounding 8.9 percent in 1991 and 8.6 percent in 1992 (UN-ECLAC 1994: 752–53). The economic turnaround bolstered the popularity of the government and reinforced the position of the neoliberals within the Menem administration.

Domestic Capital and Pension Privatization

Although the state of the economy turned around in the early 1990s, policymakers continued to be concerned about a number of issues. One of the principal concerns was the low domestic savings rate (Cottani and Demarco 1998; Cavallo 1993). Domestic savings fell sharply in Argentina in the early 1990s, dropping from 22 percent of GDP in 1989 to 19.5 percent in 1990, 16.2 percent in 1991, and 15.1 percent in 1992 (World Bank 1995c: 65). Declining domestic savings meant that Argentina depended heavily on foreign capital for investment, which many Argentine policymakers were reluctant to do given the sudden cutoff of foreign loans and the massive capital outflows they had experienced in the 1980s. Moreover, the financial liberalization measures that the government enacted in the early 1990s made it even easier for both domestic and foreign investors to quickly shift their assets overseas. The convertibility law, for example, enhanced the mobility of capital by ensuring that foreign and domestic investors alike could transfer their Argentine assets into dollars at a fixed rate of exchange.

Pension privatization appealed to Argentine policymakers because they saw it as a way to boost the country's domestic savings rates as well as to stabilize the long-term financial situation of the pension system. As Domingo Cavallo argued in a speech to the Association of Bankers of the Republic of Argentina:

We are realizing capital flows from the exterior. And for that I thank you, the bankers, for all that you have done and will surely continue to do. But our problem now is to increase domestic savings. We have to move from 13 percent, which was domestic savings last year, to levels around 20 percent. But this should not be savings captured by force, by redistribution that come from devaluations, but rather it should be voluntary savings, chosen by Argentines or generated by the institutions that we introduce to Argentine. Therein lies the importance of the pension reform. (Cavallo 1993: 461–62)

According to advocates of pension privatization, the pension reform "would have an important impact on the level and composition of national savings" (Cottani and Llach 1993: 109). A study by one of the architects of the reform estimated that the reform would gradually increase domestic savings by

2.5 percent of GDP, a 15 percent increase from its 1995 level (Cottani and Demarco 1998).

Advocates of pension privatization contended that the reform would also help them deepen and diversify Argentina's domestic capital markets. As two top policymakers in the Ministry of Economy argued, "The social security reform not only promotes an increase in national savings but also an improvement in financial intermediation that favors the quality of investment and the length of placements" (Cottani and Llach 1993: 109). The flow of funds into the private capital markets, they maintained, would reduce interest rates and make it easier for private-sector companies to fund investments (Cottani and Llach 1993: 109). The main architect of the reform, Walter Schulthess (1991: 5), similarly emphasized the positive capital markets effects of the reform in a speech to the Argentine banking community:

The [new] system of social security will also enter into the problem of the capital markets . . . at the beginning, these [pension] funds are going to grow because they will have a lot of contributions but there will practically not be any withdrawals. This will permit us to count on a good mass of money that can be used inside the capital markets with the various possibilities that this offers.

The World Bank projected that the funds accumulated in the private pension system would reach $20 billion by the year 2000 and $50 billion by 2005, creating a tremendous demand for equities, asset-backed securities, certificates of deposit and corporate and government bonds (World Bank 1994a: 103). The pension funds would become an especially important source of long-term capital, which had traditionally been in short supply on the domestic markets. This would benefit infrastructure projects owing to the "natural fit between the long term financing of such projects and the long term investment objectives of pension funds" (World Bank 1994a: 103). Pension privatization also stood to benefit the domestic insurance industry since private insurance companies would manage the disability and life insurance provided in the private pension system as well as the retirement annuities. According to World Bank (1994a: 104) estimates, domestic insurance companies would initially earn about $500 million annually in disability and life insurance premiums, and these earnings would increase over time. Moreover, once workers began to retire in the private pension system, insurance companies would also earn considerable income from the sale of retirement annuities.

Ideational Influences

The evidence that pension privatization would bring major social and economic benefits to Argentina was tenuous at best, but supporters of pension privatization nevertheless managed to persuade the top political leaders and other influential actors of the merits of the reform. Two actors—the World Bank and a group of liberal Argentine economists—played a particularly important role in promoting pension privatization in Argentina. The World Bank and the neoliberal economists assumed increasing policy-making influence in Argentina in the late 1980s and early 1990s, and they used this influence to lobby in favor of pension privatization. The experience of neighboring Chile also helped persuade Argentines of the efficacy of pension privatization. Indeed, the Chilean model was the subject of frequent discussions during this period, and Chilean pension experts made numerous visits to Argentina.

World Bank influence in Argentina increased during the 1980s and 1990s as a result of the economic problems that the country experienced. The World Bank provided badly needed financial as well as technical assistance to the country on numerous occasions during this period and, as a result, gained influence in the country. The Bank's influence extended into social as well as economic policy making. Beginning in the Alfonsín administration, the World Bank funded a major technical assistance program called the National Program for Technical Assistance for the Administration of Social Services (PRONATASS). Under this program, local technocrats carried out a series of diagnostic studies of the Argentine pension system, which would lay the groundwork for the privatization plan. PRONATASS also brought together a number of the Argentine economists who would subsequently formulate the reform.

At the end of the 1980s, the World Bank had begun to promote pension privatization as a means to address economic as well as social problems. The World Bank promoted pension privatization in part through its publications, which the Argentine policymakers researching the reform read. As one of the key architects of the pension privatization plan in Argentina later acknowledged, "The arguments for social security privatization based on the effects on the capital markets and the economic development were present in many documents of international agencies" (Demarco 2000: 5). World Bank officials also used their numerous formal and informal contacts with Argentine policymakers to promote pension privatization. Indeed, one Argentine policymaker complained that a local World Bank representative pressed them to carry out a much more sweeping privatization plan than they intended (interview with Demarco 1996). Thus, World Bank representatives had ample opportunities to make their views known, although they did not have a formal role in the policy formulation process.

Other international financial institutions also promoted pension privatization in Argentina, although they played a relatively minor role in the reform. The Inter-American Development Bank, as well as the World Bank, financed some of the transition costs of the reform, but the financing that these institutions provided paled in comparison to the transition costs of the reform. The International Monetary Fund, meanwhile, granted $4.0 billion in Extended Fund Facility financing to Argentina in exchange for the government's commitment to privatize the pension system (by January 1993) and carry out other economic reforms (Ministerio de Economía 1992). The privatization of the pension system was included in the Argentine government's letter of intent to the IMF at the instigation of the Menem administration, however, rather than at the insistence of the IMF (Brooks 1998).

The most important advocates of pension privatization in Argentina were not the international financial institutions, but rather a relatively small group of neoliberal economists within the Argentine government. These economists took over the key social security policy-making positions in Argentina during the early 1990s. Until early 1991, the secretary for social security was Santiago de Estrada, a lawyer and long-time social security specialist. De Estrada had served as the subsecretary for social security between 1967–69, and then as secretary for social security between 1976 and 1983 and again between 1989 and 1991 (interview with de Estrada 1996). De Estrada generally opposed pension privatization, although he had proposed allowing workers to invest 2 percent of their salaries in privately managed individual retirement accounts. He feared that large-scale pension privatization would undermine the finances of the public pension system, which would hurt existing pensioners (interview with de Estrada 1996).[13] Instead, he proposed a reform of the existing public pension system that would involve an increase in the minimum retirement age and a reduction in the benefits paid by the system (Isuani and San Martino 1993). This reform proposal met opposition from numerous quarters, however, and was shelved when de Estrada resigned in early 1991.

When Domingo Cavallo became minister of economy in early 1991, he had Walter Schulthess named as the new secretary of social security. Schulthess had close ties to Cavallo—they were both from Córdoba and they had worked closely together in the past (interview with Schulthess 1996). Although the Secretariat of Social Security was formally a dependency of the Ministry of Labor, Schulthess owed his position to Cavallo and reported directly to him (interview with Schulthess 1996). The Ministry of Economy took charge of the Secretariat of Social Security because of the importance of the impact that the social security system had on the economy as a whole (interview with Posadas 1996).

Schulthess was not a specialist in social security. A professor of economics at the University of Córdoba, he had worked for most of his career on issues of taxation and public finance. In the 1980s, however, he began to do consulting work on social security programs in Argentina and neighboring countries; in 1989, he was hired as a consultant for PRONATASS. When

Schulthess arrived at the Secretariat, he brought with him a small team of outside consultants, and together they began to develop the reform proposal. The entire team consisted of approximately twenty individuals, but a half dozen of these people formed the core of the team and took charge of the actual formulation of the reform proposal.

The team of consultants worked in relative isolation; indeed, for a long time most of the consultants themselves only knew the details of the program that they worked on and were kept unaware of the overall reform proposal (interviews with Posadas 1996 and with Demarco 1996). The career bureaucrats of the Secretariat for Social Security were completely shut out of the reform process in part because they were known to oppose pension privatization (interview with López 1996). Indeed, Amancio López, the director-general of economic planning of the secretary of social security, carried out an open campaign to block the privatization of the pension system until he was asked by Schulthess to resign, at which point he became a consultant to the groups seeking to block the reform (interview with López 1996).

Some of the members of the reform team had close ties to the private sector—indeed, a few of them would subsequently go to work for the private pension fund administrators—but the business community did not play an important role in the reform formulation process. The National Securities Commission was involved in the design of the reform proposal at the very early stages, but once the project was taken over by Schulthess and the Secretariat of Social Security the private sector had less direct influence (interview with Barassi 1996; Torre and Gerchunoff 1999). One of the members of the reform team commented that the reform planners were "two steps ahead of the private sector, which is not common in other reform areas in which the projects originate in some ways in the private sector. When we talked to the private sector it was like we were teaching them something. The private sector trusted fully in the development of the reform. It didn't give opinions much or pressure us much" (interview with Barassi 1996). Carlos Facal, a member of the governing board of the Argentine Association of Insurance Companies, noted that the government was not highly receptive to the private sector during the reform process "because the government did not want to be accused of defending private interests" (interview with Facal 1996).

Schulthess's reform team consisted almost exclusively of economists. As such, they represented a departure from the traditional social security policymakers in Argentina. Five of the members of Schulthess's core group, including Schulthess himself, were economists and the sixth member was an actuary. In contrast, the core group of advisers of Emilio Capuccio, who was secretary of social security under Alfonsín, consisted of four lawyers, a sociologist, and a statistician (interview with Capuccio 1996). In an interview

with the author, Schulthess discussed this change in the profile of social security policymakers:

The field of social security until 1990 was in the hands of people who specialized in
the subject, but who were lawyers and with some technical support from some actuary to do the calculations. Since we arrived here the working group has been basically economists, actuaries and sociologists. Afterwards, when we put together the
legislation, we called lawyers to edit it. First, we wanted to have an economic and
financial base. (Interview with Schulthess 1996)

The economists were highly critical of the traditional style of social security
policy making and administration. According to Schulthess:

One of the prejudices of those who have not been able to escape traditional social
security is the divorce between social objectives and economic and administrative
criteria. The problem of efficiency to which we referred previously, is one clear example of this. One observes in social security institutions and in many of their traditional functionaries a tendency to consider that the institutions will be contami-
nated by spurious objectives when one speaks of budgets, financial limitations, costs,
placement of funds. (Schulthess 1994b: 21–22)

The economists were more apt to use rigorous financial planning and more
sensitive to the implications of their policies on the economy as a whole.
Whereas the lawyers had tended to emphasize social obligations, the economists stressed the financial limitations and economic consequences of pension policy.

The economists favored pension privatization in part because they were
concerned about the larger macroeconomic implications of pension privatization. Their training in liberal economic theory had also instilled in them
a bias toward market-oriented solutions. The economists on the Argentine
reform team, unlike the Mexican economists, typically had not studied
abroad, but they had nevertheless been heavily exposed to classical economic
thought at their Argentine universities. Schulthess, for example, had received his Ph.D. from the University of Córdoba, one of the strongholds of
orthodox economic theory in Argentina. The original reform team of some
twenty members did include some economists who were skeptical of the
merits of pension privatization, but these members were gradually weeded
out of the group.

The Chilean experience with pension privatization influenced the Argentine policymakers a great deal. Argentine policymakers found Chile's
experience particularly relevant because of the many similarities between
the two countries. In the words of one key policymaker: "Chilean experience appeared neither remote nor unfeasible, given the similar cultural roots
and economic development" (Demarco 2000: 8). So crucial was the Chilean
model to the Argentine reform that one of its architects bluntly stated, "If

the Chilean case had not existed, it's probable that we still wouldn't have the reform [in Argentina]" (interview with Barassi 1996).

Throughout the late 1980s and early 1990s, Chilean pension experts traveled to Argentina to promote the Chilean model. The Chilean pension experts included the architect of the Chilean reform, José Piñera, who journeyed to Argentina to personally lobby President Menem to privatize the Argentine pension system. Chilean pension experts also promoted pension privatization through their contacts with Argentine policymakers at a variety of regional and international forums. For example, the United Nations Economic Commission for Latin America, which was based in Chile, brought together two of the principal architects of the Argentine reform with a number of Chilean pension reform experts to carry out studies of pension reform. Numerous Chilean individuals and institutions also produced glowing analyses of the Chilean reform, which were read by Argentine policymakers.

During the late 1980s and early 1990s, the Argentine media also paid a great deal of attention to their Andean neighbor and its economic achievements. News stories often contrasted Chile's sustained record of economic growth and stability to the volatility experienced in Argentina. Many observers in Argentina and elsewhere attributed the growth in Chile to the country's pension privatization scheme and hoped that privatizing their own pension system would have a similar effect (Cottani and Llach 1993: 109; World Bank 1993: 148). Proponents of pension privatization maintained that the Chilean reform had bolstered the country's domestic savings rate and capital markets, thereby providing the investment capital that fueled the Chilean economic boom. The evidence for these conclusions was relatively thin, however. As one of the architects of the Argentine reform, Gustavo Demarco (2000: 4–5), later acknowledged: "The arguments based on the effects of private pensions on savings and the capital markets were probably overweighed [*sic*] by some of the sectors promoting the reform in Argentina. . . . In most cases the conclusions were only supported by 'common sense' arguments, or on diffusion material with simple correlations of variables from the Chilean experience."

The Chilean reform was also important in that it provided a clear policy model that Argentine policymakers could use to design their reform. Indeed, Argentine policymakers initiated their reform by closely studying the Chilean scheme, traveling on one occasion to Chile to examine the reform up close (Demarco 2000; interviews with Demarco 1996, with Posadas 1996, and with Rondina 1996).[14] In addition, one of the members of the Argentine pension reform team, Mauricio Barassi, had worked with the private pension funds in Chile during the 1980s and was thus very well acquainted with the Chilean system (interview with Barassi 1996). After studying the Chilean model, the Argentine policymakers began to improvise, copying the aspects of the reform that they liked and discarding those aspects that they thought did not work well or were inappropriate for Argentina. According to Schulthess: "We used a lot from Chile; we saw what functioned well. We made some changes—a different way of presenting the problem— but we used a lot their experience" (interview with Schulthess 1996). The final privatization plan closely resembled the Chilean reform in most aspects, although it was not as far-reaching.

The Choice of a Mixed System

The reform proposal that Schulthess's team formulated envisioned the creation of a mixed public/private system. The draft legislation called for the creation of two new pension systems: a reformed public pay-as-you-go system and a completely new private system based on the method of individual capitalization. All workers under the age of forty-five would automatically become members of the two new systems, as would future entrants to the workforce, but workers older than forty-five would have the choice of joining the new systems or remaining in the old unreformed public system. Workers who joined the new systems would not be compensated for their past contributions to the pension system.

The new public system was to be financed by the employers' contribution to the system as well as by other taxes such as the value-added tax. All workers who had contributed to this system for thirty years would receive a Universal Basic Benefit (PBU) that would be equal to 1.5 times the average mandatory personal pension contribution (AMPO) for the system as a whole. The value of the basic benefit would increase by 2 percent for each year above thirty that a worker contributed to the system, but otherwise would be the same for all workers in the system, regardless of the size of their salaries (and hence their contributions to the system).

The new private pension system, in contrast, would be financed by the contributions of the workers. According to the draft legislation, each worker's monthly pension contribution would continue to be collected by the state, but it would immediately be transferred to an individual retirement account managed by a private pension fund (AFJP) of the worker's own choosing. The AFJPs would be supervised by a government agency, which would closely regulate what types of investments they would be allowed to make. The pension a worker would receive from this system upon retirement would be based on the amount of funds accumulated in his or her individual retirement account (that is, contributions plus interest earnings, minus the administrative and insurance commissions charged by the AFJPs).

The draft legislation also envisioned a number of measures intended to resolve the financial problems of the existing public pension system, which would continue to provide pensions to existing retirees as well as workers over forty-five years of age. The legislation, for example, called for tighter restrictions on access to benefits. The minimum age of retirement would be gradually raised to sixty-five years of age in both the new and old systems, and the requirements for gaining access to disability and survivors' pensions would be tightened. The reform, however, also proposed that pension benefits be adjusted to the levels stated by law and that the existing debts and obligations of the system be honored. The pension benefits would be financed by a number of taxes as well as by the revenues generated by the privatization of the state-owned petroleum company.

The Argentine reform team, unlike their counterparts in Chile and Mexico, opted to create a mixed public/private pension system for several reasons. First, and most importantly, full-scale pension privatization was prohibitively expensive. The Argentine pension system was quite mature, particularly in comparison to other Latin American countries. Pension coverage was high, the population elderly, and the benefits promised by the system relatively generous. As a result, pension expenditures and, even more importantly, future pension obligations were large. This made the transition costs of pension privatization more onerous in Argentina since the state would have to honor these public pension obligations to a large degree, even though it would lose access to the revenue from current workers that had traditionally financed its public pension expenditures. By partially privatizing its pension system, however, the Argentine government ensured that it would continue to receive a portion of the payroll contributions (in this case, the employers' contributions) that had traditionally financed the public pension system. This ensured that the government would have some funds available to pay the pensions of existing retirees.[15]

Argentine policymakers also favored partial, rather than full, pension privatization in order to ensure that the pension system continued to redistribute income. Argentina, unlike Chile in the early 1980s and even Mexico in the mid-1990s, was a full-fledged democracy, which obliged the Menem administration to consider political as well as technical factors in carrying out the reform. The Argentine social security system had always had a redistributive function, and Argentine policymakers believed that any effort to eliminate this function entirely would generate a great deal of political opposition, which would make the reform difficult to enact.[16] By preserving a redistributive public pillar in the system, the Menem administration could argue that the Argentine social security system continued to be solidaristic, which, it believed, would reduce opposition to the reform. For this reason, the Menem administration continually stressed the solidaristic aspects of the new social security system in its public pronouncements about the reform and tried to distinguish the Argentine reform from the Chilean model.[17]

The creation of a mixed system, rather than a fully private one, also made good political sense because a mixed system could be reconciled more easily with Article 14 bis of the Argentine constitution, which stipulated that "the state will confer social security benefits which will be of an integral and irrenounceable nature" ("Constituciones políticas" 1995: 8). By creating a mixed system, the Menem administration could argue that the Argentine social security system still fulfilled its constitutional requirements since the state continued to provide obligatory social security benefits to the population (Schulthess 1992: 7). Indeed, in the months before presenting the reform to the legislature, the Menem administration and its allies addressed this issue head on, crafting a joint declaration that stated, "Different forms of institutional organization with variable combinations of public and private components can be compatible with the public character of social security, as long as the delegated functions do not leave essential questions to individual choice, such as the very existence of pension benefits" (*Mesa del Diálogo Político* 1992: 1). Although various political actors challenged the constitutionality of the pension reform, their challenges ultimately proved fruitless.

The Response to the Reform

The Menem administration recognized that its reform proposal would be controversial in spite of the compromises it made in crafting the reform. The Menem administration, like the Zedillo administration in Mexico, therefore tried to build political support for the reform prior to its introduction to the legislature. In early 1992, when the reform proposal was almost finished, the Menem administration called a series of meetings with political parties and interest groups to discuss a number of issues, including the pension reform. The Menem administration did not share the details of the reform proposal with the participants in these meetings, which were dubbed the Roundtable on Political Dialogue, because it wanted to avoid a point-by-point debate (Kay 1998: 173). Instead, the discussions at these meetings centered on ten general issues having to do with the social security reform. A fair amount of dissent nevertheless emerged at these meetings, particularly with regard to the discussion about raising the minimum retirement age or partially privatizing the pension system. Even more dissent no doubt would have occurred had representatives from the Radical Party, the pensioners' movement, or the dissident labor unions participated in the forums.[18]

The controversy over the reform only deepened once the reform proposal was introduced in June 1992. Much of the business community, especially the financial sector, strongly supported the reform. Various private-sector institutions had lobbied aggressively for pension privatization since the end of the 1980s, and a number of important business associations, including the Argentine Industrial Union, the Argentine Association of Insurance Companies, and the Association of Argentine Banks, had formulated pension privatization proposals (Unión Industrial Argentina 1990, 1992; Isuani and San Martino 1993; Asociación Argentina de Compañía de Seguros 1992). When the reform was presented to the legislature, the Argentine Association of Insurance Companies issued the following statement: "We want to show our complete and enthusiastic support for the historic reform that our country proposes to enact in an area so crucial. We congratulate ourselves, not without a certain pride, for having proposed several years ago, the necessity of moving from the current pay-as-you-go system whose bankruptcy is evident, to a system of capitalization, which has proved successful in other countries of the world" (Asociación Argentina de Compañía de Seguros 1992). The private sector supported the privatization of the pension system not only because it believed it would resolve the financial problems of the pension system, but also because it would bring economic benefits. In a letter to the legislative committees that were in charge of evaluating the reforms, the Buenos Aires Stock Exchange wrote, "The private retirement funds will generate considerable amounts of domestic savings that will be directed toward investment or the working capital of companies and other profitable uses, increasing the possibilities for financing productive activities" (Bolsa de Comercio de Buenos Aires 1992: 1).

Other societal actors vigorously opposed the reform, however. The pensioners' organizations held weekly marches and demonstrations against the privatization plan and gathered more than one million signatures calling for a nationwide plebiscite to be held on the reform. The unions affiliated with the dissident labor confederation, the Congreso de Trabajadores Argentinos (CTA), joined the pensioners' associations in these campaigns against the reform. Even the main labor confederation, which was closely tied to the ruling party, grumbled about the pension privatization plans and initially threatened to carry out a massive strike to block its implementation. Opposition parties also denounced the reform as did numerous members of the ruling Peronist party and its allies, who obstructed the passage of the reform through the legislature.

The Menem administration nevertheless managed to enact its pension privatization plan, although it was obliged to make numerous concessions to critics of the reform proposal. The key to the success of the Menem administration's efforts lay in several factors. First, the pensioner's movement in Argentina, like elsewhere, was poorly organized and lacking in resources. It could therefore offer only symbolic opposition to the privatization plan. Second, although the labor movement in Argentina was quite strong, it was closely tied to the ruling party and was extremely reluctant to risk a rupture of this relationship. Thus, the main labor federation ultimately agreed to support the privatization plan, but only after obtaining significant concessions from the government. Third, the ruling party controlled a majority of the seats in the Senate and a near majority of seats in the Chamber of Deputies and had a number of mechanisms at its disposal to ensure a high level of party discipline. As a result, the Menem administration was able to gain approval of the reform proposal in the legislature with only a minimal number of votes from legislators from allied parties.

The Weakness of the Old-Age Lobby

The main pensioners' associations aggressively opposed the Menem administration's privatization plans from the beginning. The pensioners' organizations objected to the proposed reform on several grounds. First, they believed that pensioners had nothing to gain and much to lose from pension privatization. The attempt to privatize the pension system, they argued, was "to the exclusive benefit of the usurious financial sector" (Plenario Permanente de Organizaciones de Jubilados 1992: 9). Although the Menem administration assured the pensioners that their benefits would be unaffected by the reform, the pensioners' associations feared that the reform would undermine the finances of the existing public pension system, which would inevitably lead to cutbacks in their benefits (interviews with Forte 1996 and with Imizcoz 1996). Indeed, shortly after the pension reform was implemented, the Menem administration introduced a bill, entitled the Law of Pension Solidarity, which cut back pension benefits for some categories of pensioners.

The pensioners' organizations also opposed the pension privatization plan on principle. Most of the leaders of the organizations were former union activists with staunchly statist views (interviews with Forte 1996 and with Imizcoz 1996). They believed that the social security system should remain in the hands of the state and should be solidaristic in nature. In a letter to the legislative commission that was considering the reform legislation, the leaders of the General Confederation of Pensioners and Retirees wrote, "We declare ourselves against the implementation of a system based in the philosophy of capitalization and even more so if it is private, given that social security cannot be dealt with under mercantilistic principles; this is contrary to the Constitution and we understand that it breaks the concept of solidarity" (Confederación General de Jubilados 1992).

The pensioners' associations lacked the political clout to block the reform. Although the 3.7 million pensioners in Argentina represented approximately 20 percent of the country's electorate (Alonso 1998: 596), the pensioners' organization could not credibly claim to speak for many of them. The pensioners' organizations were never able to mobilize substantial numbers of pensioners for their marches and demonstrations. Indeed, the vast majority of pensioners did not participate in the pensioners' organizations in any form whatsoever.[19] The largest march held by the pensioners' organizations drew less than 20,000 people, according to *La Nación*, and pensioners represented a minority of the participants ("Movilización contra" 1993: 1).

The pensioners' organizations were also notably lacking in resources. On June 30, 1995, the Coordinating Board of Pensioners of the Argentine Republic, which directed the campaign against the reform, reported liquid assets of only $5,332 and fixed assets worth $67,740 (*Jubilados* 1996: 6). The Argentine pensioners' organizations never developed the array of products and services such as health insurance and publications that helped fund elderly associations in the United States. Nor were they able to obtain funds from foundations or other external sources. Instead, they depended entirely on their membership for contributions; yet, many of their members were not in a position to give anything. This made it impossible for the organization to hire lobbyists, make political contributions, or carry out advertising campaigns against the proposed reform.

Nevertheless, the constant marches and demonstrations held by the pensioners' movement succeeded in generating a great deal of media attention. Pensioners were typically viewed sympathetically by the population, and opinion polls typically ranked the problems of pensioners among the most important problems the country was facing (Mora y Araujo et al. 1994). The pensioners' organizations probably helped turn public opinion against the pension privatization plan, which, in turn, bolstered legislative resistance to the reform. In this way, the opposition of the pensioners' movement may have helped pressure the Menem administration into granting some concessions to critics of the privatization plan. The pensioners' organizations were ultimately too weak, however, to block the reform altogether.

Negotiating with the Unions

The labor unions also initially opposed the pension privatization plan and used their economic power and political influence to try to block it. Ultimately, the unions associated with the main labor federation, the Confederación General del Trabajo (CGT), agreed to support the reform in exchange for a number of concessions from the Menem administration. The unions struck a deal with the government largely because they did not want to risk a major rupture with the Menem administration and with the Justicialist Party (PJ) more broadly. The Argentine labor movement historically had close ties to the Justicialist Party and the labor unions obtained numerous benefits from this relationship. PJ leaders channeled patronage resources to the unions and provided the unions with policy influence. Labor leaders traditionally occupied important party posts, and the Justicialist Party regularly included a large number of labor leaders as candidates for the legislature and other political offices. The Justicialist Party also helped to establish and maintain the unions' control of the *obras sociales*, the government-sponsored, but union-run, health care and recreational programs. The obras sociales were the unions' lifeblood, supplying the vast majority of their financial resources. In the early 1990s, the obras sociales managed $2.6 billion annually in state-mandated health care contributions, whereas union dues totaled less than $800 million even under the most generous assumptions (McGuire 1997: 225).

Labor influence in the Peronist party declined sharply in the late 1980s and early 1990s. At the same time, the election of Carlos Menem as president in 1989 made their relationship with the Justicialist Party more valuable. With the Justicialist Party controlling the federal government, the amount of patronage resources available to the unions ballooned, as did the labor movement's potential policy influence. In the first years of the Menem administration, labor leaders were appointed to key policy-making posts, heading the Ministry of Labor, the Ministry of Health, the state privatization boards, and the state agency that oversaw the obras sociales, although these leaders did not always adopt policies that were to the liking of the majority of the unions (Levitsky and Way 1998). The Menem administration also resolved the debts of some of the union-run obras sociales in a way that was favorable to the unions.

The labor unions feared that a rupture with the Menem administration would jeopardize their policy influence as well as their access to patronage resources. The Menem administration exploited the concerns of the unions by linking its policies on a variety of issues to the approval of the pension reform. Menem's minister of labor, for example, declared that an agreement on wage policy would not be reached until after the pension reform had been approved ("El ministro de trabajo" 1993: 8). The most threatening action for the unions, however, was the decree deregulating the obras sociales, which posed a serious risk to the survival of many of the union-run health care programs. Labor leaders believed that the measure, the implementation of which was subsequently delayed, was linked to their opposition to the pension reform. Indeed, the measure was decided on the day after labor-affiliated legislators failed to provide the legislative committee a quorum to vote on the proposed pension reform ("Los trabajadores elegirán" 1993: 1; "El gremialismo atempera" 1993: 4). The labor leaders also feared that the Menem administration would go ahead with its veiled threats to allow private companies to compete with the obras sociales if the labor-affiliated deputies blocked the pension reform (de Simone 1993: B1).

Although the Menem administration definitely held the upper hand in its relationship with the unions, organized labor had some bargaining power. The power of the Argentine unions flowed in large part from their representation in the Chamber of Deputies. Although the number of labor leaders serving in the Chamber of Deputies dropped during the late 1980s and early 1990s, the unions continued to maintain a sizeable contingent of legislators.[20] At the time of the reform, labor-affiliated legislators accounted for 18 of the Justicialist Party's 116 members of the Chamber of Deputies and six of the party's twenty-eight votes in the joint committee that evaluated the proposed reform.[21] Because of the thin level of support for the pension reform bill, the labor leaders controlled sufficient votes to block the reform. As a result, the Menem administration was obliged to grant the labor unions substantial concessions in order to secure their support.

The Menem administration, moreover, did not want its relationship with the labor movement to deteriorate. The government depended on its relationship with the unions to maintain labor peace, which was essential to the smooth functioning of the Argentine economy. Argentina traditionally has had a powerful labor movement, with the highest unionization levels in Latin America (Lamadrid and Orsatti 1991; Collier and Collier 1991; McGuire 1997).[22] Moreover, the Argentine unions, unlike their Mexican counterparts, have had a long history of activism (McGuire 1997; Epstein 1989). Indeed, during the Alfonsín administration, the labor unions carried out thirteen general strikes to protest the government's policies and successfully blocked a large number of the Alfonsín administration's proposed reforms, including the government's proposals to democratize the unions and reform the social security system. Owing in part to the government's close ties to the unions, the CGT did not carry out a single general strike during the first three years of the Menem administration in spite of the sweeping neoliberal reforms that Menem implemented during this period. The Menem administration feared, however, that any effort to unilaterally impose a pension reform might result in a serious backlash from the labor unions that would cause considerable disruption to the economy and could potentially hurt the party's future electoral possibilities.

The negotiation of the agreement on pension reform, like other agreements negotiated with the unions during the Menem administration, was facilitated by the trust that existed between many members of the Menem administration and the labor leaders (Levitsky and Way 1998; Murillo 2001). Indeed, Menem himself had close personal ties to many of the labor leaders. This trust gave each side reason to believe that the other side would hold up its end of the bargain; although, in fact, both sides did at times renege on their agreements. The personal relationships also provided the Menem administration and the labor leaders with numerous channels of communication that they could use in addition to the formal avenues of contact. As a result, negotiations over the reform were never broken off even when the relationship between the two parties was strained. The Alfonsín administration, in contrast, had lacked these long-term relationships and multiple lines of communication. The mutual distrust that existed between the former Radical Party government and the labor unions and the absence of secondary channels of communication made it difficult for the two parties to reach agreements with regard to government policies (Levitsky and Way 1998).

In the weeks after the reform was presented to the legislature, the main Argentine labor confederation, the CGT, announced its opposition to the reform and called for a twenty-four-hour general strike to be held on July 28 to protest this and other measures. Although most of the labor leaders were not opposed to the creation of a private pension system, they believed that the private pension system should complement, rather than replace, the existing public pension system, and that participation in the private scheme should be completely voluntary. Appearing before the legislative committee that was evaluating the proposed reform, a representative of the CGT, Carlos West Ocampo, stated that "there were aspects of unconstitutionality" in the reform and that the CGT did not like the idea that "future pensioners would be obliged to contribute to a system of private capitalization" ("Intensas gestiones" 1992: 6). The CGT also objected to the fact that the proposed reform treated workers of different ages quite differently and did not compensate workers under forty-five for those contributions that they had already made to the system (Isuani and San Martino 1993; interviews with Demarco 1996 and with Sueiro 1996).

The leadership of the CGT began to negotiate with the Menem administration immediately. On July 17, after extensive discussions, the labor confederation reached an agreement with the government. In exchange for the unions calling off the strike, which would have been the first general strike during the Menem administration, the government agreed to undertake a series of measures including a revision of the pension reform legislation.[23]

The Menem administration then submitted a revised pension reform bill to Congress, which took into consideration some of the concerns expressed by the labor unions and others (Cámara de Diputados de la Nación 1992b). The most important change was the elimination of the differential treatment of workers depending on their age and the creation of an additional pension benefit to compensate workers for past contributions to the pension system. The new legislation obliged all workers, regardless of age, to transfer from the old system to a new mixed system. Under the new legislation, workers who had previously contributed to the old system would now receive a compensatory pension benefit (PC), in addition to the basic public pension and the private pension benefit that had been envisioned in the original bill.

The compensatory pension would be calculated as 2 percent of the average salary that the worker earned during the ten years prior to retirement, multiplied by the number of years in which he or she contributed to the old system (up to a maximum of thirty years). The cost of this additional benefit would be assumed by the state, a move that substantially increased the transition costs of the reform.

The new pension reform bill failed to satisfy the labor leaders, however. A spokesman for the CGT denounced the proposed changes as "merely cosmetic" and insisted that "what is behind this proposal is a big business; 150 million dollars monthly that will be turned over at the stroke of a pen to private companies, so that they can use them and make deals" ("La CGT sigue" 1992: 5). The continued disagreements over the pension reform bill and, more importantly, the proposed reforms of the labor code and the union-run health funds led the CGT in early November to hold its first general strike during the Menem administration. Shortly after this strike, the Menem administration called on representatives of business and labor to take part in a government-sponsored commission, dubbed the National Council for Production, Investment, and Growth, in order to iron out their differences over the reforms.

After a series of meetings of this commission, the government managed to reach an agreement with the CGT (Isuani and San Martino 1993; "Un proyecto consensuado" 1992: B1). This agreement involved only minor concessions to the labor leaders, however. The main concession that the government granted the leadership of the CGT in exchange for its support for the pension reform initiative was to agree to specify that nonprofit organizations, such as the unions themselves, would be allowed to establish pension funds (AFJPs) in order to manage the workers' individual retirement accounts. Although the original reform legislation had not expressly prohibited the unions from establishing AFJPs, some labor leaders insisted that the legislation guarantee them the right to run the AFJPs since they saw the pension funds as a potentially important source of revenue for the unions. At the insistence of the private sector, however, the legislation specified that workers would be free to join the AFJP of their choice in order to prevent the unions from obliging their workers to sign up with a union-run AFJP.

Although these modifications were enough to garner the support of the official leadership of the CGT, which was dominated by unions that were particularly close to Menem, the reform proposal continued to be opposed by significant sectors of the CGT. The dissidents were led by Lorenzo Miguel, the head of the powerful Metalworkers' Union (UOM), but also included a number of other dissident unions within the CGT. During the course of the next several months the Menem administration made a number of key concessions to the unions and other critics of the reform in an effort to gain the support of the dissident leaders. The government agreed, for example, to establish a state-owned AFJP, which would compete with the other AFJPs in the private pension system. The state-owned AFJP would offer workers a guaranteed return on their deposits in both dollars and Argentine pesos. At the insistence of Juan González Gaviola, a dissident PJ deputy, and some labor-affiliated deputies, the Menem administration also agreed to increase the size of the basic pension benefit, which was the most redistributive of the pensions, while decreasing the value of the compensatory pension.

The dissident members of the CGT, however, remained critical of the proposed reform, arguing that "in spite of the improvements introduced to the original pension project, it does not maintain the guarantees necessary that our pensioners require" ("Crítica de las 62" 1993: 5). The dissidents called for a general strike to be held in opposition to the reform, although the official CGT leadership resisted this measure ("Las 62 se alejan" 1993: 5). Some of the dissident unions within the CGT, along with the Congreso de los Trabajadores Argentinos, a federation of militant anti-Menemist public-sector unions, which had broken off from the CGT, also participated in the numerous marches held by the pensioners' associations in opposition to the reform. Most importantly, the labor-affiliated legislators associated with these unions obstructed the passage of the reform in the legislature, helping to deny the government the quorum necessary to vote on the bill.

The Menem administration continued to negotiate with the dissident unions within the CGT, however, and these negotiations finally bore fruit in late April 1993 on the eve of the vote on the reform in the plenary of the Chamber of Deputies. In exchange for the support of the PJ legislators who were affiliated with these unions, the government agreed to reduce the life insurance costs in the new system and make participation in the private pension system optional. This latter modification permitted workers to continue paying their social security contributions to the (reformed) public system instead of to one of the pension funds (AFJP) in the new private pension system. Workers who chose to pay their pension contributions to the public system would receive an extra pension benefit, the Additional Benefit for Permanency (PAP), from the state instead of the benefit from the private system. Table 4.2 shows the modifications made to the Argentine pension reform bill.

With this agreement, the Menem administration had finally obtained the support of all of the major component unions of the CGT, which represented 90 percent of the organized workforce. Some of the labor leaders were genuinely enthusiastic about the reform and hoped to establish AFJPs, which would provide a source of income for themselves and their unions. Indeed, some labor unions subsequently banded together to create pension funds, although the labor-affiliated AFJPs only obtained a small share of the

TABLE 4.2

Modifications to the Argentine Pension Reform Bill

	June 1992 version	August 1992 version	Final version (Sept. 1993)
Type of system created	Mixed system (public/private)	Mixed system (public/private)	Mixed system (public/private)
Is membership in the private system obligatory?	Yes, for all active workers under age 45	Yes, for all active workers	No
Value of the benefit in the private system	Depends on funds in account	Depends on funds in account	Depends on funds in account
Value of the basic benefit (PBU) in the public system?	1.5% AMPO★ for first 30 years of contributions	1.5% AMPO★ for first 30 years of contributions	2.5% AMPO★ for first 30 years of contributions
Are past contributions to the public system compensated?	No	Yes, with a compensatory pension	Yes, with a compensatory pension
Value of the compensatory pension	Not applicable	2.0% of salary★★ for each year (up to 30) of contributions	1.5% of salary★★ for each year (up to 35) of contributions
How are those who remain in the public system compensated?	Not applicable	Not applicable	With the pension for permanency (PAP)
Will the state create an AFJP to compete in the private system?	No	No	Yes, with a guaranteed return (in pesos)
Can unions and nonprofit associations create an AFJP?	Not specified	Not specified	Yes
Minimum age of retirement	65 for men, 60 for women	65 for both sexes	65 for men, 60 for women

SOURCES: Cámara de Diputados de la Nación 1992a, 1992b; *Ley 24.241* 1993.
★AMPO = Average obligatory pension contribution for the entire system.
★★The individual's average annual salary subject to pension contributions during the ten years prior to retirement.

market. However, many of the labor leaders continued to be unhappy about the reform. Nevertheless, these leaders felt obliged to give their nominal support to the reform because they did not want to risk a rupture in their relationship with the ruling party over this issue (interview with Panigatti 1996).

Controlling the Legislature

Although the support of the labor unions certainly facilitated the enactment of the pension privatization bill, it did not guarantee its passage through the legislature. The key to the enactment of the pension privatization plan was the Menem administration's relatively high degree of control of the legislature. The ruling party's near majority in the legislature and its moderately high levels of party discipline were crucial to the passage of the pension privatization plan because legislators from the main opposition parties adamantly opposed the reform bill, as did some small parties that normally supported the Menem administration. Thus, the ruling party was obliged to rely mostly on its own members to pass the reform legislation.

The Menem administration's control of the legislature was also crucial to the enactment of the reform because the government was loath to approve the pension privatization plan by decree. The decree powers of the Argentine president were the subject of much controversy, which undermined the legitimacy of any reform approved by executive decree (Ferreira Rubio and Goretti 1998). Although Menem had implemented numerous reforms by decree and repeatedly threatened to do so with the pension privatization plan as well, the government preferred to obtain legislative approval for the reform because it wanted the new system to have a solid legal foundation. Businessmen had warned the Menem administration that they would be reluctant to invest in a private pension system that had not been formally approved by the legislature. According to one legislator, "The investors in the AFJPs told us that they were not disposed to run the risk of having a pension reform by decree. . . . No investor was inclined to invest in something that didn't have juridical security" (interview with Santín 1996).

At the time of the reform, Argentina still had a strong two-party system, which consistently provided its presidents with majorities or near majorities in the legislature.[24] Since the return to democracy in 1983, the ruling party had always controlled at least 45 percent of the seats in the Chamber of Deputies. The Justicialist Party won a resounding victory in the 1989 elections, and the Menem administration's subsequent success in bringing down inflation helped it repeat its success in the legislative elections of 1991. In the wake of these elections, the Justicialist Party held 120 seats in the Chamber of Deputies (46.7 percent of the total), which, together with the 10 seats held by its new ally, the Union of the Democratic Center, gave it a majority in the lower house. The Menem administration's share of seats in the Senate, meanwhile, rose to 62.5 percent in 1992, after the provincial legislatures held elections to choose their federal senators.[25] Thus, the ruling party was in a relatively good position to enact the reform.

The prospects of the reform were also favored by the traditionally high level of party discipline prevailing within the Justicialist Party at the time. Political parties in Argentina traditionally enjoyed a relatively high level of party discipline, and recent experience has been no exception (Jones 1998; Mustapic and Goretti 1992; Fennell 1974). According to an analysis of roll-call data by Jones (1998), between 1989 and 1991, voting members of the Justicialist Party supported the majority of the party 94 percent of the time on average.[26] Jones's analysis only examines relatively controversial legislation—that is, bills in which at least 20 percent of the deputies present voted for the losing option—so the actual level of party discipline is probably even higher than he estimates. Of course, party members may express their opposition to legislation by declining to vote, rather than voting against the party. According to Jones's data, a substantial number of PJ legislators chose not to vote—only 73 percent of those Justicialist Party legislators who were present at some time during the session voted with the majority (Jones 1998). This latter indicator of party discipline is problematic, however, in that deputies may have diverse reasons for not voting. Moreover, a deputy's decision not to vote rather than to oppose legislation is itself an indication of party discipline.

The degree of party discipline that prevailed in the PJ during this period is particularly impressive considering that many of the Menem administration's legislative initiatives ran directly contrary to the traditional statist ideals of the Peronist party. Indeed, numerous PJ legislators were quite unhappy about the reforms, but voted for them anyway. According to Juan González Gaviola, a former PJ deputy, "The surprising thing is that [party] discipline is maintained many times in spite of what the ruling party legislators say they feel and think. . . . [T]hey all make criticisms and agree with the criticisms others make of a project, but at the moment of voting they all raise their hands to vote [in favor of the project]" (interview with González Gaviola 1996).

The Menem administration was able to maintain a high level of party discipline in large part by negotiating deals with the governors and provincial party bosses who controlled the political futures of the legislators from their provinces. Governors and other provincial party leaders had a great deal of influence over who ran on the party's electoral list as well as the order of the candidates on the list (Jones 1998).[27] Thus, they could determine a member's prospects of reelection. Deputies knew that if they opposed their governor or party leaders from their province on crucial issues, they were placing their political careers in jeopardy. The president and national party leaders also had some direct leverage over legislators because they controlled committee assignments, budgetary resources, and the flow of legislation as well as employment opportunities within the administration and the party itself (Jones 1998).[28] As a result, legislators had substantial incentives to stay in the good graces of national party leaders as well.

Although the Menem administration's degree of control of the legislature was relatively high, it was less than that prevailing in Mexico during the Zedillo administration. The Menem administration, unlike the Zedillo administration, did not have a majority of the seats in the Chamber of Deputies, nor was party discipline as strong in Argentina as in Mexico. Menem, un-like Zedillo, was obliged to negotiate with leaders of his own party as well as other parties in order to obtain enough votes to pass the reform bill. As a result, the Menem administration needed to make many more concessions than its Mexican counterpart.

Navigating Through the Legislature

The Menem administration initially hoped to gain rapid approval of the pension reform legislation and urged the legislature to approve the bill "with-out touching a comma." In order to try to speed the passage of the reform through the legislature, the Menem administration initially stated that cur-rent pensioners would be paid the full amounts that were owed them only after the legislation privatizing the pension system and the state petroleum company was enacted (Alonso 1998). This move backfired, however, and the reform proposal bogged down in the joint committee of the Chamber of Deputies that was responsible for evaluating it.[29] Menem's efforts to gain quick approval of the legislation antagonized legislators from all parties who were determined to give the reform bill careful consideration and invited a wide array of interest group representatives and social security experts to tes-tify on the reform before the committee (Isuani and San Martino 1993).[30]

A large number of deputies and interest groups also had strong substan-tive criticisms of the proposed bill. Some deputies, particularly those from the Radical Party and the small left-of-center parties, objected to the basic nature of the proposed reform, arguing that a move toward a system based on individual capitalization contravened the principles of social security. They contended that such systems were too risky and did not redistribute income. Many of these critics also objected to the role played by private companies in managing the pension funds, arguing that these companies would take advantage of workers. Other deputies, especially members of the Justicialist Party and some right-of-center parties, criticized particular aspects of the re-form legislation without rejecting the fundamental ideas behind the proposal.

The Menem administration was not able to gain the committee's approval of the reform bill until February 1993, more than eight months after the leg-islation had been first submitted to the legislature. The difficulties stemmed in part from the fact that the Menem administration did not control a ma-jority of the votes on the committee, which required the government to ob-tain at least one vote from a legislator from another party. Moreover, several of the Justicialist Party deputies were extremely critical of the reform and initially refused to sign on to the bill. In order to gain the support of some of the dissident deputies, the leaders of the Justicialist Party were forced to make substantial concessions, including agreeing to create a state-owned

AFJP that would offer workers a guaranteed return on their pension contributions. With these concessions, the Menem administration managed to obtain the votes of all of the members of the Justicialist Party who were on the committee, except for Luis Guerrero, who was affiliated with the Metalworkers' Union. Two members of minor parties also provided crucial votes in favor of the reform, including, surprisingly, Juan Carlos Sabio, the sole federal deputy of the Pensioners' Party.[31] Sabio had campaigned on a platform of opposition to radical reform of the pension system and had been critical of the reform bill during the deliberations of the committee, but in February he suddenly switched his vote in favor of the reform, prompting the pensioners' organizations to vociferously denounce him (interview with González Gaviola 1996; Isuani and San Martino 1995). In contrast, all of the deputies from the Radical Party who were on the joint committee opposed the bill, as did five deputies from minor parties (Cámara de Diputados de la Nación 1993a: 6870).

The tactics used by the leaders of the Justicialist Party to gain approval of the reform by the committee were the subject of a great deal of controversy. On the day of the vote in the committee, the PJ leaders used their control of the presidency of the legislature to replace a Justicialist deputy, who had left to become secretary of agriculture, with another PJ deputy. At the same time, they deferred the replacement of Federico Clérici, a deputy from the Union of the Democratic Center who had been critical of the reform before his death in January 1993 (Isuani and San Martino 1995). The leaders of the PJ also declined to take a voice vote on the reform legislation in the committee chambers, which was the parliamentary custom. Instead, the chair of the committee simply announced that he had received a copy of the committee report with the sufficient number of signatures, which included the names of a couple of deputies, including Deputy Sabio, whom Radical Party legislators claimed were not even present at the session (Isuani and San Martino 1995; Cámara de Diputados de la Nación 1993a: 6907). He then called the committee session to an end. These tactics drew sharp condemnation from the opposition parties, which accused the leaders of the PJ of "grossly violating" parliamentary rules and sought, unsuccessfully, to have the bill returned to the joint committee for further evaluation (Cámara de Diputados de la Nación 1993a: 6907).

With the approval of the legislation by the committee, the reform bill moved to the plenary of the Chamber of Deputies for a vote. The opposition, however, refused to provide a quorum to open the legislative session for consideration of the bill. In order to open a legislative session, at least 130 legislators (one more than a majority of the seats in the Chamber of Deputies) needed to be present on the floor of the legislature, which the leaders of the Justicialist Party had an extremely difficult time assembling. The PJ legislative contingent occupied 116 seats at the time, which meant that in order to attain the quorum, party leaders had to maintain a high degree of party discipline and obtain a fair amount of support from allied parties.

On three separate occasions in March and April, the Justicialist Party fell just short in its efforts to assemble a quorum for a vote on the pension reform bill. The efforts failed in part because the labor-affiliated PJ legislators associated with dissident unions within the CGT continued to oppose the reform and refused to appear for the votes. Legislators from the Radical Party and the small left-of-center parties also refused to provide the government with a quorum, as did, initially, most of the members of the provincial parties and the small right-of-center parties, with the notable exception of the Union of the Democratic Center.

In response to these failures, the Menem administration undertook intense negotiations with the reluctant members of its own party as well as with its oft-time allies in the provincial parties and the center-right Progressive Democratic Party. On April 14, the leaders of the PJ finally managed to obtain a quorum when thirteen members of the provincial parties and three members of the Progressive Democratic Party along with the vast majority of the deputies from the Justicialist Party and the Union of the Democratic Center attended the session (Dearriba 1993: 6–7).[32] Two weeks later on the eve of the vote, the negotiations with the labor-affiliated legislators finally bore fruit when they agreed to support the reform in exchange for the government's commitment to make participation in the private pension system optional. Other concessions were also granted in the hours immediately preceding the vote as the Justicialist Party leaders strived desperately to firm up support for the bill. These last-minute negotiations meant not only that legislators did not have any up-to-date financial analyses of the impact of the reform, but also that many legislators were not even certain of the exact contents of the bill (Isuani and San Martino 1995). As Socialist Party Deputy Ricardo Molinas observed during the debate:

This project still continues to be undergoing corrections in the hallways and vestibules [of the Chamber of Deputies]. For all of these reasons, we believe that it should return to the committee to be seriously studied. It is not possible to decide about a project that was brought yesterday at 1:00 in the morning with the obligation to be present on the floor [of the legislature] at 9:30 in the morning. There is not enough time even to get control of the relevant questions. (Isuani and San Martino 1995: 57; Cámara de Diputados de la Nación 1993a: 7078)

Members of both parties would subsequently complain that in its rush to approve the bill at the last minute, the government had allowed numerous contradictions, errors, and omissions to creep into the text.

The last-minute concessions helped the government pick up the necessary

TABLE 4.3

Results of the Vote to Return the Argentine Pension Reform Bill to the Committee

	In favor	Against	Absent	Total
Justicialist Party	1	105	9	115★
Radical Party	83	0	1	84
Provincial Parties	7	12	1	20
Union of the Democratic Center	4	5	0	9
Other parties	24	3	1	28
Total	119	125	12	256★

SOURCES: Cámara de Diputados de la Nación 1993a: 6827–28; Secretaria de la H. Cámara de Diputados 1993.

★ According to custom, the president of the Chamber of Deputies (a member of the PJ at the time) did not vote.

number of votes to ensure passage of the reform, however. In an effort to block the reform, the opposition first submitted a motion to return the bill to the joint committee for further evaluation. This motion was rejected by a vote of 125–119 (Cámara de Diputados de la Nación 1993a: 6827–28). (See Table 4.3). More than 90 percent of the PJ contingent voted against returning the bill to the committee, including all but three of the labor-affiliated legislators. The leadership of the Justicialist Party also picked up support from a majority of the legislators from the Union of the Democratic Center and the provincial parties, as well as a few votes from minor center-right parties. In contrast, all of the Radical Party legislators present voted to return the bill to the committee, as did the deputies from the small center-left parties. Many of the legislators from small right-wing or center-right parties, such as the Movement for Dignity and Independence (MODIN) and the Progressive Democratic Party, also voted to return the bill to the committee. A similar motion that was proposed some time later was defeated by a vote of 121–107 (Cámara de Diputados de la Nación 1993a: 6987). The pension reform bill itself was finally put to a vote at 2:00 A.M. the morning of April 30 after a day and a half of debate. The motion was enacted by a show of hands with 135 legislators present, after opponents of the reform left the chamber in an unsuccessful attempt to deny the Justicialist Party a quorum.

With the approval of the reform bill in general, the Chamber of Deputies moved a week later to consider the bill chapter by chapter. The Radical Party and other opponents of the reform proposal again declined to provide a quorum for this session, which meant that Justicialist Party leaders had to assemble 130 deputies for the votes on each chapter. The PJ leaders continued to have a difficult time assembling the quorum, and individual members of the Justicialist Party and allied parties exploited these difficulties by demanding a variety of modifications to the reform bill in return for their support. Many of these demands were promptly granted. The leadership of the Justicialist Party, for example, agreed to increase the Additional Pension for Permanency, which was to be paid to workers who chose to continue to make their individual pension contributions to the public system rather than the private system. The Menem administration had hoped to keep the PAP relatively low in order to encourage workers to switch to the private pension system, but, at the insistence of labor-affiliated legislators, the PAP was increased from 0.5 percent to 0.85 percent of the average salary that a worker earned during the ten years prior to retirement (multiplied by the number of years in which he or she contributed to the reformed public system).

Female legislators from various parties, meanwhile, insisted that the minimum age of retirement for women be reduced. The female deputies argued that women had a double workday because of their domestic responsibilities, "which implied greater wear and a premature exhaustion of their capacity for work" (Isuani and San Martino 1995: 63; Cámara de Diputados de la Nación 1993b: 278). The leadership of the Justicialist Party initially rejected this proposal on the grounds that it would increase the financial costs of the public system and reduce the pension benefits available to women in the private system (Isuani and San Martino 1995). In response the female deputies left the chamber, thus depriving the PJ of its quorum. The chastened PJ leadership then backed down and acceded to the female deputies' wishes, setting the minimum age of retirement for women at sixty years of age, as opposed to sixty-five years of age for men.

Once the reform bill had received full approval from the Chamber of Deputies, it moved to the Senate for consideration. Although some Justicialist Party senators wanted to modify various aspects of the bill, the Menem administration blocked this plan because it would have required the government to subsequently return the bill to the Chamber of Deputies for consideration, which it was loathe to do. Instead, the Menem administration promised to draw up additional legislation that would correct some of the errors contained in the text as well as modify certain aspects of the bill to which the leaders of the PJ objected. The senators of the Justicialist Party thus reluctantly agreed to approve the pension reform bill as it had been sent to them from the Chamber of Deputies.

Obtaining the approval of the bill proved to be considerably easier in the Senate than in the Chamber of Deputies, owing to the large majority that the Menem administration enjoyed in the upper chamber. Although the majority of the senators from the provincial parties as well as all of the Radical Party senators opposed the bill and tried to deny the leaders of the PJ a quorum for the vote, their efforts failed owing to the strong party discipline of the ruling party. All of the senators from the Justicialist Party save one voted in favor of the bill, as did two senators from a provincial party. Thus,

TABLE 4.4

The 1993 Argentine Pension Reform

	Former system	New system
Operating basis	Public pay-as-you-go	Public pay-as-you-go and private fully funded
Employer contribution	16%	16%★
Worker contribution	10%	11%
State contribution	Earmarked taxes plus treasury revenues to cover the deficit	Earmarked taxes plus treasury revenues to cover the deficit
Recipient of contributions	Public pension system	Public pension system and the AFJPs★★
Pension benefit levels	70–82% of former salary indexed for inflation★★★	Undefined
Value of the minimum pension	Variable	Variable
Minimum retirement age	60 for men; 55 for women	65 for men; 60 for women
Minimum years of contributions required for retirement	20 years	30 years

★Subsequently reduced by 30 to 80 percent depending on region and industry.
★★The AFJPs receive the workers' contribution of those who opt for the private pension system. The public pension system receives the employer's contribution from all workers and the individual contribution of those workers who choose to remain strictly in the public system.
★★★Although the law guaranteed these benefits, they had not been delivered in recent years.

on Sept. 23, 1993, the bill finally received full legislative approval, more than fifteen months after it had first been sent to the Chamber. (See Table 4.4 for a summary of the 1993 reform.)

In the months that followed, the Menem administration made a number of adjustments to the bill. The most controversial of these measures was the elimination of the provision stipulating that the state-run AFJP would provide a guaranteed rate of return in dollars on funds deposited there. The private sector lobbied aggressively for the elimination of this guarantee, arguing that the private pension funds would not be able to compete with a state-run institution offering such a guarantee. Although Menem had repeatedly promised the labor unions as well as PJ legislators that he would not veto this guarantee, Menem eventually sided with the private sector, contending that "it's not possible for an official institution like the [AFJP] Banco Nación to have advantages over the rest of the institutions. This is disloyal competition" ("Se eliminó" 1994: 1B). The Menem administration chose to nullify the provision by *decree*, which enabled the government to argue that it had kept its promise not to *veto* the provision. This measure neverthe-less provoked widespread criticism inside as well as outside of the Justicialist Party.

Conclusion

The roots of social security privatization in Argentina, as in Mexico, lie in the economic challenges that the country faced at the beginning of the 1990s. The Menem administration's decision to privatize its pension system re-sponded not only to the growing financial problems of the country's social security system, which were much more severe in Argentina than in Mex-ico, but also to the Argentine government's concerns about its increasing de-pendence on unstable foreign capital flows. By privatizing its pension sys-tem, the Menem administration hoped to bolster Argentina's domestic saving rate, stimulate its capital markets, and place its pension system in a more se-cure long-term financial position.

Ideas about the economic efficacy of pension privatization spread in Ar-gentina through several main channels. First, the Chilean experience con-vinced many observers in neighboring Argentina that pension privatization would bring substantial economic benefits. The World Bank, meanwhile, worked hard to convince Argentine policymakers of the merits of pension privatization. The most important proponents of pension privatization in Argentina, however, were the neoliberal economists who came to dominate the key social security policy-making positions during the early 1990s. These economists independently formulated the reform proposals and actively lob-bied political leaders to embrace the pension privatization plans.

The Menem administration in Argentina, unlike the Zedillo administra-tion in Mexico, chose not to undertake full-scale privatization, opting in-stead to create a mixed public/private system. The scope and maturity of the Argentine pension system made full-scale privatization too expensive, and the Menem administration reasoned that partial privatization would be more politically as well as financially viable. The Menem administration did eventually manage to secure legislative approval for its proposed reform, but only after it made numerous concessions to opponents of the reform in the legislature. These concessions were necessary because the Menem admin-istration, unlike the Zedillo administration, held only a near-majority of the seats in the Chamber of Deputies and party discipline in Argentina was some-what weaker than in Mexico. Many of the concessions were obtained by the Argentine labor unions, which had a greater tradition of activism and inde-pendence than their Mexican counterparts. The final pension privatization legislation thus represented a much milder version of the original proposal, but it nevertheless constituted a dramatic change in the way in which retirement income is provided in Argentina.

The overall impact of the reform will not be known for many decades, but recent developments have not been encouraging. The massive fiscal costs of the reform, and the accompanying reduction in employers' social security taxes, contributed to the severe financial problems that Argentina confronted at the end of the 1990s. As Chapter 8 discusses, the Argentine government responded to this crisis by reducing the contributions that people make to the private pension system and forcing the pension fund administrators to lend the government money. The result has been a private pension system teetering at the edge of bankruptcy that inspires little confidence among the population as a whole.

CHAPTER 5

The Politics of Aborted Reform:
Pension Policy in Brazil in the 1990s

THE BRAZILIAN social security system suffered from serious financial difficulties in the 1990s, but Brazil, unlike Argentina and Mexico, did not privatize its pension system. Instead, the Brazilian government opted to modify its existing public pension system by lowering benefits, raising contributions, and tightening pension eligibility requirements. This chapter will seek to explain why the Brazilian government attempted to amend rather than privatize its existing public pension system, and why these efforts largely failed.

One key difference between Brazil and Argentina and Mexico was the economic climate. Brazil had a higher domestic savings rate than Argentina and Mexico and major internal sources of long-term capital, which reduced the economic incentives to privatize. Moreover, large existing public pension obligations made pension privatization in Brazil, as in Argentina, extremely expensive. The ideational climate was also less favorable for pension privatization in Brazil. Neoliberal economists within the Ministry of Finance and other government agencies did advocate pension privatization, but the traditional social security specialists within the Ministry of Social Insurance vigorously opposed these efforts. The Ministry of Social Insurance continued to play a large role in social security policy making in Brazil, and the employees of this institution successfully countered the claims of the supporters of pension privatization.

Perhaps more importantly, the political impediments to pension privatization were also greater in Brazil than most other countries in the region. In order to create a compulsory private pension system, the Brazilian government needed to amend the constitution, which would have required the support of three-fifths of the members of both chambers of the legislature. This would have been difficult to achieve given the unpopularity of pension privatization, the relatively small portion of seats in the legislature held by the ruling party, and the weak party discipline prevailing in Brazil. To complicate matters, the largest Brazilian labor federation, unlike its counterparts in Argentina and Mexico, was closely tied to the opposition and threatened to use its considerable political and economic resources to resist any effort to privatize the pension system. Thus, Brazilian policymakers concluded that any effort to privatize the pension system would almost certainly be doomed to failure.

The pension system's growing financial problems did lead the Brazilian government to repeatedly attempt to undertake more modest reforms of the public pension system, but these efforts were stymied by the same political factors that impeded pension privatization. Most of the proposed reforms, like privatization, required a constitutional amendment, which the government was hard pressed to obtain given its lack of control over the legislature. Although the administration of President Fernando Henrique Cardoso did manage to approve a pension reform in the waning days of his first term, this bill was so watered down by its opponents that members of the government considered the passage of the reform at best a symbolic victory.

The Origins of Social Security in Brazil

Brazil, like Argentina, was one of the pioneers in the development of social security programs in Latin America, and by the 1980s it had one of the highest levels of social security coverage in the region. The first pension programs for private-sector workers were established in the 1920s, although pension programs for civil servants and the military date from the previous century. The Brazilian government established the social security programs largely in order to co-opt the increasingly militant labor movement (Malloy 1979; Cohn 1981). Proponents of social security argued that the programs would help defuse the mounting social conflict by improving the living conditions of workers. Eloy Chaves, the federal deputy who authored the legislation that granted social security benefits to railroad workers in 1923, presented his bill as a form of "class collaboration" and an alternative "to the class struggle which is advised by radicals and by other minds which are disturbed by strange and complicated passions" (Malloy 1979: 47).[1]

The Brazilian social security system, like that of Argentina, developed in a highly fragmented and inequitable manner. Social security coverage, which included not only retirement benefits but also life and disability insurance and funeral and medical benefits, was first provided to relatively privileged categories of workers. These workers included both state employees and private-sector laborers who worked in key areas of the economy such as railroad and dock workers and merchant seaman. In the 1930s, the Brazilian government

gradually extended social security benefits to other members of the organized urban workforce, but rural workers, domestic employees, and the self-
employed remained uncovered. Moreover, considerable differences existed
even among those included in the system. Most occupational categories had
their own social insurance fund—by 1940, there were ninety-five different
institutions (Malloy 1979: 102)—and the social security funds by and large
provided different levels of benefits. As elsewhere in Latin America, the military and civil servants, along with certain privileged private-sector workers,
received the most lucrative benefits (Malloy 1979: 107–13).

   Although the inequities and inefficiencies of the social security system engendered a great deal of criticism, reform was slow to come. During the late
1940s and 1950s, social security technocrats made various attempts to unify
the different systems and to extend coverage to the working population as a
whole. These efforts, however, were blocked or subverted by the employees
and beneficiaries of the existing systems who were loath to give up control of
the social security funds or their traditional pension privileges (Malloy 1979;
Cohn 1981; Hochman 1988). It was not until the military took power again
in the mid-1960s that the Brazilian government was able to push through
major social security reforms. In 1967, the military government merged the
six main social security funds that served private-sector workers into a single
institute in spite of protests of the groups that had traditionally benefited
from the existing systems. The military regime subsequently extended social
security coverage to rural workers and to domestic employees.

   The reforms substantially boosted the coverage of the Brazilian social security coverage system, making it one of the most extensive systems in Latin
America. By 1980, the social security system covered 87 percent of the population, as opposed to only 27 percent in 1970 (Mesa-Lago 1991b: 50). The
reforms also reduced, but did not eliminate, the internal inequities of Brazil's social security system. Although the 1967 reform had consolidated the
pension systems serving urban private-sector workers and standardized their
benefits, it had not touched the systems belonging to public-sector employees. The military and state and federal employees continued to maintain
separate pension systems, which provided substantially higher benefits to
their members than did the system serving private-sector workers. Moreover, both urban private-sector workers and public-sector employees earned
higher benefits than did rural workers, who had their own largely noncontributory pension system.

Emerging Financial Problems

   Although the Brazilian social security system experienced financial problems from its inception, these problems deepened considerably in the 1980s
and early 1990s, putting pressure on the government to carry out some type

of reform. The financial difficulties stemmed in large part from the maturation of the Brazilian pension system. In the 1950s, the system had more than 8 contributors for every pension recipient, but the system's dependency ratio fell to 4.2 to 1 in 1970 and 2.5 to 1 in 1990 (Britto 1993: 11). Demographic trends played only a small role in the maturation of the pension system. Although the birth rate dropped and life expectancy rose considerably during this period, the Brazilian population remained relatively young. People over sixty years of age represented only 6.7 percent of the Brazilian population in 1990, as opposed to 13.1 percent in Argentina (World Bank 1994b: 344). Whereas Brazil's population dependency ratio (that is, the ratio of the population over sixty to that between twenty and fifty-nine) was approximately 6.7 to 1 in the late 1980s, the Brazilian pension system's dependency ratio (that is, the ratio of pensioners to contributors) was approximately 2.5 to 1 (World Bank 1995a: xii).

The rapid maturation of Brazil's pension system stemmed mainly from the system's lax requirements for gaining access to retirement pensions.[2] The standard retirement age was sixty-five years of age for men and sixty years for women (five years earlier in the case of rural workers), but only five years of contributions were required to be eligible for a pension.[3] To make matters worse, all workers could retire early based on time of service—men could retire after thirty years of service and women could retire after twenty-five years of service, regardless of their age. Moreover, some privileged categories of workers, such as journalists, pilots, and university professors, could retire even earlier. A substantial percentage of the members of the system took advantage of these provisions for early retirement. Indeed, in 1990, 62 percent of the pensioners in the subsystem serving urban private-sector workers had retired early (Oliveira, Beltrão, and Medici 1994: 68). Workers who retired under the time of service provisions had an average age upon retirement of 54.9 years for men and 53.3 years for women. As a result, they received their pensions for an extraordinarily long time—an average of 17.6 years for men and 22.4 years for women—which put a great deal of financial strain on the pension system (Barbosa and Mondino 1994: 169).

The financial difficulties of the Brazilian pension system also stemmed from the system's relative generosity. Brazilian pension benefits, as a percentage of workers' salaries, were considerably higher than those in other Latin American countries and substantially exceeded what the members contributed to the system (World Bank 1995a). The basic pension benefit was set at 70 percent of a worker's average salary in the three years prior to the retirement, but this was increased by 1 percent for each year of contributions over the minimum required for old-age pensions, and 6 percent for each year of contributions over the minimum required for time-of-service pensions. As a result, a 100 percent salary replacement rate was quite common in Brazil (World Bank 1995a: 62). Retired civil servants, moreover, were entitled to any increases received by active workers, and pensioners, unlike active workers, did not pay social security contributions, which meant that the net income of many workers increased upon retirement.

The actual value of the benefits that pensioners received varied considerably. The military and state employees typically earned the largest benefits, whereas rural workers generally received the minimum pension. In 1995, the average benefit paid out by the system for private sector workers equaled 1.7 minimum wages, whereas the average benefit paid out by the system for civil servants was worth 14 times the minimum wage (Ministério da Previdência 1997: 21). Certain privileged subgroups, such as employees of the legislature or the judiciary, earned pension benefits worth approximately 35 times the minimum wage (Ministério da Previdência 1997: 21).

The 1988 constitution further increased pension benefits.[4] The constitution required that benefits be adjusted monthly to take inflation into account. It also set the minimum pension equal to the minimum wage (previously it had been half the minimum wage), which led to a 30 percent cost increase for the system as a whole since a large number of pensioners earned the minimum benefit (World Bank 1995a: xiii). Partly as a result, the average benefit rose 78 percent in real terms between 1988 and 1996 (*Informe de Previdência Social* 1997b: 1). The rise in benefit levels, along with a sharp increase in the number of pensioners, led benefit expenditures in the main pension system, the National Social Security Institute (INSS), to rise by 136 percent in real terms between 1990 and 1996. By 1996, pension spending in the main pension system equaled 5.5 percent of GDP, up from 2.6 percent in 1988. Pension spending on employees of the federal, state, and municipal governments, meanwhile, totaled an estimated 6 percent of GDP in 1996 (Ministério da Previdência 1997: 22; *Informe de Previdência Social* 1997b: 2). Table 5.1 presents key financial indicators for the Brazilian pension system.

The main pension system was financed principally by contributions from workers and their employers, although some taxes on sales and corporate profits were also earmarked for the system.[5] Evasion of payments was widespread, however. According to a World Bank (1995a: 46) study, the evasion rate averaged 40.6 percent between 1984 and 1991. Evasion was encouraged by the poor monitoring of compliance with payments, the lax requirements for gaining access to pensions, and the relatively high levels of contributions required. Recent economic trends, such as rising unemployment and the growth of the informal sector, also contributed to the high rates of evasion. The high levels of inflation that the country experienced in the late 1980s and early 1990s, meanwhile, eroded the real value of the contributions and taxes that were collected by the pension system.

The main pension system's revenue had initially been more than sufficient to cover the system's expenditures in spite of the traditionally high levels of evasion. As the dependency ratio of the pension system declined, how-

TABLE 5.1

Financial Indicators of the Main Brazilian Pension System

	1990	1991	1992	1993	1994	1995	1996
Pension contributions★	$27.0	$24.4	$24.0	$29.6	$31.4	$37.9	$41.8
Pension benefit expenditures★	$18.3	$19.1	$20.8	$28.0	$31.7	$39.0	$42.6
Surplus (deficit)★	$8.7	$5.3	$3.2	$1.6	($0.3)	($1.1)	($0.8)
Contributions (as a percent of GDP)	5.2	4.9	4.8	4.4	4.7	5.0	5.4
Expenditures (as a percent of GDP)	3.2	3.5	3.8	4.4	4.7	5.2	5.5
Average monthly pension benefit★★	$120	$123	$123	$155	$170	$202	$214
Pension spending on civil servants★	$8.2	$6.3	$5.8	$11.0	$13.7	$16.9	$17.1

SOURCES: *Informe de Previdência Social* 1997a, 1997b; Ministério da Previdência 1997.
★ In billions of constant December 1996 reais.
★★ In constant December 1996 reais.

ever, the pension system ran into financial difficulties. To complicate matters, the pension system had failed to invest the surpluses that it had generated when the dependency ratio had been favorable. Instead, the surpluses had been channeled into the social security system's health care programs, which had traditionally run a deficit. The economic crisis of the late 1980s and early 1990s also took its toll on the pension system's finances (Draibe and Matijascic 1999). Between 1988 and 1993, the revenue of the system stagnated. Although the system's income began to grow again after economic stability returned in 1993, the growing revenues did not keep pace with increased expenditures.

In 1995, the main pension system ran a deficit for the first time in many years.[6] The size of the pension deficit was expected to increase rapidly in the years ahead, owing to the projected aging of the Brazilian population. The growing financial problems threatened the Brazilian government's economic program, which depended on keeping government spending in check. In the early 1990s, Brazil was still struggling to keep inflation under control, which required fiscal restraint. The Brazilian government was therefore under considerable pressure to reform its pension system, but considerable disagreement existed on what sort of reform to enact.

The Debate over Privatization

Pension privatization had a variety of advocates within Brazil. The business community, particularly the financial sector, generally supported partial pension privatization, although the fragmented nature of the Brazilian business community prevented it from speaking with a single voice (Weyland 1996a). A variety of business organizations made their views known to government policymakers, and some even went so far as to formulate their own pension privatization proposals (Carvalho Filho 1993; Weyland 1996b; interview with Trabuco 1997). In 1993, for example, the Federation of Industries of the State of São Paulo (FIESP), which was, perhaps, the most important business organization in Brazil, proposed a partial pension privatization plan (Carvalho Filho 1993; Kay 1998). Other business associations, such as the National Confederation of Industry (CNI), the Brazilian Federation of Banks (FEBRABAN), the Brazilian Institute of Capital Markets (IBMEC), and an association of private pension funds, ANAPP, also called for partial pension privatization (Weyland 1996b; V. Pinheiro 2000; interview with Trabuco 1997).

The World Bank also actively promoted pension privatization in Brazil. To do so, it carried out studies and formulated reform proposals, financed technical assistance programs, hired Brazilian policymakers on consulting contracts, and sponsored the participation of Brazilians in World Bank conferences, workshops, and seminars. In the mid-1990s, for example, the World Bank carried out a major study of the Brazilian pension system and recommended a series of reforms including the gradual partial privatization of the system (World Bank 1995a: xxi; interviews with Cechin 1997 and with Carvalho 1997). However, the World Bank did not make loans to Brazil conditional on the privatization of the country's pension system. It sought instead to exert influence principally by promoting its ideas. In the words of the Brazilian secretary of social security, the World Bank's role was confined to "the diffusion of ideas and the promotion of debates about [the World Bank's propositions] and, principally, the construction of a rhetoric of privatization to facilitate its ideas" (V. Pinheiro 2000: 2).

Many liberal economists in Brazil also advocated pension privatization. During the 1970s and 1980s, the Brazilian economics community increasingly absorbed liberal economic ideas. Before the 1970s, most Brazilian economists received their training in Brazil or at the United Nations Economic Commission for Latin America in Chile where structuralist and other heterodox views dominated. Since the 1970s, however, many Brazilians have received their training in the United States, where orthodox views predominate. Indeed, by 1991, 46 percent of Brazilian economics professors had received their master's or Ph.D. degrees in the United States, and only 40 percent of the faculty members had been trained exclusively in Brazil (Loureiro 1997: 189). Moreover, many of the Brazilian faculty members who had been trained exclusively in Brazil studied at institutions such as the Getulio Vargas Foundation of Rio de Janeiro and Catholic University of Rio de Janeiro, which emphasized orthodox economic theory (Loureiro 1997).[7] Beginning in the 1990s, a number of liberal economists affiliated with these institutions began to formulate pension privatization proposals (V. Pinheiro 2000; Carvalho Filho 1993). Some pension privatization proposals also emanated from liberal economists in other universities, such as the University of São Paulo, which was a more ideologically diverse institution.

Pension privatization also had important advocates among liberal economists inside the Brazilian government (interviews with Carvalho Filho 1997, with Cechin 1997, and with Moraes 1997; Weyland 1996b; Coelho 1999). In recent years, economists have increasingly dominated a number of Brazilian ministries and agencies including the Ministry of Finance, the Ministry of Planning, the Central Bank, and the National Economic and Social Development Bank (Loureiro 1997). During the late 1980s and early 1990s, these economists and other Brazilian policymakers aggressively promoted market-oriented economic policies in order to cope with the severe economic crisis that had gripped the country since the early 1980s. Beginning under the Collor administration, the Brazilian government moved to reduce the role of the state in the economy, cutting state expenditures, slashing barriers to foreign trade and investment, and, gradually, privatizing state-owned corporations.

Liberal economists within the Ministry of Finance and other economics and planning agencies argued that the state's role in the provision of social security should be cut back as well. Privatizing the social security system, they maintained, would place the system on more solid financial footing, reducing its vulnerability to future demographic changes. It would also help the government to increase the domestic savings rate and bolster the local capital markets. Indeed, Cardoso himself acknowledged the potentially important role that private pension funds could play in the economy (Leite and Alvarenga 1996: 27). Proponents of pension privatization in Brazil, like elsewhere, often pointed to the Chilean model to back up their claims about the benefits of pension privatization. They also visited Chile as well as Argentina and Uruguay to study the pension privatization schemes in those countries.

During the administration of President Fernando de Collor de Mello, advocates of pension privatization drafted a pension privatization proposal, but this proposal was abandoned in the face of overwhelming opposition from both inside and outside the government (interviews with Carvalho Filho 1997 and with Moraes 1997; Weyland 1996b). Other partial pension privatization proposals surfaced during the administration of Itamar Franco as part of the constitutional revision that took place during that period. These proposals emanated from IPEA and the Executive Commission of Fiscal Reform, both of which had ties to the Ministry of Economy, yet they foundered in the face of staunch resistance (Coelho 1999: 130–31). At the outset of the administration of Fernando Henrique Cardoso, some policymakers also contemplated a partial privatization of the system, but this idea was shelved in the face of opposition. Finally, in 1997, Cardoso created a commission headed by Andre Lara Resende, a prominent Brazilian economist and the head of the National Development Bank (BNDES), to study social security reform (Coelho 1999: 135−38). This commission formulated a pension privatization plan, but it, too, ran aground.

Efforts to privatize the Brazilian pension system have failed to prosper in Brazil for a number of reasons. First, the economic incentives to privatize were weaker in Brazil than elsewhere. Although Brazilian policymakers were concerned about the country's domestic capital sources, this issue never reached the same degree of salience that it did in Argentina and Mexico. The Brazilian domestic savings rate remained high by regional standards in the 1990s: between 1990 and 1995, domestic savings averaged 21.8 percent of gross domestic product in Brazil, as opposed to 15.9 percent for the region as a whole (World Bank 1995c: 1996, 1997). Thus, Brazilian policymakers did not feel the same degree of pressure to find new ways to boost the country's domestic savings rate, as did policymakers in Argentina and Mexico. Moreover, Brazil, unlike other Latin American countries, already had a large network of pension funds, which provided the country with an important source of long-term capital. A variety of state-owned and private corporations had established pension funds in order to provide their employees with a supplement to the benefits delivered by the public social security system. The pension funds served only 5 percent of the population, but they controlled a substantial amount of financial capital, which they channeled into a variety of investments. By 1995, these funds had assets of $59 billion, which equaled 9.7 percent of the country's GDP ("The Oldest" 1997: 11). The existence of these ample sources of domestic capital meant that the macroeconomic rationale for pension privatization was weaker in Brazil than in some neighboring countries.

Brazilian policymakers were also quite concerned about the fiscal costs of the privatization scheme. Brazil, like Argentina, had a high level of existing pension obligations, which the state would need to pay by itself if workers began to direct their social security contributions to private pension funds. Estimates of the implicit pension debt ranged between 188 and 250 percent of GDP in Brazil (V. Pinheiro 2000: 22). President Cardoso stated, "I recognize that [pension privatization] like it exists in Chile is easy to talk about and difficult to do. What will we do with those people who already have the right to a pension? The state will pay [their pensions] all by itself? . . . It's not easy" (Leite and Alvarenga 1996). Vinícius Pinheiro (2000: 22), the secretary of social security in Brazil, similarly argued that the transition costs of pension privatization "would be unbearable for the public accounts in the short run" regardless of any potential positive long-term effects that it might have on the economy.

The effort to privatize the pension system also encountered problems in Brazil because proponents of privatization within the Brazilian government met powerful internal opposition. Neoliberal economists in Brazil, in contrast to Argentina and Mexico, did not have control over the key social security policy-making positions. Although there were numerous advocates of pension privatization in the Ministry of Finance, social security policy in Brazil continued to be made principally through the Ministry of Social Insurance (MPAS), which was dominated by traditional social security specialists (Coelho 1999; interviews with Moraes 1997 and with Carvalho 1997). Most of the bureaucrats within the Ministry of Social Insurance vigorously opposed the pension privatization proposals both for ideological reasons and because they feared that privatizing the pension system would reduce the ministry's responsibilities and resources (Weyland 1996b; interview with Carvalho Filho 1997). The professional politicians who headed the Ministry of Social Insurance in the 1990s tended to adopt a more ambiguous posture. They were open to discussing the issue, but they generally hindered rather than helped actual pension privatization efforts.

The resistance of the Ministry of Social Insurance to the privatization plans prevented supporters of pension privatization from dominating the discourse about pension reform in Brazil, the way that they did in Argentina and Mexico. Opponents of privatization within the Ministry of Social Insurance questioned whether a Chilean-type reform would bring the benefits that its supporters claimed. The secretary for social security reported that "inside the Ministry of Social Insurance, arguments against the privatization reform were developed based on the effects observed in Chile and Argentina. In this sense, the Chilean show case was used as the opposite in the discussion of the Brazilian reform" (V. Pinheiro 2000: 22). Critics of pension privatization within the Ministry of Social Insurance called attention to the massive transition costs, large administrative expenses, and high evasion rates of the Chilean model. They suggested that even its long-term economic benefits were in doubt. In this way, proponents of pension privatization in Brazil were placed on the defensive and failed to gain the ideological hegemony that they enjoyed in Argentina and Mexico.

Even more importantly, the political impediments to pension privatization were greater in Brazil than in Argentina or Mexico. The ruling party in Brazil, unlike its counterparts in Argentina and Mexico, did not have close ties to the main labor federation, the Central Unica dos Trabalhadores (CUT), which meant that it was unlikely to be able to convince the unions to go along with pension privatization. Indeed, the CUT, along with the pensioners' associations and various other interest groups, had repeatedly declared its opposition to any effort to privatize the pension system. The Brazilian labor movement represented a potentially major hindrance to pension privatization because it was relatively strong and militant. An estimated 25–30 percent of the workforce was unionized and many of those workers who were not organized were sympathetic to the unions' goals and participated in strikes and demonstrations (Cardoso 1997; Comin 1996; McGuire 1997; ILO 1997). The unions therefore had the potential to create major economic disruptions in response to policies they opposed.

The Brazilian legislature represented an even larger obstacle to pension privatization. The ruling party in Brazil, unlike in Argentina and Mexico, controlled only a very small portion of seats in the legislature. Thus, in order to enact a pension privatization bill, the government would have needed to obtain a substantial number of votes from allied parties—a particularly difficult task given the low level of party discipline prevailing among the government's allies. To complicate matters further, full-scale pension privatization or even some forms of partial pension privatization would have required a constitutional amendment, which necessitated the support of three-fifths of both chambers of the legislature.[8] A large majority of legislators, however, were known to oppose pension privatization—in one survey 70 percent of the members of the Chamber of Deputies stated that they were against the partial privatization of the system (Lamounier and de Souza 1995; interview with Almeida 1997). The government therefore concluded that, in the words of the then-secretary for social security, "any attempt [to privatize the pension system] would suffer a strong rejection from society, including from the government's base of support" (interview with Moraes 1997).

The Brazilian government did try to encourage the development of private pension funds in ways that were less likely to encounter political resistance. The government, for example, made contributions to private pension funds tax deductible under some circumstances. It also allowed the level of benefits provided by the public pension system to gradually deteriorate, which encouraged workers to seek additional social security coverage from private institutions.

The main thrust of the social security reform in Brazil was directed at modifying the public system rather than privatizing it, however. Policymakers argued that cutting back benefits in the public pension system was necessary regardless of whether the government decided to privatize its pension system or not (interview with Cechin 1997). Moreover, benefit cutbacks, unlike privatization, would result in short-term as well as long-term fiscal savings for the government. Policymakers also believed that modifying the public system would be politically easier than privatization. Indeed, surveys of the legislature revealed broad support for restricting early retirement, creating a ceiling on benefits and eliminating privileged pension schemes (Lamounier and de Souza 1995; "O congreso diz" 1995: 30).

The same political factors that obstructed the privatization of the pension system contributed to the evisceration of the government's proposed modifications of the public pension system. The proposed reforms encountered problems because the Cardoso administration had only weak control over the legislature given the fragmentation of the Brazilian party system and the weak party discipline. To make matters worse, the government needed to amend the constitution in order to enact many of its desired reforms, which required a super-majority vote. In addition, the labor unions, pensioners' associations, and some smaller interest groups initiated a strong campaign against the reforms, helping to build legislative opposition to the proposed reforms. After repeated failures, the Cardoso administration did manage to enact a social security reform bill, but this bill had been excised of many of its most important features.

Constitutional Barriers to Reform

The 1988 Brazilian constitution was extremely detailed on the issue of social security. It set forth the requirements for obtaining a pension, specified the standard age of retirement, and provided for early retirement based on time of service for all workers. It even stipulated that certain groups, such as rural workers and teachers, would be eligible to retire at a younger age or after fewer years of service than others. The constitution also specified how retirement benefits were to be calculated. It required that pensions be based on the average salary earned during the last three years of employment, and that the benefits be corrected monthly to compensate for increases in the cost of living. In the case of public servants, the constitution also required that pension benefits be adjusted to take into account any increases in the salary of active workers.

The detailed nature of the constitution meant that most changes in pension benefits or eligibility requirements would require a constitutional amendment, not an easy matter in Brazil. Constitutional amendments in Brazil required the support of three-fifths of both the Chamber of Deputies and the Senate in two consecutive sessions of each body. Before being voted on by the chamber as a whole, however, constitutional reform legislation first needed to be approved by Committees on Constitution and Justice (CCJ) of each chamber as well as by a special committee in the Chamber of Deputies. If one of the chambers altered the constitutional reform legislation that the other one had already approved, the bill would have to return to the original chamber for further consideration by the relevant committees as well as the chamber as a whole. The movement of constitutional reform legislation between the two chambers, which was sometimes referred to as "ping pong," could continue indefinitely (Melo 1997a).

The 1988 constitution also allowed members of the legislature to call for votes on specific provisions of a constitutional reform bill, and these votes, known as *destaques para votação em separado*, would be subject to the same constitutional hurdles as the vote on the entire bill. It was relatively easy to propose these destaques in the Chamber of Deputies, where only 10 percent of the chamber needed to support a destaque in order for it to be brought to a vote. By proposing numerous destaques, legislators could drag out the reform process, obliging the government to assemble repeatedly the three-fifths majority necessary to maintain its constitutional reform proposal intact. By unbundling the legislation, the destaques made it relatively easy for opponents of the reform to block the most controversial parts of the legislation, particularly since legislators were reluctant to take a public position in favor of the controversial aspects of the reform bill. Moreover, by law, constitutional reform bills, including the destaques, required roll-call votes, which meant that legislators could be held accountable for their votes (Figueiredo and Limongi 1998).

The 1988 constitution did provide for a brief period of constitutional revision beginning in October 1993, during which the super-majority requirement for constitutional amendments would be lifted. The Brazilian government failed to take advantage of this opportunity to modify the social security system, however. Although the administration of President Itamar Franco prepared a series of social security reform proposals as part of the constitutional revision process, these proposals ran into stiff opposition in the legislature and were ultimately dropped (Weyland 1996b; interviews with Moraes 1997 and with Balera 1997).

Thus, when the Cardoso administration took power in early 1995, social security policy in Brazil continued to be circumscribed by the dictates of the constitution. The Cardoso administration immediately prepared legislation that aimed not only to reform the pension system but also to deconstitutionalize social security. The proposed legislation sought to excise from the constitution most of the articles that specified the requirements for obtaining pensions or set forth how the pensions were to be calculated. These requirements would instead be laid out in a complementary law project, which would only need the support of an absolute majority of the Chamber of Deputies and the Senate (in two sessions of the legislature) in order to be approved or subsequently modified.

The Cardoso administration's constitutional reform bill did seek to make a number of additions to the text of the constitution itself, however. For example, it sought to ban early retirement based on time of service. It also sought to equalize the rules governing retirement in the public and private sector and to prohibit the adoption of special concessions in the granting of pensions, except in the cases of workers who labored in activities that were detrimental to their health. These changes would be gradually phased in for active workers, but current pensioners would be unaffected by the new rules.

The high barriers to amending the constitution repeatedly frustrated the Cardoso administration's reform plans. On a number of occasions, the Cardoso administration obtained the support of a majority of the legislators for its reform bill, but it fell short of the three-fifths majority required for constitutional reform. On other occasions, the administration passed the reform legislation as a whole, but was unable to consistently assemble the three-fifths majority necessary to block measures (destaques) that sought to excise individual provisions of the legislation. The government's plans to reform the social security system were also hindered by its single-minded emphasis on de-constitutionalizing social security. Many politicians and interest groups were reluctant to eliminate articles from the constitution when they did not know what was going to replace them. To do so, they felt, would be to give the government a blank check since Brazilian presidents had substantial control over ordinary legislation, owing to their formidable decree powers as well as their agenda-setting and veto authority (Melo 1998; Beltrão 1996).

Interest Group Opposition

A variety of interest groups resisted the Cardoso administration's efforts to modify Brazil's public pension system, just as they had blocked earlier reform efforts during the Collor and Franco administrations. Groups that traditionally enjoyed special pension privileges opposed the reforms that sought to reduce or eliminate their privileges. Many of these groups, such as congressmen, the military, and the judiciary, had substantial political influence, which they used to try to exempt themselves from the reforms. Federal deputies, for example, refused to vote in favor of reforms that sought to curb the benefits offered by their special pension scheme, and members of the judiciary used the numerous legal resources at their disposal to oppose reforms that affected their benefits. The military was probably the most successful of the privileged interest groups in resisting efforts to cut back its benefits and merge its pension scheme with the general pension system. This success was at least partly a result of the military's political clout. When asked why the military had been able to resist being included in the recent social security reform proposal, the secretary for social security responded, only partly in jest, that it was because the Ministry of Social Security, unlike the military, did not have any armored divisions (interview with Moraes 1997).

Reform efforts in Brazil also encountered substantial opposition from associations representing the employees of the social security system, such as the National Association of Social Security Auditors (ANFIP). Although ANFIP had only 10,000 members, of which only 3,700 were in active service, it had substantial political influence within the legislature as well as within the social security ministry (Melo 1997b; interview with França 1997). ANFIP controlled a great deal of economic resources, which it used to mount an aggressive advertising and lobbying campaign against the government's reform proposals. It also took advantage of its expertise in the area of social security to provide technical assistance to its allies in the legislature in an effort to defeat or amend the proposed reforms (interviews with França 1997, with Ribeiro 1997, and with Jorge 1997).

Organizations of pensioners represented another source of opposition to the government's proposed social security reforms. The pensioners' associations, which were led by former union leaders, opposed the reforms on the grounds that they would "limit the public system to a platform incapable of providing a subsistence level income to its members" ("Cobap informa" 1995: 2; Melo 1997b; interview with Cota 1997). The Brazilian pensioners' organizations, like their counterparts in Argentina and Mexico, were poorly institutionalized, which undermined their efforts to block the reforms. Although Brazil had 19.6 million pensioners (Ministério da Previdência 1997: 22), the pensioners' organizations could not claim to represent very many of them. Only a small proportion of the retired population participated in the pensioners' organizations and an even smaller percentage attended marches or demonstrations. The pensioners' organizations, which typically depended on contributions from their members, were also notably lacking in financial resources.[9] Nor did the pensioners' associations command technical expertise in social security. As a result, they did not enjoy a great deal of influence in the legislature, which prevented them from playing a major role in the legislative negotiations over social security reform. Nevertheless, the numerous marches and demonstrations against the reforms that they organized generated substantial media attention to their cause and may have helped galvanize opposition to the reforms.

Labor Opposition

The broadest and most effective interest group resistance to the reforms came from the labor movement, particularly from the public-sector unions, which had the most to lose from the reforms. The public-sector unions, which were highly militant and encompassed most state employees, represented some of the most powerful unions in Brazil (Cheibub 2000). The Brazilian government sought on various occasions to gain the support of the unions for their proposed reforms, but the ruling party's lack of ties to the main labor federation made an agreement difficult to reach. The ruling party in Brazil did not have the kind of long history of cooperation with the labor unions that in Argentina and Mexico had helped build trust, created personal ties, and spawned multiple channels of communication between the government and the labor unions. As a result, negotiations between the government and the main labor federation in Brazil were marked by uneasiness and were prone to breakdown.

When the Cardoso administration announced its plans for a social security reform in early 1995, the reform proposal was immediately attacked by some of the unions, which threatened to carry out a general strike. Labor opposition to the proposed reform helped bog down the proposal in the legislature. In an effort to unblock the reform, the Cardoso administration initiated negotiations with the unions, and in January 1996 the government announced that it had reached a tentative agreement with the two main labor federations—the CUT and Força Sindical—and with other parties ("Reforma da previdência social" 1996; Evelin 1996). In exchange for the labor unions' support for the reforms, the government made substantial concessions, including agreeing to maintain special pension privileges for civil servants and for elementary and secondary schoolteachers.

This accord quickly fell apart, however, because the CUT was closely tied to the principal opposition party, the Partido dos Trabalhadores (PT), which vigorously opposed the reform. Under intense pressure from the PT as well as from the public-sector unions, the leader of the CUT, Vicente Paulo da Silva, retracted the agreement shortly after he had given his verbal commitment to the deal. By March 1996, the head of the CUT was denouncing the government's reform proposal as "terrible" and "unacceptable" ("Projeto é inaceitável" 1996: 4). Força Sindical continued to back the general principles behind the reform, however. Força Sindical's continued support for the reform was due not only to its closer ties to the government, but also to the fact that it was composed almost entirely of private-sector unions, which had less to lose from pension reform.

After the collapse of the agreement, the CUT and its member unions helped frustrate the government's repeated efforts to approve the social security reform bill in the legislature. The CUT represented a wide variety of urban and rural, public- and private-sector unions, which had considerable pull within the legislature. The teachers' unions were particularly effective in lobbying the legislature (interviews with Ribeiro 1997 and with Moraes 1997). As one observer noted, almost every federal deputy has a mother or a sister who is a teacher, which made the deputies sensitive to the concerns of the teachers' unions (interview with França 1997). Other sectors of organized labor such as the confederation of rural unions and the union of social security employees also played an important role in building opposition to the reforms (Weyland 1996b; Melo 1997b). In order to defeat the reforms, the unions went so far as to carry out campaigns against legislators in their home districts to dissuade them from voting for the bill.

The CUT and its member unions had influence not only because they could influence the electoral prospects of legislators, but also because they had the potential to disrupt the economy, which legislators wanted to avoid. The unions repeatedly threatened to carry out strikes in opposition to the social security reform bill and other proposed constitutional reforms. Creston Portilho, a spokesperson for the Brazilian private-pension fund industry, argued that legislators on the committee had repeatedly delayed approving a social security reform because they "were worried that voting a social security amendment onto the floor . . . meant risking strikes and protests similar to those . . . set off by the French government's social security reform proposals and those legislators weren't willing to take on that level of political responsibility" (Kepp 1995: 16). A high-ranking official of the Ministry for Social Security, Celecino de Carvalho Filho, also ascribed the difficulties in passing the reform partly to the opposition of the unions, arguing that the government should have done more to gain their support (interview with Carvalho Filho 1997).

Weakness in the Legislature

Although constitutional barriers and labor opposition helped obstruct the enactment of social security reform in Brazil, the largest obstacle to reform was the president's lack of control of the legislature. Control of the legislature was crucial to the enactment of social security reform in Brazil because the government's reform proposal was highly controversial, which made it practically impossible for the Cardoso administration to obtain support from opposition parties. Indeed, it was even difficult for the government to obtain a high degree of support from members of the ruling coalition.

The Brazilian party system is highly fragmented, which has deprived the ruling party of legislative majorities in recent years (Mainwaring 1991, 1995, and 1999; Nicolau 1996).[10] At the time of his election, Fernando Collor de Mello's party, which was little more than a personal electoral vehicle, held only 8 percent of the seats in the Chamber of Deputies and 6 percent of the seats in the Senate. After his 1994 election, Cardoso's party controlled only 12.1 percent of the seats in the Chamber of Deputies and 16.7 percent of the seats in the Senate, in spite of his impressive electoral victory. The number of seats controlled by the ruling Brazilian Social Democratic Party (PSDB) went up during Cardoso's term because of frequent party-switching by deputies, but even at the end of his first term, the PSDB held less than 20 percent of the seats in the lower chamber.

The ruling party's relative weakness in the legislature forced Brazilian presidents to assemble broad and unwieldy coalitions in order to govern. Fernando Collor formed a coalition that ranged from three to five parties, whereas Itamar Franco, who had no party of his own, cobbled together a coalition of as many as seven parties. Cardoso's initial electoral coalition consisted of three parties—the Brazilian Social Democratic Party (PSDB), the Party of the Liberal Front (PFL), and the Brazilian Labor Party (PTB)—which won 36 percent of the seats in the Chamber of Deputies and 42 percent of the Senate. The Party of the Brazilian Democratic Movement (PMDB) joined the government at the start of Cardoso's mandate, which gave the ruling coalition 56 percent of the seats in the Chamber of Deputies and 69 percent of the seats in the Senate (Meneguello 1997). When the Brazilian Progressive Party (PPB) joined the government a year later, the ruling coalition came to control more than three-fourths of the seats in the lower chamber and more than 85 percent of the Senate.

The various coalitions were so broad, however, that they were difficult to hold together, particularly on controversial issues such as social security reform. The coalitions often grouped political parties from very different places on the political spectrum, which led to frequent disagreements over policy. Presidents, moreover, had little control over legislators from other parties. Legislators from parties that were not part of the president's original electoral coalition were particularly likely to act independently since their political fortunes were not closely tied to the government. In order to obtain votes, Brazilian presidents frequently had to dispense political patronage or enact modifications to the legislation in question.

The difficulty of obtaining votes from all of the members of the ruling coalition was magnified by the undisciplined nature of Brazilian parties. Political parties in Brazil traditionally exhibited low levels of party discipline compared to other Latin American or European parties (Neto and Santos 1997), and this has continued to hold true in recent years. Studies carried out by Samuels (1996) and Mainwaring and Pérez Liñán (1996) of the 1987–88 Brazilian Constitutional Congress found that party discipline was low even compared to the notoriously undisciplined U.S. Congress. The only exceptions were left-wing parties, such as the Partido dos Trabalhadores (PT) and the Democratic Labor Party (PDT). According to Mainwaring and Pérez Liñán's (1996) calculations, less than 75 percent of the legislators *present* voted with the majority of their party on controverted roll-call votes during the Brazilian Constitutional Congress.[11] Moreover, a large percentage of deputies failed to show up for the votes at all, which is often a sign of a lack of party discipline. According to Mainwaring and Pérez Liñán's (1996) data, less than 55 percent of *all* legislators voted with the majority of their party, owing to the large number of absentees.

Figueiredo and Limongi (1995) report higher degrees of party discipline in roll-call votes in the Brazilian Chamber of Deputies between 1989 and 1994, but these levels are still substantially below those found in Argentina (Jones 1998).[12] Moreover, Figueiredo and Limongi (1995) define a controverted vote more loosely than do the other scholars, which tends to increase the reported scores of party discipline.[13] According to their calculations, less than 90 percent of the voting members of non-left-wing parties supported the positions of their parties on roll-call votes.[14] Unfortunately, Figueiredo and Limongi do not report the percentage of all legislators who voted with the majority of their party, but this figure would no doubt be substantially lower, owing to the high levels of absenteeism in the Brazilian legislature.

Brazilian parties typically had low levels of party discipline in large part because the country's political institutions did not favor party discipline (Mainwaring and Pérez Liñán 1996; Ames 1995, 2001). National party leaders in Brazil, unlike those in Argentina and Mexico, had relatively little control over the selection of their parties' candidates. Most candidates were chosen at state party conventions in which the leaders of the national party had relatively little influence. Moreover, incumbent deputies were automatically entitled to a place on the ballot, whether they had supported the party in the legislature or not.

National party leaders also had relatively little control over which candidates were elected. For elections to the Chamber of Deputies, Brazil used an open-list proportional representation system in which voters selected a single candidate from a lengthy party list. Although a party's representation in the Chamber of Deputies depended on the number of votes for the party's candidates, the order in which candidates were chosen from this list to occupy the seats in the lower chamber depended on the number of votes that they received. Senators, meanwhile, were elected by plurality in a direct popular vote in which personal popularity tended to matter as much as or more than the party label. Thus, both senators and deputies had ample incentives to cater to the interests of their local electorate rather than the desires of national party leaders, and party leaders had few mechanisms at their disposal to compel party discipline.

Career patterns of Brazilian policymakers also tended to weaken party discipline. Most legislators did not remain in the Chamber of Deputies for long—in recent years, only 15 percent of federal deputies had already served more than two terms (Samuels 1998). Politicians typically built their careers at the municipal or state level rather than at the national level (Samuels 1998). Congressmen therefore tended to focus on pleasing local constituencies, particularly the governor, even when the interests of local constituencies conflicted with those of national party leaders.[15] Indeed, when Brazilian members of congress were asked with whom they would vote if there were a conflict between their party's position and the needs of their state, 49.5 percent of the respondents answered that they would side with their state and only 31.3 percent responded that they would vote with their party (Mainwaring 1991: 33).

Legislative Battles over Reform

The small proportion of seats held by the ruling party and the weak party discipline prevailing among the governing coalition made it very difficult for the Cardoso administration to assemble sufficient votes to pass the social security reform bill. Numerous members of the ruling coalition voted against the bill or simply failed to attend the sessions when the bill was being voted on, leading Cardoso to complain that "the difference between President Clinton and me is that he has an organized majority against him and I have a disorganized majority in my favor" (*Veja* 1996: 13). On the whole, the latecomers to the ruling coalition—the PMDB and the PPB—exhibited the least party discipline, but even the PSDB, the PFL, and the PTB experienced substantial defections on some of the votes.

The Cardoso administration's social security reform proposal encountered problems in the legislature from the outset. The government's first defeat took place in the Committee on the Constitution and Justice of the Chamber of Deputies. Here, critics of the reform proposed dividing the reform bill into several pieces—a highly unusual move given that the sole purpose of the committee was to rule on the constitutional admissibility of the proposal (interviews with Almeida 1997 and with da Silva 1997). The Cardoso administration opposed this proposal, but it lost the vote, 24 to 22, when 8 of its allies on the committee, including 3 members of the PMDB, defected. In some cases, traditional allies of the Cardoso administration defected because the government had refused to grant them the administrative posts that they desired for their parties ("First Defeat" 1995; "Susto na largada" 1995; Suassuna and Silva 1995). As a result, three sections of the reform proposal were broken off for separate consideration. The bulk of the reform proposal, however, continued to be contained in a single bill, which was renamed Constitutional Amendment Project 33-A. After extended negotiations with legislators from the PMDB and other parties, the Cardoso administration obtained the approval of the CCJ for the admissibility of this bill in late April 1995, several months after it was first presented to the committee.

The main reform bill then passed to a special congressional committee that was established specifically to evaluate the social security reform proposal. This committee's treatment of the bill was delayed for almost five months because of the government's preoccupation with the economic reforms as well as disagreements over the composition of the committee (Melo 1998; "Stephanes tentou" 1995: 3). Once the committee began its hearings in September 1995, it got bogged down because of disagreements within the government's support coalition in the legislature. Although members of the governing coalition held most of the seats on the committee, many of these members were highly critical of the reform proposal. Among the critics of the reform proposal were the president of the committee, Jair Soares of the PFL, who was a former minister of social security, and the rapporteur of the committee, Euler Ribeiro of the PMDB. Rejecting the Cardoso administration's pleas to approve the proposal rapidly, the committee called on a wide variety of interest groups and social security experts to testify. The committee also proceeded to make a large number of changes to the bill, including a controversial amendment that would have maintained the legislators' own privileged pension system.

The Cardoso administration responded by putting intense pressure on the leaders of the committee to move faster and to withdraw some of their proposed modifications of the reform bill. The leaders of the committee resisted this pressure for the most part, however, which caused their relations with the Cardoso administration to deteriorate. Addressing the rapporteur of the committee, who was in charge of making modifications to the bill, the minister of social security, Reinhold Stephanes, denounced the committee as "a circus of which Your Excellency is the clown" (*Veja* 1996: 13). In an effort to unblock the reform, the Cardoso administration opened up negotiations with the labor unions and the pensioners' associations, but these negotiations quickly foundered. Nevertheless, the committee incorporated into the reform proposal the concessions that the government had granted to the unions in the negotiations.

By early February 1996, the committee had still not approved a reform proposal, even though the committee had originally established a November 1995 deadline for completion of their mission. Under pressure from the government and the leaders of his party to approve the proposal, Soares preferred to resign his position as president of the committee and leave the PFL. The leader of the Chamber of Deputies, Luis Eduardo Magalhães, then dissolved the committee and shifted the responsibility for revising the reform proposal to the chamber floor, although he retained Ribeiro as the rapporteur. Magalhães justified this measure by arguing that the committee had already met more than the forty times prescribed by the chamber's regulations, but opponents of the reform criticized this move as highly irregular. A proposal by the opposition to return the social security reform bill to the committee was defeated by a vote of 311 to 152.

In early March, party leaders brought Ribeiro's modified reform proposal to a vote in the full chamber, but it failed to obtain the support of three-fifths of the legislature. In order to pass the bill, the government needed 308 votes, but only 294 deputies voted in favor of the bill, with 190 votes against and 8 abstentions (*Diário da Câmara dos Deputados* 1996a: 5951). The Cardoso administration lost this vote largely because of defections from allied parties—fifty-nine members of the governing coalition voted against the reform bill, including thirty-eight deputies from the PMDB. A substantial percentage of the members of the right-wing PPB, which habitually supported the government, also voted against the reform, as did all of the left-wing parties in the legislature.

According to the rules of the legislature, the Chamber of Deputies should have voted on the government's original reform proposal after the defeat of Ribeiro's version of the reform bill (Melo 1998; interviews with Almeida 1997 and with da Silva 1997). Instead, the president of the Chamber of Deputies appointed Michel Temer, the leader of the PMDB, as the new rapporteur of the bill, and Temer proceeded to assemble a new version of the reform bill, based in part on the numerous amendments that various legislators had proposed to the original legislation. This caused a great deal of criticism from opponents of the reform, which sought to block the move in the courts, but the Brazilian Supreme Court (STF) ultimately upheld the legality of the action. The new version of the reform bill, which was more faithful to the original proposal than Ribeiro's version, was voted on by the legislature on March 22. Surprisingly, it was approved by a vote of 351 deputies in favor, 139 opposed, and 2 abstentions (*Diário da Câmara dos Deputados* 1996b: 7539).

The Cardoso administration managed to gain approval of the new bill by engaging in old-fashioned patronage politics, trading government resources and administrative appointments for the votes of key deputies ("Foi dando" 1996; "O presidente riu" 1996). All of the deputies from the state of Rondônia, for example, switched their votes on the social security reform bill after the Cardoso administration promised them resources for rural electrification and the rebuilding of a highway in the state. More significantly, the leader of the PPB and mayor of São Paulo, Paulo Maluf, agreed to join his party to the ruling coalition in exchange for a ministerial appointment for a member of his party and 3.36 billion reais in federal aid to help pay São Paulo's debts. Partly as a result of this agreement, the PPB delivered seventy-one votes for the reform bill on March 22, as opposed to only fifty-seven on the earlier vote. Thanks to the lobbying efforts of Temer and the government's willingness to bargain, the Cardoso administration also won the votes of seventy-five members of the PMDB, as opposed to only fifty-three of its members on the previous vote.

The government's victory was short-lived, however. Opponents of the reform proposed 226 votes on individual provisions of the reform as permitted under the 1988 constitution, and, over the course of the next several months, 25 of these destaques were brought to a vote (Figueiredo and Limongi 1998). In order to defeat most of the destaques, the government needed to obtain the support of three-fifths of the legislature, which it was unable to achieve on eight of the votes. In this way, the opposition managed to excise some of the most important parts of the reform, including the provisions that required public servants to be at least fifty-five years of age in order to receive a pension and that would have prevented the pensions of civil servants from being automatically adjusted to keep pace with increases in the salaries of active workers. The opposition also managed to defeat provisions that eliminated the special pension systems of university professors and members of the legislature.

The government lost the votes in part because it grew reluctant to make the bargains necessary to hold its coalition together over the long series of votes (Meireles and Filgueiras 1996; "Government Faces Defeat" 1996: 2). Numerous legislators were also loath to vote in favor of the unpopular reforms because they were competing in the upcoming municipal elections. Of the parties in the governing coalition, the PMDB and the PPB again provided the lowest level of support for the reforms, but the PTB, the PFL, and the PSDB also registered a substantial number of defections ("Ministérios não renderam" 1996: 33).

The government managed to obtain a fairly high level of relative, but not of absolute, party discipline on the social security reform votes that took place in the Chamber of Deputies in 1996 (Figueiredo and Limongi 1998). Almost 90 percent of the voting members of the ruling coalition supported the government's position on these votes. The problem was that many members of the ruling coalition expressed their opposition by failing to show up for the votes. Only 77.1 percent of the legislators from the ruling coalition supported the government's position on all social security reform votes held in 1996, and only 71.7 percent supported the government on those votes that the government lost. This hurt the government since it needed to obtain the support of three-fifths of the entire legislature, not just of those present.

In the wake of these defeats, the Cardoso administration decided to try to present a new version of the reform bill in the Senate, where the government had a stronger base of support. This tactic proved successful, but it delayed the consideration of the reform until after the October municipal elections. The Senate's consideration of the new reform bill was then postponed even further because Cardoso did not want it to interfere with the government's proposal to amend the constitution to permit his own reelection, which was being discussed in the legislature during the first half of 1997. As a result, the Senate Committee on the Constitution and Justice did not rule on the new reform bill until July 1997, and it did not come to a vote on the Senate floor until late September 1997.

Although the Senate's reform bill involved much more sweeping changes than the legislation approved by the Chamber of Deputies, it was enacted by the Senate relatively easily, thanks to Cardoso's strong base of support in the Senate. At the time of the vote, the government's most faithful supporters, the PSDB, the PTB, and the PFL, controlled approximately half of the eighty-one seats in the upper chamber, which meant that they only needed to pick up a handful of votes from senators in other allied parties in order to pass the bill. As it turned out, fifty-nine senators voted in favor of the bill, whereas only twelve senators opposed it, in the first round of voting. The passage of the reform bill in the Senate was also aided by the stricter rules the upper chamber placed on the presentation of destaques (Figueiredo and Limongi 1998). In order to present a destaque in the Senate, legislators needed to have the support of the majority of their colleagues, which prevented opponents of the reform from placing the most controversial parts of the reform legislation to a vote.

The new reform bill established a minimum retirement age of sixty years for men and fifty-five for women, which was to apply to workers in both the public and private sectors, with exceptions only for primary and secondary schoolteachers.[16] In order to retire at these ages, workers would have to demonstrate that they had contributed for a minimum of thirty-five years (thirty years in the case of women). Otherwise they would have to wait until they were sixty-five years of age (sixty years of age for women) to receive a pension, the value of which would depend on the number of years of contributions. The bill also mandated that the pensions of public-sector workers could no longer exceed the value of their salary prior to retirement, and it reduced the pensions of high-salaried civil servants by as much as 30 percent. Almost all of these changes were to be phased in, however, so as to preserve the acquired rights of active workers.

Because the legislation passed by the Senate represented a new version of the reform, the bill needed to be returned to the Chamber of Deputies for its approval. The Cardoso administration knew that obtaining the approval of the lower chamber would be difficult given the resistance that it had encountered on the previous attempt. The government therefore began an intense campaign to obtain votes for the proposal in the Chamber of Deputies. In order to persuade reluctant legislators to vote for the bill, the Cardoso administration released $545 million in funds for housing and draining projects in the legislators' districts, including $113 million to the districts of deputies from the PFL and $90 million to the districts of members of the PPB ("Key Reforms Approved" 1998: 76). According to one opposition deputy, the government dispensed more than $300 million in the hours immediately preceding the reform (Lago 1998).

This campaign paid off, as the lower chamber approved the bill by a vote of 346 to 151 in the first round of voting in early February. As previously, the Cardoso administration received strong support from his own party and the PFL, but much weaker support from the other members of the governing coalition. More than 90 percent of the legislators from the PFL and the PSDB voted in favor of the legislation, whereas only about 70 percent of the members of the PMDB and the PPB gave him their votes ("Fidelidade do PFL" 1998).

Once again, however, the opposition succeeded in undoing some of the key aspects of the reform by proposing votes on individual provisions of the reform bill. The opposition, for example, managed to eliminate the article that instituted a minimum age of retirement of sixty years of age (fifty-five in the case of women) for private-sector workers, a provision that the Ministry of Social Security had termed the "fundamental axis of the social security reform" (Lima and Jungblut 1998). The government fell 1 vote short of the required 308 votes to maintain this provision when 98 legislators from the ruling coalition, most of whom belonged to the PMDB and the PPB, voted with the opposition. Critics of the reform subsequently managed to eliminate the provision that reduced the pensions of public-sector workers. The Cardoso administration had originally hoped to cut the pensions of high-salaried civil servants by as much as 30 percent, but it subsequently agreed to reduce the cut to no more than 23.6 percent in an effort to obtain enough votes to maintain the provision. The government nevertheless fell two votes short of the three-fifths majority needed to enact the proposed reduction, owing in large part to seventy defections by legislators from the PPB and the PMDB ("Problemas pessoais" 1998).

Although the Cardoso administration finally managed to enact the bill at the end of 1998 when the last destaques were withdrawn or defeated, the integrity of the reform had been severely compromised. The social security reform bill enacted by the Cardoso administration in late 1998, unlike the reforms implemented in much of the rest of the region, represented only a minor adjustment in the existing system. (See Table 5.2.) The reform failed to cut benefit levels for public- or private-sector workers, many of whom will continue to receive benefits equal to their former salaries. Nor did it establish a minimum retirement age for private-sector workers, making Brazil one of the few countries in the world with no minimum retirement age. Although the government did manage to set a minimum retirement age of sixty years for male civil servants and fifty-five years for female civil servants, these retirement ages remained under those prevailing in much of the region. Perhaps the most important achievement of the reform was the requirement that workers, in the future, must prove that they have made at least thirty-five years of contributions (thirty years for women) in order to retire early. This measure, like the others, will only be gradually phased in, however, which will limit the financial savings of the reform in the medium

TABLE 5.2

The 1998 Brazilian Social Security Reform

	Prior to the reform	After the reform
Standard retirement age	65 for men; 60 for women (five years less for rural workers)	65 for men; 60 for women (five years less for rural workers)
Minimum retirement age for private-sector workers	None	None
Minimum retirement age for civil servants	None	60 for men; 55 for women
Requirements for retiring early	35 years of service (30 for women)	35 years of contributions (30 for women)
Privileged pension schemes	Military; schoolteachers; university professors; judiciary; legislators	Military; schoolteachers

term. Moreover, workers who cannot prove that they have made that many years of contributions will still be able to retire at the standard retirement age. The reform also eliminated the special pension systems belonging to legislators, the judiciary, and university professors, but these changes will have mostly a symbolic impact since the number of people benefiting from these systems was relatively small.

In response to the severe financial crisis that struck Brazil in late 1998, the Cardoso administration submitted an additional social security reform bill to the legislature. This legislation sought to increase the social security contributions of high-earning civil servants and would have required civil servants to continue to make social security contributions equal to 11 percent of their salary after they retired. The reform bill was defeated in the legislature even though it did not seek to modify the constitution and therefore only required a simple majority to be approved. The government resubmitted the bill to the legislature in early 1999 and managed to gain approval of a modified version of the legislation, but the Brazilian Supreme Court subsequently ruled that the bill was unconstitutional.

Conclusion

Political obstacles thus prevented the Brazilian government from enacting a major social security reform in the 1990s in spite of the numerous efforts it made toward this end. Brazil, unlike Argentina and Mexico, needed to amend its constitution in order to reform its social security system, which was difficult to do given the high barriers to constitutional reform and the government's weak control of the legislature. The ruling party in Brazil, un-like its counterparts in Argentina and Mexico, only held a small portion of the seats in the legislature, and party discipline was traditionally weak, mak-ing it difficult for the Cardoso administration to hold its governing coalition together.

The failure of the Brazilian government to enact a major social security reform will only increase the pressure on the government to reform its sys-tem in the years ahead. The minor reforms that the government has enacted to date have not solved the financial problems afflicting the country's pen-sion system. Indeed, in 1999, the main social security system serving private-sector workers generated a deficit of 10 billion reais, while the systems serv-ing federal employees racked up a deficit of 20 billion reais (Soares 1999: 56). These deficits are expected to continue to grow as the country's population ages rapidly in the coming decades, putting pressure on the Brazilian govern-ment to enact further reforms. The recent election of Luiz Inácio Lula da Silva as president of Brazil may actually make some types of public pension re-forms more likely. Lula has placed pension reform high on the agenda, and the ties between Lula's Partido dos Trabalhadores and organized labor may enable the government to persuade the unions to acquiesce to some tight-ening of pension eligibility requirements or cutbacks in benefits. The PT's traditionally high levels of party discipline should also facilitate the enact-ment of parametric reforms, although gaining legislative approval for such reforms will not be easy given the small share of seats that the PT controls in the legislature. The Brazilian government is unlikely to privatize its pen-sion system any time soon, however. The political, as well as financial, bar-riers to privatization remain formidable, and Lula has not yet shown the de-sire or the ability to surmount them.

CHAPTER 6

*The Politics of Pension
Privatization Around the World*

THE NATIONS examined in the previous three chapters represent only a few of the many countries that have debated pension reform in the last decade. From Australia to Zimbabwe, pension reform has been high on the policy agenda, and a significant number of nations have gone so far as to privatize their pension systems. This chapter analyzes how well the economic, ideational, and political factors discussed in the previous chapters explain pension reform outcomes in this larger sampling of countries. Two methods are used to examine these arguments: a qualitative survey of the politics of pension reform in a variety of nations in Latin America and the postcommunist world; and a quantitative analysis of the determinants of pension privatization in middle- and high-income countries worldwide.

The analyses find a considerable amount of support for the arguments made in the previous chapters. Both the quantitative and the qualitative analyses indicate that nations have privatized their pension systems partly in response to concerns about high public pension spending and low domestic savings rates. The quantitative and the qualitative analyses also suggest that the Chilean model and the World Bank have played an important role in persuading policymakers to privatize their pension systems. In addition, the chapter presents quantitative and qualitative evidence that ruling parties that control a large percentage of seats in the legislature have a much easier time enacting sweeping pension privatization schemes. Finally, a fair amount of case study evidence, but not quantitative evidence, exists to suggest that sweeping pension privatization is more likely where economists dominate the key social security policy-making positions and where the ruling party is relatively disciplined.

The chapter begins with an examination of the role played by macroeconomic factors in pension reforms in Latin America and the postcommunist world. It then analyzes the key ideational and political factors that have shaped pension reform outcomes in these two regions. Finally, the chapter provides a series of statistical tests of the main arguments.

The Economic Burden of Public Pensions

Growing public pension expenditures put social security reform on the agenda not only in Argentina, Brazil, and, to a lesser extent, Mexico, but also in a number of other countries in Latin America. Uruguay, which had broad social security coverage, an aging population, and a fully mature pension system, had the most serious financial difficulties. Uruguay's pension expenditures rose dramatically in the 1980s and 1990s, and by 1996, they had reached an estimated 15 percent of the country's gross domestic product, which was far and away the highest level in Latin America (Palacios and Pallarès-Miralles 2000). The burgeoning public pension expenditures wreaked havoc on the country's finances and prompted numerous efforts at reform. The Uruguayan minister of economy sought to justify one of those reform efforts in 1992, arguing:

We Uruguayans confront a very critical situation. The major cause of this is the volume that the state spends and the impossibility of covering those expenses with genuine resources. . . . If measures are not taken, the deficit can only be dealt with by printing more and more money, which amounts to extracting more and more money from people through the inflation tax. . . . We have decided to do what anybody would do in our place. The first and most important measure to be taken is a deep reform of our social security system. (qtd. in Filgueira and Moraes 1999: 12)

Although Uruguay clearly had the most pressing financial problems, some other Latin American countries were also burdened with large public pension expenditures, which hindered economic growth. By the mid-1990s, public pension spending in Costa Rica, Nicaragua, and Panama totaled approximately 4 percent of GDP, prompting each of these countries to seek to reform their systems (Palacios and Pallarès-Miralles 2000). In Costa Rica, for example, the Exposition of Motives for the Reform cited in particular "the growth in costs, associated with the maturation of the system" (*Proyecto de Ley* 1999: 3). In Nicaragua, the government argued that the reform was aimed at "resolving the grave problems and the economic and social inviability [of the system]. . . . The worst that could occur in Nicaragua, would be to enter the next millenium with a worn-out pay-as-you-go system that runs deficits by nature and is hardly apt to deal with the accelerated changes that are taking place" (Instituto Nicaragüense de Seguridad Social 2000: 1-2).

Public pension systems in Eastern Europe had even more serious financial difficulties than the Latin American systems. East European countries have long had large public pension expenditures because of their elderly populations, broad social security coverage, and mature pension systems. In the early 1990s, however, East European countries underwent transitions to market economies, which caused unemployment to rise sharply. Many East European countries sought to alleviate the rising unemployment by loosening their pension eligibility requirements, which led to a wave of retirements. By the mid-1990s, public pension expenditures in Eastern Europe had reached an average of 8.5 percent of GDP (Palacios and Pallarès-Miralles 2000). In some countries, such as Poland and Slovenia, public pension spending totaled approximately 14 percent of gross domestic product. Moreover, the public pension expenditures were expected to rise considerably in the years ahead. According to some World Bank pension experts, "Reasonable baseline projections envisage that the pension burden [of the postcommunist nations] will grow well above 14 percent of GDP within a few decades, or even above 16 percent of GDP with expected fertility and mortality changes. Such growth is likely to generate social and political unrest, and unless managed successfully, could undermine growth in employment" (Lindeman, Rutkowski, and Sluchynsky 2001: 9). Rising pension expenditures thus placed pension reform high on the policy agenda in the postcommunist world as well.

Many of the Latin American and Eastern European countries with high pension expenditures opted to privatize their pension systems. As discussed in Chapter 2, pension privatization may gradually reduce public pension spending by shifting responsibility for the payments of pensions away from the state and toward private pension funds. Pension privatization may also reduce the vulnerability of the pension system to future demographic changes by shifting (at least partially) the pension system from a pay-as-you-go basis to a fully funded basis. In fully funded systems, unlike pay-as-you-go systems, payroll taxes do not necessarily have to be increased as the ratio of workers to pensioners declines.

Public pension expenditures can only explain some of the variance in pension privatization, however.[1] As Table 6.1 indicates, the Latin American countries that have privatized their pension systems tended to have higher public pension expenditures than those that have not privatized their pension systems. Nevertheless, some Latin American countries with low public pension expenditures, such as Mexico, Peru, Colombia, El Salvador, and the Dominican Republic, have privatized their pension systems, whereas other nations with high public pension expenditures, such as Brazil and Panama, have eschewed pension privatization. The same is true outside of Latin America. The postcommunist countries that have privatized their pension

TABLE 6.1

Public Pension Spending and Pension Reform

	Public pension spending (as a percent of GDP)	Year
Argentina	6.2	1994
Bolivia	2.5	1995
Chile	4.0	1980
Colombia	1.1	1994
Costa Rica	3.8	1996
Dominican Republic	0.4	1987
El Salvador	1.3	1996
Mexico	0.4	1996
Nicaragua	4.3	1996
Peru	1.2	1996
Uruguay	15.0	1996
Latin American privatizers	**3.65**	
Brazil	4.9	1995
Ecuador	1.0	1997
Guatemala	0.7	1995
Honduras	0.6	1994
Panama	4.3	1996
Paraguay	0.1	1986
Venezuela	0.5	1990
Latin American nonprivatizers	**1.73**	
Bulgaria	7.3	1996
Croatia	11.6	1997
Estonia	7.0	1995
Hungary	9.7	1996
Kazakhstan	5.0	1997
Latvia	10.2	1995
Macedonia	8.7	1998
Poland	14.4	1995
Postcommunist privatizers	**9.24**	
Postcommunist nonprivatizers	**5.99**	

SOURCES: Palacios and Pallarès-Miralles 2000; World Bank 1994.

systems have tended to have higher public pension expenditures than those postcommunist countries that have eschewed privatization. But many Eastern as well as Western European countries with high public pension expenditures have declined to privatize their pension systems. Indeed, Western European countries have substantially higher levels of public pension spending (as a percentage of GDP) than Latin American countries, but they have, to date, mostly eschewed pension privatization.[2]

It is also problematic to attribute the privatization schemes to the financial difficulties that some countries were experiencing with their public pension systems since the immediate effect of the privatization schemes was to worsen these financial difficulties. With the implementation of the privatization scheme in Mexico, all members of the Mexican Social Security Institute (IMSS) ceased to contribute to the system, but the IMSS continued to have to pay the pensions of existing retirees. As a result, the IMSS pension system began to run a large deficit for the first time. In Argentina, the privatization scheme similarly aggravated the public pension system's already large financing gap by allowing active workers to make their personal pension contributions to private pension funds instead of to the public pension system. The privatization schemes should eventually reduce the state's pension obligations in both countries, but these reductions will take place only gradually as current pensioners and older workers pass away.[3] Both countries could have alleviated the financial difficulties much more quickly by undertaking parametric reforms exclusively (that is, by cutting benefits, tightening eligibility requirements, or raising contribution rates in their public pension systems), rather than privatization. Thus, financial problems alone cannot explain why these two countries (or any countries for that matter) opted to privatize their pension systems rather than, or in addition to, carrying out some other type of reform.

Financial problems did clearly put pension reform on the agenda, but this made parametric reform, and not just privatization, more likely. Many countries with high public pension expenditures have opted to seek to cut back this spending by tightening pension eligibility requirements or by changing the formula that they use to calculate pension benefits. A bivariate probit analysis reveals that the level of public pension spending is a statistically significant determinant of the likelihood of cutbacks in public pension benefits.[4] Nations with high public pension expenditures are more likely to cut back their pension benefits than countries with low public pension expenditures. Indeed, cutbacks in benefits have been more common in Western Europe and the former Soviet bloc where the economic burden of the public pension systems have been the highest. Of the thirty-six reforms that took place in the 1990s that involved some form of cuts in benefits, twenty-five occurred in Western Europe and the postcommunist nations (Schwarz and Demirgüç-Kunt 1999; *International Social Security Review* 1996). Most of the remaining cutbacks took place in Latin American nations, many of which had high levels of public pension expenditures or had opted to privatize their pension systems and, as a result, needed to tighten their pension eligibility requirements.[5]

Boosting Domestic Savings

As the case studies of Argentina and, especially, Mexico demonstrated, many policymakers have opted to privatize their public pension systems, instead of carrying out parametric reforms, partly in order to boost their sagging domestic savings rates and reduce their dependence on unstable foreign capital. Indeed, the Mexican government went so far as to spell out this aim in the legislation that privatized the pension system (Cámara de Diputados de los Estados Unidos Mexicanos 1996a: 202). Both Argentina and Mexico traditionally had relatively low savings rates, and these savings rates suffered a sharp decline during the early 1990s. Brazilian policymakers, in contrast, had fewer macroeconomic incentives to privatize in part because the country's domestic savings rate was high by regional standards and Brazil already had a large source of long-term investment capital.

Chronically low or falling domestic savings has also provided impetus to pension privatization efforts in other Latin American countries. Bolivia's domestic savings rate, for example, averaged a mere 9.3 percent between 1990 and 1995. Proponents of pension privatization in Bolivia maintained that privatizing the pension system would help boost the country's pitiably low savings rate (Pérez 2000; Mercado Lora 1998). The president of Bolivia, Gonzalo Sánchez de Lozada, argued that his pension privatization plan would "mean the development of domestic savings, capital formation, a stock and bond market almost overnight" (Bowen 1996: 12). El Salvador, Nicaragua, and the Dominican Republic also suffered from extremely low, or even negative, domestic savings rates in the 1990s, and policymakers in these countries hoped that their pension privatization plans would help ameliorate this situation. The Nicaraguan Social Security Institute in its statement of the motives for the reform, argued that pension privatization would "raise domestic savings; improve the productivity of capital; stimulate the GDP growth owing to the [growth in] savings and employment" (Instituto Nicaragüense de Seguridad Social 2000). A similar rationale undergirded the reform in El Salvador. According to the statement of motives that accompanied the pension privatization legislation, the Salvadoran reform sought "to generate domestic savings in the long run, the destiny of which will be the financing of productive activities for the country" ("Exposición de motivos" 1997: 9). The legislation that privatized the pension system in the Dominican Republic, meanwhile, noted that the reform would "raise the capacity of national and individual savings and the sustainability of social and economic development" (Secretaría de Estado de Trabajo 2001: 1).

Other countries, such as Colombia and Peru, traditionally had reasonably high domestic savings rates, but experienced sharp drops in these rates shortly before they enacted their pension privatization plans. The domestic savings rate in Colombia, for example, declined steadily beginning in 1988, reaching a low of 19.2 percent in 1993, the year the system was privatized. In Peru, the domestic savings rate dropped from 21.6 percent in 1990 to 14.9 percent in 1992, the year before the system was privatized. Increasing the domestic savings rate was one of the primary goals of the reforms, according to key policymakers in both of these countries. Nelson (1998: 3) concluded from her interviews with top policymakers in Colombia that "the main attraction of pension reform for the Gaviria government was the opportunity to increase long-term savings."[6] In a detailed study of the Colombian social security reform, González Rossetti and Ramírez (2000: 38) note that Colombian president César Gaviria saw his pension privatization plan "as a component of the economic reforms made by his government and a strategy to boost internal savings." A similar macroeconomic rationale for pension privatization was present in Peru. Carlos Boloña (1995: 52), one of the main architects of the Peruvian reform as the then-minister of finance, wrote that the privatization plan would "foment savings and national investment contributing to economic growth." Peruvian President Alberto Fujimori, meanwhile, argued that "without a doubt, the creation of the [private pension system] will generate huge reserves which shall be absorbed by our capital markets" (Conradt 1993: 35).

In the postcommunist countries, policymakers also hoped that pension privatization would boost their domestic savings rates and bolster the local capital markets. Bulgaria, Croatia, and Macedonia all had quite low domestic savings rates throughout the 1990s, whereas Kazakhstan and Latvia experienced sharp declines in their domestic savings rates in the mid-1990s, shortly before they enacted their reforms. The main architect of the reform in Kazakhstan, Grigori Marchenko, viewed pension privatization as a way to both boost domestic savings and jump start the capital markets (interview with Andrews 1998; Orenstein 1999). A desire to raise the domestic savings rate and bolster the local capital markets also reportedly motivated the reforms in Hungary and Poland (interview with Palacios 1998; Nelson 2001; Müller 1999: 78; Golinowska 1999). Indeed, the Hungarian government sought to finance the transition costs of its privatization plan through taxes and expenditure reduction rather than debt specifically in order to boost the domestic savings rate (Palacios and Rocha 1998: 27). In both Hungary and Poland, the domestic savings rates dropped sharply in the early 1990s when pension privatization first came on the agenda, although the savings rate rebounded shortly before these countries enacted their reforms.

As Table 6.2 shows, those countries that have privatized their pension systems have tended to have lower domestic savings rates than those countries that have eschewed privatization. In Latin America, the domestic savings of the countries that privatized their pension systems averaged 13.5 percent of

TABLE 6.2

Domestic Savings Rates Around the World, 1990–1995

(gross domestic savings as a percent of GDP)

	1990	1991	1992	1993	1994	1995	1990–95
Argentina	19.7	16.2	15.2	16.7	16.9	17.6	17.1
Bolivia	11.4	10.1	7.7	7.3	8.8	10.6	9.3
Colombia	24.6	23.4	19.3	19.2	19.6	19.4	20.9
Costa Rica	20.5	24.2	24.0	22.7	23.2	23.3	23.0
Dominican Republic	15.2	14.5	10.9	19.1	18.4	18.3	16.1
El Salvador	1.2	2.1	2.2	3.8	4.6	4.2	3.0
Mexico	22.0	20.4	18.3	17.0	16.9	22.5	19.5
Nicaragua	−2.1	−10.6	−13.9	−9.2	−3.5	0.8	−6.4
Peru	21.6	14.9	14.3	15.6	19.0	19.3	17.5
Uruguay	17.0	16.7	14.2	14.1	13.1	12.8	14.7
Latin America privatizers*	**15.1**	**13.2**	**11.2**	**12.6**	**13.7**	**14.9**	**13.5**
Brazil	21.4	20.5	21.4	22.3	22.5	20.5	21.4
Ecuador	22.9	23.8	25.0	21.7	22.0	19.7	22.5
Guatemala	9.8	10.7	9.1	8.9	8.4	8.8	9.3
Honduras	19.5	20.0	19.0	21.6	27.0	27.0	22.4
Panama	21.4	18.7	22.7	24.5	28.0	28.2	23.9
Paraguay	16.3	17.1	21.7	20.9	20.7	18.3	19.2
Venezuela	29.5	23.8	21.2	18.5	22.7	23.4	23.2
Latin America nonprivatizers	**20.1**	**19.2**	**20.0**	**19.8**	**21.6**	**20.8**	**20.3**
All middle income	**24.8**	**24.1**	**24.3**	**23.5**	**24.1**	**24.0**	**24.1**
All high income	**22.6**	**22.2**	**21.8**	**21.4**	**21.7**	**21.8**	**21.9**
All countries	**23.3**	**22.9**	**22.6**	**22.2**	**22.6**	**22.7**	**22.7**

SOURCE: World Bank (2000).

*Excludes Chile.

GDP between 1990 and 1995, as opposed to 20.3 percent in those countries that have not privatized their pension systems.[7] Not all of the Latin American countries with low domestic savings rates have privatized their pension systems. Guatemala, for example, suffered from quite low domestic savings rates throughout the 1990s. The Guatemalan government did propose pension privatization plans, but opponents of the reforms blocked them. Costa Rica, in contrast, opted to privatize its pension system even though it had a relatively high domestic savings rate. There is some evidence to suggest that the Costa Rican government privatized its pension system partly in order to increase its domestic savings rate even though it was clearly better off in this regard than most Latin American countries. President Miguel Angel Ro-

dríguez argued that Costa Rica's new private pension system would constitute "a source of financing for the productive apparatus and would stimulate
the capital markets and the stock market" ("Costa Rica-fondos de pensiones" 2000). One of the architects of the Costa Rican reform, Ronulfo Jiménez, similarly maintained that "the funds going into the individual accounts
will provide, in the long-term, a source of national savings that could invigorate the economy" (Muñoz 2000).

On average, domestic savings rates have been much lower in those regions where pension privatization has had a prominent position on the policy agenda. In Latin America, where almost every major country has considered pension privatization, domestic savings averaged 16.4 percent of GDP
between 1990 and 1995. In the postcommunist countries where pension
privatization has also been widely considered, domestic saving rates averaged
17.6 percent. In contrast, domestic savings rates averaged 36.1 percent in
East Asia and the Pacific, 22.7 percent in the Middle East and North Africa,
and 21.7 percent among high-income OECD countries during this period.
In none of these latter regions did pension privatization occupy a prominent
position on the policy agenda.

Diffusion of the Chilean Model

Beliefs in the economic efficacy of pension privatization have been trans-
mitted in part by Chile's experience with pension reform. In the two decades after privatizing its pension system in 1981, Chile experienced a sharp
increase in its domestic savings rate, a stock market boom, and robust economic growth. Observers commonly attributed the country's economic
prosperity to the pension privatization scheme, although the evidence for
this is inconclusive. By the end of the 1980s, policymakers throughout Latin
America and in many other areas of the world were carefully studying the
Chilean model and contemplating similar reforms in their own countries.

Chilean pension experts played an important role in promoting pension
privatization throughout Latin America. Pension experts affiliated with Chilean universities, such as Catholic University of Santiago and the University
of Chile, and Chilean think tanks such as the Corporation for Research,
Study, and Development of Social Security (CIEDESS), the Center for Public Studies (CEP), and the Institute of Liberty and Development (ILD), have
provided technical assistance on pension privatization to a wide variety of
Latin American countries. The Superintendency of Pension Fund Administrators (SAFP) in Chile has also promoted pension privatization throughout Latin America, as have private companies such as Socimer, a Chilean-
based investment bank, and PrimAmérica, a Chilean consulting firm founded
by former executives of a Chilean pension fund. PrimAmérica, for example,

helped draw up pension privatization proposals in El Salvador, Honduras, Bolivia, Ecuador, Panama, Paraguay, and Guatemala among other countries (intervews with Iglesias 1996 and with Acuña 1997).

Perhaps the most influential Chilean advocate of pension reform has been José Piñera. Piñera has traveled throughout Latin America, meeting with ministers and presidents in his effort to promote pension privatization (interview with Piñera 1997). According to both Carlos Boloña, the former minister of economy in Peru, and Mario Roggero, an important legislative advocate of pension privatization, Piñera played a key role in persuading President Fujimori in Peru to support pension privatization (Roggero 1993; Boloña Behr 1997). Indeed, Fujimori gave his approval to the pension privatization project at the end of a three-hour meeting with Piñera (Roggero 1997: 41). Boloña recounts, "At the time of the reform, the president of Peru was very concerned. He wasn't convinced that we should privatize the pension system. So we brought José [Piñera] to talk to him, to discuss what privatization had done for Chile. And, of course, José was able to convince him that privatization was in Peru's best interest. The reform might not have been signed into law without José's assistance" [Boloña Behr 1997: 1].

Piñera also reportedly helped convince Colombian president-elect César Gaviria and his economic advisers of the merits of pension privatization during a 1990 visit to that country (Santos 1997; Hommes 1995: 11; Nelson 1998: 3). According to Juan Manuel Santos (1997: 42), the former minister of trade in Colombia:

The arguments and results presented by Piñera [at a presentation on pension reform in Colombia] made a deep impression on those who knew about the problem and on Colombian public opinion. That day Piñera met with the President elect and with his team of economic advisers. It was an intense meeting of five hours after which the economic team of Gaviria was convinced of the necessity of pushing the pension reform and of working on the basis of the Chilean scheme of private pensions.

Shortly after Piñera's visit, several of the key architects of the Colombian reform traveled to Chile to study the Chilean reform (Santos 1997).

The Chilean reform has typically been the point of departure for Latin American countries that have privatized their pension systems, although some countries have modified it substantially. In Argentina and Mexico, policymakers started out by closely studying the Chilean reforms. The initial drafts of the pension reform legislation closely replicated the Chilean laws, but policymakers in both countries subsequently introduced changes in order to adapt it to their own countries and correct what they perceived to be weaknesses of the Chilean scheme. Although policymakers in Argentina and Mexico emphasize the innovative aspects of their reforms, they also acknowledge their debt to the Chilean model. Bolivian President Gonzalo

Sánchez de Lozada similarly acknowledged that the Bolivian pension reform "is something that we have received and copied from Chile," although he noted, "Obviously, we have made changes, taking advantage of the Chilean experience" ("Goni: Ley de pensiones" 1996: 9). In Colombia, the government also modified the Chilean reform in important ways. The original Colombian reform proposal, however, was so close to the Chilean model that one World Bank adviser joked that they had taken the Chilean reform legislation and used the search and replace function on a computer to substitute the word "Chile" with "Colombia" (interview with von Gersdorff 1998).

Chilean pension experts have also promoted pension privatization outside of Latin America and countries in other regions have studied the Chilean reform. The Chilean model has been less influential outside of Latin America, however, because countries outside the region have not shared the cultural and institutional ties that bind Latin American countries to Chile. The media outside of Latin America tend not to pay much attention to Chile, and economic and cultural links are relatively limited. Policymakers outside of Latin America have had only infrequent contact with Chilean policymakers because they do not belong to the regional institutions that regularly bring Latin American policymakers in contact with each other. Although Chilean pension experts have consulted on proposed reforms in Eastern Europe and other regions, they have done so on a much lesser scale than they have done in Latin America. Furthermore, much of the literature on the Chilean reform is in Spanish, which limits its accessibility to policymakers outside of the region. As a result, outside of Latin America, policymakers and the public as a whole have tended to be less familiar with the Chilean pension reform and the Chilean model in general.

Policymakers outside of Latin America have also been less apt to view Chile as a model for their own countries. Outside of Latin America, the Chilean success story seems less spectacular—indeed, numerous East Asian countries have enjoyed higher growth and savings rates than Chile over the past several decades. Chile's small size and, by first-world standards, undeveloped economy have also limited its relevance as a policy model for many countries. As one Chilean pension expert put it: "It's easier for Peru and Argentina to accept the reform of a relatively small and poor country like Chile. . . . It has little relevance for Germany, France, the United States, etc. that a reform has been successful in a poor and small country like Chile—a country that is better known for its tremendous financial and political swings. Perhaps if [Chile] had been a more stable or bigger country there would have been more credibility" (interview with Schmidt-Hebbel 1997). Policymakers in regions outside of Latin America have been more inclined to look toward their own neighbors or the advanced industrialized countries for models of policy reforms. In Eastern Europe, for example, opponents of pension privatization urged policymakers to stick with a European model of social security, rather than a foreign, Latin American model (Palacios and Rocha 1998; Inglot 1995; Müller 1999).

Chile is no longer the sole focal point for diffusion of pension privatization, however. The spread of pension privatization schemes throughout Latin America and much of the postcommunist world means countries now have a large number of variations on the Chilean model to consider. Analyses of the merits of pension privatization continue to focus in large part on the Chilean model, however, because Chile is the only country to have a relatively lengthy experience with pension privatization. Nevertheless, over time the Chilean model will probably decline in relevance as data begin to accumulate about the effects of pension privatization schemes in other countries.

The Role of the World Bank

The World Bank has also played an important role in persuading policymakers of the merits of pension privatization. The most significant contribution of the World Bank was to create an ideational climate that was propitious for pension privatization. Through its publications, seminars, and consulting missions, the World Bank has exposed the problems of the existing state-run pension systems and highlighted the benefits of pension privatization. The World Bank has also provided loans that have reduced some of the financial obstacles to pension privatization, but these loans have covered only a tiny portion of the transition costs of the reforms. Thus, the World Bank has not provided significant financial incentives for countries to privatize their pension systems.

The World Bank has been particularly influential in those countries where it has carried out pension reform missions. The pension reform missions enabled World Bank representatives to maintain extended contacts with host country social security policymakers, to carry out sophisticated analyses of the problems facing the country's public pension system, and to formulate detailed privatization proposals. The technical assistance provided by the World Bank has also given domestic advocates of pension privatization the upper hand in their struggles with opponents of privatization.

The World Bank carried out pension reform missions in both Argentina and Mexico during the late 1980s and early 1990s, which gave impetus to the pension privatization efforts in these countries. The pension reform missions financed preliminary studies of the problems facing the public pension system in both countries that ultimately led to the formulation of pension privatization proposals. World Bank officials in both countries also used their formal and informal contacts with policymakers in the two countries to encourage them to privatize their pension systems. Finally, the World Bank provided some financing to ease the implementation costs of the reforms in both countries, although the World Bank financing represented only a small portion of the overall transition costs.

The World Bank has also promoted pension privatization elsewhere in Latin America. Indeed, the World Bank has provided technical assistance and financing for all of the pension privatization schemes that have been implemented in Latin America to date, except for the Chilean reform, which was undertaken before the World Bank had embraced pension privatization (interviews with Schwarz 1998, with Palacios 1998, and with Vittas 1998). In El Salvador, the World Bank financed a study by a Chilean consulting firm, which recommended the gradual privatization of the Salvadoran pension system. This plan was eventually implemented, although somewhat more quickly than the World Bank-financed proposal had envisioned (Mesa-Lago and Müller 2002). At the invitation of the Salvadoran government, the International Finance Corporation of the World Bank also commented on the draft legislation and regulations and invested $1 million in one of the private pension fund administrators (Conger 1998).

The World Bank also helped plan the Bolivian pension privatization scheme (interview with von Gersdorff 1998). During the early 1990s, the World Bank, along with the U.S. Agency for International Development helped finance a pension reform team that identified the problems of the existing pension system and formulated a pension privatization plan (interview with Iglesias 1996; Müller 2002: 48–49). Then in 1995, the International Development Agency of the World Bank provided a $9 million credit to the Bolivian government to help carry out the pension reform as well as a reform of the financial markets. The loan provided technical assistance to help establish the regulatory structure for the private pension system, to create a new Superintendency of Pensions that would supervise the system, and to restructure the existing public pension systems (World Bank 1995c). A detailed study of the pension reform process in Bolivia concluded that international organizations led by the World Bank "play[ed] an important role in the [pension privatization] process" in that country (Gray-Molina, Pérez de Rada, and Yañez 1999: 41).

The World Bank has provided some Latin American countries with financing and technical assistance for parametric reforms, but it has shown a decided preference for privatization. Not all countries have chosen to heed the advice of the World Bank, however. A World Bank pension reform mission in Brazil recommended that the Brazilian government carry out a combination of parametric reforms and partial privatization (World Bank 1995a). Brazilian policymakers sought to carry out the parametric reforms that the World Bank recommended, but eschewed pension privatization.

Other countries have opted to carry out less sweeping pension privatization plans than the World Bank advocated. The World Bank clashed with policymakers in Uruguay and Venezuela over their relatively modest pension privatization plans and ultimately withdrew its support for the reforms (interviews with Palacios 1998 and with Márquez 1998). The Uruguayan government, however, persisted with its own privatization plans, and the World Bank, along with the Inter-American Development Bank, ultimately financed some of the transition costs of the reform.

The World Bank played an important role in placing pension privatization on the agenda in Costa Rica, but here too its specific privatization proposal was ultimately rejected. During the mid-1990s, the World Bank carried out an extensive study of the public pension system in Costa Rica and recommended radical privatization. A World Bank report on the Costa Rican pension system argued that limited reform "simply delays problems rather than really solving them once and for all" (Demirgüç-Kunt and Schwarz 1995: 29). Although the report's authors acknowledged that radical privatization might be more costly than limited reform, they maintained that its benefits were higher as well. Specifically, they claimed that the radical reform would reduce evasion, produce higher returns, and "generate savings for the economy" (Demirgüç-Kunt and Schwarz 1995: 29). The World Bank's proposal was ultimately discarded in favor of a more modest privatization scheme, however.

The World Bank has also participated actively in pension privatization efforts in Eastern Europe and the former Soviet Union. The bank has provided financing and technical assistance to facilitate pension privatization efforts in Hungary, Poland, Kazakhstan, Latvia, and Croatia, for example.[8] The World Bank did not become directly involved in the reform in Kazakhstan until after the decision to privatize the system had been made (Orenstein 1999; interview with Andrews 1998).[9] Nevertheless, the World Bank helped shape the ideational climate in Kazakhstan. The reform's principal architect, Grigori Marchenko, read *Averting the Old Age Crisis* and attended World Bank conferences on pension reform, both of which, he acknowledges, influenced his thinking about pension reform (Orenstein 1999: 24). During the later stages of the planning process, the World Bank became directly involved in the reform process, sending a technical assistance team to Kazakhstan that was successful in convincing the government to enact a number of modifications to the scheme. The World Bank also facilitated the Kazakh reform by lending the country $300 million to help implement the privatization plan (Orenstein 1999: 24).

In Poland, the World Bank assisted in the creation and funding of the Plenipotentiary for Social Security Reform, which planned and implemented the pension privatization scheme in that country (Nelson 2001; Müller 1999;

Orenstein 1999). The Director of the Plenipotentiary, moreover, was a Polish economist on leave from his position at the World Bank (Golinowska 1999). After the enactment of the reform, the World Bank, along with the United States Agency for International Development, sponsored trips to Latin America and elsewhere so that Polish government officials, parliamentary deputies, journalists, and trade unionists could learn more about privatized pension systems (Müller 1999; Orenstein 1999).

The World Bank played an equally important role in the Hungarian reform. World Bank officials had discussed pension privatization with Hungarian policymakers as early as 1992, but it did not begin to actively promote pension privatization in Hungary until the mid-1990s (Ferge 1999). In 1995, the World Bank published a study that detailed the main problems of the existing Hungarian pension system and proposed partial privatization (Palacios and Roche 1998; Ferge 1999; Müller 1999). That same year, the World Bank began to fund the working group of the Hungarian Ministry of Finance that was developing a privatization proposal (Ferge 1999; Müller 1999; Orenstein 1999). The World Bank's financial and technical assistance helped strengthen the Ministry of Finance in negotiations with other governmental and societal actors, although the World Bank tried to maintain a relatively low profile (Orenstein 1999; Ferge 1999). Subsequently, the World Bank became heavily involved in funding and participating directly in an interministerial working group on pension reform that worked out differences within the government with regard to the reform (Nelson 2001; Ferge 1999; Orenstein 1999; Müller 1999). The World Bank also brought in international pension experts from a variety of countries to serve as consultants on the reform and helped finance the transition costs of the reform after the privatization plan was implemented (Holzmann 2000).

The World Bank also contributed to the enactment of recent privatization schemes in Bulgaria and Croatia. The Bank sponsored a 1995 conference that brought pension experts from Chile and elsewhere to Croatia and led the incoming prime minister to endorse partial pension privatization (Müller 2002: 85). The World Bank also provided technical assistance to the Croatian government and helped finance the transition costs of the reform. As in Poland, a World Bank employee, Zoran Anušic, headed the Croatian government's reform team (Müller 2002: 91). The World Bank also helped persuade the Bulgarian government to privatize partially its pension system instead of limiting itself to parametric reforms of its existing public pension system (Müller 2002: 96–101).

Other international financial institutions have played a much less important role in pension privatization. The International Monetary Fund (IMF) has made some credits contingent on the implementation of pension privatization schemes, but it has not aggressively promoted pension privatization. Indeed, the IMF was initially skeptical about the merits of pension privatization in part because of its concern with the high transition costs. The Inter-American Development Bank (IADB) has facilitated pension privatization in a number of Latin American countries by providing technical and financial assistance, but it has not been involved in nearly as many countries as the World Bank. Nor has the IADB promoted pension privatization as vigorously as its larger counterpart. Other regional development banks, such as the Asian Development Bank, have played only a minor role in promoting pension privatization.

The Rise of the Economists

The rise of liberal economists to the top social security policy-making positions in many countries has also hastened the privatization of pension systems. In the 1980s and 1990s, liberal economists seized control of the finance ministries in many countries in Latin America, Eastern Europe, and elsewhere. The liberal economists often sought to promote pension privatization from their base within the economics ministries, but these efforts frequently ran into opposition from the lawyers and other social welfare specialists who traditionally controlled the key social security policy-making institutions. As a result, supporters of pension privatization in the Ministry of Finance and elsewhere frequently tried to have their like-minded colleagues appointed to the main social security policy-making posts as well. Where they succeeded, pension privatization proposals typically prospered. Where the traditional social security experts retained control of the social security institutions, however, they often managed to stall or defeat efforts to privatize the pension systems.

A variety of factors have determined whether liberal economists have managed to gain control of the main social security policy-making posts. Certainly, the political clout wielded by the finance ministers has mattered a great deal, but so have other factors, such as the personal and political ties of the existing social security officials as well as the composition of the governing party or coalition. For our purposes, the key point is that the rise of liberal economists to the top social security policy-making positions is not purely an endogenous phenomenon. Presidents did not simply appoint the market-oriented economists to the key social security policy-making positions because they wanted them to privatize the pension systems. In some cases, presidents were initially quite skeptical of pension privatization and needed to be persuaded of its benefits. In other cases, presidents did not appear to have any clear views on pension privatization before the economists began to promote it as the solution to a number of social and economic problems. The liberal economists that came to occupy key social security policy-making positions in many countries have thus been able to shape policy as well as implement it.

Market-oriented economists gradually took control of most of the key social security policy-making posts in both Argentina and Mexico during the 1990s. These economists by and large favored pension privatization and used their newfound influence to lobby in favor of it. In both Argentina and Mexico, the economists ultimately managed to gain approval for their pension privatization schemes in spite of the opposition of the traditional social security experts who were marginalized from the key decision-making posts. In Brazil, by contrast, the traditional social security experts have continued to control key pension policy-making posts within the Ministry for Social Insurance and have used their influence to resist efforts to privatize the Brazilian pension system.

Elsewhere in Latin America pension privatization has also prospered where neoliberal economists have been able to displace the traditional social security specialists from the key pension policy-making positions. In Chile, economists within the National Planning Office (ODEPLAN) began to advocate pension privatization shortly after the Pinochet regime came to power in 1973 (Borzutzky 1983; Piñera 1991). Social security experts and their allies in the Ministry of Labor and the Superintendency of Social Security successfully resisted these plans at the outset. Market-oriented economists, however, gradually took over the key social security policy-making posts in the Ministry of Labor and marginalized the Superintendency from the social security policy-making process. In 1978, José Piñera, a Harvard-trained economist, was appointed minister of labor and quickly assembled a team of liberal economists, which formulated and pushed through a sweeping pension privatization plan (interview with Piñera 1997).

In Bolivia, the Ministry of Finance began to promote pension privatization during the administration of Jaime Paz Zamora. The minister of labor, as well as the minister of health who was officially responsible for the pension system, vigorously opposed pension privatization, however, and they managed to prevent it from advancing during the Paz Zamora administration (Gray-Molina, Pérez de Rada, and Yañez 1999; Pérez 2000). When Gonzalo Sánchez de Lozada was elected president in 1993, however, he shifted responsibility for pension policy to a new National Secretariat of Pensions, which was located in the Ministry of Capitalization, the government ministry in charge of the privatization of state-owned companies. The Sánchez de Lozada administration appointed an economist, Marcelo Mercado, who was known to support pension privatization, as the head of a new National

Secretariat of Pensions (Gray-Molina, Pérez de Rada, and Yañez 1999). The bureaucratic reorganization helped reduce resistance to the privatization of the pension system by reducing the social security policy-making influence of the traditional social security specialists. As a result, the Sánchez de Lozada administration finally managed to push through the pension privatization plan in late 1996.

In Colombia, liberal economists within the Ministry of Finance, the National Planning Agency, and the Central Bank also promoted pension privatization (Hommes 1995; Santos 1997; Nelson 1998; González Rossetti and Ramírez 2000). The director of the Social Security Institute, Cecilia López, opposed the pension privatization plan, but in mid-1992, she resigned and was replaced by Fanny Santamaría, a top official from the Ministry of Finance (Nelson 1998: 4; González Rossetti and Ramírez 2000: 38). At the same time, Luis Fernando Ramírez, a former deputy minister in the Ministry of Finance, was appointed as head of the Ministry of Labor. Both Santamaría and Ramírez became important proponents of pension privatization; with their assistance, advocates of pension privatization managed to see the proposal enacted.

In Peru, the main push for pension privatization came from the minister of economy, Carlos Boloña. Boloña and a small team of economists pushed through a pension privatization plan in spite of the efforts of the minister of labor to slow down the reform (Roggero 1997; Arce 2001). President Alberto Fujimori was initially skeptical of the pension privatization plan, but his doubts were overcome by the proponents of pension privatization within the Ministry of the Economy and the Chilean pension experts. The head of the Peruvian Social Security Institute, Luis Castañeda Lossio, also initially opposed the Peruvian pension privatization plan, although he subsequently reversed his position (Ortiz de Zevallos et al. 1999: 38). In the wake of the reform, control of the public social security system was shifted from the Peruvian Social Security Institute, which was traditionally under the control of the Ministry of Labor, to the new Office for Pensions Normalization, which came under the jurisdiction of the Ministry of Finance (Müller 2002: 41).

In the former Soviet bloc, neoliberal economists located in the ministries of finance have also pushed pension privatization against the objections of the traditional social security experts (Nelson 2001; Müller 1999). This was the case in Hungary, Poland, Croatia, and, to a lesser extent, Kazakhstan. Surprisingly, however, in Bulgaria, the minister of labor, who was a former vice president of the postcommunist trade union, took the lead role in promoting pension privatization (Müller 2002: 97). In the Czech Republic, the Ministry of Finance did not actively promote pension privatization, and the Ministry of Labor and Social Affairs, which was the principal ministry in charge of pension policy, opposed it (Müller 1999). This may explain in part why the Czech Republic eschewed privatization in favor of making minor adjustments to its public pension system.

In Hungary, the Ministry of Finance initially advocated broad privatization of the pension system (Ferge 1999; Müller 1999). Both the Pension Insurance Fund, which administered the public pension system, and the Ministry of Social Welfare vigorously opposed this proposal; they advocated instead parametric reforms of the existing pay-as-you-go system (Ferge 1999; Nelson 2001). In April 1996, the Ministry of Finance and the Ministry of Social Welfare managed to reach an agreement on a scaled-back version of the Ministry of Finance's earlier pension privatization proposal. The traditional social security experts and the governing board of the Pension Insurance Fund continued to oppose this partial pension privatization plan, but they could not prevent it from being implemented (Müller 1999; Ferge 1999).

In Poland, the Ministry of Finance also promoted pension privatization in spite of the objections of the Ministry of Labor and Social Policy (Nelson 2001; Orenstein 1999; Müller 1999; Golinowska 1999).[10] The minister of labor, Leszek Miller, initially succeeded in blocking the pension privatization plan, but in 1996, Andrzej Baczkowski, who was supportive of the privatization plans, replaced him as minister. Baczkowski jump-started the privatization plans, creating a single office, the Plenipotentiary for Social Security Reform, to oversee the privatization effort. The pension privatization plans were briefly put in jeopardy when Baczkowski died unexpectedly and was replaced by someone who was skeptical of the merits of pension privatization. Supporters of pension privatization, however, managed to transfer the Plenipotentiary out of the Ministry of Labor and attach it to the prime minister's office, which helped the reform to go forward (Nelson 2001; Orenstein 1998; Müller 1999).

In Kazakhstan, the head of the National Securities Commission was the most important advocate of pension privatization, but some members of the Ministry of Finance were also quite interested in pension privatization because they wanted to develop the country's capital markets (interview with Andrews 1998). The initial minister of labor opposed pension privatization, but he was replaced with an official from the Ministry of Finance who supported the privatization plan (interview with Andrews 1998). To facilitate the reform, the government also set up an interministerial commission on pension reform early in the reform process, and this commission helped prevent conflicts over the reform from erupting within the government (Orenstein 1999). Some officials from the social security institute did oppose the reform, but they could provide relatively little resistance to it owing to the authoritarian nature of the regime (Orenstein 1999; interview with Andrews 1998).

The case studies from both Latin America and the postcommunist world thus show how economists within the Ministry of Finance and other economics agencies typically favored pension privatization. Their efforts to promote pension privatization, however, met resistance from the lawyers and other social security specialists who have long dominated the key social security policy-making positions in many countries. The traditional social security specialists used the influence afforded them by these positions to campaign, often successfully, against pension privatization. The fate of social security privatization proposals has therefore often turned on whether the economists were able to seize control of the key pension policy-making positions from the traditional social security specialists.

Executive Control of the Legislature

Pension privatization proposals have often encountered resistance within the legislature even in those countries where the executive branch has been united in its support for privatizing the pension system. In order to enact social security legislation, the executive has typically needed to wield a good deal of control over the legislature, as the case studies of Argentina, Brazil, and Mexico show. The strength and discipline of the ruling party was very high in Mexico, moderately high in Argentina, and low in Brazil, and this shaped the ability of presidents in each of those countries to enact their proposed pension reforms.

The strength and discipline of the ruling party matter because pension privatization has proved to be highly controversial in most countries, which has frustrated efforts to enact reforms by consensus.[11] As a result, the ruling party has been obliged to depend largely on the votes of members of its own party. Where the ruling party has been relatively unified and has held a majority or near majority of the seats in the legislature, it has typically been able to enact pension privatization legislation. Presidents have had a much more difficult time gaining legislative approval for pension reforms in instances where the ruling party has held a small minority of seats in the legislature or where the ruling party has been split.

In Ecuador, President Sixto Durán Ballén's party, the Partido Unidad Republicano, held only a few seats in the Chamber of Deputies when he proposed a constitutional reform that would have allowed him to privatize the pension system. Durán Ballén attempted to stitch together a coalition of various parties in support of the proposed reforms, but, as in Brazil, this coalition proved difficult to achieve. Durán Ballén then submitted the proposed reforms to a national plebiscite where they were resoundingly defeated. Subsequently, the administrations of Presidents Germán Abdalá Bucaram and Gustavo Noboa tried to enact pension privatization legislation, but these initiatives also failed to prosper, owing in part to the presidents' weak control of the legislature. The Noboa administration did manage to enact a modest pension privatization bill at the end of 2001, but major pieces of this reform were subsequently ruled unconstitutional.

Pension privatization proposals should have fared better in Venezuela during the presidency of Carlos Andrés Pérez and in Paraguay during the presidency of Juan Carlos Wasmosy because the ruling party held a near majority of seats in the legislature during both of these administrations. In both cases, however, splits within the ruling party impeded the passage of the pension privatization bills. In Paraguay, the ruling Partido Colorado was badly split between supporters of Wasmosy and the allies of Luis María Argaña whose supporters had nearly left the party when Wasmosy was chosen as the party's presidential candidate. After Wasmosy was elected president, Argaña's faction of the Partido Colorado struck a deal with the two main opposition parties to exclude supporters of Wasmosy from the key leadership posts in the legislature. Argaña's faction of the Partido Colorado and the two opposition parties together controlled thirty-five of the forty-five seats in the Senate and sixty-four of the eighty seats in the Chamber of Deputies, and they used these majorities to block many of the Wasmosy administration's initiatives, including the proposed privatization of the pension system.

Internal conflicts also divided the ruling party, Acción Democrática, when the Pérez administration in Venezuela proposed a pension privatization plan. Venezuela had traditionally enjoyed extremely high levels of party discipline because national party leaders have strict control over access to the ballot, which they can use to reward compliant legislators and punish defectors (Crisp 1997; Coppedge 1994). As Crisp (1997: 172) points out, however, the "factors that promote party discipline among legislators do not apply to the president"; as a result, conflicts may emerge between the president and the party leadership that controls the votes of the representatives of the party in the legislature. This is what occurred during the Pérez administration. Pérez did not consult extensively with party leaders and failed to appoint many party members to ministerial positions in his administration. The neglect of party leaders eventually prompted a backlash by members of Pérez's party, which began to block his reform measures, including the pension privatization proposal, and ultimately impeached him (Corrales 2000).[12] Subsequently, the administration of President Rafael Caldera did manage to reach an agreement on a modest pension privatization plan through negotiations with a diverse group of political and social actors, but this plan was shelved once Hugo Chávez came to power.

The weak level of party discipline in Colombia similarly hindered the enactment of pension privatization in that country, although the president was finally able to gain approval of the reform. At the time of the reform, President César Gaviria's Liberal Party (PL) controlled 54 percent of the seats in the Colombian Chamber of Deputies and 56.9 percent of the seats in the Senate, but this was partly offset by its low level of party discipline. Colombia has traditionally had low levels of party discipline because the country's electoral laws grant party leaders relatively little control over the ballot and the political careers of party members (Archer and Shugart 1997; Mainwaring and Shugart 1997). In order to secure the support of many legislators from his own party, the Gaviria administration was obliged to carry out extended negotiations and make substantial concessions to critics of the reform.

The Gaviria administration first proposed the privatization of the pension system in 1990, but this proposal ran into substantial opposition in the legislature, including among members of Gaviria's own party (Hommes 1995). The government decided to withdraw this initial proposal, but in September 1992, the Gaviria administration submitted another proposal to the Colombian legislature that called for the full privatization of the pension system along the lines of the Chilean model. The new proposal also met substantial opposition in the legislature, however, and in December 1992 it, too, was withdrawn. The following year it was resubmitted with a number of changes, including the creation of a solidarity tax to aid low-income workers and reductions in proposed increases of the minimum retirement age and the number of years of contributions workers needed to qualify for a pension (Mesa-Lago 1994: 148). The revised proposal also encountered problems in the legislature, and it was only enacted in December 1993 after undergoing major changes. The most important modification was the stipulation that the existing public pension system would remain open and would compete with the new private system for members.

The presidents of Nicaragua, El Salvador, and Bolivia, in contrast, had a relatively high degree of control over their legislatures when they proposed pension privatization bills. The ruling parties in Nicaragua, El Salvador, and Bolivia all held just under a majority of the seats in the legislature and had a relatively high degree of party discipline. Party discipline in Nicaragua, El Salvador, and Bolivia was high in part because electoral laws granted party leaders in these countries control over access to the ballot (Mainwaring and Shugart 1997). In each of these countries, the presidents were able to pass sweeping pension privatization bills by gaining the support of all or nearly all of the legislators from their own parties and picking up a few votes from members of allied parties.

In Nicaragua, the Alianza Liberal of President Arnoldo Alemán, controlled approximately 45 percent of the seats in Nicaragua's National Assembly at the time of the reform. The main opposition party, the Frente Sandinista de Liberación Nacional (FSLN), opposed the reform as did some legislators from smaller parties, but the Alianza Liberal was able to pass the reform bill with the votes of its own legislators and a handful of votes from members of small allied parties. No members of the FSLN voted in favor of the reform, but a few members of this party did help provide the ruling party with a quorum, which prompted accusations that the FSLN had struck a deal with the ruling party to allow passage of the reform (Barberena 2000b).

In El Salvador, President Armando Calderón Sol's party, the Alianza Republicana Nacionalista (ARENA), controlled 46 percent of the seats in El Salvador's unicameral legislature, but it too was able to count on support from a small allied party, the conservative Partido de Conciliación Nacional (PCN). The reform bill was first submitted to the legislature in September 1996, but it soon bogged down in the committee, which was equally divided between supporters and opponents of the reform. In order to break a deadlock on the committee evaluating the pension reform bill, in December 1996 the ruling party expelled a committee member from the Movimiento de Unidad (MU) who had opposed the reform (Mesa-Lago 1999). This gave supporters of the reform a majority of the votes in the committee, and they immediately moved the reform legislation to the plenary where it was approved by a voice vote ("Pensions Privatization" 1997: 44).

In Bolivia President Sánchez de Lozada's party, the Movimiento Nacionalista Revolucionario (MNR), controlled approximately 63 percent of the seats in the Senate, but only 40 percent of the seats in the Chamber of Deputies at the time of the reform. The MNR, however, had formed an alliance with two smaller parties, the Unión Cívica Solidaridad (UCS) and Movimiento Boliviano Libre (MBL), which provided it with a large working majority in the Chamber of Deputies as well as in the Senate. This large majority proved to be crucial when the government finally submitted its pension privatization bill to the legislature in mid-1996 after several years of delay. The main opposition parties, Acción Democrática Nacionalista (ADN), Movimiento de la Izquierda Revolucionaria (MIR), and Conciencia de Patria (CONDEPA), vigorously resisted the pension privatization plan, and one of the parties in the governing coalition, the MBL, also denounced the reform, but to little avail. With the votes of the members of his own party and the UCS, Sánchez de Lozada managed to obtain the rapid passage of the bill in both chambers of the legislature.

At first glance, the president's control of the legislature appears to have been less important in Chile and Peru since these countries' pension systems were privatized by executive decree when those countries were under authoritarian rule. Nevertheless, in both cases the executive's control of the legislature (or main law-making institution) facilitated the implementation of the reform. In Chile, the military junta, which served as the de facto legislature in the wake of the 1973 coup, initially resisted proposals to privatize the pension system (Borzutzky 1983). The most important opposition came from Air Force General Gustavo Leigh, who was a powerful member of the military junta. As one advocate of pension privatization later recounted:

The first presentation that we delivered on the area of social security . . . was probably in February or March 1974. And when it was argued that pension funds were going to be administered by the private sector, Leigh almost jumped over the desk. He contended that the proposal was crazy. . . . So Leigh said, "Well, we have to study this issue in depth" and this and that, and there was no bill, no nothing. (Castiglioni 2000: 16)

In 1978, however, General Augusto Pinochet consolidated his control of the junta by forcibly removing Leigh from the military junta. The following year government policymakers began work on the sweeping pension privatization proposal, which was sanctioned by the military junta in November 1980.

In Peru, President Alberto Fujimori's party, Cambio 90, initially held less than 18 percent of the seats in the legislature, which made the prospects for gaining legislative approval of pension privatization quite dim. Fujimori therefore opted to use his delegated decree powers to partially privatize the country's pension system in November 1991 (Ortiz de Zevallos et al. 1999). This measure was bitterly opposed by many legislators, who sought to overturn the decree and block the enactment of the enabling legislation in the legislature (Neves 1994). Before they could do this, however, Fujimori carried out a self-coup, suspending the constitution and closing down the legislature. The Fujimori regime then formulated a much more sweeping pension privatization plan, which would have closed down the existing public pension system and required all future entrants to the labor force to join the new private system. The Fujimori administration published this plan but declined to enact it for fear that it might hurt his party in the elections that were to be held in November 1992 to choose a new national assembly (Ortiz de Zevallos et al. 1999; Burgos 1992). Fujimori's political party won 55 percent of the seats in the legislature in these elections, which might have been sufficient to enact his proposed pension reform. Nevertheless, Fujimori opted to take no chances: in December 1992, shortly before the new legislature was seated, he issued a new decree privatizing the pension system. Fujimori's control of the legislature, however, was still important because it prevented the assembly from overturning his decree. The new legislature did pass a bill that sought to eliminate the retroactive portions of the pension reform, but Fujimori vetoed this legislation (Neves 1994).

The president's degree of control of the legislature proved to be less crucial to the enactment of pension privatization bills in Costa Rica and Uruguay. The Costa Rican and Uruguayan governments, unlike those of other

Latin American countries, managed to build a relatively high degree of consensus for their proposed pension reforms, which meant that it was not necessary for their presidents to dominate the legislature in order to enact the measures. This consensus-building process, however, resulted in reforms that were timid by regional standards.

Shortly after taking office in May 1998, Costa Rican President Miguel Angel Rodríguez established a Forum on Concertation that brought together a variety of social actors in an effort to achieve a broad consensus on pension reform as well as on other proposed reforms (*Proyecto de Ley* 1999). The government then sent its reform proposal to the pension commission that was established within this forum, which was made up of thirty representatives from diverse sectors of the Costa Rican population (Mesa-Lago and Müller 2002). In September 1998, this commission reached an agreement on a reform proposal that established a relatively small private pension system to complement the existing public pension system. Under the reform proposal, the new private pension system was to receive obligatory contributions equal to 4.25 percent of each worker's salary, which was redirected from other contributory social programs. The reform proposal earned support not only from President Rodríguez's party, the Partido Unidad Social Cristiano, which held a near majority of the seats in the legislature, but also from the main opposition party, the Partido de Liberación Nacional. The legislature made only minor changes to the reform bill before enacting it in December 1999 by a vote of forty-two to three (Herrera 1999).

Under the leadership of President Julio María Sanguinetti, the Uruguayan government also managed to obtain a relatively high degree of consensus in the legislature for its pension reform. Uruguay had attempted to reform its pension system on numerous occasions in the late 1980s and early 1990s, but these measures had run into political roadblocks. During the administration of President Luis Alberto Lacalle (1990–95) of the Partido Nacional, four reform efforts were defeated in the legislature, whereas one other measure was approved and then repealed in a plebiscite ("Entre las conductas" 1995). One of the main causes of these failures was the president's weakness in the legislature—the Partido Nacional held only 39 percent of the seats in the Chamber of Deputies, which meant that it needed the support of one of the other two principal parties in order to pass the reform.

Sanguinetti, who took office in 1995, faced a similar problem since his party, the Partido Colorado, held only 32 percent of the seats in the Chamber of Deputies and 35 percent of the Senate. In the wake of the 1994 election, however, Sanguinetti forged an alliance with the largest opposition party, the Partido Nacional, and passage of social security reform was set down as a precondition to the maintenance of the alliance. Even before taking office, the Sanguinetti administration commenced negotiations over the reform with a broad spectrum of political parties and social actors (Filgueira and Moraes 1999). The Sanguinetti administration was unable to reach an agreement with the main left-wing party, the Frente Amplio, but it did gain the support of the Partido Nacional as well as a small center-left party, Nuevo Espacio, which provided it with more than enough votes to pass the reform. The reform bill, which was passed only five months after Sanguinetti took office, received the votes of twenty-two out of thirty members present in the Senate and fifty-nine out of eighty-six members present in the Chamber of Deputies ("La reforma de la seguridad social" 1995: 10; "Senado votó" 1995: 7). The reform proposal suffered relatively few modifications in the legislature, but it was modest to begin with compared to the reforms enacted elsewhere in Latin America. The reform required only high-income members of the population to participate in the private pension system—other workers could participate on a voluntary basis—and it exempted several privileged pension schemes from the reform altogether.

The executive's control of the legislature has proved to be an important factor in the enactment of pension reform in some of the postcommunist countries as well. In Bulgaria, Croatia, and Hungary, for example, the ruling party enjoyed a large majority in parliament, which facilitated the passage of the pension privatization bills. In Hungary, the ruling party was able to use its large parliamentary majority to push through the pension reform over the objections of the opposition parties. Prime Minister Gyula Horn's party, the Hungarian Socialist Party, held 54 percent of the seats in the National Assembly at the time of the reform. Moreover, it had formed an alliance with a liberal party, the Alliance of Free Democrats, which controlled another 18 percent of the seats. The government needed this majority because all of the major opposition parties, including the right-wing Young Democrats, voted against the reform (Ferge 1999). Parliament passed the reform rather quickly and made few significant changes to the reform bill, in part because major modifications had been implemented before the proposal reached parliament. The parliament had insisted that the main social actors involved come to an agreement on the reform before submitting it to parliament, and the labor unions, employers' associations, and the government had then hammered out an accord that involved significant concessions on all sides (Orenstein 1999; Müller 1999). In spite of this agreement and the large parliamentary majority held by the government, the reform was enacted by a relatively slim margin—only 55 to 58 percent of the members present voted in favor of the reform (Ferge 1999).

In authoritarian Kazakhstan, President Nursultan Nazarbaev wielded almost complete control over the parliament and this substantially facilitated pension reform in that country. Although most members of the Assembly and the Senate were formally independents, the vast majority of them were closely aligned with the government. Moreover, the 1995 constitution sub-stantially limited the powers of the parliament in any event (Olcott 1997). When Nazarbaev submitted his pension privatization plan to the parliament in May 1997, he labeled it "urgent." This meant that parliament had only one month to pass the law or risk being dissolved, in which case the reform would be implemented by decree (Orenstein 1999; interview with Andrews 1998). Members of parliament feared being punished by voters in the up-coming elections if they supported the reform, but the potential political consequences of voting against the reform were even more serious. Many members of parliament therefore chose to express their concerns about the reform or even their opposition to it, but in the end they voted over-whelmingly for it within the prescribed time period (Orenstein 1999: 27). The parliament did enact a few changes to the reform bill, including elimi-nating a proposed increase in the minimum retirement age, but most of these modifications were relatively minor (Orenstein 1999; interview with Andrews 1998).

The Polish government managed to achieve a higher degree of consen-sus behind its pension privatization than did Hungary or Kazakhstan, which meant that the executive's control of the legislature was less crucial, although not irrelevant, to the enactment of the Polish pension reform. The effort to reform the pension system in Poland dragged on for several years because of intragovernmental disputes, and as a result, the reform legislation had to be enacted by two separate governments. The initial government was an al-liance between two left-of-center groups dominated by former communists: the Democratic Left Alliance and the Polish Peasant Party. Together, these two groups held 66 percent of the seats in the lower chamber and 73 percent of the Senate at the time of the election. The coalition government did not need to use its legislative strength to push through the reform, however, be-cause the government had been able to build a broad consensus behind the reform by the time the initial legislation was submitted to parliament in mid-1997. The initial reform legislation received the support of 90 percent of the legislature's deputies—indeed, only a few right-wing deputies from the op-position Solidarity movement voted against the reform (Orenstein 1999).

The center-left government was unable to enact all of the necessary leg-islation before the elections that were held in September 1997, however. These elections resulted in a victory for the Solidarity Election Action, an electoral alliance of thirty-six centrist and right-wing parties, and therefore a change in government, which complicated the plans to implement the pension reform. Solidarity Election Action formed a governing coalition with another right-of-center party, the Freedom Union, and together these two blocs controlled 57 percent of the seats in the lower chamber of parlia-ment and 59 percent of the seats in the Senate. The government's strength in the legislature proved to be important because the parliamentary consensus that had been built up began to crumble. The new government embraced the central aims of the reform but insisted on making some changes to the remaining legislation, which antagonized the center-left parties, such as the Democratic Left Alliance, that had designed the original reform (Orenstein 1999). Although the center-left parties were reluctant to oppose directly the pension reform legislation, they did seek to slow it down in the parliament and enact modifications. Ultimately, the governing coalition had to rely on its own deputies to pass some of the final pension reform legislation, which became law in late 1998 (Orenstein 1999).

The political fate of pension privatization has thus hinged to a large extent on the executive's degree of control of the legislature. In most countries—Costa Rica and Poland being notable exceptions—opposition parties have bitterly opposed the pension privatization legislation, which has obliged the executive to rely on members of his own party to enact the reforms bills. Where the ruling party has controlled a large number of seats in the legislature and enjoyed high levels of party discipline, pension privatization proposals have advanced without undue difficulty. In countries where the ruling party has controlled only a minority of the seats or where party discipline has been weak, presidents have struggled, often unsuccessfully, to pass their pension privatization bills.

Quantitative Analyses of Pension Privatization

In order to test the arguments contained in this book, I carried out a series of quantitative analyses of the determinants of pension privatization worldwide. I limited the sample to middle- and upper-income countries with populations above one million partly because of the difficulty of finding reliable data for low-income countries and nations with tiny populations.[13] It also made little sense to include low-income countries in the analyses since many low-income countries lack the minimum requisites to privatize their pension systems. In order to privatize their pension systems, countries need some minimal level of financial infrastructure and expertise. A private pension system also requires a mass of formal-sector workers who earn sufficient income to make pension contributions that are large enough for the private pension funds to manage profitably. Many countries with low incomes and tiny populations lack these requirements. Indeed, some low-income countries do not even have public pension systems, which obviously precludes pension privatization.

The initial tests consisted of binomial probit analyses in which the dependent variable was coded as 1 if a country enacted legislation that partially or fully privatized its pension system between 1990 and 2000, and 0 if it did not.[14] The sample comprised a total of eighty-two countries, including seventeen nations that privatized their pension systems to some degree.[15] I excluded countries that privatized their pension systems in the 1980s from the sample on the grounds that they were unlikely to enact a privatization scheme in the 1990s since their systems had already been, at least, partially privatized. I also excluded from the analyses countries that enacted add-on schemes on the grounds that these schemes, which constitute a form of welfare state expansion, are governed by a different political and economic logic than that of pension privatization. Inclusion of the countries that privatized their pension systems in the 1980s or enacted add-on schemes during any period does not significantly change the results, however.

The following independent variables were used in the initial probit analysis of the determinants of pension privatization worldwide:

Public pension spending: The economic burden of public pension spending was measured by public pension expenditures as a percent of gross domestic product. These data were taken from Palacios and Pallarès-Miralles (2000) and the World Bank (1994b) and represent various years in the 1990s. Figures for a few of the countries represent estimates based on regional averages.

Domestic savings rate: The sufficiency of local capital sources was measured by the average domestic savings rate between 1990 and 1998. These data were culled from the World Bank (2000). In order to minimize problems of endogeneity, only the years before a nation privatized its pension system were included for those countries that enacted pension privatization schemes.

Ruling party's share of seats: The executive's degree of control of the legislature was measured as the average percentage of seats held by the ruling party in the lower chamber during the 1990s. Data are from Europa Publications (various years).

World Bank missions: World Bank influence over pension policy was measured by whether a country had hosted a World Bank pension reform mission. This variable was coded as 1 if the country in question hosted a World Bank pension reform mission during the 1990s and 0 if it did not. Data are from Schwarz and Demirgüç-Kunt (1999).

Latin American country: A dummy variable was also included for Latin American countries on the grounds that these countries were particularly likely to privatize their pension systems because of regional diffusion of the Chilean model. This variable was coded as 1 if a country was in Latin America and 0 if it was not.

Unfortunately, the absence of worldwide data on party discipline precluded the inclusion of this variable in the analysis. Nor do the analyses

TABLE 6.3
The Determinants of Pension Privatization Around the World
(probit analyses)

	Model 1	Model 2	Model 3	Model 4	Model 5
Constant	-7.749**	-7.550**	-3.015**	-7.715**	-8.230**
	(-3.154)	(-2.972)	(-2.416)	(-3.038)	(-3.030)
Public pension spending	0.423**	0.481**	0.243**	0.482**	0.504**
(as a percent of GDP)	(3.030)	(3.109)	(3.248)	(3.159)	(3.048)
Gross domestic savings	-0.036	-0.102*	-0.079*	-0.101*	-0.099*
(as a percent of GDP)	(-1.448)	(-2.241)	(-2.271)	(-2.184)	(-2.160)
Ruling party's share of seats in the	0.045*	0.053**	0.030*	0.055**	0.059**
legislature	(2.454)	(2.622)	(2.152)	(2.661)	(2.682)
Latin America	3.359**	3.600**	2.600**	3.774**	3.620**
	(3.213)	(3.254)	(3.580)	(3.237)	(3.236)
World Bank pension reform mission	2.621**	3.006**		2.700**	2.894**
	(2.932)	(2.973)		(2.433)	(2.734)
World Bank loans/GDP			2.241		
			(0.408)		
Economic recession				0.383	
				(0.549)	
Hyperinflation					0.890
					(1.394)
Number of observations	82	81	81	81	79
Percent correctly predicted	91.5	96.3	84.0	95.1	93.7
Log likelihood (initial)	-18.061	-15.453	-24.516	-15.303	-14.319
Log likelihood (at convergence)	-56.838	-56.145	-56.145	-56.145	-54.759

* <.05; ** <.01 (two-tailed t-tests).
t-statistics in parentheses.

test for the effect of the presence of economists in the key social security policy-making positions because of the absence of comprehensive cross-national data on this topic.

The first column of Table 6.3, labeled Model 1, displays the results of the initial probit analysis. As is evident from the table, the variables in the initial analysis all had the expected signs and most of them were statistically significant at the 0.05 level or better. The model correctly predicts 91.5 percent of the cases, including 13 of the 17 cases of privatization and 62 out of the 65 cases of nonprivatization. The mistaken predictions included Albania, Panama, and Honduras, which were predicted to have more than a 50 percent probability of privatizing their pension systems but did not do so. Bulgaria, Latvia, Macedonia, and Sweden, meanwhile, were all predicted to have less than a 50 percent chance of privatizing their pension systems, but each of these nations did, in fact, enact a modest pension privatization scheme.

The coefficient of public pension expenditures had a positive sign as expected and was statistically significant at the 0.01 level. This indicates that the likelihood that a nation will privatize its pension system increases as its public pension spending rises. The substantive effect of this variable is powerful. The probability that a nation will privatize its pension system is less than 2 percent if all variables are held at their means. However, a one standard deviation increase in public pension expenditures from 5.1 percent of GDP to 9.5 percent of GDP (holding all other variables at their means) boosts the probability that a nation will privatize its pension system from less than 2 percent to 39 percent.

The variable that measures the ruling party's share of seats in the legislature was also positive and statistically significant at the 0.05 level. This suggests that, as predicted, the probability of pension privatization rises as the ruling party's control of the legislature increases. The substantive effect of changes in the ruling party's degree of control of the legislature is not as powerful as changes in public pension expenditures, but it nevertheless makes an important contribution to explaining variation in pension privatization. If we increase the ruling party's share of the seats in the legislature by one standard deviation from its mean (from 49 percent to 71 percent) and hold all other variables at their means, the probability that a nation will privatize its pension system rises from less than 2 percent to 12 percent.

The ideational variables also performed as expected. The regional dummy variable for Latin America was positive and statistically significant at the 0.01 level, indicating that, other things being equal, Latin American nations are more likely to privatize their pension systems. The previous chapters have argued that the Latin American bias toward pension privatization is largely a result of regional diffusion of the Chilean model, but other factors that are unaccounted for in this analysis might also lead Latin American nations to have a tendency to privatize their pension systems. The Latin America dummy variable had a strong substantive effect on the likelihood of pension privatization. If we increase this variable by one standard deviation from its mean (and hold all other variables at their means), the probability that a nation will privatize its pension system rises from less than 2 to 21 percent. Other things being equal, Latin American nations have a 69 percent probability of privatizing their pension systems.

The World Bank pension reform mission variable also had a positive sign, and its coefficient was statistically significant at the 0.01 level. Its substantive effect was also relatively large. Ceteris paribus, nations that host World Bank pension reform missions have an approximately 20 percent likelihood of privatizing their pension systems, as opposed to a minimal likelihood for those countries that do not host pension reform missions. The objection might be made that the correlation between World Bank missions and pension privatization is endogenous—that is, governments request World Bank pension reform missions because they intend to privatize their pension systems. The case studies, however, suggest that governments request World Bank pension missions because they are interested in carrying out some type of pension reform, not because they are necessarily committed to privatizing their pension systems. Indeed, in many instances, countries hosting World Bank pension reform missions have declined to privatize their systems, opting for parametric reforms or no reforms at all. In other instances, World Bank pension reform specialists have been able to convince the governments to privatize their pension systems in spite of their initial reluctance. The likelihood that the World Bank will be able to persuade governments to privatize their pension system increases when a country hosts a pension reform mission because World Bank pension reform specialists obtain increased access to local policymakers, which they can use to promote pension privatization. Moreover, pension reform missions also enable World Bank pension specialists to carry out detailed analyses of the problems afflicting the public pension systems, which they can use to trumpet the benefits of privatization.

The one variable that did not perform as well as expected was the domestic savings rate variable. The coefficient of this variable had a negative sign as predicted, but it was not statistically significant at conventional levels. The lack of statistical significance of this variable, however, is due to a single outlier—Albania—and there are strong theoretical reasons for excluding Albania from the analysis. Albania suffered from a great deal of political and economic instability during the 1990s, which made it difficult to privatize its pension system. This may explain why the country did not privatize its pension system even though it presumably had substantial economic incentives to do so, given its extraordinarily low domestic savings rate (-16.3 percent). As Model 2 of the table shows, if we exclude Albania from the analysis, the domestic savings rate variable achieves statistical significance at the 0.05 level. (Excluding Albania has only a minimal effect on the other variables.) The exclusion of the Albanian case also slightly improves the explanatory power of the model. Even with the exclusion of the Albanian case, the substantive effect of the domestic savings rate on the likelihood of pension privatization is modest. If we decrease the domestic savings rate by one standard deviation from its mean (from 21.4 percent to 12.4 percent) while holding all other variables at their means, the likelihood that a nation will privatize its pension system rises from less than 1 percent to 6 percent.

To test alternative explanations of pension privatization, the statistical model was reestimated with a number of additional variables. First, I included a variable that measured the value of World Bank loans to each country between 1990 and 1998 divided by that country's gross domestic product during this period. I included this variable in order to test whether the World Bank's influence was based on the financial inducements it could offer, rather than on the Bank's ability to persuade nations of the merits of pension privatization. The assumption was that if the World Bank had influence principally because of the financing it provided, the likelihood that a country would privatize its pension system would rise as the amount of World Bank loans increased. As Model 3 indicates, a statistical analysis provides little support for this alternative hypothesis. Although the World Bank loans variable had the expected sign, it did not approach statistical significance. Moreover, the explanatory power of the model declined significantly when this variable rather than the World Bank pension missions variable was included in the analysis.[16] This finding provides support for the argument that World Bank influence is more ideational than material in nature.

Second, I included additional variables to see whether economic crisis had a statistically significant effect on the likelihood of pension privatization. A country was coded as having suffered an economic crisis if it experienced hyperinflation (measured as an annual inflation rate of more than 100 percent) or a serious economic recession (measured as a downturn of more than 5 percent in GDP in a single year) at any point between 1980 and 1998. Additional tests examined whether pension privatization was correlated with the average inflation rate or the average growth in GDP between 1990 and 1998.[17] All of these variables, which were measured with World Bank (2000) data, had the expected sign, but none of them proved to be statistically significant at conventional levels. (Models 4 and 5 of the table present the results of two of the economic crisis dummy variables.) These findings suggest that economic crisis has, at best, a weak relationship with the likelihood of pension privatization. As noted earlier, however, economic crisis may affect the probability of pension privatization indirectly through its effect on some of the other variables that have been stressed in this study.

The model was also estimated with a variable measuring the level of authoritarianism, although the results are not presented here. Surprisingly, the level of authoritarianism, which was measured as average Freedom House scores on civil and political liberties between 1992 and 1998 (see Gastil various years), had a negative sign.[18] This suggests that authoritarian regimes are less likely than democratic regimes to privatize their pension systems. The coefficient of this variable was not statistically significant, however. Moreover, this result should be interpreted with caution because the level of authoritarianism is highly positively correlated with the ruling party's share of seats in the legislature (r = .55) and highly negatively correlated with public pension expenditures (r = .52).

The analysis also tested the effect of labor strength on the likelihood of pension privatization. Labor strength was measured by the percentage of the nonagricultural workforce represented by unions based on data from the ILO (1997). This variable had a positive and statistically significant coefficient, which suggests, surprisingly, that countries with high unionization rates may be more likely to privatize their pension systems than countries with weak unions. This finding should be viewed with caution, however, given the poor quality of data on unionization rates in many developing countries and the fact that the analysis is based on a reduced sample of countries.[19] Moreover, the unionization rate variable was highly correlated with public pension expenditures (r = .42), which makes it difficult to assess its effects accurately.

Many of the variables that help determine whether a country privatizes its pension system would also presumably influence the degree of privatization. I would expect countries with low domestic savings rates, for example, to be more likely to enact sweeping pension privatization schemes in order to maximize the potential effects of the reform on domestic savings. I would also expect Latin American nations, meanwhile, to be more likely to follow the Chilean model more closely than countries in other regions. Finally, I would expect presidents that dominate their legislatures to be in a better position to enact full-scale pension privatization schemes than presidents that have only weak support in the legislature. However, one would not expect countries with high public pension expenditures to be more likely to adopt sweeping pension privatization measures because of the high costs of such schemes for countries with large public pension obligations. Nor would we necessarily expect that the existence of a World Bank mission would lead to full-scale rather than partial privatization, given the World Bank's endorsement of partial privatization.

TABLE 6.4

The Determinants of Pension Privatization Around the World

(OLS regression analyses)

	Model 1	Model 2
Constant	−0.077	−0.0319
	(−0.745)	(−0.307)
Public pension spending (as a percent of GDP)	0.0073	0.0068
	(1.245)	(1.174)
Gross domestic savings (as a percent of GDP)	−0.0051★	−0.0074★★
	(−2.150)	(−2.845)
Ruling party's share of seats in the legislature	0.0027★	0.0030★★
	(2.384)	(2.629)
Latin America	0.255★★	0.234★★
	(3.958)	(3.644)
World Bank pension reform mission	0.119★	0.127★★
	(2.486)	(2.685)
Number of observations	82	81
Adjusted r-squared	0.329	0.361

★<.05; ★★<.01 (two-tailed t-tests).
t-statistics in parentheses.

In order to test these hypotheses, a series of Ordinary Least Squares regression analyses were carried out using the index of pension privatization presented in Chapter 1 as the dependent variable. Countries were assigned scores on this index ranging from 0 (no privatization) to 1 (full privatization) following the methodology described in Chapter 1. The independent variables remained identical to those used in the earlier probit analyses.

The results of the analyses, which are presented in Table 6.4, suggest that some of the aforementioned variables do influence the degree as well as the likelihood of pension privatization. Indeed, a couple of the variables performed substantially better in the OLS regression analyses than they did in the probit analyses. As Model 1 of Table 6.4 indicates, the coefficient of domestic savings rate had the expected sign and achieved statistical significance even with the inclusion of the Albanian case. Moreover, the domestic savings variable reached a high level of statistical significance when Albania was excluded from the sample, as Model 2 shows. This suggests that the countries with low domestic savings rates are not only more likely to privatize their pension systems than countries with high domestic savings rates, but they also tend to carry out more sweeping pension privatization schemes. According to Model 2, a one standard deviation (9 percent) decrease in the domestic savings rate leads to a 6.7 percent increase in the degree of privatization. The Latin American dummy variable also achieved a higher level of statistical significance in the OLS regression analyses than in the probit analyses, which indicates that Latin American countries also tend to carry out more sweeping pension privatization schemes than non-Latin American countries. Surprisingly, the variable measuring the ruling party's share of seats did not perform any better in the OLS regression analyses than in the probit analyses. Thus, it is not clear that presidents whose political party dominates the legislature tend to implement more sweeping pension privatization schemes than presidents who have a weaker base of support in the legislature.

As expected, two of the other variables performed more poorly in the OLS regression analyses than in the probit analyses. The public pension expenditure variable fell below conventional levels of statistical significance, although it continued to have the expected sign. This result suggests that countries with high public pension expenditures tend to adopt more modest pension privatization schemes—an issue that will be explored in more depth in Chapter 7. The World Bank pension mission variable also declined somewhat in statistical significance in the OLS regression analyses, although it remained highly significant. This finding, too, is not entirely unexpected. As discussed earlier, the World Bank has provided support for partial as well as sweeping pension privatization schemes; it recently went on record as actually preferring partial privatization. Thus, it is not surprising that countries that host World Bank pension missions may tend to implement modest pension privatization schemes as frequently as, or more frequently than, sweeping schemes.

Conclusion

This chapter used qualitative as well as quantitative methods to test the arguments laid out in Chapter 2. Both approaches provided support for most of the hypotheses, and, in all instances, at least one of the approaches provided persuasive evidence to back the arguments. A considerable amount of qualitative and quantitative evidence exists to suggest that policymakers have privatized their pension systems in order to achieve certain macroeconomic goals. The case studies showed that policymakers in a variety of countries were seriously concerned about their low savings rates and burgeoning public pension expenditures and viewed pension privatization as an effective means to address these problems. The statistical analyses, meanwhile, found that countries with low domestic savings rates and high levels of public pension expenditures were more likely than other countries to privatize their pension systems. The quantitative analyses also found that countries with low savings rates tend to adopt more sweeping pension privatization schemes and that countries with high public pension expenditures often opt for parametric reforms of their public pension systems.

The macroeconomic benefits of pension privatization are still very much under debate, however. Chapter 2 argued that three factors—the emergence of the Chilean model and the rising influence of both the World Bank and market-oriented economists—have helped persuade numerous political leaders that pension privatization would bring substantial social and economic benefits in spite of the relatively meager empirical evidence to this effect. As the case studies showed, in many Latin American and postcommunist countries, economists have taken over the key policy-making positions within the social security and labor ministries and have used these positions to promote pension privatization. The World Bank, meanwhile, has provided funding and technical assistance to facilitate pension privatization efforts in many countries and has championed the benefits of pension privatization through its conferences, publications, and formal and informal contacts with policymakers in developing countries. The case studies also showed how the Chilean model influenced the views of policymakers, especially in other Latin American countries. Chilean pension experts promoted the Chilean model especially aggressively in Latin America, helping persuade many governments to base their own reforms on the Chilean scheme.

The quantitative analyses presented in this chapter provided support for some of the ideational claims in the study. The analyses found that, other things being equal, Latin American countries have been more likely to enact pension privatization schemes along the lines of the Chilean model. This study attributes this finding largely to the effect of regional diffusion, although other potential interpretations for this finding are also plausible. In addition, the quantitative analyses found that those countries that had hosted World Bank pension reform missions were statistically more likely to enact pension privatization schemes. No correlation was found between pension privatization and the amount of credit that individual countries received from the World Bank, however, which suggests that World Bank influence was more ideational than material.

The case studies presented here also showed that executives who have proposed pension privatization have often faced considerable opposition within their own parties, as well as overwhelming resistance from the political opposition. As a result, executives have typically needed to wield a high degree of control of the legislature in order to obtain passage of their pension privatization plans. The statistical analyses supported this observation, finding that the likelihood of pension privatization increased as the ruling party's share of seats in the legislature rose. Thus, political as well as economic and ideational factors shaped the likelihood of pension privatization in the 1990s.

CHAPTER 7

Institutions, Interest Groups,
and Pension Privatization

UNLIKE THE FACTORS discussed in the previous chapters, institutions and interest groups have not played a decisive role in determining whether countries have opted to privatize their pension systems. However, they have shaped how countries have chosen to privatize their pension systems. Pension privatization schemes have varied in myriad ways, differing not only in the extent to which the existing public pension system has been reformed or abandoned, but also in the rules governing the new private systems. It is not possible to understand fully what led countries to opt for a particular type of privatization scheme without taking into account the role played by these interest groups and institutions.

Institutions have shaped the pension privatization schemes by placing political and financial constraints on reform possibilities. Regime type, for example, has helped determine the degree of privatization that is politically feasible: authoritarian regimes have typically found it easier than democratic regimes to implement sweeping privatization schemes. The level of existing commitments of the public pension systems, meanwhile, has limited the degree of public pension privatization that is financially feasible. Countries with a high level of public pension commitments have typically been obliged to opt for partial, rather than full, pension privatization. The constitutional rules governing social security have also limited the degree of pension privatization that is feasible by obliging governments in some countries to amend their constitutions in order to carry out full-scale pension privatization.

Interest groups have played an equally important role in shaping pension privatization schemes, although they have typically not been able to block or push through the schemes on their own. Organized labor, business associations, and the beneficiaries of privileged pension programs have all lobbied hard and, often successfully, to convince the government to structure the reforms in ways that favor their interests. The beneficiaries of privileged public pension schemes, such as the military, the judiciary, and other state employees, have often managed to exclude themselves from the privatization schemes altogether, or, at least, to maintain certain privileges. The labor movement, meanwhile, has sometimes managed to reduce the scope of the privatization schemes and to create some role for itself in the administration of the new system. The labor movement has been especially successful in modifying the pension privatization schemes where the unions have close ties to the ruling party. Finally, the business community has, at times, managed to block aspects of the pension privatization legislation that would have reduced the profitability of the private pension systems for investors.

Regime Type

A number of scholars have suggested that authoritarian regimes may be better positioned to adopt sweeping pension privatization schemes than democratic regimes (Malloy 1985; Mesa-Lago 1997b, 1999; Mesa-Lago and Müller 2002). The statistical analyses presented earlier found no correlation between the level of democracy and the likelihood of pension privatization, however. This is because authoritarian regimes are no more likely to choose to privatize their pension systems than democratic regimes. Indeed, military-based authoritarian regimes may be less likely than democratic regimes to seek to privatize their pension systems, given the military's traditional reluctance to give up its own privileged pension programs.

Nevertheless, if an authoritarian regime does opt to privatize its pension system, it is more likely to be able to carry out a sweeping pension privatization plan, as Mesa-Lago and Müller (2002) suggest. Sweeping pension privatization plans are much less likely to get watered down in the legislature in authoritarian regimes than in democratic regimes. Many authoritarian regimes do not maintain legislatures, and those authoritarian regimes that do have legislatures usually stack them with supporters of the regime who routinely pass any legislation that is submitted to them. Thus, in authoritarian regimes few, if any, concessions, need to be made during the legislative process. Nor do authoritarian regimes usually need to make concessions to interest group opponents of the privatization plans, such as labor unions or pensioner's associations. Indeed, authoritarian regimes are frequently free to implement whatever pension privatization plan they desire, ignoring or stifling any resistance they may encounter. Even semiauthoritarian regimes are in a privileged position when it comes to enacting sweeping pension privatization plans since such regimes typically silence or emasculate the opposition by restricting civil and political liberties.

TABLE 7.1

Institutional Determinants of the Degree of Pension Privatization

	Type of pension system	Degree of privatization	Degree of democracy★	Implicit pension debt (as a percent of GDP)	Public pension spending (as a percent of GDP)
Partial Privatizers					
Argentina	Mixed	.27	2.5	305.4	6.2
Bulgaria	Mixed	.17	2.5	NA	7.3
Colombia	Parallel	.35	3.0	34.8	1.1
Costa Rica	Mixed	.36	1.5	93.9	3.8
Croatia★★	Mixed	.26	4.0	350	11.6
Estonia★★	Mixed	.16	1.5	NA	7.0
Hungary	Mixed	.26	1.5	213	9.7
Latvia	Mixed	.20	1.5	NA	10.2
Macedonia★★	Mixed	.35	3.0	NA	8.7
Poland	Mixed	.22	1.5	220	14.4
Sweden	Mixed	.14	1.0	370	11.4
United Kingdom	Mixed	.20	1.5	184	8.3
Uruguay	Mixed	.15	2.0	289.4	15.0
Total		**.24**	**2.1**	**228.9**	**8.2**
Broad Privatizers					
Bolivia	Private	1.00	3.0	30.9	2.5
Chile	Private	.95	6.0	100	4.0
Dominican Republic★★	Private	.90	2.5	21.5	0.4
El Salvador	Private	.90	3.0	8.7	1.3
Kazakhstan	Private	1.00	5.5	88	5.0
Mexico	Private	1.00	4.0	37.0	0.4
Nicaragua★★	Private	1.00	3.0	32.9	4.3
Peru	Parallel	.58	5.5	44.5	1.2
Total		**.92**	**4.1**	**45.4**	**2.4**

SOURCES: Palacios and Pallarès-Miralles 2000; Mesa-Lago 1997a; James and Brooks 2001; Gastil various years.

★This scale ranges from 1 (most free or democratic) to 7 (least free or democratic). Scores correspond to the year the pension system was privatized.

★★These schemes have been enacted, but have not yet been implemented. As a result, the figures for degree of privatization represent estimates.

Table 7.1 provides support for these arguments. As the table indicates, those countries that enacted relatively sweeping pension privatization schemes during the 1990s tended to grant their citizens fewer political and civil liberties than those countries that created more modest mixed public/ private pension systems. The partial privatizers—that is, those countries that privatized less than 50 percent of their pension system—had an average score

of 2.1 on Freedom House's rating of civil and political rights. The broad privatizers—those countries that privatized more than 50 percent of their system—had an average score of 4.1 on the Freedom House index. (The Freedom House index ranges from 1 to 7, with 1 being the most democratic and
7 being the least democratic.) A few relatively democratic countries were
able to implement broad pension privatization schemes, but most of the
countries that enacted sweeping pension privatization regimes were governed by authoritarian or semiauthoritarian regimes. In contrast, virtually all
of the countries that enacted mixed systems were democratic.

Case studies of pension privatization in Latin America and the postcommunist world show how authoritarian political institutions facilitated the
implementation of sweeping pension privatization plans. Indeed, the very
first pension privatization plan, Chile's sweeping reform of 1981, was implemented by executive decree in a highly authoritarian context. In the
wake of the 1973 coup in Chile, the military regime led by General Augusto
Pinochet closed the legislature, suspended the constitution, and committed
widespread violations of human rights. General Pinochet also gradually as-
serted control over the military regime by purging the governing junta of his
rivals. The concentration of authority in the executive branch enabled the
government to plan and implement a sweeping pension privatization plan,
which completely phased out the existing public pension system. Opposition political parties and labor unions, which had been banned or severely
weakened in the wake of the coup, were unable to present serious resistance
to the plan. The only group that had power to demand changes to the bill
was the military itself, which successfully lobbied to be exempted from the
privatization plan (Piñera 1991; interview with Piñera 1997).

The authoritarian nature of political institutions in Kazakhstan also facilitated the implementation of a sweeping pension privatization scheme in that
country. President Nursultan Nazarbaev, the former first secretary of the
Communist Party of Kazakhstan, has ruled Kazakhstan since independence
with near dictatorial powers.[1] In 1995, Nazarbaev dissolved the existing legislature, which had challenged some of his policies, and replaced it with a
more pliant body. The Nazarbaev regime also replaced the Constitutional
Court, which had questioned the legitimacy of some of his actions, with a
new institution whose rulings are subject to presidential veto. Finally, Nazarbaev placed significant limits on civil and political liberties and routinely im-
prisoned critics of his regime. The highly authoritarian nature of Kazakhstan's
political institutions meant that opponents of the regime's sweeping pension
privatization plan could not present significant resistance to the reform proposal, although it was highly unpopular. Trade unions and pensioner associations criticized the reform proposal, but the government largely ignored
them. Numerous legislators also voiced some discontent with the privatiza-

tion plan, but in the end most of them voted overwhelmingly for the reform legislation without enacting significant modifications to it (Orenstein 1999).

When Mexico and Peru undertook their reforms, they were also governed by semiauthoritarian regimes, which facilitated the enactment of rather sweeping reforms. The final reforms were more modest than most of the reforms enacted by highly authoritarian regimes, but they were nevertheless broader reforms than those typically enacted by democratic countries. In Mexico, President Ernesto Zedillo used his party's traditionally iron control of the legislature and of the labor movement to push through a sweeping pension privatization bill. Nevertheless, he was obliged to make a number of concessions, most of them minor, to opponents of pension privatization. In Peru, President Alberto Fujimori used his authoritarian powers to overcome opposition to his pension reform. Nevertheless, Fujimori was obliged to take constitutional and political considerations into account when planning the reform; as a result, the Peruvian reform, like the Mexican plan, was somewhat more modest than the Chilean or Kazakh reforms.

Fujimori first sought to privatize the Peruvian pension system by decree in November 1991, but his privatization plan was challenged both in Congress and before the Tribunal of Constitutional Guarantees. Such challenges were rendered moot in April 1992, however, when Fujimori, with the support of the military, carried out a self-coup, closing down the legislature and suspending the constitution. Shortly thereafter, the Fujimori administration published a more sweeping pension privatization proposal, which would have phased out the public pension system. The Fujimori administration ultimately backed off from this proposal, however, because of concerns that it was unconstitutional and that it would hurt the regime in the new legislative elections that it had called for November 1992. Instead, Fujimori opted for a privatization plan that maintained the existing public pension system, but forced it to compete with a new private pension system. This plan nevertheless represented a relatively sweeping change to the Peruvian pension system and went beyond his original privatization proposal in a number of different aspects (Boloña Behr 1995). The Fujimori regime opted to enact the pension privatization plan by decree in December 1992 before the new legislature was seated, which prevented legislators from modifying the proposed reform. Moreover, opponents of the reform could not overturn the decree because allies of Fujimori dominated the new legislature, unlike the old one. Labor unions, pensioner's associations, and opposition parties vigorously demonstrated against the privatization plan, but there was little they could do to prevent it from being implemented.

Democratic governments, by contrast, have typically had a much more difficult time enacting sweeping pension privatization schemes because the democratic institutions have provided opportunities for opponents of the reforms to block or alter them. In Argentina, Colombia, Poland, and Hungary, for example, critics of the proposed privatization plans managed to water down the reforms considerably. The Sanguinetti administration in Uruguay and the Rodríguez administration in Costa Rica, meanwhile, had to make numerous compromises in order to achieve a broad consensus behind their reforms. Democratic governments in Bolivia, El Salvador, Nicaragua, and the Dominican Republic did manage to enact relatively sweeping pension privatization plans, although in some cases they used somewhat undemocratic methods to do so. The government of El Salvador, for example, only managed to gain legislative approval of its reform after the president of the legislative committee that was evaluating the reform expelled a member of the opposition from the committee on the grounds that he had not attended earlier meetings (Mesa-Lago 1999: 145).

Level of Public Pension Commitments

The level of existing commitments of the public pension systems shapes pension reform by placing limits on the degree of pension privatization that is financially feasible.[2] A number of different factors, including the generosity, maturity, and coverage of the public pension system as well as population demographics determine the level of existing public pension commitments. Countries that have older populations, broader coverage, and more mature and generous pension systems tend to have larger existing public pension commitments.

Pension privatization is considerably more expensive in countries that have high levels of existing pension commitments. A government that privatizes its pension system typically ceases to receive pension contributions from workers that switch to the private system, but it must continue to pay the pensions of existing retirees and it typically must compensate workers for their previous contributions to the public pension system as well. Thus, pension privatization is a very expensive undertaking where existing public pension commitments are quite large.

Countries with high levels of pension commitments have therefore typically opted to create mixed public/private pension systems rather than carry out full privatization schemes. In mixed systems, the government typically continues to receive a portion of the pension contributions made by workers and their employers, whereas in fully private systems the entirety of the pension contributions typically flows to the private system. This reduces the transition costs of pension privatization.

By contrast, countries with low public pension obligations have frequently opted to privatize fully their pension systems. These countries have faced lower transition costs, which has made full-scale privatization financially feasible. Countries with both low and high levels of public pension commitments have also reduced the transition costs of pension privatization by reneging on some of their public pension commitments. They have, for example, sought to raise the minimum retirement age, reduce the benefits paid by the public system, and pay only limited, if any, compensation to workers who switch to the private system for their past contributions to the public system.

The standard measure of a country's existing pension commitments is the implicit pension debt, which takes into account the government's commitments to both active workers and retirees. Unfortunately, estimates of the implicit pension debt are available only for a relatively limited number of countries (Kane and Palacios 1996; James and Brooks 2001; Palacios and Pallarès-Miralles 2000). Moreover, these estimates vary considerably depending on the methodology used.[3] The implicit pension debt, however, tends to be highly correlated with a country's current public pension expenditures ($r = .86$ in a sample of forty countries for which I have data on both variables). This analysis therefore uses public pension spending interchangeably with the implicit pension debt as a measure of a country's existing public pension commitments.

As Table 7.1 shows, the countries that partially privatized their pension systems had public pension expenditures that equaled 8.2 percent of GDP on average and implicit pension debts that equaled 228.9 percent of GDP. By contrast, public pension spending equaled only 2.4 percent of GDP and the implicit pension debt averaged only 45.4 percent of GDP in those countries that enacted broader pension privatization schemes.[4] In Latin America, the countries that have relatively high public pension commitments have typically opted to partially privatize their public pension systems. Neither Argentina, nor Uruguay, nor Costa Rica ever seriously contemplated fully privatizing their pension system in part because of the high transition costs involved.[5] Chile constitutes a partial exception to this pattern since it opted to fully privatize its pension system in spite of the country's relatively high level of public pension commitments. The Chilean government was running a major fiscal surplus at the time of the reform, however, which made full-scale privatization more feasible. Moreover, there is little evidence that the Chilean government was fully aware of the costs of its pension privatization plan (Borzutzky 1983).

Eastern European countries have also opted to create mixed public/private systems in part to reduce the transition costs of pension privatization. Indeed, in the last decade, Hungary, Poland, Latvia, Bulgaria, Croatia, Macedonia, and Estonia have all enacted legislation creating mixed pension systems. Eastern European countries typically have high public pension commitments, whether measured by public pension spending or the implicit pension debt, which has made full-scale pension privatization largely unaffordable. In Hungary, the Finance Ministry initially wanted to carry out a full privatization scheme, but other policymakers argued that Hungary's high level of public pension commitments made such a plan financially unfeasible (Orenstein 1999: 33).

Those countries that have lower levels of public pension commitments have tended to choose full-scale privatization. In recent years, Bolivia, El Salvador, Mexico, Nicaragua, Kazakhstan, and the Dominican Republic have all enacted full privatization schemes. Peru and Colombia are partial exceptions to this pattern since both countries created parallel systems—in which the public and private systems compete for members—rather than fully private systems, although both countries had relatively low levels of public pension commitments. Nevertheless, neither Peru nor Colombia opted for a mixed system, which typically involves a lesser degree of privatization. Moreover, both the Colombian and the Peruvian governments attempted to create fully private systems at earlier stages of the reform process, but political considerations obliged them to keep their public pension systems open. Thus, the existing level of public pension obligations, whether measured by the implicit pension debt or current public pension spending, has constrained the degree of pension privatization in both Latin America and the post-communist world.

Constitutional Rules on Social Security

In many countries, constitutions have also placed constraints on pension reform. Constitutional rules, for example, have made it difficult to tighten pension eligibility requirements and cut back pension benefits in some countries. The 1988 Brazilian constitution specified the standard age of retirement and the way in which pension benefits were to be calculated, which obliged the Brazilian government to amend the constitution in order to enact a relatively minor parametric reform of its public pension system. Constitutional rules have also limited the changes that can be made to the financing methods used by the pension systems. For example, the constitutions of a number of Latin American countries, including Costa Rica, Ecuador, El Salvador, Guatemala, Honduras, and Uruguay, stipulate that the financing of social security benefits should be tripartite—that is, financed by employers, employees, and the state ("Constituciones políticas" 1995). This means that any effort to eliminate the employer's contribution, as was done in Chile, might be ruled unconstitutional.

Most importantly, some constitutions have limited the degree of pension privatization that is politically feasible. Many Latin American constitutions stipulate that the state or a particular state agency will provide social security benefits. Such provisions have not necessarily precluded pension privatization because the language of constitutions can be interpreted in very different ways. Nevertheless, they have made full-scale pension privatization more vulnerable to constitutional challenges. Some Latin American governments have opted to create mixed or parallel pension systems partly in order to avoid potential challenges to the constitutionality of their reforms. Other Latin American governments have sought to amend the constitution in order to make pension privatization clearly constitutionally acceptable, but this has not been easy to accomplish, given the barriers to constitutional reform.

Constitutional rules made it much easier to carry out a sweeping pension privatization plan in Mexico than in Brazil, or even Argentina. The Mexican constitution is relatively succinct on the issue of social security. Article 123 of the Mexican constitution states simply, "The Law of Social Security is of public utility and will include insurance for invalidity, old-age, life" ("Constituciones políticas" 1995: 116). The constitution does not specify that the state should be responsible for providing these pensions, which meant that the Mexican government did not need to amend its constitution in order to privatize the country's pension system.

The Argentine constitution, meanwhile, is more ambiguous. Article 14 bis stipulates: "The state will confer social security benefits, which will be of an integral and irrenounceable nature. In particular, the law will establish: obligatory social security which will be the responsibility of provincial or national entities with financial and economic autonomy, managed by the beneficiaries with state participation" ("Constituciones políticas" 1995: 8). The constitution also states that old-age and retirement pensions were to be adjusted for inflation ("Constituciones políticas" 1995: 8). As the Menem administration realized, these constitutional provisions left open the possibility that a full-scale pension privatization scheme might be ruled unconstitutional. By proposing a mixed public/private system, however, the Menem administration eliminated any grounds that opponents of the reform might have to challenge the reform's constitutionality (Schulthess 1992: 7). Under the Argentine reform, the state continues to provide retirement pensions as well as other social security benefits. Partly as a result, constitutional challenges to the reform have not prospered.

The Brazilian constitution was much more detailed on the issue of social security than were the constitutions of Argentina or Mexico. The constitution did not specifically prohibit privatization of the pension system, but many of the existing constitutional provisions, such as the articles that stipulate how benefits are to be calculated, were incompatible with a fully private pension system. The Cardoso administration sought to amend the constitution in order to implement some parametric reforms of the public pension system, but these efforts were largely unsuccessful in part because of the large barriers to constitutional reform.

The Ecuadoran government has also encountered difficulties in trying to reform its pension system because of the constitutional rules governing social security in Ecuador. Article 29 of the Ecuadoran constitution states that social security "will be provided via an autonomous institution. The State, the employers and the insured will have equal representation on its administrative organism" ("Constituciones políticas" 1995: 60). The government of President Sixto Durán Ballén sought to amend the constitution in order to clear the way for a sweeping pension privatization plan, but this proved difficult to do. The government first sought to amend the constitution via the legislature, which required the approval of two-thirds of the members of the legislature in two separate sessions of Congress. The high barriers to constitutional reform and Durán Ballén's small base of legislative support led the government's proposal to founder in the legislature, however. Durán Ballén then submitted this and eleven other proposed constitutional amendments to a national plebiscite, as permitted by the Ecuadorian constitution. All twelve proposed constitutional amendments were defeated at the polls, including the constitutional amendment that would have opened up the way to privatize the pension system. This latter amendment was rejected by 60 percent of the voters.

Another effort to privatize the Ecuadorian pension system was undertaken after President Gustavo Noboa took office in 2000. This time, however, the government sought to create a mixed public/private system, which they argued would not require a constitutional amendment. The new privatization effort initially bore fruit when legislation creating a mixed public/private system was approved in late 2001. In the spring of 2002, however, the Constitutional Tribunal ruled that the privatization legislation was unconstitutional, which left the reform in doubt.

Constitutional rules also reportedly played a role in the decision of the Peruvian government to create a parallel public/private system rather than a fully private pension system. Article 14 of the 1980 Peruvian constitution stipulated that "the existence of other public and private entities in the area of insurance is not incompatible with the aforementioned [autonomous social security] institution as long as they offer better or additional benefits and there exists the consent of the insured" (*Constitución Política del Perú* 1980: 22). Shortly after his self-coup in 1992, the Fujimori administration published a pension privatization proposal that would have required all future entrants to the workforce to join a new private pension system. According to Carlos Boloña, then-minister of economy, the Fujimori regime subsequently backed away from its plan to phase out the public pension system and make membership in the new private pension system mandatory because of concerns that this would be unconstitutional (Boloña Behr 1995: 218; Cruz-Saco 1995). The Fujimori regime's concern about the constitutional acceptability of its pension privatization scheme continued even after the new system was implemented. Indeed, when the Fujimori regime created a new constitution in 1993, it changed the language governing social security to make it more consistent with the existence of a private pension system.

Colombia's pension privatization plan also suffered some modifications partly in order to ensure the constitutionality of the proposal. The administration of César Gaviria originally proposed a sweeping pension privatization plan that would have phased out the existing public pension system. This proposal came under attack partly on constitutional grounds, however (Mesa-Lago 1994: 136–49). Article 48 of the 1991 Colombian constitution states that "social security can be provided by public or private entities, in conformity with the law," which would seemingly clear the way for any type of pension privatization ("Constituciones políticas" 1995: 27). Nevertheless, the constitution also states that social security will be governed by the principles of "universality and solidarity" and that the state "will progressively expand social security coverage," and critics of the proposal argued that it violated both of these constitutional provisions ("Constituciones políticas" 1995: 27). These constitutional concerns, combined with the government's difficulty in obtaining legislative support for the initiative, led the Gaviria administration to alter the proposal in a number of ways. As in Peru, the reform was changed to make membership in the private system voluntary for future as well as current workers, and a solidarity fund was created to help subsidize the incorporation of low-income workers into the public pension system.

Constitutional concerns have similarly shaped pension reforms in Eastern Europe. In Hungary, the government initially planned to require all active workers below a certain age to join the new private pension system. Some members of the reform team were concerned that such a provision might be ruled unconstitutional, however, since these workers already had acquired rights in the old system (Nelson 2001). To circumvent this constitutional obstacle, the government decided to make membership in the new private pension system voluntary for existing members of the labor force regardless of their age, but mandatory for new entrants to the labor force, who did not have any acquired rights. In Poland, some members of the government were also concerned that the proposed pension privatization plan would not pass constitutional muster (Nelson 2001). In order to assuage these concerns, the government opted to have the state underwrite any deficits in the private pension funds. The government also defended the constitutionality of the reform by pointing out that the state would continue to provide pensions in the new social security system (Nelson 2001).

Constitutional provisions have thus constrained pension privatization schemes in a number of important ways in both Latin America and Eastern Europe. A number of governments have opted to scale back their privatization plans rather than try to amend their constitutions or risk seeing their privatization plans ruled unconstitutional. In the few cases that governments have sought to amend their constitutions in order to carry out major pension reforms, the proposed amendments suffered serious defeats. Nevertheless, constitutional rules on social security have not precluded pension privatization altogether. On the contrary, numerous governments enacted pension privatization schemes by adjusting the reform proposals to ensure that they would pass constitutional muster.

Interest Group Opposition to Pension Privatization

As numerous scholars have noted, social security reforms create winners and losers, and the interest groups that represent the potential losers will typically mobilize on their behalf (Williamson and Pampel 1993; Pierson 1994). Interest groups will try to influence social security reforms by pressuring the executive to modify or withdraw its reform proposals or by lobbying members of Congress, including members of the executive's own party, to block or alter the executive's proposed reforms. In applying pressure, interest groups have a variety of political resources at their disposal. Some interest groups can apply pressure by carrying out strikes or demonstrations. Other interest groups may control large numbers of votes or financial resources that they can use to influence electoral outcomes. The ability of interest groups to block or alter policy proposals is dependent not only on their control of political resources but also on their willingness to use these political resources to achieve their policy objectives. Interest groups will typically fight battles with varying levels of intensity depending on what is at stake.

A variety of interest groups have opposed pension privatization and have taken numerous different measures to block or alter the proposed schemes. The opponents of the reforms have included pensioners' organizations, labor unions, and groups that have traditionally benefited from privileged public pension schemes, such as the judiciary and the military. These groups have had varying degrees of success in their efforts to modify pension reforms, but none of these groups has been able to block the reforms by themselves.

The ability of these interest groups to extract concessions from the government has depended to a large degree on their organizational strength and political influence. Pensioner's associations have provided important symbolic resistance to the reforms, but they have typically lacked the organizational, technical, and financial resources necessary to block the reforms or even force important modifications. Powerful beneficiaries of privileged public pension schemes have at times been able to persuade the government to exempt their schemes from the privatization plans, but they have not prevented the reforms from being applied to the rest of the population. The labor movement, particularly when it has close ties to the ruling party, has exercised the greatest influence over the reforms as a whole. Labor unions at times have obliged the government to scale back its privatization plans or limit its efforts to tighten eligibility requirements for pensions, but the unions, too, have typically not been able to block the reforms outright.

Pensioners' Associations

Organizations of pensioners have vigorously opposed efforts to privatize the public pension systems in Latin America and Eastern Europe.[6] The pensioners' associations have opposed the reforms in part because they de-fund the public pension systems on which the pensioners depend. Proponents of privatization schemes have frequently assured pensioners that their existing benefits will be maintained, but the leaders of the pensioners' organizations have typically been skeptical of these assertions. They commonly believe that the elderly will inevitably be asked to shoulder some of the enormous transition costs of privatization through increased taxes or benefit cuts (Kay 1998; Ortiz de Zevallos et al. 1999: 40; Gray-Molina, Pérez de Rada, and Yañez 1999: 41; interviews with Imizcoz 1996 and with Forte 1996). Moreover, the leaders of the pensioners' organizations often argue that the funds that pay the transition costs of pension privatization should instead be used to improve the meager benefits of existing pensioners (interviews with Alonso 1997, with Imizcoz 1996, and with Cota 1997).

Ideology has also played an important role in the decisions of the pensioners' organizations to oppose pension privatization. In many countries, pensioners' associations are tied closely to the labor unions, and the leaders of the organizations are typically former union activists who tend to be critical of neoliberal policies in general (interviews with Alonso 1997, with Imizcoz 1996, and with Cota 1997). Leaders of the pensioners' organizations in Argentina and Mexico, for example, denounced the privatization schemes as neoliberal projects that were being imposed by foreign actors such as the World Bank and the International Monetary Fund (MUNJP 1995; interviews with Alonso 1997 and with Imizcoz 1996). The leaders also frequently argue that the privatization schemes violate the basic principles of social security since the reforms undermine the solidaristic function of the pension system (Ortiz de Zevallos et al. 1999: 40; Kay 1998; MUNJP 1995).

The pensioners' organizations have typically not played a significant role in the pension privatization process in Latin America, however (Alonso 1998; Madrid 1999; Gray-Molina, Pérez de Rada, and Yañez 1999; interviews with Alonso 1997, with Imizcoz 1996, and with Forte 1996). Governments have usually not consulted with the pensioners' associations when they have planned the privatization proposals, nor have they commonly included the pensioners' associations in the negotiations over the reforms that have taken place in tripartite commissions. The main pensioners' organizations have also been largely excluded from the negotiations that have taken place on the reforms in the legislature, although they have frequently testified before the legislative committees evaluating the reforms. In some countries, pensioners' organizations may have shaped public opinion on the reforms and influenced the actions of other more powerful actors. Nevertheless, the pensioners' associations per se have not been able to block or modify the proposed reforms.

The pensioners' associations have failed to play a significant role in the reform process in part because they lack political clout. Latin American pensioner's organizations do not typically have high-level political contacts and are notably lacking in financial and technical resources. Owing to their poor financial situation, the pensioners' associations have been unable to hire lobbyists, make campaign contributions, carry out advertising campaigns, or undertake other costly measures that would enhance their political influence. Nor could the pensioners' associations hire the technical personnel necessary to analyze the reform proposals and respond with their own counterproposals (Kay 1998).

Owing to their lack of political contacts and technical and financial resources, the main strategy of the pensioners' associations has been to hold public protests against the reforms. The pensioners' associations, however, have not typically been able to mobilize large numbers of people. Most Latin American countries still have relatively young populations and low levels of social security coverage, which means that pensioners represent a very small percentage of the population. Only in Cuba and the Southern Cone do pensioners constitute more than 3 percent of the population as a whole (World Bank 1994b). Moreover, the pensioners' associations have not been able to mobilize even a small proportion of the population that they claim to represent. Most pensioners are not members of pensioners' associations, and only a small percentage of the so-called members attend political marches and demonstrations.

Latin American pensioners' associations were unable to mobilize large numbers of people to protest the privatization of the pension systems in part because of the traditional barriers to collective action. The assurances that Latin American governments gave to the elderly population that their benefits would not be affected by the pension privatization schemes also probably undermined the efforts of pensioners' associations to mobilize the elderly against the reforms.[7] The Uruguayan pensioners' movement, which is easily the strongest in Latin America, mobilized a large number of people in the late 1980s and early 1990s to help defeat pension reform measures that would have directly reduced existing pension benefits (Papadópulos 1992; Filgueira and Moraes 1999). With regard to the pension privatization scheme, however, the labor and social security minister, Ana Lía Piñeyrúa, repeatedly stressed that "under no circumstances will these reforms impact those who are already retired." These statements may have undermined the efforts of the pensioners' movement to build resistance to the privatization measures (Kay 1998: 180; Filgueira and Moraes 1999).

The pensioners' associations have played a similarly marginal role in the pension privatization process in the postcommunist countries in spite of the fact that pensioners represent a much larger proportion of the population in this region (Orenstein 1999; Müller 1999; Nelson 2001). Because they lack ties to the established parties, pensioners' associations in the postcommunist countries have relatively little political influence, which has limited their ability to shape the reforms (Orenstein 1999). Moreover, in Eastern Europe, as in Latin America, the governments' decisions to exclude existing pensioners and older workers from the reforms played an important role in defusing opposition to the privatization measures (Orenstein 1999; Müller 1999; Nelson 2001). In Kazakhstan, pensioners' associations did mobilize to protest the privatization measures, but these demonstrations were prompted in part by the failure of the state to make timely payments to existing pensioners (Orenstein 1999).

Beneficiaries of Privileged Programs

Beneficiaries of privileged public pension schemes have provided another source of actual or potential opposition to the pension privatization measures. Public pension systems in Latin America have traditionally contained special pension schemes that have provided generous benefits to certain privileged categories of workers, such as the military, the judiciary, teachers, and state employees in general (Mesa-Lago 1978, 1989). The beneficiaries of the privileged pension systems have often received higher pensions and have typically been able to retire at younger ages and with fewer years of contributions than the members of the main public pension systems. The maintenance of these special benefits tends to be incompatible with pension privatization, however, since pensions in the private systems are based largely on what each person has contributed to an individual retirement account. Indeed, advocates of pension privatization have often argued that the private pension systems are more equitable since they prevent powerful interest groups from putting pressure on the state to grant them special benefits.

The beneficiaries of privileged pension schemes often have well-organized associations that represent them, and they frequently control important political or economic resources. Indeed, as Mesa-Lago (1978) has shown, these groups typically have privileged pension schemes precisely because they control key political or economic resources. The beneficiaries of the privileged pension schemes have not typically been able to block the pension privatization proposals as a whole, however; nor have they usually tried to do so. Instead, they have sought to maintain their existing privileges by persuading the government to exclude them from the privatization schemes.

The most powerful of these interest groups have frequently been exempted from the reforms. At times, Latin American governments have excluded certain categories of workers from the privatization schemes from the outset in order to forestall their opposition to the reforms. The architect of the Uruguayan reform, Ariel Davrieux, justified the exclusion of notaries, bank employees, university professors, the police, and the military from the reform by arguing that "it was not worth it . . . to risk a good reform by challenging the most powerful groups" (Filgueira and Moraes 1999: 16). In Mexico, the government similarly decided to avoid potential political opposition from state employees and petroleum workers by excluding them from its sweeping privatization plans (interviews with Cerda 1997 and with Cajiga 1997). In other cases, governments have backed away from plans to incorporate the groups into the privatization schemes because of powerful resistance from these groups. State oil workers in Colombia, for example, carried out a two-day strike to convince the government to let them maintain their privileged public pension scheme (Franco Agudelo 1994; interview with Von Gersdorff 1998). Polish miners, meanwhile, won some concessions from the government after occupying the Ministry of Labor for two days (Orenstein 1999). In most cases, these groups have promptly ceased to lobby against the privatization measures once they have been exempted from the reforms.

The military has been excluded from the privatization schemes more frequently than any other group. The exclusion of the military from most privatization schemes is partly a result of technical factors, which complicate the transformation of the military's retirement program into a system based on individual capitalization. The principal obstacles to the inclusion of the military are political, however. In Latin America, the military continues to wield a great deal of political power and has used this power to resist any effort to eliminate its special retirement benefits. In Chile, the architects of the pension privatization plan had initially proposed including the military in the scheme only to encounter adamant opposition to this idea from the leadership of the armed forces, which had veto power over legislation (Piñera 1991; interviews with Gazmuri 1997 and with Larraín 1997). The governments of most Latin American countries have excluded the military from the privatization plans from the beginning, however, partly in order to avoid antagonizing the leaders of the armed forces (interviews with Schulthess 1996, with Moraes 1997, and with Iglesias 1996). To date, the military has been excluded from every privatization scheme in Latin America except the Bolivian reform, and even in Bolivia the military was incorporated into the new private system under special conditions.[8] In Eastern Europe, where the military is politically weaker, it has had less success in maintaining its privileged pension systems. The Polish military, for example, was unable to block the government's efforts to include it in the reforms, although only younger members of the military will participate in the private pension system (Orenstein 1999: 58).

Various other powerful interest groups have also been able to obtain exemptions for themselves. The judiciary and some other public-sector employees in Costa Rica used their political clout to retain their traditional pension privileges (Jiménez 2000: 264–65). Schoolteachers and some other state employees in Colombia similarly managed to exempt themselves from the reforms in that country. Schoolteachers and civil servants also managed to hang onto many of their traditional privileges in Brazil when that country implemented its parametric reform of the public pension system. In the postcommunist countries, members of the powerful *nomenklatura* have also retained their benefits in numerous instances. In Poland, for example, judges and prosecutors managed to maintain their existing privileges. The government of Kazakhstan, meanwhile, chose to extend special benefits to employees of the interior ministry and the state investigations office (the former KGB), although it rejected efforts to grant privileges to other groups, including steel workers, miners, prosecutors, and judges (Orenstein 1999: 28).

The Labor Movement

The labor movement has typically been the most important interest group opponent of pension privatization. Labor leaders have opposed the pension privatization schemes for a variety of reasons. Many leaders have argued that the privatization schemes reduce or eliminate benefits that the labor movement struggled to gain over the course of the last century. Indeed, the privatization schemes have stripped away many of the pension guarantees that the state formerly provided and have frequently tightened restrictions on gaining access to pensions by raising the minimum retirement age or increasing the required years of contributions. Labor leaders have also opposed the pension privatization schemes in some instances because the schemes have reduced labor's access to patronage resources. In many countries, the privatization schemes have eliminated the role of the labor unions in the management of the public pension funds, thus depriving the labor leaders of a source of revenues that they had used to reward allies and punish their enemies. Finally, the privatization schemes endanger the jobs of the employees of the public social security systems. As a result, unions representing these workers have frequently spearheaded the resistance to the privatization schemes.

Not all labor unions have opposed pension privatization, however. Some unions, like Força Sindical in Brazil and the unions built by the anticommunist opposition in Eastern Europe, have embraced pension privatization and other market-oriented reforms for ideological reasons (Orenstein 1999; Nelson 2001; L. Pinheiro 1997: A9; Força Sindical n.d.). Certain unions have also endorsed pension privatization because they have believed that they could benefit from it. Indeed, in a number of countries, entrepreneurial unions, including the Solidarity Labor Movement in Poland and the Electrical Workers' Union and the Construction Workers' Union in Argentina, have become major stockholders in the new private pension funds (Ensignia 1996; Ensignia and Díaz 1997). The trade unions that are genuinely enthusiastic about pension privatization represent a distinct minority of the organized workforce, however. In most countries, the largest labor unions and federations have vigorously opposed pension privatization or acquiesced to it only grudgingly.[9]

Labor unions have undertaken a variety of steps to impede pension privatization. They have publicly denounced the reform proposals, lobbied legislators and government officials to oppose the reforms, and held numerous strikes and demonstrations against the measures. In Bolivia, for example, the main labor federation, the Central of Bolivian Workers (COB), carried out a series of general strikes in an effort to defeat the pension privatization bill ("La COB se juega" 1996: 9; "La COB anuncia semana" 1996: 6). In Nicaragua, the main labor federation, the National Front of Workers (FNT), similarly carried out protests and even shut down the legislature for one day in an attempt to block the privatization of the pension system in that country (Barberena 2000b). The main labor federations in Peru, Colombia, Uruguay, El Salvador, Guatemala, Paraguay, Ecuador, and Kazakhstan also carried out major campaigns to block their governments' pension privatization proposals (Ensignia and Díaz 1997).

Organized labor has not typically been able to impede pension privatization, however. Pension privatization measures have passed in numerous Latin American countries, including Peru, Colombia, Uruguay, Bolivia, El Salvador, and Nicaragua, in spite of the vigorous objections of the labor movement. Although labor unions have helped defeat pension privatization proposals in a few countries, there is no evidence that union opposition was the crucial factor. Indeed, other factors, especially the government's internal divisions and the ruling party's weakness in the legislature, appear to have played a much more important role than union opposition in the defeat of pension privatization proposals in Brazil, Ecuador, Guatemala, Paraguay, and Venezuela. The labor movement may have contributed to the defeat of the privatization measures in these countries by influencing the views and actions of important political actors such as legislators and government officials, but it has depended on these actors to actually block the reforms.

The labor movement has not been able to block the pension privatization schemes in large part because it lacks sufficient political clout. Labor leaders typically do not have the high-level political contacts enjoyed by members of the private sector. Nor do the unions usually have the technical personnel necessary to contribute in a sophisticated way to public policy debate on this issue (Ensignia 1996; Kay 1998). Unions do enjoy some organizational and economic resources, but these resources have declined in recent years. Unionization rates, which were never particularly high in Latin America, fell sharply in the late 1980s and early 1990s in part because of the decline of the economic sectors in which labor had traditionally been strong. A recent International Labor Organization study of union membership reported that the unionization rate in the region dropped from 22.9 percent in the late 1980s to 14.7 percent in the early 1990s (ILO 1997). Unionization rates have also fallen in the postcommunist countries from 76.4 percent in the 1980s to 53.3 percent in the 1990s (ILO 1997).[10] The declining unionization rates have undermined the labor movement's political influence by reducing its ability to sponsor political campaigns and disrupt the economy. The shrinking number of union members, combined with the unions' low public approval ratings in many countries, have also made politicians more willing to implement measures that the unions oppose.

Although the labor movement has not typically been able to block pension privatization plans, labor unions have sometimes been able to obtain significant concessions on the proposed pension reforms. Organized labor has sought different types of concessions. For example, it has often sought to maintain an important public component in the pension system, pressuring the government to make membership in the private system voluntary or to create a government-owned pension fund that competes with the private pension funds in the new pension system. It has also tried to oblige the government to raise the minimum pension and to provide numerous guarantees in the event of the failure of one of the private pension funds. In addition, it has sought to reduce or eliminate measures that would tighten eligibility requirements for pensions, such as proposed increases in the minimum retirement age. Finally, the labor unions have sought concessions that would benefit the unions themselves. They have pressed the government to allow the unions to run pension funds and to have a role in the supervision of the new pension system. They have also tried, unsuccessfully, to convince the government to establish corporate, as opposed to individual, affiliation with pension funds, which would allow the unions to oblige their members to join a union-affiliated pension fund.

Those unions that have close ties to the ruling parties have typically received the most important concessions. Labor unions and ruling parties with close ties have large incentives to avoid a confrontation over pension reform (Lange and Garrett 1985; Levitsky and Way 1998; Burgess 1999; Murillo 2000, 2001). Ruling parties with close links to labor typically benefit from the unions' campaign contributions and mobilization drives as well as the unions' ability to maintain labor quiescence. The labor unions, for their part, may benefit from government policies and state patronage resources, which the ruling party, as the head of government, controls. Thus, the unions and the government both have incentives to reach an agreement over social security reform through negotiations, rather than engage in a winner-take-all battle over the issue that could damage their relationship. The more dependent the ruling party is on labor, the greater the concessions the ruling party may be willing to make in order to prevent a rupture in the relationship. In contrast, the more dependent the labor movement is on the ruling party, the fewer concessions the ruling party may be willing to make since it knows that the labor movement is unlikely to risk a rupture in the relationship.

If the labor movement does not have ties to the party in power, open confrontation over social security reform is much more likely to occur. In this case, the costs of confrontation for both parties are lower since no relationship is at risk. Moreover, the potential benefits of confrontation are higher for both actors since a victory by either side not only would further its policy interests, but also would lead to the weakening of an opposing political force. Cooperation on this issue would also be difficult in the absence of close ruling party-labor ties because both sides would have reason to fear that the other side would renege on its agreements, since they had no history of cooperation between them. As Levitsky and Way (1998) argued, historical ties between the unions and the ruling party build trust and other forms of social capital, which facilitate cooperation. Because of their long history of cooperation, both union and ruling-party leaders have reason to believe that the other side will fulfill its promises.[11]

The absence of ties between the main Brazilian labor federation, the Central Unica dos Trabalhadores (CUT), and the Brazilian government impeded efforts to find a concerted solution to the impasse over pension reform in Brazil. The labor confederations in Argentina and Mexico, in contrast, had close ties to the political party that initiated the pension privatization process in those countries. In both of the countries, the main labor federations initially opposed the pension privatization plans. The close links between the unions and the governing parties, however, facilitated the negotiation of agreements in which the governments made certain concessions to the unions in exchange for their support for the reforms.

In Eastern Europe, close ties between organized labor and the governing party have also enabled reforms to be negotiated rather than imposed. In Hungary, the National Confederation of Hungarian Trade Unions, the largest labor federation, initially opposed the partial privatization of the pension system and threatened to call a strike in order to block the privatization plans (Orenstein 1999; Müller 1999). The ruling socialist party, which had close ties to the labor federation, immediately initiated negotiations with the labor unions, and the close ties between the ruling Socialist Party and the unions helped the two parties reach an agreement.[12] Indeed, Sandor Nagy, a Socialist Party leader and a former head of the National Confederation of Hungarian Trade Unions, played a key role in bringing about this agreement (Orenstein 1999; Nelson 2001). In order to gain the support of the unions for the privatization proposal, the government agreed to loosen pension eligibility requirements, reduce the amount of contributions to the private system, and expand state guarantees in the new private pension system. The Socialist Party also promised to postpone the reform of the disability insurance system and to maintain the existing method of allocating seats to the board of the Pension Insurance Fund, the union-dominated organization that managed the public pension system (Orenstein 1999; Nelson 2001). When a center-right government took power in May 1998, however, it reneged on some of these concessions and eliminated the Pension Insurance Fund altogether, bringing the administration of the pension system under the direct control of the government (Orenstein 1999).

Pension reform in Poland was more consensual than in most of the other countries. The Solidarity Labor Movement, one of the two most important labor federations, had been a strong opponent of communism and supported market-oriented reforms, including pension privatization. Solidarity proposed its own pension privatization plan in 1995 and subsequently endorsed the government's proposal, although significant sectors of Solidarity were critical of pension privatization. More surprisingly, the formerly communist labor federation, the All Poland Trade Unions Alliance, also endorsed pension privatization—albeit somewhat grudgingly. It did so in large part because of its strong ties to the ruling political coalition, the Alliance of the Democratic Left, which had proposed the pension privatization bill (Orenstein 1999; Nelson 2001). When the Alliance of the Democratic Left lost power midway through the reform process, however, the All Poland Trade Unions Alliance became more critical of the reforms and subsequently sought to delay the approval of the reform, although it did not outright oppose it (Orenstein 1999: 54). Both labor federations sought to negotiate a variety of concessions through the Tripartite Council that brought together business, labor, and the state (Orenstein 1999; Müller 1999; Nelson 2001). The labor federations, for example, blocked the government's attempt to equalize the retirement age, and they opposed the plan to do away with pension privileges for certain occupational categories. Overall, the Solidarity federation gained greater concessions for its unions, however, in large part because of its ties to the electoral coalition that took power when the final details of the reform were being worked out (Orenstein 1999: 56).

The labor movement has thus shaped the contents of social security privatization plans in both Latin America and East Europe, although it has not usually been able to block pension privatization altogether. Unions that have close ties to the ruling parties have typically engaged in negotiations with the government over the reforms, and these negotiations have often led to important concessions. Unions without ties to the ruling party have usually engaged in more direct confrontations over the reforms, but these unions have rarely won major concessions. As a result, pension privatization proposals have tended to be somewhat more sweeping where the unions and the ruling parties lack a tradition of cooperation.

The Private Sector

Not all interest groups have opposed pension privatization plans. Throughout Latin America and Eastern Europe, the business community, particularly the financial sector, has supported pension privatization, often quite vigorously. Business interests have actively lobbied governments to privatize their pension systems in many instances, and members of the private sector have often managed to shape the content of pension privatization legislation. The business community, however, has not typically been able to dictate the terms of the reforms. Nor has it been able to push through pension privatization proposals unilaterally. Indeed, in many instances, the business community's efforts to promote pension privatization have been to no avail.

The Latin American business community began to embrace pension privatization in the late 1980s in the wake of the Chilean reform. To promote pension privatization, many business associations formulated privatization proposals, which they shared with the government and the media. In Mexico, for example, the most important business associations, including the Mexican Association of Stockbrokers (AMCB), the Employers' Confederation of the Mexican Republic (COPARMEX), and the Business Coordinating Council (CCE), formulated pension privatization proposals in the early

1990s (Bertranou 1994; Laurell 1995; Hazas 1995; Arias Jiménez 1995). In Argentina, meanwhile, the country's most important business association, the Argentine Industrial Union (UIA), rejected the parametric reforms that were proposed by the undersecretary for social security in 1990, calling the proposals "pale palliatives that do not modify in any manner the structure or the inefficiency of the actual system" (Unión Industrial Argentina 1990). The UIA, along with the Argentine Association of Insurance Companies, and the Association of Argentine Banks, proposed much more sweeping pension privatization plans (Unión Industrial Argentina 1992; Isuani and San Martino 1993; Asociación Argentina de Compañía de Seguros 1992).

The business community has also promoted pension privatization through its informal contacts with government officials. In many countries, members of the business community enjoy a high level of access to key government officials, which they have used to encourage them to privatize the pension system. In Bolivia, some members of the private sector had direct access to President Sánchez de Lozada, which they used to lobby him on this issue (Gray-Molina, Pérez de Rada, and Yañez 1999: 42). In Peru, President Fujimori distanced himself somewhat from the business community, but the private sector had a great deal of influence within the Ministry of Economy (Ortiz de Zevallos et al. 1999; Arce 2001). Indeed, the minister of economy who carried out the reform, Carlos Boloña, had come from the private sector and after leaving office became an investor in one of the newly created private pension funds.[13] According to recent studies of the Bolivian and Peruvian reforms, pressure from the private sector played an important role in breaking deadlocks within the executive branch over the reform proposals (Gray-Molina, Pérez de Rada, and Yañez 1999; Ortiz de Zevallos et al. 1999; Arce 2001).

The degree of private-sector participation in the actual planning of the reforms has varied widely, however. In some instances, members of the business community have participated on the government committees that plan the reform proposals. In Kazakhstan, two members of the private sector sat on the government working group that helped plan the reform, and in Hungary a prominent investment banker was charged with drawing up portfolio management rules for the private pension funds (Orenstein 1999). In many instances, however, the reforms were planned with only minimal participation of the business community. In Chile, Argentina, and Uruguay, for example, small teams of technocrats planned the reforms with relatively little interaction with the private sector (Kay 1998; interviews with Piñera 1997, with Gazmuri 1997, with Larraín 1997, with Demarco 1996, with Barassi 1996, and with Posadas 1996).

Even where governments have planned the reforms by themselves, however, they have often sought out the views of the key actors in the business

community. The Mexican government presented a preliminary privatization plan to a Mexican business association for comments when it first proposed privatizing the pension system in 1990 (Bertranou 1994, 1995). When
the government launched another attempt to privatize the pension system in
1995, it held a series of meetings with business and labor and then convened
a tripartite commission to study the general outlines of the reform. In Hungary and Poland, the government formally submitted a draft of its reform
proposal to commissions composed of representatives of business, labor, and
the state, which negotiated various changes to the reform bill. The Argentine government, meanwhile, used tripartite commissions both to discuss
the general principles that should guide the reforms and to negotiate some
changes to the reform proposal after the reform had been introduced to the
legislature.

The business community has also used its influence to lobby legislators to
approve pension privatization legislation. In numerous countries, members
of the business community have given congressional testimony in favor of
pension privatization bills. Members of the business community have also
used their personal contacts with legislators to urge them to vote in favor of
the bills.

The private sector has sought not only to enact pension privatization legislation but also to shape the content of the legislation in a manner that serves
the interests of the business community as a whole. Business associations in
Argentina and Mexico, for example, blocked measures that would have allowed labor unions to choose the pension funds to which workers belonged.
In addition, sectors of the business community have at times been able to
convince the government or the legislature to tailor the pension privatization legislation to favor their narrow sectoral interests. A leader of the Argentine insurance industry, for example, managed to convince an influential
legislator to successfully propose tightening the restrictions on who would
qualify for survivors' pensions in the new pension system (interview with
Facal 1996). The banking community in Mexico and El Salvador, meanwhile, successfully defeated efforts to ban banks from participating in the
private pension fund industry. Similarly, the preexisting voluntary private
pension funds industry in Hungary successfully prevailed on the government
to use its regulatory and organizational structure in the new private pension
system, which saved the existing pension funds considerable start-up costs
(Orenstein 1999; Müller 1999).

In many instances, however, the business community has failed to achieve
its goals. The private sector, for example, pushed for much broader pension privatization schemes than it was able to achieve in Colombia, Peru,
and Mexico. The business community was also unable to block amendments
to the pension privatization legislation that established state-owned pension

funds in Argentina and Mexico. Nor was it able to prevent the government from substantially raising the employer's contribution rates in El Salvador and Colombia. Some sectors of the business community have also failed to obtain the right to participate fully in the new pension systems of some countries. The Chilean banking industry, for example, was banned from directly managing the new private pension funds in that country, and the Mexican insurance industry failed to obtain the permission of the government to manage the life and disability insurance policies in Mexico's private pension system.

The private sector has often not even been able to convince the government to privatize the pension system. Private-sector support is clearly not a sufficient condition for pension privatization to take place since the business community has promoted pension privatization in many countries that have failed to privatize their pension systems. The most important Brazilian business association, the Federation of Industries of the State of São Paulo (FIESP), called for pension privatization in 1993, and other Brazilian business associations subsequently formulated pension privatization plans, but these proposals have gone unheeded (Carvalho 1993; Kay 1998; Weyland 1996b; interview with Trabuco 1997). In Venezuela, the Chamber of Commerce of Caracas proposed a pension privatization plan as early as 1989, but to little avail ("Proposición de la Cámara" 1989). Business groups in the Czech Republic, Paraguay, and Ecuador have also unsuccessfully lobbied their governments to privatize their pension systems.

Business support is not a necessary condition for pension privatization either, since some countries have privatized their pension systems without active pressure from the business community. In Chile, the business community did not lobby the government to privatize the pension system and was largely unaware of the pension privatization plans of the government prior to the announcement of the reform (interviews with Piñera 1997, with Gazmuri 1997, and with Larraín 1997). According to Kay (1998: 204), business "did not take a prominent role in advocating reform" in Uruguay either. Indeed, two of the most important Uruguayan business associations, the Higher Business Council and the Christian Association of Businessmen, did not even endorse the government's proposed reform until after it had been introduced to the legislature (Kay 1998: 204).

Pension privatization does not appear to be closely correlated with business strength or influence either. Business is presumably stronger in those countries that have economy-wide peak associations since such associations serve to unify the private sector and coordinate its lobbying efforts. There does not appear to be any correlation between the existence of economy-wide peak associations and pension privatization, however. Some of the countries that have privatized their pension systems—such as Colombia and

Uruguay—do not have economy-wide peak associations, whereas some of the countries that have not privatized their systems, including Venezuela, Ecuador, Panama, and Paraguay, do have economy-wide peak associations (Schneider 1998b).

Business is also commonly thought to have more influence in countries governed by right-wing business-allied parties. Countries governed by right-of-center ruling parties do not appear to be any more likely to privatize their pension systems than countries governed by left-of-center parties. Indeed in many countries, center or center-left parties, many of which have close ties to the labor movement, have enacted the pension privatization schemes. In Hungary and Poland, left-of-center political parties, which had close ties to the formerly communist labor unions, enacted the legislation privatizing the countries' pension systems. In Bolivia, Argentina, and Mexico, centrist political parties with long traditions of economic populism and, in the latter two cases, close ties to the labor movement, implemented the pension privatization schemes. In all three of these countries, traditionally right-of-center political parties with close ties to the business community voted against the pension privatization plans. In Uruguay and Costa Rica, the pension privatization measures achieved a relatively high degree of consensus, obtaining support from some left-of-center parties as well as right-of-center parties. Only in El Salvador and Nicaragua did right-wing parties enact pension privatization schemes over the objections of the left-wing opposition.

Conclusion

Institutions and interest groups have thus played an important role in shaping pension privatization plans, even if they have typically not determined whether countries would privatize their pension systems. Institutions, including the type of regime, constitution, and public pension system prevailing in each country, have placed limits on the degree of pension privatization that is financially and politically feasible. Countries with democratic political institutions have tended to implement more limited pension privatization schemes than countries with authoritarian institutions because they have faced greater political obstacles to enacting sweeping reforms. Similarly, countries with highly developed public pension systems have tended to implement more limited privatization schemes because of the higher transition costs these countries face. Finally, countries with constitutions that constrain the adoption of a fully private pension system have tended to opt for partial pension privatization.

Interest groups, especially business, labor, and the beneficiaries of privileged public pension programs, have also influenced pension privatization plans in important ways. The business community has helped persuade governments to privatize their pension systems and, at times, has been able to shape the reform legislation in ways that benefit parts or all of the private sector. The beneficiaries of privileged pension programs, meanwhile, have often managed to have themselves excluded from the pension privatization plans. Finally, organized labor has frequently managed to water down the pension privatization plans or obtain a role for itself in the administration of the new pension systems. Organized labor has been most successful in obtaining these concessions where it has close ties to the ruling party. None of these groups, however, has determined the fate of proposed reforms on its own.

CHAPTER 8

Implications for Theory and Policy

THE FINDINGS of this study have a number of implications for existing theories of market-oriented reform. As Chapter 2 discussed, existing theories of market-oriented reform in developing countries have ascribed a preeminent causal role to economic crisis (Bates and Krueger 1993; Haggard and Kaufman 1995; Weyland 2002). This study, however, suggests that economic crisis may not play an equally important role in all areas of policy reform. Policymakers tend to enact economic stabilization measures and some first-generation structural reforms in response to economic crises because they believe that such measures will help them overcome the crises. There is little reason to expect that policymakers would enact second-generation reforms, such as pension, labor, health, or education reform, in response to economic crises, however, because most of these reforms would do little to combat crises. Indeed, some second-generation reforms, such as pension privatization, may actually make the crises worse in the short to medium term by reducing government revenues or increasing fiscal expenditures.

Some might argue that second-generation reforms are part of a general neoliberal package, and the countries that enact first-stage reforms are therefore likely to enact second-generation reforms as well. In fact, to the contrary, second-generation reforms are not part of the standard neoliberal package.[1] Second-generation measures were noticeably absent from the so-called Washington consensus on policy reform (Williamson 1990), and considerable disagreement exists on what should be the content of the second-stage reforms. To date, second-generation reforms have proven to be much less popular than the first-generation reforms. In Latin America and the Caribbean, for example, twenty-four countries enacted major financial reforms, twenty-three countries implemented major trade reforms, and fourteen countries privatized a substantial number of state companies between 1985 and 1995, but only five countries reformed their pension systems or their labor laws during this period (IADB 1996a: 80; Lora and Pagés 1996: 7). Other second-generation reforms, such as those affecting the social sectors, have also lagged behind the first-generation reforms. It may be that many Latin American nations will eventually adopt second-generation reforms. Nevertheless, two decades have already elapsed since the outbreak of the debt crisis in Latin America, which suggests that any relationship that exists between the second-generation reforms and economic crisis is a relatively weak one.

The quantitative analyses presented in this book found no clear evidence that economic crisis, as measured either by inflation or economic recession, has directly contributed to the enactment of pension privatization schemes in Latin America. Most of the countries that privatized their pension systems were not in the midst of economic crises at the time, nor had they experienced economic crises within two or three years prior to the reforms. Moreover, countries that had experienced economic recession or hyperinflation in the 1980s or 1990s were not significantly more likely to privatize their pension systems than countries that had not experienced such economic crises.

Economic crises may have indirectly contributed to the wave of pension privatization schemes by aggravating the financial problems of pension systems, jeopardizing foreign capital flows, and undermining domestic savings. In some countries, economic crises may also have built support for pension privatization by causing disenchantment with the existing state-led development model and by bolstering the policy-making influence of the World Bank and of market-oriented economists. As Chapter 2 argued, however, economic crisis is only one of the many factors that affect these variables, which partly explains why only a weak statistical relationship exists between economic crisis and pension privatization.

This study nevertheless found a great deal of evidence that specific macroeconomic problems have led governments to privatize their pension systems. In particular, it showed that countries with low domestic savings rates and high public pension expenditures were more likely to privatize their pension systems. Policymakers have viewed pension privatization, rightly or wrongly, as a means to boost their domestic savings rates and reduce the long-term economic burden of public pension expenditures, both of which are seen as necessary to compete in an increasingly globalized world economy.

These findings suggest that the concepts of economic crisis and market-oriented reform need to be disaggregated and that the economic crisis hypothesis should be reformulated to specify more precisely the relationship between different types of reforms and different kinds of economic problems. The challenge for scholars is to identify which types of reforms are associated with which types of problems. Do second-generation reforms tend to be related more to the specific problems affecting the particular sector that they involve (for example, pensions, health, or the civil service) than to macroeconomic problems in general? Are all types of first-generation structural reforms associated with general economic crises or only certain measures? Are first-generation reforms also associated with the specific problems affecting their particular sectors? Improved specification of the relationship between particular types of economic problems and policy responses will yield a more accurate and more useful theory of the determinants of market-oriented reform.

Ideas and Policy Reform

The decisions of policymakers to privatize their pension systems or undertake other reforms cannot be divorced from the realm of ideas. A purely functionalist account of decision-making is obviously insufficient. For any given economic problem, a variety of possible policy solutions typically exist. Ideas not only determine what the range of possible policy solutions are, but they also suggest, correctly or incorrectly, what costs and benefits are associated with each type of policy solution. Ideas thus help policymakers decide what they must do to maximize their interests in an uncertain world.

The challenge for theorists is to show how and where ideas matter. Scholars should be able to show how ideas can explain variance in policy outcomes not only across time but also across polities. Theorists should also be able to generate hypotheses that will allow them to test for the effects of ideas. One way to do this is by specifying under what circumstances ideas will diffuse, which is the approach taken in this book.

This study has shown that ideas about the efficacy of pension privatization have diffused through three main channels: the World Bank; neoliberal economists; and regional diffusion of the Chilean model. Each of these factors played an important role in persuading political leaders that pension privatization would bring major economic benefits even though empirical studies of pension privatization have not found conclusive evidence that such benefits exist. Pension privatization has therefore been more likely to take place where the Chilean model has been more salient and where the World Bank and market-oriented economists have had more influence. This suggests that the success of policy ideas is at times related more to the salience of the ideas and the influence of their advocates than to the merits of the ideas themselves.

The literature on market-oriented reform in developing countries has paid relatively little attention to the role that regional diffusion has played in economic reform.[2] Although some scholars have suggested that the policy successes of the Chilean reforms encouraged other Latin American nations to adopt similar measures, they have not provided much in the way of theoretical or empirical evidence to back up this assertion. The failure of scholars to explore systematically the role of diffusion may be a product of the case study orientation of most research on economic reform in Latin America, since patterns of regional diffusion often become most apparent in large-n studies.

This study found substantial evidence of a pattern of regional diffusion in the spread of pension privatization. Pension privatization has been promoted in Latin America more than any other region, and Latin American policymakers have repeatedly stressed the importance of the Chilean model in shaping their thinking on this issue. In many Latin American countries, policymakers initiated the reform process by studying the Chilean privatization scheme and used the Chilean legislation as a point of departure for their own measures. Latin American policymakers have been particularly inclined to privatize their pension systems both because they have been better acquainted with the Chilean model than their counterparts outside the region, and because they have been more inclined to view the Chilean experience as relevant to their own countries.

Recent studies of diffusion suggest that patterns of diffusion may change over time. Indeed, in the last five years, pension privatization has spread like wildfire from Latin America to Eastern Europe and the former Soviet Union. Over time, the Chilean model may become less relevant, as new models of pension privatization or other types of pension reform emerge.[3] Nevertheless, in the last two decades, the Chilean model has been the main reference point in the area of pension privatization.

The influence of the Chilean model was particularly notable with regard to pension reform because Chile was the first country to privatize its pension system, and much of the alleged evidence of the economic benefits of pension privatization has been based on studies of the Chilean reform. Nevertheless, some evidence suggests that the Chilean model has also contributed to the spread of other types of economic and social policy reforms. Latin American countries have adopted reforms more quickly than countries in other regions of the world in the last fifteen years. Moreover, those countries that border Chile have implemented the reforms most quickly of all. Between 1985 and 1995, Argentina, Bolivia, and Peru (along with Nicaragua, which started out with a very low rating) registered the greatest changes in the region on the Inter-American Development Bank's index of economic reform, perhaps because the Chilean model was particularly salient in neighboring countries (IADB 1997: 95–96).[4]

Although the demonstration effects of the Chilean reforms appear to have played some role in the spread of market-oriented reforms in Latin America, much work remains to be done in order to understand the precise mechanisms by which neoliberal policies have diffused. The literature on the diffusion of innovations suggests that personal communications play an important role in the spread of ideas. According to Rogers (1995: 18), "Dependence on the communicated experience of near peers suggests that the heart of the diffusion process consists of the modeling and imitation by potential adopters of their network partners who have adopted previously." These communications often take place through policy networks—communities of policymakers who share an interest in a particular issue area (Mintrom and Vergari 1998; Knoke 1990; Walker 1981). Epistemic communities, or networks of experts with similar training and values and a shared policy enterprise, represent one kind of policy network, which have played an important role in some policy reforms (Haas 1992; Adler and Haas 1992).

This study found that a policy network of neoliberal economists, which resembled an epistemic community in many ways, played an important role in the spread of pension privatization in Latin America. During the last two decades, economists have gradually come to dominate social security policy making in many Latin American countries, displacing the traditional social security experts who were typically trained as lawyers. The economists have tended to advocate pension privatization in part because they have usually received training in neoclassical economics, which emphasizes the efficiency of market-oriented solutions. Economists also tend to be supportive of pension privatization because, unlike the traditional social security experts, they tend to be very concerned with the macroeconomic impact as well as the social impact of the pension system.

Some studies argue that networks of economists promoted other kinds of neoliberal reforms in individual Latin American countries (Centeno and Silva 1998; Centeno 1994; Conaghan, Malloy, and Abugattás 1990; Valdés 1995; Hira 1998; Biglaiser 1998; Silva 1991; Domínguez 1997). Much research remains to be done to assess how important these policy networks are in promoting reform, however. Specifically, we need to better understand why the networks of economists have come to power, and we need to know how much policy-making autonomy these economists actually have. To what degree is the rise of economists exogenously or endogenously determined? To what extent are the economists actually able to influence the direction of policy?

This study has suggested that both exogenous and endogenous factors have influenced appointments in the area of social security policy, and different groups within the government have struggled to control these positions. It has also argued that the top social security policymakers have had a considerable degree of autonomy in designing the social security reforms. Thus, it matters a great deal who is appointed to the top policy-making posts in these areas. Policymakers may have a particularly large amount of latitude in crafting social security reforms because there tends to be less consensus about the consequences of these reforms, and the top political leaders are therefore less likely to have firm views on these topics. Further research, however, is needed in order to assess whether policymakers have an equal level of policy-making autonomy with other second-generation reforms as well.

This study also found a great deal of evidence that the World Bank has played an important role in the spread of pension privatization around the world. Other studies have argued that the international financial institutions have played a similarly important role in the spread of other market-oriented reforms (Stallings 1992; Kahler 1992; Williamson and Haggard 1994; Biersteker 1995; Edwards 1995). Nevertheless, further research is needed to assess whether the international financial institutions are more influential in some policy areas than in others. The World Bank, for example, may be particularly influential with regard to second-generation reforms, such as pension privatization, because these measures are not part of the standard neoliberal reform package and they tend to require extensive technical assistance to implement. Many of the stabilization measures and first-generation structural reforms do not require the same degree of technical planning. Moreover, countries may be more likely to undertake stabilization measures and first-generation structural reforms even without the World Bank's encouragement, particularly if they are facing a severe economic crisis.

We also need to better understand the exact mechanisms through which the international financial institutions exercise policy influence. What are the most effective means of influence? Where and under what circumstances is the World Bank likely to propagate its views? This study argued that the World Bank's influence in pension policy has been more ideational than material. It suggested that through its publications, workshops, conferences, technical assistance, and formal and informal contacts with policymakers, the World Bank has helped persuade many policymakers that privatizing their pension systems would bring their countries numerous economic as well as social benefits. The World Bank's pension reform missions have been particularly influential because they have provided the World Bank with direct access to the key policymakers and the essential financial and demographic data, which the World Bank used to propagate its views. Further research is needed, however, to identify the mechanisms of World Bank influence in other policy areas.

Political Institutions and Market Reform

Many of the early studies of the politics of economic reform in developing countries argued that regime type was an important determinant of the fate of economic reform. Early studies of social security reform in Latin America, for example, suggested that only authoritarian regimes would be able to implement sweeping reform measures (Rosenberg and Malloy 1978; Malloy 1985). According to this literature, only authoritarian regimes had the strength and autonomy to carry out neoliberal reforms, which often re-quired the repression of labor or the political opposition in general (Shea-han 1980; Kaufman 1986). More recent studies have cast doubt on these ar-guments, however. A variety of scholars have documented cases of successful reform by democratic governments (Haggard and Kaufman 1995; Williamson 1994; Bates and Krueger 1993), and statistical analyses have found no cor-relation between regime type and economic performance (Remmer 1986, 1990; Przeworski and Limongi 1993, 1997).

My research echoes the recent findings in that it finds no correlation be-tween regime type and pension privatization per se. This study, nevertheless, suggests that regime type does indeed matter. Both democratic and author-itarian regimes have privatized their pension systems, but the nature and the outcome of the privatization process have varied considerably between them. In the authoritarian regimes, political participation in the reform pro-cess has been kept to a minimum and the privatization proposals have been approved rapidly and largely as their architects had intended. Democratic governments, by contrast, have generally taken much longer to approve so-cial security reforms and have allowed a much greater degree of participa-tion in the reform process. In democratic regimes, social security reforms have typically been enacted only after the architects of the reforms have made substantial concessions to critics of the reform proposals. Democratic governments in Latin America have not privatized their pension systems by decree. Instead, they have sought legislative approval for their pension re-form measures, at times carrying out meaningful negotiations with a variety of political and social actors in an effort to obtain broad support for the re-form proposals. As a result, the reforms enacted by democratic governments have typically been much less sweeping than those enacted by authoritarian regimes.

The ability of democratic governments to enact pension privatization schemes hinges to a large extent on the executive's degree of control of the legislature. The unpopularity of pension privatization makes it difficult to obtain votes from legislators from opposition parties or even allied parties. The strength and internal discipline of the ruling party in the legislature therefore becomes a key determinant of the political viability of pension re-form. This finding coincides with the conclusions of Haggard and Kaufman (1995) and others who suggest that reform is more likely in two-party sys-tems, largely because the ruling party is more likely to hold a majority of seats in the legislature in these systems.

None of these findings applies to all types of reforms, however. Economic stabilization measures or basic structural reforms, such as trade liberalization and the privatization of state-owned enterprises, typically do not require leg-islative approval, and when implemented in the context of a crisis, they may even enjoy broad, popular support. As a result, democratic governments may not need to control a large number of seats in the legislature in order to enact these reforms and may have no more trouble enacting them than do authoritarian regimes. In contrast, the second-stage reforms typically do require legislative approval under democratic rule (Naím 1995; Nelson 1995). Moreover, these reforms tend to be highly unpopular in large part because the benefits tend to be long term and diffuse whereas the costs are immediate and concentrated. Democratic regimes may therefore have a harder time carrying out sweeping second-stage reforms than do authoritarian regimes, and in most instances they may only be able to do so where they control a large percentage of seats in the legislature.[5]

These findings again point to the importance of disaggregating the concept of reform in studies of policy change in developing countries. Much of the confusion regarding the relative abilities of democratic and authoritarian regimes to enact reforms may be the result of the lumping together of different types of reforms that are governed by different procedures and often have varying distributions of costs and benefits. Contradictory findings regarding the importance of the executive's support in the legislature may also be due to the conflation of first- and second-stage economic reforms.[6]

Implications for Welfare State Literature

This study also has some theoretical implications for the literature on the welfare state. As noted in Chapter 1, the existing welfare-state literature focuses almost exclusively on the advanced industrial democracies of Western Europe, North America, and the Antipodes. By focusing solely on these countries, welfare-state scholars limit the explanatory reach of their theories and introduce the potential of selection bias into their analyses. There is no reason to believe that the industrialized countries are representative of the total universe of countries with regard to the determinants of pension reform. Although some of the variables that explain the development and reform of the welfare state in the industrialized countries may explain social policy outcomes in the developing world, others may not. It is therefore essential for scholars with more general theoretical ambitions to test their theories of social policy on developing as well as industrialized countries.

This study suggests that some of the variables that welfare-state theorists have identified as being crucial to understanding social policy outcomes in the industrialized world may not be as important in Latin America and other developing areas. The dominant branch of welfare-state theory, the power-resources approach, has traced the development of varying social policy regimes to differences in the relative strength of business and labor (Stephens 1979; Korpi 1983; Esping-Andersen 1985, 1990). As Chapters 6 and 7 show, however, the relative political strength of business and labor cannot explain reform patterns in Latin America. The quantitative analyses in this book found that countries with low unionization rates are not more likely to enact pension privatization schemes than countries with high unionization rates—indeed, countries with low unionization rates may actually be less likely to enact such schemes. Nor are Latin American countries with well-organized business communities (as measured by the existence of an economy-wide peak association) more likely to privatize their pension systems. Moreover, the case studies in this book reveal that neither business nor labor has played a decisive role in determining whether pension privatization schemes were enacted.

The case studies of the Latin American and Eastern European reforms, however, also show that both business and labor can shape the content of the privatization proposals, even if they do not determine whether they are enacted. In Latin America and Eastern Europe, the labor movement has been particularly influential where it has close ties to the ruling party. Where labor unions and the ruling party have historical links, there has typically been more cooperation and less confrontation on the issue of pension reform. Ruling parties that are tied to organized labor have been more willing to grant the unions concessions, and the unions that have close ties to the ruling party have been more inclined to agree to support the pension privatization schemes in exchange for such concessions.

In most instances, however, Latin American unions have not had close ties to the political parties that have sought to implement pension privatization measures, and the unions have vigorously, but typically unsuccessfully, opposed the reforms. By contrast, most recent pension reforms in the industrialized countries have been negotiated rather than imposed, and labor unions as well as employers' associations have played crucial roles in these negotiations (Myles and Pierson 2001; Rhodes 2001; Hinrichs 2001). Labor unions, for example, helped bring about the establishment of private pension systems that supplement the existing public pension systems in Denmark, the Netherlands, and Australia, and they even grudgingly supported the pension privatization schemes that were negotiated in Sweden (K. Anderson 2001). The unions also signed off on many of the parametric reforms of the public pension systems that occurred in numerous other industrialized countries during the 1990s (Myles and Pierson 2001; Hinrichs 2001).

Labor unions in Latin America may have opposed pension reform more vigorously than their Western European counterparts because unions representing privileged public- and private-sector workers tend to dominate the labor movement in Latin America. These groups tend to be the biggest beneficiaries of the existing public pension systems and are therefore typically quite hostile to pension privatization measures or other reforms that seek to reduce or eliminate their privileges. In contrast, Western European labor movements typically represent a larger portion of the economically active population, and the pension systems in these countries tend not to be as skewed in favor of privileged groups of workers. Thus, Western European labor movements may be more likely to support reforms that they view as necessary to restore the financial health of the pension system as a whole. Further research, however, is needed to better understand both the varying responses of labor movements to pension reform in the two regions and what role these responses play in shaping the reforms.

Institutions may also have played a more important role in shaping pension reform in Western Europe than in Latin America. A number of studies of European countries have found that certain kinds of political institutions have made pension reform more difficult by providing opportunities to opponents of reforms to block the reform proposals. As Chapter 2 discussed, however, the kinds of political institutions that are said to make reform more difficult (for example, presidential systems, bicameral legislatures, federal systems, and proportional representation) are present in many of the Latin American countries that have privatized their pension systems. Thus, such institutions cannot explain the variance in pension privatization within Latin America. It may be that these institutions do not shape pension reform as much in Latin America as they do in industrialized countries because these institutions tend to be weaker in the developing world. In Latin America, for example, presidents have at times circumvented or manipulated the legislature and other political institutions in order to obtain approval of their reform proposals.

As the case studies in this book have shown, however, even in Latin America some institutions clearly do shape pension reform outcomes. The constitutional rules governing social security, for example, have obliged some Latin American countries to opt for partial rather than full privatization. The structure of the political party system and the rules governing control of the ballot, meanwhile, have influenced the prospects for pension privatization through their effect on the executive's degree of control of the legislature. Perhaps the most important institutional determinant of the nature of pension reform, however, is the scope of the existing public pension system. The scope of the existing public pension system places significant limits on the type of privatization schemes that countries may enact. Pension privatization is particularly expensive for countries with mature and highly developed public pension systems because they have large existing public pension commitments. Countries with mature public pension systems have therefore tended to enact partial rather than full-scale pension privatization schemes in order to reduce the transition costs involved. They have also slowed down the speed of the transition and deferred some of the transition costs (Devesa-

Carpio and Vidal-Meliá 2001: 28). Finally, they have frequently slashed the transition costs of the privatization schemes by reneging on some of their existing pension commitments (Mesa-Lago and Müller 2002).

Nevertheless, some welfare-state scholars exaggerate the importance of institutional barriers to pension privatization (Pierson 1994, 1996; Myles and Pierson 2001). Pierson (1994: 72), for example, has argued that high transition costs are likely to create "insurmountable political difficulties" to pension privatization in countries with mature pension systems. However, numerous Latin American and Eastern European countries with mature pension systems, and even a few industrialized countries, have privatized their pension systems in spite of the high transition costs involved.[7] Moreover, the statistical analyses in this book found that countries with mature pension systems were more likely, rather than less likely, to privatize their pension systems. This is because countries with mature public pension systems tend to have very high levels of pension spending, which puts pressure on them to enact some type of reform. Although most countries with high levels of public pension spending have opted for parametric reforms of their pension systems, some of these countries have sought to reduce the long-term economic burden of public pension spending by privatizing their systems. The maturity of public pension systems thus constrains the scope of pension privatization schemes, but it does not prohibit them altogether.

Whereas interest groups and institutions are less important than welfare-state theorists would predict in determining social policy outcomes outside of the industrialized world, other variables are more important than they would suggest. Welfare-state theorists, for example, have largely ignored the role played by factors such as domestic capital shortages, World Bank influence, and the ascent of market-oriented economists in bringing about pension reform. This study has shown that Latin American and Eastern European countries have privatized their pension systems partly in order to boost their sagging domestic savings rates and reduce their vulnerability to cutoffs of foreign capital. It has also demonstrated how the World Bank and market-oriented economists helped persuade political leaders in Latin America and Eastern Europe that pension privatization would bring numerous benefits to their countries.

These same variables may also play an important role in shaping pension reform outcomes in the industrialized countries. The industrialized countries, by and large, have had higher domestic savings rates and more stable access to capital than their less-developed neighbors, which may explain in part why they have found pension privatization less appealing. The absence of support for pension privatization among the industrialized countries may also stem from the lower degree of influence of the World Bank and market-oriented economists in these countries, not to mention the lesser salience of the Chilean model. The industrialized countries may thus have eschewed pension privatization not because the political or institutional barriers to pension privatization are insurmountable, but rather because the economic and ideational climate has been less propitious for pension privatization in the industrialized world. The statistical analyses presented in this book, which examine the determinants of pension privatization in both industrialized and developing countries, provide support for the argument that these economic and ideational variables have been important not only in Latin America but around the world as well. Nevertheless, further research is needed in order to assess how well these arguments apply to the industrialized countries alone.

Lessons from Latin America

What lessons does Latin America's experience with pension privatization have to offer the rest of the world? Many analysts have focused on the positive aspects of Latin America's experience with private pension systems. Indeed, the Chilean private pension system and most of the other private pension systems in Latin America have performed well in a number of areas. The private pension systems, for example, have generated high returns, attracted a large number of members, and built up an impressive amount of assets in the short time that they have been in operation. Nevertheless, the Latin American private pension systems have also suffered from some serious deficiencies. In most countries, the private systems have experienced high rates of evasion and large administrative costs, both of which will reduce the pensions that they pay out over the long run. The new systems have also increased the financial risks borne by workers without eliminating the threat of political interference in the pension system. Finally, the pension privatization measures have failed to improve the coverage of the social security systems, and there is relatively little evidence that they have brought major economic benefits to the countries that implement them. Thus, it is not clear that the new systems represent a major improvement over the previous systems.

The private pension systems have certainly been successful in that they have attracted a large and growing number of members. As discussed in Chapter 1, many of the reforms have obliged future members of the workforce and some or all of current members of the labor force to join the private pension system. Even where people have been granted a choice, however, they have typically opted to join the private pension systems. Workers have opted for the private system in part because of the high returns that the private pension systems have enjoyed, but also because many Latin American governments actively encouraged people to join the private systems and offered special incentives for those who did. In Chile, for example, workers flocked to the private pension system partly because the contribution rates in this system were lower than in the public system and the state carried out a massive propaganda campaign to convince people to switch (Borzutzky 1983). Those who have remained in the public pension system in Chile and elsewhere have typically been elderly, often low-income, workers. One exception to this trend is Colombia, where the public system has been strengthened and continues to service the majority of the workforce. In Uruguay, too, most people continue to belong exclusively to the public system, largely because membership in the private system would require an additional social security contribution for low-income workers. In the rest of the Latin American countries, however, at least three-quarters of the covered population belong to the private pension systems. Table 8.1 presents indicators of the performance of private pension systems in Latin America in a number of different areas.

The growing memberships of the private pension systems have helped them accumulate a tremendous amount of assets. At year-end 2001, the private pension system in Chile alone had more than $35.4 billion in funds under management, which was equal to 55 percent of the country's gross domestic product (FIAP 2002). Other Latin American countries have fewer funds under management in part because their private pension systems have not been in existence for nearly as long as the Chilean system. Nevertheless, they control a substantial and growing quantity of assets. The Mexican private pension system, for example, had more than $27.1 billion in assets as of December 31, 2001, and the Argentine pension system controlled almost $20.8 billion in assets at this time (FIAP 2002). In all cases, the assets of the private pension systems equaled at least 4.5 percent of their country's gross domestic product, making them important new sources of capital for their developing economies.

Perhaps the most significant achievement of the private pension systems to date has been the high returns that they have generated. As Table 8.1 indicates, in most countries the private pension systems have yielded annual returns of more than 10 percent above inflation since their inception, and in no country did these returns fall below 6 percent (FIAP 2002; Devesa-Carpio and Vidal-Meliá 2001: 12). In Chile, the private pension system generated returns of 10.7 percent between May 1, 1981, and December 31, 2001, and in Bolivia, Colombia, and El Salvador the systems have generated real returns of more than 11 percent since their inception. These returns are substantially above what a public pay-as-you-go pension system might be expected to return. Indeed, in all of the countries, the rate of return of the private pension systems substantially exceeded annual growth in gross

TABLE 8.1

The Performance of Private Pension Systems in Latin America

(at year-end 2001)

	Argentina	Bolivia	Colombia	Chile	El Salvador	Mexico	Peru	Uruguay
Total funds accumulated (as percent of GDP)	$20,786 mil. (7.7%)	$936 million (11.2%)	$4,955 million (6.1%)	$35,461 mil. (55.4%)	$768 million (5.5%)	$27,146 mil. (4.5%)	$3,622 million (6.6%)	$1,045 million (5.5%)
Contributors	2,561,620	631,671	2,111,607	3,450,080	492,221	11,864,672	1,089,654	293,697
Affiliates	8,843,089	691,590	4,336,379	6,427,656	919,805	26,518,534	2,732,071	596,964
Contributors/ affiliates	29.0%	91.3%	48.8%	53.7%	53.5%	44.7%	39.9%	49.2%
Contributors/ labor force	18.0%	20.4%	10.5%	58.0%	19.5%	29.1%	10.3%	23.0%
Affiliates/ labor force	62.2%	22.4%	21.6%	108.0%	36.5%	65.1%	25.9%	46.8%
Number of pension funds	12	2	6	7	3	13	4	4
Market share of largest three	58.5%	100%	64.8%	79.0%	100%	36.7%	76.4%	86.8%

Investment portfolio of pension funds	Public 70% Corporate 12% Financial 14% Foreign 2%	Public 73% Corporate 13% Financial 10%	Public 49% Corporate 14% Financial 25%	Public 35% Corporate 18% Financial 33% Foreign 13%	Public 80% Corporate 2% Financial 18%	Public 88% Corporate 8% Financial 2%	Public 14% Corporate 37% Financial 44% Foreign 5%	Public 61% Corporate 6% Financial 22%
Annual real rate of return (dates)	7.97% (7/94–12/01)	11.10% (5/97–12/00)	11.78% (4/94–12/01)	10.70% (5/81–12/01)	12.62% (1/98–12/01)	9.34% (7/97–12/01)	6.00% (6/93–12/01)	10.82% (4/96–12/01)
Average management fees	1.50%	0.50%	1.57%	1.48% (excludes fixed commission)	1.69%	1.62% (excludes commissions on balances)	2.39%	1.98%
Average insurance fees	0.77%	1.71%	1.92% (state-managed)	0.78%	1.28%	2.5% (state-managed)	1.34%	0.76%
Fees as a percent of contributions	20.6%	18.1%	25.9%	18.4%	22.9%	32.5%	31.8%	18.1%
Net income of AFPs (as a percent of mgmt fees)	$101.8 million (12.3%)	$0.8 million (8.0%)	NA	$228.1 million (50.5%)	$0.4 million (0.9%)	$305.0 million (28.1%)	$58.5 million (40.9%)	$3.2 million (12.3%)

SOURCES: FIAP 2002; AIOS 2001; Mesa-Lago 2001.

domestic product per capita, an indicator that can be used as a proxy for the implicit rate of return of a pay-as-you-go system (Devesa-Carpio and Vidal-Meliá 2001: 12).

It is not clear that these high returns can be maintained, however. Indeed, in recent years, the returns have typically been lower than their historical average (Mesa-Lago 2001: 85; AIOS 2001: 24–25). The high returns generated in the 1980s and most of the 1990s resulted in large part from the elevated real interest rates that prevailed on government bonds in Latin America during this period. As the table indicates, most of the assets of the pension funds have been invested in government securities. In Argentina, Bolivia, El Salvador, and Mexico public debt represented more than 70 percent of the assets held by the private pension funds at year-end 2001. Most of the remaining assets in these systems, as well as in the other systems, are concentrated in corporate bonds and bank certificates of deposits, both of which paid out high real interest rates throughout most of the 1980s and 1990s. The high returns do not appear to be the result of the expert management of the funds invested. Some studies have shown that in Chile and Peru, at least, the returns of the private pension systems have lagged behind the performance of some relevant benchmarks (Srinivas, Whitehouse, and Yermo 2000; CB Capitales 1999).

Many observers are concerned that the excessive concentration of the pension fund industry in a few funds might undermine the long-term performance of the private pension system. At year-end 2001, three or fewer pension funds accounted for more than half of the members of the private pension systems in all of the Latin American countries, save Mexico, and more than three-quarters of the members of the private pension systems in Bolivia, Chile, El Salvador, Peru, and Uruguay.[8] Critics fear that the lack of competition in the system will reduce the incentives of the pension fund managers to maintain high returns and low costs. There is also some evidence to suggest that larger funds may be less efficient on average than the smaller funds. A study of British pension funds, for example, found that larger funds tended to have lower returns than smaller funds, and a long-term study of the Chilean pension system came to somewhat similar conclusions (Blake 2000; Mesa-Lago 2001: 78).

More importantly, the high commissions that the pension fund administrators have charged have partly offset the high returns generated by the private pension systems.[9] As Table 8.1 indicates, in all of the countries except Bolivia, the pension funds charged management commissions of at least 1.5 percent of each worker's monthly salary at year-end 2001 (FIAP 2002).[10] Moreover, the pension fund managers in some countries also charged additional commissions. In Mexico, for example, pension fund managers charged an average annual commission of 0.38 percent on the balances in workers' individual retirement accounts. According to one study, if these commissions and other factors are taken into account, the average annual real return of the AFPs in Chile declines from approximately 11 percent to 5.1 percent between 1982 and 1998, an annual yield below that corresponding to bank certificates of deposit in Chile during this period (CB Capitales 1999).[11]

The commissions have been high in part because of marketing costs of the private pension fund administrators (AFPs). Marketing costs averaged 29 percent of total expenses of the AFPs between July 2000 and June 2001 (AIOS 2001: 17−18). The pension funds compete to attract customers, which involves a great deal of advertising and large sales forces—in Argentina and Mexico, for example, the AFPs employed more than 10,000 salespeople at year-end 2001 (FIAP 2002). Frequent transfers between the AFPs, which are encouraged by the salespeople, have also pushed up the administrative expenses of the pension funds. During 2001 alone, 412,683 people switched pension funds in Argentina and 235,245 people transferred from one pension fund to another in Chile. The private pension funds have also charged high fees in order to reap large profits. Between July 2000 and June 2001, the private pension fund administrators took home profits equivalent to 27 percent of their total management commissions (AIOS 2001: 20). All of the private pension systems generated net profits during this period, but the AFPs did particularly well in Mexico, registering profits of $305 million, or 28 percent of their management fees (AIOS 2001: 17).

In most countries, the private pension fund administrators also deduct funds from each worker's paycheck in order to pay their life and disability insurance premiums.[12] The life and disability insurance premiums have declined over time, but they still remain quite high in some countries. The premiums range from a low of approximately 0.8 percent of each worker's salary on average in Argentina, Chile, and Uruguay, to 1.71 percent in Bolivia and 2.5 percent in Mexico. The insurance premiums and the management commissions together divert a substantial amount of funds from each worker's individual retirement account. In Peru and Mexico, for example, 35 percent of the funds deducted from each worker's paycheck is spent on these fees instead of being deposited in a worker's retirement account. Even in Chile and Uruguay, the countries with the lowest management and insurance commissions, the fees represented 18 percent of each worker's pension contributions at year-end 2001. If these fees remain high, they will substantially reduce the amount of funds in each worker's account upon retirement. Indeed, one study estimated that if the current level of fees were cut in half, workers would be able to finance 10 percent higher pensions upon retirement (Devesa, Rodríguez, and Vidal 2001).

Evasion has also undermined the high returns of the private pension systems. Proponents of pension privatization had argued that workers would be more likely to contribute to the private pension systems because pension benefits would be more closely linked to contributions. The shift to private pension systems has not led workers to make their social security contributions more regularly, however. On the contrary, evasion rates have risen in many instances (Mesa-Lago 2001: 74–75). At year-end 2001, less than half of the affiliates were contributing to the private pension systems in most countries (FIAP 2002). The situation was particularly bad in Argentina where only 29 percent of the affiliates were contributing to the private pension system, owing in part to the severe economic crisis that had afflicted the country. Throughout Latin American, evasion rates are particularly high among women, the uneducated, agricultural workers, people under twenty-five years of age, and employees of small businesses (Devesa-Carpio and Vidal-Meliá 2001). The high evasion rates mean that many workers who are officially enrolled in the private pension systems will not have sufficient funds in their individual accounts to support themselves upon retirement. Moreover, some of these workers will not even have made enough contributions to qualify for a minimum pension.

It is difficult to predict the overall impact of pension privatization on the level of pension benefits in Latin America, but a few general observations can be made. First, if the current rates of return are maintained, average pensions may well be higher in the new private pension systems than they were in the public systems. To date, the Chilean private pension system has paid out pensions that are approximately 50 percent higher than they were in the old public system (Devesa-Carpio and Vidal-Meliá 2001: 9). Nevertheless, the effects of the reforms will vary considerably among different sectors of the population. The wealthy will typically receive higher pensions than previously because the private pension systems, unlike many of the public systems, do not have ceilings on benefits. Many of the former beneficiaries of privileged public pension schemes, meanwhile, will fare more poorly in the new systems since the privatization measures eliminated the special privileges that they had enjoyed. Women may also fare more poorly in the new systems because they often have prolonged absences from the labor market during child-raising years; therefore, they will make fewer contributions than men. Women will also be hurt because they live longer than men and often have lower minimum retirement ages, which means that the funds in their individual retirement accounts will have to be stretched out over a longer period of time.

The overall impact of the privatization schemes on income distribution is difficult to assess. The new private pension systems do not, for the most part, redistribute income, but much of the redistribution that took place under the previous systems was directed toward certain middle-income sectors (for example, state employees) rather than the poor. Some aspects of the reforms, such as the elimination of ceilings on benefits, will clearly have a negative impact on income distribution, but other aspects, such as the elimination of the privileged pension schemes, will have a positive impact.

The most worrisome issue regarding income distribution relates to the coverage of the private pension systems. As Chapter 1 discussed, the social security systems of the less developed Central American, Caribbean, and Andean nations, have traditionally only covered a relatively small proportion of the population. Moreover, even the more developed nations of the region have typically not provided pension benefits to many of the poorest groups of the population, including domestic servants, agricultural workers, and the self-employed. A few of the recent pension privatization schemes have sought to address the issue of coverage. Colombia and Uruguay, for example, granted subsidies to low-income workers to help them join the pension systems. Bolivia, meanwhile, used the proceeds from the partial privatization of some state-owned companies to establish a small noncontributory pension for all Bolivians above the age of sixty-five.[13] Most of the Latin American countries that have privatized their pension systems have done little or nothing to expand the coverage of their systems, however. As a result, pension coverage has shown no change or has actually shrunk in most of the countries that have privatized their pension systems (Mesa-Lago 2001: 74). Moreover, the high evasion rates in the private pension systems mean that many workers who are officially covered by the pension systems will not have made sufficient contributions to qualify even for a minimum pension. This problem was made even more acute by the decisions of many countries to require workers to contribute for a larger number of years in order to be eligible for a minimum pension.

It is clear that the pension privatization measures have increased the financial risks borne by workers. In the public systems, the state guaranteed workers a certain pension (usually measured as a percentage of each worker's salary) provided that the workers met the basic eligibility requirements, which were usually not especially stringent. In the new private systems, however, workers are not guaranteed any pension benefit beyond the minimum set by law, and the requirements for receiving a minimum pension have been tightened.[14] In the private systems, the size of the pension benefits that workers will receive depends on the amount of funds that they have accumulated in their individual retirement accounts. Thus, if the rate of return on the funds in these accounts is poor, many workers could be left with meager pensions.

Proponents of pension privatization argue that workers face fewer political risks in the private systems, even if they face greater financial risks. They point out that Latin American governments frequently intervened in their public social security systems, diverting the revenues of these systems and adjusting the benefits and contribution levels as they saw fit. Such interference, proponents of privatization maintain, is much less likely to take place in a private pension system. Argentina's recent experience, however, demonstrates that governments may interfere with private pension systems, much as they have done with the public systems. In particular, it suggests that the large pool of capital controlled by the private pension funds is particularly tempting for governments facing a serious economic crisis. During 2001, the Argentine government, under the leadership of Minister of Economy Domingo Cavallo, repeatedly forced the private pension funds to lend money to the government to help it through the crisis. The government not only pressured the pension funds to purchase treasury bonds but also obliged them to transfer $2.3 billion in fixed-term deposits to a state-owned bank so that this bank could purchase government securities. Then, the government obliged all local bondholders, including the pension funds, to trade their dollar-denominated high-interest government bonds for lower-interest loans. Finally, the government ceased to make interest payments on these loans altogether. To make matters worse, it slashed the amount that workers must contribute to the pension funds from 11 percent to 5 percent in order to free up more spending money for the population. The result has been the virtual bankruptcy of the private pension system in Argentina.[15] One pension industry consultant remarked, "It's probably the first failure of a Latin American pension system . . . What you've seen since 1994 is a gradual return to what the system had tried to get away from—a reliance on the federal government to honour pensions" (Catan 2002).

Proponents of pension privatization have also argued that the privatization schemes will bring major macroeconomic benefits, but Latin America's experience with pension privatization has provided only mixed evidence of these benefits to date. There is little evidence to suggest that the private pension systems have had positive effects on the domestic savings rates of Latin American countries so far, although it is clearly too early to tell whether they will do so in the future. The private pension systems have channeled substantial amounts of resources into the local capital markets, which has stimulated their growth. In many countries, however, the private pension funds have invested a large portion of their assets in government bonds; as a result, the pension privatization measures have not benefited the capital markets as much as many advocates of privatization predicted.

The fiscal costs of the pension privatization schemes, meanwhile, have often exceeded the expectations of the architects of the reforms, which has put a major strain on government finances. The tremendous costs of the Argentine pension privatization plan, for example, helped contribute to that country's devastating financial crisis. According to Arenas de Mesa (2000), the fiscal costs of the transition in Chile averaged 6.1 percent of GDP between 1981 and 1989, and 4.8 percent of GDP between 1990 and 1998, and they are expected to average 4.1 percent of GDP per year between 1999 and 2037. The transition costs of pension privatization will probably be lower in other Latin American countries, but they will nevertheless be quite large. Schmidt-Hebbel (1995), for example, estimates that the transition costs in Colombia will rise from approximately 0.93 percent of GDP in 1995 to a high of 2.61 percent of GDP in 2013 and then gradually decline thereafter (Schmidt-Hebbel 1995). In Bolivia, the transition costs were expected to reach a peak of 2.72 percent in 1998 and gradually decline to 0.18 percent of GDP in 2037 (Mesa-Lago 2000: 31–32). Any positive capital markets effects that have been generated by the pension privatization schemes must therefore be weighed against the considerable fiscal costs that these schemes incur.

Pension privatization thus does not appear to be the panacea that some of its advocates have argued. It may well bring benefits to some groups and individuals, but at considerable costs to others. It may also remedy some existing economic problems, while creating new ones. Whether the total benefits of the privatization schemes exceed the total costs will remain unknown for decades, and even then estimates of the net impact of the reforms may depend on a variety of assumptions and counterfactuals. The tremendous wave of pension privatization that has occurred in the last decade therefore represents an unprecedented policy experiment. It is the workers of today— peasants, factory employees, salespeople, and state bureaucrats—who will reap the benefits or suffer the consequences.

Notes

CHAPTER 1 *The Politics of Retiring the State*

1. For insightful reviews of these literatures, see Geddes 1995; Kaufman 1999.

2. A few quantitative analyses of the determinants of economic reform do exist. See, for example, Remmer 1998; Roberts and Wibbels 2000; Crisp and Johnson 2001.

3. For exceptions, see Naím 1995; Nelson 1995; Graham 1999; Manzetti 1999; Madrid 2003.

4. The interviews did not use a standard set of questions. Instead, they typically aimed at gathering information on topics that the interviewees knew intimately.

5. Throughout this study, I use the term "social security" in the narrow sense to refer exclusively to retirement, survivors', and disability pensions. Outside of the United States, the term "social security" typically refers to a broad range of social programs, including health care, unemployment insurance, and family assistance programs.

6. These measures, which will be referred to here as add-on schemes, represent welfare-state expansion in the sense that they increase the size of publicly mandated benefits. Not surprisingly, add-on schemes are not typically as politically controversial as pension privatization.

7. For this reason, even the most broadly privatized systems, like the Chilean system, are commonly referred to as multipillar systems.

8. Some studies eschew the term "pension privatization" in favor of "structural reform" or "systemic reform" or they refer to a shift to "multipillar" or "fully funded" or "defined contribution" systems.

9. These stylized stages correspond only roughly to the actual reform process in most countries. The different phases of the reform process overlap with one another in most cases, and economic, ideational, and political factors usually play at least some role at each of the stages discussed above.

10. See, for example, the excellent studies by Esping-Andersen 1985, 1990; Pierson 1994; Garrett 1998; Hicks 1999; Huber and Stephens 2001. For useful surveys of the welfare-state literature, see Shalev 1983; Pierson 2000.

11. See, for example, Immergut 1992; Mares 1997; Bonoli 2000; Wood 2001; Myles and Pierson 2001.

12. For important exceptions, see the insightful analyses on the development of the welfare state in Latin America by Mesa-Lago 1978, 1989, and by Malloy 1979.

13. Mesa-Lago's 1978 study continues to be the authoritative volume on the development of social security in Latin America.

14. For a contrasting approach, see Mesa-Lago 1978.

15. For detailed analyses of the content of the pension privatization schemes, see Mesa-Lago 1994, 1997a, 2001; Mesa-Lago and Bertranou 1998; Queisser 1998; Devesa-Carpio and Vidal-Meliá 2001.

16. In this study, this type of reform will frequently be referred to as "full privatization."

17. Workers who make less than 7,500 Uruguayan pesos per month, however, are entitled to contribute 50 percent of the contributions that they make (on the first 5,000 Uruguayan pesos that they earn each month) to the private system instead of to the public system.

18. In Mexico, active workers were obliged to switch to the private system, but at the time of their retirement they will be allowed to choose between their private pension and a public pension based on the rules prevailing prior to the reform.

19. The financial community in Latin America has complained that the state-owned pension fund administrators represent unfair competition, but only in Uruguay has the state-owned administrator seized control of a large share of the market to date.

20. This index was first published in Madrid 2002.

21. James and Brooks (2001) also propose an index of pension reform, but their index fails to take into account whether membership in the private system is optional or mandatory and what sorts of incentives, if any, are provided for individuals to join the private system. As a result, it yields inaccurate scores: reforms creating parallel systems, such as in Colombia and Peru, are given the same scores as reforms creating fully private systems, as in El Salvador and Chile. Their index is also problematic in that it is based on a calculation of what percentage of a worker's future pension benefit will come from the private system, which makes it highly dependent on the economic assumptions used.

22. In the case of Argentina, the reduction in the employer's contribution was not part of the pension legislation, but it occurred at approximately the same time as the reform.

23. On the broadest level, the subject of this study—the dependent variable in social science parlance—is social security reform in general, and parts of the manuscript discuss some of the determinants of a variety of types of reforms (for example, parametric reforms). Nevertheless, the focus of this study is on a particular type of social security reform: pension privatization.

CHAPTER 2 *Explaining Pension Privatization in the 1990s*

1. Advocates of pension privatization correctly point out that the privatization schemes have reduced the *political* risks faced by workers by making it more difficult for the state to intervene in the pension system. As Chapter 8 discusses, however, members of the private pension systems continue to face some political risks.

2. Not surprisingly, many analyses from a power resources perspective also identify other important variables. See, for example, Huber and Stephens 2001.

3. Although the power resources approach was developed largely to explain the expansion of the welfare state in the industrialized countries, some theorists have suggested that it should be able to explain its present-day evolution as well (Esping-Andersen 1990: 21; Pierson 1994).

4. Applying the power resource approach to Latin America is complicated by the fact that Latin American party systems, unlike European systems, are not typically structured along class lines (Dix 1989; Collier and Collier 1991; Mainwaring and Scully 1995).

5. For a skeptical view, see Corrales 1997–98.

6. The average number of capital controls maintained by OECD governments fell from more than 0.8 in 1970 to approximately 0.3 in 1990 (Garrett 1995: 662), whereas the average number of capital controls maintained by governments in Latin America dropped from 1.78 in 1970 to 0.83 in 1994 (IMF, various years). Capital restrictions are counted here as restrictions on payments for capital transactions; bilateral payments arrangements with members of the IMF as well as with nonmembers; and advance import deposits.

7. The rising vulnerability of countries to capital outflows has led countries to adopt a variety of market-oriented reforms in order to attract or retain increasingly mobile capital.

8. Empirical analyses have not found clear evidence that pay-as-you-go systems reduce private savings (Aaron 1982; World Bank 1994b; Thompson 1998). Proponents of pension privatization, nevertheless, argue that "even if existing pay-as-you-go systems have had little negative impact on savings relative to the no-pension state, they are an opportunity lost to increase long-term saving through large mandatory funded plans" (World Bank 1994b: 126).

9. A World Bank study estimated that the cumulative transition cost of the Chilean reform will total a whopping 126 percent of gross domestic product, whereas the cumulative cost of the Colombian reform is projected to reach 86.5 percent of gross domestic product (Schmidt-Hebbel 1995).

10. As Chapter 7 discusses, public pension expenditures tend to be highly correlated with the implicit pension debt, which measures the present value of a country's public pension commitments to both retirees and active workers. These commitments determine the transition costs of pension privatization.

11. Pierson (1994: 71–72) refers to this as the "double-payment" problem.

12. This risk is reduced to the extent that the pension funds invest abroad. However, most of the countries that have privatized their pension systems have placed low limits on the funds that can be invested in other countries.

13. Some economists also argue that it is full funding rather than privatization per se that promotes savings (Orszag and Stiglitz 2001). Publicly managed systems may be fully funded—indeed, most Latin American pension systems started out as funded systems and some of them continue to be partially funded systems.

14. This is not to say that the advocates of pension privatization who occupy key positions in the World Bank and developing-country governments never benefit from the privatization schemes. In fact, in a number of cases, the advocates of pension

privatization have had close ties to the financial firms that establish private pension funds, and some of these pension privatization enthusiasts have subsequently gone to work for the pension funds.

15. A number of studies have argued that the spread of social security programs across the globe resulted in part from policy emulation (Heclo 1974; Collier and Messick 1975; Kuhnle 1981; Strang and Chang 1993; Usui 1994).

16. The Chilean reform, like many other pension privatization schemes, strictly limited the amount of resources that the private pension funds could invest abroad.

17. The latter studies have typically attributed the growth in the Chilean savings rate to increased corporate savings that were generated by the Chilean economic boom of the late 1980s.

18. International institutions may also provide indirect financial inducements to policymakers themselves to carry out reforms since such individuals may hope to work for the international institutions in the future, and they may believe that their employment opportunities hinge on their support for the institutions' policies.

19. Nelson (1990: 331) observes that "by the 1980s, in almost all developing countries some senior officials (and/or influential private economists) had spent some time as staff members of the IMF, the World Bank, or the regional development banks. At a minimum, that experience introduced a broader perspective, some familiarity with adjustment efforts in other countries, and an understanding of (if not agreement with) perspectives in international financial circles."

20. The World Bank has formally supported a multipillar approach to pension reform from the beginning, but there has been a great deal of division within the institution over the appropriate size of the public pillar. Although some staff members have supported full-scale privatization a la Chile, which would relegate the public pillar to the provision of a minimum pension, others have advocated partial privatization—that is, the retention of a sizable public pillar (interviews with Schmidt-Hebbel 1997, with Demarco 1996, and with Vittas 1998).

21. Some countries have also committed themselves to privatize their pension systems as well as to undertake other reforms in exchange for major financial assistance from the International Monetary Fund, but there is no evidence to suggest that the IMF has insisted that the countries commit to privatizing their pension systems in order to receive IMF loans. Indeed, the IMF has traditionally favored parametric pension reforms over privatization because of its concern about the fiscal costs of pension privatization.

22. Not all World Bank staffers are convinced of the benefits of pension privatization, however, and even many supporters of pension privatization are skeptical that it will boost a country's domestic saving rate. Recently, a public dispute over these issues broke out between the World Bank's former chief economist, Joseph Stiglitz, and other World Bank staff members. See Orszag and Stiglitz 2001; Holzmann et al. 2001.

23. Some authors distinguish between technocrats, whom they view as nonpolitical bureaucrats, and technopols, who tend to participate actively in politics (typically at the highest levels) and become involved in policy making in areas that are far removed from their area of expertise (Domínguez 1997; Williamson and Hag-

gard 1994). For the purposes of this analysis, however, the relevant distinction is not between technocrats and technopols, but between economists and those public policymakers trained in other fields.

24. Neoliberal economists, like any members of an epistemic community, typically have some differing causal and principled beliefs as well.

25. Markoff and Montecinos (1993: 41) argue, however, that the economics training is largely ceremonial since "little of the professional training of economists contributes to the actual decisions of economists as ministers."

26. Kahler (1990: 59) notes, "The internationalization of economic training through the Bretton Woods institutions and the graduate departments of American and European universities, has clearly increased the economic viability of orthodoxy by creating a cadre of economists in many developing countries who can understand its outlines and are attracted (in part) to its coherence."

27. Institutional variables may be more important in the industrialized countries than in Latin America because political institutions such as the judiciary or legislature are typically more difficult to circumvent in the former countries. I thank Steve Levitsky for this observation.

28. A few Latin American countries—Mexico, Venezuela, and, since 1997, Bolivia—use both proportional representation and single-member districts to elect the lower chambers of their legislatures.

29. These figures do not include Chile or Peru, which did not have operating legislatures at the time that they privatized their pension systems.

30. These figures again exclude Chile and Peru for the aforementioned reasons.

31. Opponents of pension privatization tried to hold a referendum calling for the annulment of the privatization bill, but the electoral court ruled that such a measure was unconstitutional because the executive had a legal monopoly on social security initiatives (Kay 1999; Filgueira and Moraes 1999).

32. The way in which the constitution is interpreted is just as important as the actual language of the constitution, however, since similar constitutions in different countries have been subject to quite different understandings. Tradition or precedent typically plays an important role in determining how constitutions are interpreted, but so does the composition and autonomy of the judiciary.

33. Even in Chile many members of the military opposed the pension privatization plan, and it was only approved after the government agreed to exclude the military's own pension program from the privatization scheme.

34. Authoritarian regimes may have less to gain from submitting their proposed reforms to the legislature, since the legislatures in such regimes may be viewed as illegitimate in any event. Moreover, obtaining the approval of the legislature may not be possible since many authoritarian regimes, like the Pinochet regime in Chile, do not maintain legislatures.

35. The ruling party's share of seats in the legislature may not be a good indicator of the ruler's control of the legislature in authoritarian regimes, however, since authoritarian rulers often control most or all of the major political parties. Moreover, as noted above, in some authoritarian regimes legislatures do not exist at all, which enables the executive or ruling junta to wield de facto legislative powers.

CHAPTER 3   *The Politics of Sweeping Privatization: Mexico*

1. For a contrasting view, see Dion 2000.

2. A substantial number of small and medium-sized industrial companies, particularly those associated with the National Chamber of Industry of the Transformation (CANACINTRA), did oppose some of the neoliberal reforms, however, in large part because many of these companies benefited from state subsidies and protection. In 1985, the head of CANACINTRA, Carlos Mireles García, argued that Mexico's entry into the General Agreement on Tariffs and Trade represented a threat to medium-size and small enterprises "because we do not really have the infrastructure, because we do not have an integrated plant to be able to compete and that will take years" (qtd. in Puga 1993: 196).

3. For a detailed account of Salinas's effort to privatize the Mexican pension system, see Bertranou 1994, 1995.

4. This study estimated that the pension privatization plan would increase the savings rate by 1.8 percent in five years and 5.1 percent after forty years. Some estimates were even higher. One influential proponent of pension privatization, Agustín Carstens (1997: 256) of the Bank of Mexico, for example, suggested that reform could "double financial savings in Mexico" and supply half of the planned 6 percent increase in Mexico's domestic savings rate by 2000. See also the projections by Solís and Villagómez 1999: 153–54.

5. For a detailed analysis of the role played by technocrats in the Mexican social security reform, see González Rossetti and Mogollon 2000.

6. Salinas himself viewed the 1992 pension reform as incomplete. In the final interview of his term, Salinas noted that an overhaul of the social security system was one of two major reforms that he had left pending—the other was a reform of the judiciary system (qtd. in Laurell 1995: 9).

7. Borrego was a seasoned politician who had served as president of the PRI, as governor of the state of Zacatecas, and as federal deputy—in the latter position he also served as president of the Chamber of Deputies.

8. For political reasons, the Zedillo administration refused to characterize the pension reform as a form of privatization and publicly denied that it was based on the Chilean model.

9. Unpublished poll data provided to the author by *Reforma.*

10. The MUNJP had also opposed the SAR. The founder of the organization, Eduardo Alonso Escárcega, denounced the SAR as a "threat to workers" and a "project inspired in what was born eleven years ago in Chile under the pressure of bullets and torture" ("Que se dijo" 1992: 56).

11. The principal labor confederations remained loyal to the government, denouncing the rebellion. Alberto Juárez Blancas, the general secretary of the CROC, expressed his "full backing of the initiative" and described opponents of the reform as a "group of mafiosos who take care of their particularistic interests, like the workers of IMSS" (Becerril 1995a: 11).

12. Out of this struggle sprang the Foro Sindicalismo ante la Nación, an ad-hoc group of unions belonging to both official and unofficial labor federations that

adopted a more independent posture vis-à-vis the government and the main labor federations.

13. The International Labor Organization, in contrast, estimated that 31 percent of the nonagricultural workforce in Mexico was unionized in 1991, down from 54.1 percent in 1989 (ILO 1997).

14. Under the privatization plan, employers continued to contribute an amount equal to 5 percent of each worker's salary to INFONAVIT, which remained under the control of the unions. Workers who do not receive assistance from INFONAVIT in purchasing a house would gain access to these funds upon retirement.

15. President Zedillo subsequently denounced the PAN for voting against the reform, arguing that society "has the maturity to distinguish between those who . . . have only tried to take political advantage of the difficult situation" of recent months (Alemán Alemán 1995a: 12).

16. For analyses of the reform, see Kurczyn 1996; Ulloa Padilla 1996a, 1996b; and the special issue of *Gaceta de Economía* 1997.

17. See, for example, Garduño Espinosa and Llanos Samaniego 1996: 8.

CHAPTER 4   *The Politics of Partial Privatization: Argentina*

1. Advocates of social security programs were influenced by the social welfare measures undertaken by the German Chancellor Otto von Bismarck. One member of the Chamber of Deputies chided the government for not having done more to forestall the disastrous strikes of 1912, arguing that the president "should have seen the storm that had been gathering for a long time" and taken measures to adapt "those beautiful German laws" to Argentina (Isuani 1985: 84).

2. In discussing the legislation that created pension funds for railroad employees, one Argentine senator bluntly remarked, "This project has as its immediate objective to favor railroad employees, but also, simultaneously, to favor the social good and public service. . . . [T]here can be no doubt that this project will contribute to reducing the number and the magnitude of strikes" (Isuani 1985: 87).

3. The largest labor federation, the Confederación General de Trabajo (CGT), swelled from 520,000 members in 1945 to 2.3 million members in 1954 (Rock 1987: 263).

4. In addition, Perón extended health benefits to many categories of workers, creating the union-run health care and recreational programs known as *obras sociales*.

5. Most of the noncontributors were rural or independent workers who belonged to the newly created program for these workers (Feldman, Golbert, and Isuani 1988: 101).

6. Fifty-four different categories of workers were able to retire early because their field of employment led to a shortened life span (Schulthess 1992: 6).

7. In 1991, 64 percent of pensioners received the minimum pension, which was equivalent to US$150 per month (Schulthess 1994a: 4).

8. See also the polling data reported in Otaegui 1993.

9. In July 1989, 43 percent of the population identified inflation as the most serious problem facing the country as opposed to only 17 percent in August 1986 (Mora y Araujo 1991: 220).

10. Menem later commented on his lack of candor in the campaign, noting that "the three golden rules of conduct are: 1) Be perfectly informed; 2) Keep that information secret; 3) Act with the benefit of surprise. This is what I did all my life. . . . If I say to the people: 'I'm going to privatize the telephone companies, the railroads and the national airlines,' I would have the whole labor movement against me. There still was not a clear realization what was necessary to do. When journalists, during the campaign, asked me if I was going to privatize or not, I said to them: 'I'm neither a privatizer nor a statist" (Interview in *Gente*, April 1, 1993, qtd. in Nun 1994: 109).

11. Acuña (1994: 51) argues that "the decision to put the ministry of economy in the hands of the Bunge & Born group represents the 'foundation' of Menemism."

12. Gerchunoff and Torre (1996) maintain that the Argentine government carried out revenue-generating structural reforms, like the privatization of state-owned enterprises, at the same time as stabilization in order to generate revenues to alleviate the severe fiscal crisis that the government was experiencing.

13. When he resigned, de Estrada stated, "In the future the income of the pension system will continue to deteriorate. And for that reason, my resignation was a moral duty, since the economic adjustment is being paid for by the pensioners" (qtd. in "La verdad sobre" 1991: 1).

14. The policy team also studied other social security systems, like those of the United States and Brazil, but to a lesser extent than the Chilean model (interview with Rondina 1996).

15. In order to reduce the transition costs of pension privatization even further, the Menem administration also initially chose not to grant workers in the new private system (that is, workers under forty-five years of age) any compensation for their past contributions to the public social security system. The Menem administration was obliged to amend this plan under intense political pressure.

16. The principal beneficiaries of the redistribution carried out by the pension system in the past have been politically powerful groups rather than the poorest sectors of the population.

17. Although Argentine policymakers continually emphasized the solidaristic aspects of the new pension system, they had doubts about the effectiveness of the pension system as a mechanism for income redistribution. Schulthess expressed these concerns in a 1991 speech to a conference organized by the insurance industry: "With this [public] pillar precisely what we want is to reinforce, within the possibilities that the social security system has, the aspect of income redistribution. I say 'within the possibilities' because I am convinced that a social security system offers very little from this perspective" (Schulthess 1992: 7).

18. At approximately the same time that these meetings were taking place, the Radical Party released a document that denounced the Menem administration's privatization plans and proposed its own plan for the reform of the pension system (Unión Cívica Radical 1992).

19. The pensioners' organizations claimed to have 1 million members, but this figure is almost surely inflated. Moreover, most of the members participated only in social or recreational activities, which was the primary purpose of the organizations (interviews with Forte 1996 and with Imizcoz 1996).

20. The number of labor-affiliated legislators fell from thirty-five in the 1983–85 legislature to eighteen in the 1991–93 legislature (Etchemendy 1995: 144).

21. Author's calculations based on data from Laborda (1993: 5) and Secretaría de la Honorable Cámara de Diputados de la Nación (1993).

22. The Argentine unionization rate declined beginning in the 1980s, dropping from approximately 40 percent of the labor force in the mid-1980s to between 25 and 30 percent in the early 1990s, but Argentina remained one of most unionized countries in the region (Lozano 1995; ILO 1998; McGuire 1996). The bargaining power of the Argentine labor movement was also enhanced by the fact that 73 percent of formal-sector workers in Argentina were covered by a collective contract (McGuire 1998).

23. The text of the agreement is reprinted in Furman and Alfieri 1992: 3. See also "Para el gobierno" 1992: 5.

24. Between 1983 and 1995, the Radical Party and the Justicialist Party controlled more than 80 percent of the seats in the Chamber of Deputies, and no other party held more than 5 percent of the seats in the lower house. In 1995, however, a left-of-center coalition, FREPASO, won 9.7 percent of the seats in the Chamber of Deputies.

25. In Argentina, half of the Chamber of Deputies is renewed in direct elections held every two years. Senators, however, are chosen by the provincial legislatures for nine-year terms, with one-third of the Senate renewed every three years.

26. The Radical Party maintained an even higher degree of party discipline during this period—98 percent of the UCR deputies voted in support of the majority position of the party.

27. Party leaders will not always use their influence to support the president's legislative initiatives, however. Indeed, the party leaders, especially provincial party leaders, may oppose the initiatives and try to influence legislators to vote against the initiatives.

28. Two labor-affiliated PJ legislators who had refused to attend the sessions to vote on the pension reform bill unexpectedly had their congressional staff reduced and another deputy was threatened with expulsion from the party for "repeated absences" ("Otra denuncia" 1993: 2).

29. For a detailed account of the reform process in the legislature, see Isuani and San Martino 1995. See also Alonso 1998; Torre and Gerchunoff 1999.

30. Alberto Natale, a deputy of the Progressive Democratic Party (DP), which usually supported the Menem administration, complained that "the Government spent two years studying the pension reform and now they want Congress to approve it in a week" ("Opinión contraria" 1992: 6). José Rodríguez, a labor leader and Peronist deputy, expressed his opposition in even stronger terms, stating, "We deputies are not a doormat on which the members of the Executive Branch can wipe their feet" ("Reparos legislativos" 1992: 1).

31. Deputy Sabio, as well as Humberto Romero, a PJ deputy, partially dissented from the report, however.

32. One PJ deputy who had left the legislature to take a post in the Menem administration quit his position to return to the legislature in order to help party lead-

ers attain the quorum. Shortly after performing this service, he left the legislature again to return to the Menem administration.

CHAPTER 5   *The Politics of Aborted Reform: Brazil*

1. The Brazilian policymakers were influenced by the Argentine social security legislation, which was apparently brought to them by an English railroad engineer (Malloy 1979: 175).

2. Requirements for gaining access to disability pensions were also relatively lax and various studies found a great deal of fraud in this area (World Bank 1995a: 2–3).

3. A 1992 law established a timetable for gradually increasing the required years of contributions to fifteen years in 2012.

4. The 1988 constitution did not specify how these increased expenditures were to be paid for, leading one observer to describe the charter as a "romantic rebellion against the discipline of mathematics" (World Bank 1995a: xi).

5. The pension benefits of tenured civil servants, who belonged to a separate pension system, were financed out of general treasury revenues, and their contributions equaled only 5 to 7 percent of their salaries (World Bank 1995a: 8).

6. The pension systems serving federal, state, and municipal employees always ran deficits since they were primarily financed out of the annual budget rather than by contributions. In 1996, the pension system serving federal employees collected only $2.6 billion reais, whereas it spent $17.1 billion reais on pensions (Ministério da Previdência 1997: 25).

7. Eighty percent of the faculty members at both the Getulio Vargas Foundation and the Catholic University of Rio de Janeiro received doctorates in North America, many of them at the University of Chicago (Loureiro 1997).

8. According to various experts, partial pension privatization would only require a constitutional amendment if it sought to make membership in the private system obligatory (interviews with Moraes 1997, with Balera 1997, and with Novaes 1997).

9. On October 31, 1996, the largest pensioners' confederation, the Brazilian Confederation of Pensioners (COBAP) had approximately $15,000 in liquid assets and $11,000 in fixed assets (COBAP 1997: 20).

10. In the early 1990s, as many as nineteen parties held seats in the Chamber of Deputies and the effective number of parties in the lower chamber exceeded eight (Mainwaring 1997: 74; Nicolau 1996: 36). For an analysis of the causes of party system fragmentation in Brazil, see Nicolau 1996.

11. Mainwaring and Pérez Liñán (1996) define a controverted vote as one in which at least 25 percent of the legislators present vote against the winning side. Samuels (1996), who defines a controverted vote as one in which only 10 percent of the legislators vote against the winning side, reports higher degrees of party discipline because of these and other methodological differences.

12. See also Figueiredo and Limongi 2000.

13. Figueiredo and Limongi (1995) define a controverted vote as one in which more than 10 percent of the legislators voting opposed the majority, and at least one of the leaders of the seven largest parties urged their members to vote in a way different from the other major parties.

14. These figures are Mainwaring and Pérez Liñán's (1996: 24) recalculations of data presented by Figueiredo and Limongi (1995).

15. Not surprisingly, state-level party discipline tends to be substantially higher than national-level party discipline (Samuels 1996; Mainwaring and Pérez Liñán 1996).

16. Although the Senate had initially agreed to preserve the special pension systems enjoyed by legislators and the judiciary, it subsequently voted to eliminate these privileges in the face of a great deal of criticism.

CHAPTER 6 *The Politics of Pension Privatization Around the World*

1. As Chapter 7 discusses, public pension expenditures also help explain why some countries opted for partial rather than full-scale pension privatization.

2. As noted in Chapter 1, only the United Kingdom and, more recently, Sweden have opted to partially privatize their pension systems, substituting private pension benefits for public benefits. A few other OECD countries, namely Switzerland, the Netherlands, Denmark, and Australia, have added a mandatory private pillar to their existing public pension systems without (at least, initially) reducing the benefits offered by their public pension systems.

3. As discussed in Chapter 1, even the long-term financial benefits of pension privatization are contingent on the successful performance of the private pension systems over the long run.

4. In this probit analysis, the coefficient of public pension spending was 0.10 and it had a standard error of 0.0328, which made it statistically significant at the .01 level (two-tailed t-test). The universe of cases consists of ninety-one middle- and high-income countries for the period 1992–97. Data are from Schwarz and Demirgüç-Kunt 1999; *International Social Security Review* 1996; the World Bank 1994b; and Palacios and Pallarès-Miralles 2000. Of course, this statistical model is underspecified since numerous factors other than the level of public pension spending presumably shape the likelihood of parametric reform. A complete analysis of the determinants of parametric reform is beyond the scope of this study, however.

5. As noted previously, a number of Latin American countries tightened the eligibility requirements in their public pension systems in order to reduce the transition costs of pension privatization and to equalize the eligibility requirements in the private and public systems.

6. Colombian President Alvaro Uribe Vélez (1993: 19), one of the key backers of the reform while serving in the Colombian Senate, has written that "the pension reform seduces me because of its macroeconomic effects—its impact on savings. Colombia is a country with a very low savings rate. I do not see a sufficiently valid reason to sacrifice the opportunity to improve [the savings rate] substantially."

7. The domestic savings rates of the Latin American countries that privatized their pension systems averaged 14.9 percent during the three years before they enacted their reforms (World Bank 2000).

8. In contrast, the World Bank played no real role in the Czech Republic, which may help explain in part why the country opted to reform its pay-as-you-go pension system rather than privatize it (Müller 1999).

9. The U.S. Agency for International Development was active in the reform from the beginning, however.

10. Surprisingly, pension privatization was first proposed in Poland by a couple of social security experts, one of whom was the president of the country's social insurance fund, ZUS. Nevertheless, most social security experts, who were typically professors of social security law, opposed pension privatization, with the notable exception of those experts whose training was in economics (Hausner 2001; Nelson 2001; Müller 1999).

11. As Chapter 2 noted, political leaders have been reluctant to privatize their pension systems by decree because of their desire to establish a solid legal foundation for the new private pension systems.

12. Corrales (2000: 129) argues that the divisions within the ruling party in Venezuela were not caused by the reforms themselves, but rather by Pérez's neglect of party leaders. Indeed, party leaders largely agreed with the objectives of the reforms, and the party nominated a reformer as its candidate in the subsequent presidential elections.

13. This includes all countries that the World Bank (2000) lists as having a gross domestic product per capita of more than $2,000 in 1995.

14. Unfortunately, the absence of annual data for many of the variables under study precluded a cross-sectional time series analysis.

15. The countries that enacted pension privatization schemes during this period were Argentina, Bolivia, Bulgaria, Colombia, Costa Rica, Croatia, El Salvador, Hungary, Kazakhstan, Latvia, Macedonia, Mexico, Nicaragua, Peru, Poland, Sweden, and Uruguay.

16. The coefficient of the World Bank loans variable becomes negative (but not statistically significant) if the World Bank pension mission variable is also included in the statistical analysis.

17. Unfortunately, data were not available before 1990 for a number of countries in the sample.

18. Measuring authoritarianism as a dichotomous variable does not significantly change the results.

19. Data on unionization rates were only available for sixty-two countries.

CHAPTER 7 *Institutions, Interest Groups, and Pension Privatization*

1. Nazarbaev became president of Kazakhstan in 1990 before the country became independent. He has governed the country since 1989 when he became the first secretary of the Communist Party of Kazakhstan.

2. The author first elaborated this argument in Madrid 1998 and 1999, based in part on the arguments that Pierson laid out in his 1994 book. James and Brooks (2001) subsequently developed a similar argument, but used the implicit pension debt, rather than current public pension spending, as the measure of a country's existing public pension commitments.

3. See, for example, the varying estimates of the implicit pension debt in OECD countries that are reproduced in Palacios and Pallarès-Miralles (2000: 32).

4. This relationship also appears to hold for those countries that added on pri-

vate pension schemes since Australia, which added on a very large private pension system, had lower public pension spending and a smaller implicit pension debt than Switzerland, the Netherlands, and Denmark, all of which created smaller private pension systems.

5. In describing the motives for its reform, the Costa Rican government noted that the "fiscal cost of [the Chilean reform] turned out to be extraordinarily elevated," which precluded adopting the Chilean reform in Costa Rica (*Proyecto de Ley* 1999: 4). The main architect of the reform in Costa Rica, Ronulfo Jiménez, has similarly written, "The Chilean reform opened up a fiscal cost that [Costa Rica] was not in a condition to pay" (Jiménez 2000: 254).

6. Surprisingly, in Croatia, the pensioners' association supported the pension privatization plan (Müller 2002: 88).

7. Existing pensioners were exempted from the privatization schemes not so much to avoid political opposition, but rather because there was no feasible way to include them since it was clearly too late for them to begin contributing to a private pension fund.

8. The inclusion of the Bolivian military took place only after negotiations with the leadership of the armed forces during which the commander in chief warned that the military would listen but would not accept impositions ("FF.AA. escuchan pero" 1996: 9).

9. Some major labor federations with close ties to the ruling party have endorsed pension privatization, but they have typically done so reluctantly.

10. The unionization rate is a poor measure of labor strength in the postcommunist countries, however. Under communism, many countries had high unionization rates because union membership was mandatory, but the unions had little political clout then and do not have that much more influence today.

11. Trust is particularly important since the agreements cannot typically be spelled out in legally enforceable contracts. Indeed, because of delicate legal or political considerations, the agreements may be implied rather than explicitly stated. No president, for example, would be willing to sign a contract stating that he or she will grant the labor leaders a certain number of jobs or will channel government resources to the unions in return for the unions' support for a proposed social security reform.

12. The Hungarian parliament had voted to make consideration of the reform proposal contingent on its acceptance by the Interests Reconciliation Council, the tripartite council that brings together business, labor, and the state, so most of the negotiations took place within this council (Orenstein 1999; Müller 1999).

13. As Chapter 4 notes, one of the key planners of the Argentine privatization scheme, Mauricio Barassi, had also come from the private sector and went to work for one of the private pension funds after the enactment of the reform.

CHAPTER 8 *Implications for Theory and Policy*

1. It is questionable whether a standard neoliberal package even exists with regard to the first-generation reforms, given that reforming nations have opted for very different policies with regard to such issues as capital controls and exchange rates.

2. For notable exceptions, see Simmons and Elkins 2001; Weyland 2001.

3. In recent years, a new kind of pension system, called "notional defined contribution" (NDC), has started to spread in Europe. Italy, Latvia, Poland, and Sweden have already established NDC systems, and a number of other countries have similar reforms on the agenda. In NDC systems, the pension contributions that workers make to the public pension system are credited to fictitious interest-bearing accounts in their name. NDC systems thus hive a defined contribution system onto the existing public pay-as-you-go pension system.

4. This index evaluates the performance of Latin American countries with regard to trade policy, tax policy, financial policy, privatization, and labor legislation.

5. This does not mean that authoritarian regimes are more likely to *propose* second-stage reforms. Indeed, authoritarian regimes may be less apt to hear or respond to signals from the citizenry about the problems afflicting certain government institutions.

6. Remmer (1998), for example, found that presidents with weaker electoral bases were actually more likely to agree to IMF-sponsored reform packages, but her findings apply only to first-stage economic reforms (especially, stabilization policies).

7. Some of the Latin American and Eastern European countries that privatized their pension systems had more mature pension systems than some industrialized countries.

8. In Mexico, the law specified that no private pension fund administrator could hold the accounts of more than 17 percent of the members of the system during the first four years of the system's operation, and no more than 20 percent thereafter.

9. These fees have tended to increase over time (Mesa-Lago 2001: 80).

10. In Bolivia the government set the fees at 0.5 percent of each worker's salary when it took bids to establish the pension fund administrators. The pension privatization legislation in the Dominican Republic similarly set commissions at a maximum of 0.5 percent of each worker's salary, but it also allowed a commission of up to 30 percent to be charged on annual returns that exceed the interest rate of bank certificates of deposit.

11. This calculation also takes into account the fact that returns were higher in the 1980s than the 1990s when a larger amount of funds had been accumulated in the private system.

12. In Mexico and Colombia, life and disability insurance is provided by the state rather than by private insurance companies, but deductions are still made from each worker's salary in order to finance the costs of the insurance.

13. This noncontributory pension, which was independent of the private pension system, was originally set at US$248 a year, but it was subsequently scaled back to only US$60 annually (Müller 2002: 54–55).

14. In all of the private systems, the state does set guidelines about how the pension assets may be invested and also typically provides some guarantees to workers in the event of the bankruptcy of a pension fund manager.

15. The Argentine labor minister, Graciela Camaño, recently proposed that contributions to the private pension system be made entirely voluntary.

Works Cited

INTERVIEWS

Acuña, Rodrigo. Director of PrimAmérica Consultores (a private pension reform consulting company). Santiago de Chile. Jan. 16, 1997.

Almeida, Sandra. Adviser on questions of social security to the Brazilian Chamber of Deputies. Brasília. Mar. 21, 1997.

Alonso Tejeda, Blanca. President of the Movimento Unificador Nacional de Jubilados y Pensionados (MUNJP). Mexico City. June 6, 1997.

Andrews, Emily. Staff economist at the World Bank. Washington, D.C. May 15, 1998.

Audry, Alejandro. Federal deputy from the Partido Revolucionario Institucional (PRI). Mexico City. Apr. 29, 1997.

Baeza, Eduardo. Advisor to former federal deputy Oscar Parrilli. Buenos Aires. Nov. 1, 1996.

Balera, Wagner. Professor of social security law at Catholic University of São Paulo. São Paulo. Feb. 23, 1997.

Barassi, Mauricio. Former adviser to the secretary of social security. Buenos Aires. Oct. 15, 1996.

Cajiga, Gerardo. Director of affiliation and collection of the Mexican Social Security Institute (IMSS). Mexico City. June 2, 1997.

Capuccio, Emilio. Former undersecretary of social security. Buenos Aires. Dec. 3, 1996.

Carvalho Filho, Celecino de. Adviser to the minister of social security. Brasília. Mar. 18, 1997.

Cechin, José. Executive secretary of the Ministry of Social Security. Brasília. Mar. 19, 1997.

Cerda, Luis. Adviser to the secretary of finance. Mexico City. May 7, 1997.

Cota, Maria Machado. President of the Confederação Brasileira de Aposentados e Pensionistas (COBAP). Brasília. Mar. 21, 1997.

Da Silva, Silvio Avelino. Adviser to Special Committees in the Chamber of Deputies. Brazil. Mar. 24, 1997.

Dávila, Enrique. Coordinator of advisers of the Subsecretariat of Expenditures, Secretariat of Finance and Public Credit (SHCP). Mexico City. June 13, 1997.

De Estrada, Santiago. Former undersecretary of social security. Buenos Aires. Dec. 5, 1996.

Demarco, Gustavo. Former advisor to the secretary of social security. Buenos Aires. Oct. 25, 1996.

Fable, Luis. Adviser to the Congressional Commission on Finance and Public Credit. Mexico City. May 26, 1997.

Facal, Carlos. Director of Berkeley International Corp. and former member of the governing board of the Argentine Association of Insurance Companies. Buenos Aires. Oct. 18, 1996.

Forte, Antonio. Former president of the Coordinating Board of the Pensioners of the Argentine Republic. Buenos Aires. Oct. 18, 1996.

França, Alvaro Sólon de. President of the National Association of Social Security Auditors (ANFIP). Brasília. Mar. 20, 1997.

García Sainz, Ricardo. Former director-general of the Mexican Social Security Institute (IMSS). Mexico City. May 23, 1997.

Gazmuri, Renato. Director of AFORE Banamex and former official in the Chilean Ministry of Labor. Mexico City. June 12, 1997.

González Gaviola, Juan. Former federal deputy from the Justicialist Party. Buenos Aires. Nov. 15, 1996.

Guzmán, Eduardo. Federal deputy from the Partido del Trabajo (PT). Mexico City. Apr. 28, 1997.

Iglesias, Augusto. Director of PrimAmérica Consultores (a private pension reform consulting company). Santiago de Chile. Dec. 23, 1996.

Imizcoz, Carlos. Former press secretary of the Coordinating Board of the Pensioners of the Argentine Republic. Buenos Aires. Sept. 25, 1996.

James, Estelle. Staff economist at the World Bank. Washington, D.C. May 14, 1998.

Jorge, Eduardo. Federal deputy from the Partido dos Trabalhadores (PT). Brasília. Mar. 20, 1997.

Larraín, Luis. Former official in the Chilean Ministry of Labor. Santiago de Chile. Jan. 16, 1997.

López, Amancio. Former director-general of economic planning of the Secretariat of Social Security. Buenos Aires. Oct. 22, 1996.

López Angel, Carlos. Adviser to the Parliamentary Contingent of the Partido de la Revolución Democrática (PRD). Mexico City, June 5, 1997.

Márquez, Gustavo. Economist at the Inter-American Development Bank. Washington, D.C. May 16, 1998.

Martínez, Gabriel. Director of planning, Mexican Social Security Institute (IMSS). Mexico City. June 10, 1997.

Moraes, Marcelo Viana de Estevão. Secretary of social security, Ministry of Social Security. Brasília. Mar. 17, 1997.

Novaes, Wladimir. Professor of social security law. São Paulo. Feb. 23, 1997.

Palacios, Robert. Staff economist at the World Bank. Washington, D.C. May 14, 1998.

Panigatti, Edgar. Former social security advisor to the Metalworkers' Union (UOM). Buenos Aires. Dec. 3, 1996.

Piñera, José. Former minister of labor of Chile. Santiago de Chile. Jan. 15, 1997.

Posadas, Laura. Former adviser to the secretary of social security. Buenos Aires. Oct. 4, 1996.

Ribeiro, Euler. Federal deputy from the Partido do Movimento Democrático Brasileiro (PMDB). Brasília. Mar. 20, 1997.

Rondina, Eduardo. Former adviser to the secretary of social security. Buenos Aires. Dec. 2, 1996.

Sáenz Garza, Miguel Angel. Technical secretary for the Commission on Social Security of the Chamber of Deputies (and former president of the National Social Security Workers Union). Mexico City. May 8, 1997.

Santín, Eduardo. Former federal deputy from the Radical Party. Buenos Aires. Nov. 25, 1996.

Schmidt-Hebbel, Klaus. Former World Bank staff economist. Santiago de Chile. Jan. 17, 1997.

Schulthess, Walter. Former secretary of social security. Buenos Aires. Nov. 6, 1996.

Schwarz, Anita. Staff economist at the World Bank. Washington, D.C. May 14, 1998.

Sueiro, Carlos. Former federal deputy from the Justicialist Party and secretary-general of the Custom Workers Union. Buenos Aires. Nov. 15, 1996.

Trabuco, Luiz Carlos. President of the National Association for Private Social Insurance. São Paulo. Mar. 3, 1997.

Urdapilleta, Jorge. Federal deputy from the Partido de Acción Nacional (PAN). Mexico City. Apr. 24, 1997.

Vittas, Dmitri. Staff economist at the World Bank. Washington, D.C. May 15, 1998.

Von Gersdorff, Herman. Staff economist at the World Bank. Washington, D.C. May 15, 1998.

PRINTED WORKS

Aaron, Henry. 1982. *The Economic Effects of Social Security*. Washington, D.C.: Brookings Institution.

Acosta Córdova, Carlos. 1995. "El único ahorro." *Proceso*, Nov. 6.

Acuña, Carlos. 1994. "Politics and Economics in the Argentina of the Nineties." In *Democracy, Markets and Structural Reform in Latin America*, ed. William C. Smith, Carlos Acuña, and Eduardo Gamarra. New Brunswick, N.J.: Transaction Books.

Adler, Emanuel. 1991. "Cognitive Evolution: A Dynamic Approach for the Study of International Relations and Their Progress." In *Progress in Postwar International Relations*, ed. Adler and Beverly Crawford. New York: Columbia University Press.

Adler, Emanuel, and Peter M. Haas. 1992. "Conclusion: Epistemic Communities, World Order, and the Creation of a Reflective Research Program." *International Organization* 46, no. 1 (winter): 367–90.

Agosín, M. R., G. Crespi, and L. Letelier. 1996. "Explicaciones del aumento del ahorro en Chile." Centro de Investigación Económica, Banco Interamericano de Desarrollo. Mimeo.

Albarrán de Alba, Gerardo. 1995. "Las reformas al IMSS metieron en aprietos al PRI y al PAN." *Proceso*, Dec. 11.

Alemán Alemán, Ricardo. 1995a. "Censuró Ernesto Zedillo a quienes votaron en contra de las reformas a la Ley de Seguro Social." *La Jornada*, Dec. 12.

————. 1995b. "Iniciativa para evitar el colapso del IMSS." *La Jornada*, Nov. 2.

Alonso, Guillermo. 1998. "Democracia y reformas: Las tensiones entre decretismo y deliberación. El caso de la reforma previsional Argentina." *Desarrollo Económico* 38, no. 150 (July–Sept.): 595–626.

Ames, Barry. 1995. "Electoral Strategy Under Open-List Proportional Representation." *American Journal of Political Science* 39, no. 2: 406–33.

————. 2001. *The Deadlock of Democracy in Brazil.* Ann Arbor: University of Michigan Press.

Anderson, Charles W. 1971. "Comparative Policy Analysis: The Design of Measures." *Comparative Politics* 4: 117–31.

Anderson, Karen M. 2001. "The Politics of Retrenchment in a Social Democratic Welfare State: Reform of Swedish Pensions and Unemployment Insurance." *Comparative Political Studies* 34, no. 9 (Nov.): 1063–91.

Arce, Moises. 2001. "The Politics of Pension Reform in Peru." *Studies in International Comparative Development* 36, no. 3 (fall): 90–116.

Archer, Ronald P., and Matthew Soberg Shugart. 1997. "The Unrealized Potential of Presidential Dominance." In *Presidentialism and Democracy in Latin America*, ed. Scott Mainwaring and Matthew Soberg Shugart. Cambridge: Cambridge University Press.

Arellano, José Pablo. 1985. *Políticas Sociales y Desarrollo: Chile 1924–1984.* Santiago: CIEPLAN.

Arenas de Mesa, Alberto. 2000. "El sistema de pensiones en Chile: Resultados y desafios pendientes." Secretaria de Hacienda, Gobierno de Chile. Mimeo. URL: http://www.finteramericana.org.

Arias Jiménez, Recaredo. 1995. "Propuesta para la modernización del seguro de invalidez, vejez, cesantía en edad avanzada y muerte." In Cámara de Diputados (Mexico), *Foro: Beneficios, Costos y Financiamento de la Seguridad Social.* Mexico City: Cámara de Diputados (July).

Arrau Pons, Patricio. 1994. "Fondos de pensiones y desarrollo del mercado de capitales en Chile: 1980–1993." *Serie Financiamiento del Desarrollo* 19. Santiago: United Nations Economic Commission for Latin America.

Ascher, William. 1997. "The Evolution of Postwar Doctrines in Development Economics." In *The Post-1945 Internationalization of Economics*, ed. A. W. Coats. Durham, N.C.: Duke University Press.

Asociación Argentina de Compañia de Seguros. 1992. Letter to the Comisiones de Previsión y Seguridad Social y Presupuesto y Hacienda de la H. Cámara de Diputados de la Nación. June 30. Mimeo.

Asociación International de Organismos de Supervisión de Fondos de Pensiones (AIOS). 2001. *Boletín Estadístico AIOS* 5 (June).

Aziz Nassif, Alberto. 1994. "The Mexican Dual Transition: State, Unionism, and the Political System." In *Regional Integration and Industrial Relations in North America*, ed. Maria Lorena Cook and Harry C. Katz. Ithaca, N.Y.: ILR Press.

Azpiazu, Daniel, and Adolfo Vispo. 1994. "Algunas enseñanzas de las privatizaciones en Argentina." *Revista de la CEPAL* 54 (Dec.).

Babb, Sarah. 2001. *Managing Mexico: Economists from Nationalism to Neoliberalism.* Princeton, N.J.: Princeton University Press.

Barberena, Edgard. 2000a. "Aprobada ley de pensiones." *El Nuevo Diario*, Mar. 16.
————. 2000b. "Sesión abortada." *El Nuevo Diario*, Mar. 15.
Barbosa, Fernando de Holanda, and Guillermo Mondino. 1994. "El sistema de seguridad social en Brasil: Por qué es importante reformarlo." *Estudios* (Oct.–Dec.): 155–73.
Barrientos, Armando. 1998. *Pension Reform in Latin America*. Aldershot, Eng.: Ashgate Publishing.
Basáñez, Miguel. 1997. "Actitudes y opiniones electorales: Latino barómetro 1995." Paper delivered at the meeting of the Latin American Studies Association, Guadalajara, Mexico, Apr.
Bates, Robert H., and Anne O. Krueger, eds. 1993. *Political and Economic Interactions in Economic Policy Reform*. Oxford: Blackwell.
Beattie, Roger, and Warren McGillivray. 1995. "A Risky Strategy: Reflections on the World Bank Report, *Averting the Old Age Crisis*." *International Social Security Review* 48, nos. 3–4.
Becerril, Andrea. 1995a. "Las cúpulas obrera y empresarial lanzaron duras críticas al SNTSS." *La Jornada*, Nov. 25.
————. 1995b. "Rosado: Todos los recursos legales, contra la privatización de pensiones." *La Jornada*, Nov. 1.
————. 1995c. "Salvados, puntos medulares de la seguridad social: Rosado." *La Jornada*, Dec. 9.
Beltrão, Kaizo Iwakami. 1996. "As tentativas recentes de reforma no Brasil." Rio de Janeiro: Escola Nacional de Estatística. Mimeo.
Bennett, Colin J. 1991. "What Is Policy Convergence and What Causes It?" *British Journal of Political Science* 21, no. 2 (Apr.).
Berry, Frances Stokes, and William D. Berry. 1992. "Tax Innovation in the States: Capitalizing on Political Opportunity." *American Journal of Political Science* 36, no. 3 (Aug.): 715–42.
Bertranou, Julián F. 1994. "Decisiones públicas y formulación de políticas en el México contemporaneo: Análisis de la formulación del sistema de ahorro para el retiro." Master's thesis. FLACSO, Mexico City.
————. 1995. "La política de la reforma a la seguridad social en México: Análisis de la formulación del sistema de ahorro para el retiro." *Estudios Sociológicos* 13, no. 37: 3–23.
Biersteker, Thomas J. 1995. "The 'Triumph' of Liberal Economic Ideas in the Developing World." In *Global Change, Regional Response: The New International Context of Development*, ed. Barbara Stallings. Cambridge: Cambridge University Press.
Biglaiser, Glen. 1998. "U.S. Influence in the Economics Profession in Latin America." Paper delivered at the annual meeting of the American Political Science Association, Boston, Mass. Sept.
Blake, D. 2000. "Financial System Requirements for Successful Pension Reform." *Discussion Paper*. Oxford: The Pensions Institute, Birbeck College. URL: http://www.pension-institute.org.
Boloña Behr, Carlos. 1995. *Dueño de tu Jubilación?* Lima: Instituto de Economia de Libre Mercado.
————. 1997. "Testimony: Pension Reform in Peru." Excerpts from a conference

sponsored by The Cato Institute and the Economist on the Global Pension Crisis, London, Dec. URL: http://www.pensionreform.org/articles/carlos_bolona.html

Bolsa de Comercio de Buenos Aires. 1992. Letter to the Comisiones de Previsión y Seguridad Social y Presupuesto y Hacienda de la Cámara de Diputados. July 1. Mimeo.

Bonoli, Giuliano. 2000. *The Politics of Pension Reform: Pensions and Policy Change in Western Europe.* Cambridge: Cambridge University Press.

Borzutzky, Silvia. 1983. "Chilean Politics and Social Security Policies." Ph.D. dissertation, University of Pittsburgh.

Bowen, Sally. 1996. "Andean Struggle for Reform." *Financial Times,* May 1.

Britto, Antônio. 1993. "Discurso do senhor ministro da previdência social, deputado Antônio Britto." *Previdência em Dados* 8, no. 1 (Jan.–Mar.): 5–14.

Brooke, James. 1994. "Quiet Revolution in Latin Pensions." *New York Times,* Sept. 10.

Brooks, Sarah. 1998. "Social Protection and the Market: The Case of Pension Reform in Argentina." Paper delivered at the XXI International Congress of the Latin American Studies Association, Chicago, Ill., Sept.

———. 2000. "Social Protection and the Market: A Political Economy of Pension Reform in Latin America and the World." Paper delivered at the XXII International Congress of the Latin American Studies Association, Miami, Fla., Mar.

Bruhn, Kathleen. 1997. *Taking on Goliath.* University Park: Pennsylvania State University Press.

Bruno, Michael, and William Easterly. 1996. "Inflation's Children: Tales of Crises that Beget Reforms." *American Economic Association Papers and Proceedings* 86 (May).

Burgess, Katrina. 1999. "Loyalty Dilemmas and Market Reform: Party-Union Alliances under Stress in Mexico, Spain and Venezuela." *World Politics* 52 (Oct.): 105–34.

Burgos, Hernando. 1992. "Fondo privado de pensiones: Quién gana, quién pierde." *Quehacer* 79 (Sept.–Oct.): 62–70.

Cámara de Diputados de la Nación (República Argentina). 1992a. *Trámite Parlamentario* 27 (June 5).

———. 1992b. *Trámite Parlamentario* 82 (Aug. 27).

———. 1993a. *Diario de Sesiones* (Apr. 28–29).

———. 1993b. *Diario de Sesiones* (May 5–6).

Cámara de Diputados de los Estados Unidos Mexicanos. 1992. *Diario de los Debates* Comisión Permanente 1, no. 8 (Feb. 10).

———. 1995a. *Diario de los Debates* 2, no. 18 (Nov. 9).

———. 1995b. *Diario de los Debates* 2, no. 30 (Dec. 7).

———. 1996a. *Diario de los Debates* 2, no. 4 (Mar. 20).

———. 1996b. *Diario de los Debates* 2, no. 13 (Apr. 19).

Camp, Roderic A. 1990. "Camarillas in Mexican Politics: The Case of the Salinas Cabinet." *Mexican Studies/Estudios Mexicanos* (winter).

———. 1996. *Politics in Mexico.* 2d ed. Oxford: Oxford University Press.

Campbell, Donald T. 1975. "Degrees of Freedom and the Case Study." *Comparative Political Studies* 8 (July): 178–93.

Canitrot, Adolfo. 1994. "Crisis and Transformatiion of the Argentine State (1978–1992)." In *Democracy, Markets and Structural Reform in Latin America*, ed. William C. Smith, Carlos Acuña, and Eduardo Gamarra. New Brunswick, N.J.: Transaction Books.

Cardoso, Adalberto Moreira. 1997. "Un referente fora de foco: Sobre a representatividade do sindicalismo no Brasil." *Dados* 40, no. 2: 169–98.

Carey, John M. 2000. "Party Unity in Legislative Voting." Paper presented at the meeting of the American Political Association, Washington, D.C., Sept.

Carey, John M., and Matthew S. Shugart. 1995. "Incentives to Cultivate a Personal Vote: A Rank Ordering of Electoral Systems." *Electoral Studies* 14, no. 4: 417–40.

———, eds. 1998. *Executive Decree Authority*. Cambridge: Cambridge University Press.

Carstens, Agustín. 1997. "The Reform of Social Security in Mexico." A paper delivered at the Social Security Reform: Conference Proceedings, Conference Series 41, Federal Reserve Bank of Boston, Boston, Mass., June.

Carvalho Filho, Celecino de. 1993. "Propostas de reforma de seguridade social: Uma visão crítica." *Previdência em Dados* 8, no. 4 (Oct.–Dec.): 5–29.

Castiglioni, Rosanna. 2000. "Welfare State Reform in Chile and Uruguay: Cross-class Coalitions, Elite Ideology, and Veto Players." Paper delivered at the meeting of the Latin American Studies Association, Miami, Fla., Mar.

Catan, Thomas. 2002. "Argentina's Pensions System Vision in Tatters." *Financial Times*, Apr. 28.

Cavallo, Domingo. 1993. Speech to the Association of Banks of the Argentine Republic. Rpt., *Las Estrategias del Desarrollo*. Buenos Aires: Asociación de Bancos de la República Argentina.

CB Capitales. 1999. URL: http://www.cb.cl.

Centeno, Miguel A. 1994. *Democracy Within Reason*. University Park: Pennsylvania State University Press.

Centeno, Miguel A., and Patricio Silva, eds. 1998. *The Politics of Expertise in Latin America*. New York: St. Martin's Press.

Cerda, Luis, and Gloria Grandolini. 1997. "México: La reforma al sistema de pensiones." *Gaceta de Economía* (supplement) 2, no. 4 (spring): 63–105.

Cerda, Luis, and José María Rivera Cabello. 1996. "La reforma mexicana de pensiones: Experiencias derivadas de su concepción." Paper prepared for delivery at the regional seminar of the UN Economic Commission for Latin America entitled "Situación actual y perspectivas de las reformas a los sistemas de pensiones." Santiago de Chile, Oct.

"La CGT sigue en contra." 1992. *Clarín*, Aug. 10.

Chand, Sheetal K., and Albert Jaeger. 1996. "Aging Populations and Public Pension Schemes." *International Monetary Fund Occasional Paper* 147. Washington, D.C.

Cheibub, Zairo B. 2000. "Reforma administrativa e relações trabalhistas no setor público." *Revista Brasileira de Ciências Sociais* 15, no. 43 (June): 116–46.

Coats, A. W., ed. 1997. *The Post-1945 Internationalization of Economics*. Durham, N.C.: Duke University Press.

"La COB anuncia semana conflictiva." 1996. *Presencia* (Sección de Economía) Nov. 11.

"La COB se juega hoy por la seguridad social." 1996. *Presencia* (Sección de Economía), Nov. 12.

"Cobap informa." 1995. *Jornal do Aposentado* 4, no. 78 (Oct. 1–15).

Coelho, Vera Schattan P. 1999. "A reforma da previdência e o jogo político no interior do executivo." *Novos Estudos CEBRAP* 55 (Nov.): 121–42.

———. 2001. "Poder executive e reforma da previdência na América Latina." *Novos Estudos CEBRAP* 61 (Nov.): 77–92.

Cohen, Benjamin J. 1996. "Phoenix Risen: The Resurrection of Global Finance." *World Politics* 48 (Jan.): 268–96.

Cohn, Amélia. 1981. *Previdência Social e Processo Político no Brasil*. São Paulo: Editora Moderna.

Colander, David, and Reuven Brenner. 1992. *Educating Economists*. Ann Arbor: University of Michigan Press.

Collier, David, ed. 1979. *The New Authoritarianism in Latin America*. Princeton, N.J.: Princeton University Press.

Collier, David, and James Mahoney. 1996. "Insights and Pitfalls: Selection Bias in Qualitative Research." *World Politics* 49 (Oct.): 56–91.

Collier, David, and Richard E. Messick. 1975. "Prerequisites Versus Diffusion: Testing Alternative Explanations of Social Security Adoption." *American Political Science Review* 69 (Dec.): 1299–1315.

Collier, Ruth Berins, and David Collier. 1991. *Shaping the Political Arena*. Princeton, N.J.: Princeton University Press.

Comin, Alvaro Augusto. 1996. "Sindicatos y centrales sindicales en Brasil en los años 80 y 90." *América Latina Hoy* 14: 93–103.

Comisión Tripartita para el Fortalecimiento de la Seguridad Social. 1995. "Comisiones técnicas: Conclusiones." Mexico City: IMSS.

Conaghan, Catherine M., James M. Malloy, and Luis A. Abugattás. 1990. "Business and the 'Boys.'" *Latin American Research Review* 25, no. 2: 3–30.

Confederação Brasileira de Aposentados e Pensionistas (COBAP). 1997. *Anais*. Brasilia: Cobap. (Jan.)

Confederación General de Jubilados Retirados y Pensionistas del País. 1992. "Consideraciones generales." Buenos Aires. July 7.

Conger, Lucy. 1998. "The Long View: Latin America's Pension Boom." *Impact* (summer). URL: http://www.ifc.org/publications/

"O congreso diz sim." 1995. *Veja*, Feb. 22.

Conradt, Katherine. 1993. "Fujimori on Peru." *Latin Finance* 46.

Constitución Política del Perú. 1980. Lima: Editorial Desarrollo.

"Constituciones políticas de América Latina." 1995. *Perfiles Liberales*. Special ed.

Coppedge, Michael. 1993. "Parties and Society in Mexico and Venezuela." *Comparative Politics* (Apr.): 253–74.

———. 1994. *Strong Parties and Lame Ducks: Presidential Partyarchy and Factionalism in Venezuela*. Stanford, Calif.: Stanford University Press.

Corporación de Investigación, Estudio y Desarrollo de la Seguridad Social (CIEDESS). 1995. *El Ahorro Previsional: Impacto en los Mercados de Capitales y de la Vivienda*. Santiago de Chile: CIEDESS.

Corrales, Javier. 1997–98. "Do Economic Crises Contribute to Economic Reform? Argentina and Venezuela in the 1990s." *Political Science Quarterly* 112, no. 4: 617–44.

———. 2000. "Presidents, Ruling Parties and Party Rules: A Theory on the Politics of Economic Reform in Latin America." *Comparative Politics* (Jan.): 127–49.

Correa, Salvador. 1995. "Efímera rebelión: Durante 20 horas los dirigentes obreros se volvieron combativos." *Proceso*, Jan. 9.

Corsetti, Giancarlo, and Klaus Schmidt-Hebbel. 1995. "Pension Reform and Growth." *World Bank Policy Research Working Paper* 1471. Washington, D.C.: World Bank.

"Costa Rica—fondos de pensiones." 2000. EFE News Services. Apr. 25.

Cottani, Joaquín, and Gustavo Demarco. 1998. "The Shift to a Funded Social Security System: The Case of Argentina." In *Privatizing Social Security*, ed. Martin Feldstein. Chicago: University of Chicago Press.

Cottani, Joaquín, and Juan J. Llach. 1993. "Ahorro nacional, ahorro externo y financiamiento de la inversión durante la reforma económica: El programa de la Argentina." *Estudios* (July–Sept.): 95–114.

Craig, Ann L., and Wayne Cornelius. 1995. "Houses Divided: Parties and Political Reform in Mexico." In *Building Democratic Institutions: Party Systems in Latin America*, ed. Scott Mainwaring and Timothy R. Scully. Stanford, Calif.: Stanford University Press.

Crisp, Brian F. 1997. "Presidential Behavior in a System with Strong Parties: Venezuela, 1958–1995." In *Presidentialism and Democracy in Latin America*, ed. Scott Mainwaring and Matthew Soberg Shugart. Cambridge: Cambridge University Press.

Crisp, Brian F., and Gregg B. Johnson. 2001. "Ideology vs. Institutions as Determinants of Economic Policy." Dept. of Political Science, University of Arizona. Mimeo.

"Crítica de las 62 organizaciones." 1993. *La Nación*, Feb. 25.

Cruz-Saco, María Amparo. 1995. "The Pension System Reform in Peru: The Economic Rationale versus the Political Will." Paper prepared for delivery at the meeting of the Latin American Studies Assocation, Washington, D.C. Sept.

Cruz-Saco, María Amparo, and Carmelo Mesa-Lago, eds. 1998. *Do Options Exist? The Reform of Pension and Health Care Systems in Latin America*. Pittsburgh, Pa.: University of Pittsburgh Press.

Cutright, Phillips. 1965. "Political Structure, Economic Development and National Social Security Programs." *The American Journal of Sociology* 70 (Mar.): 537–50.

Dearriba, Alberto. 1993. "Reforma previsonal a escena." *Página 12*, Apr. 15.

De la Garza, Enrique. 1994. "The Restructuring of State-Labor Relations in Mexico." In *The Politics of Economic Restructuring*, ed. María Lorena Cook, Kevin J. Middlebrook, and Juan Molinar Horcasitas. La Jolla: Center for U.S.-Mexican Studies, University of California at San Diego.

Demarco, Gustavo. 2000. "The Argentine Pension System Reform and the International Experience." Paper delivered at the Woodrow Wilson Center Conference on Learning from Foreign Models in Latin American Policy Reform, Washington, D.C. Sept. Forthcoming in *Learning from Foreign Models in Latin American Policy Reform*, ed. Kurt Weyland. Washington, D.C.: Woodrow Wilson Center, Johns Hopkins University Press.

Demirgüç-Kunt, Asli, and Anita M. Schwarz. 1995. "Costa Rican Pension System: Options for Reform." *World Bank Policy Research Working Paper* 1483 (June). Washington, D.C.: World Bank.

De Simone, Eduardo. 1993. "Compromiso con el FMI para aprobar la reforma previsional." *La Nación*, Feb. 17.

Devesa, J. E., A. Lejárraga, and C. Vidal. 2000. "The Internal Rate of Return of the Pay-As-You-Go System: An Analysis of the Spanish Case." *Center for Pensions and Social Insurance Research Report* 33. URL: http://www.pensions-Research.org/papers/

Devesa, J. E., R. Rodríquez, and C. Vidal. 2001. "Assessing Administrative Charges for the Afiliate in Individual Account Systems." University of Valencia. Mimeo.

Devesa-Carpio, José, and Carlos Vidal-Melía. 2001. "The Reformed Pension Systems in Latin America." *World Bank Pension Reform Primer*. Washington, D.C.: World Bank. URL: http://www.worldbank.org/pensions

Diamond, Peter, and Salvador Valdés-Prieto. 1994. "Social Security Reforms." In *The Chilean Economy: Policy Lessons and Challenges*, ed. Barry Bosworth, Rudiger Dornbusch, and Raúl Laban. Washington, D.C.: Brookings Institution.

Diário da Câmara dos Deputados (República Federativa do Brasil). 1996a. 51, no. 39 (Mar. 7).

———. 1996b. 51, no. 50 (Mar. 22).

Díaz-Alejandro, Carlos. 1983. "Open Economy, Closed Polity?" In *Latin America in the World Economy*, ed. Diana Tussie. London: Gower Press.

DiMaggio, Paul, and Walter Powell. 1983. "The Iron Cage Revisited." *American Sociological Review* 48, no. 2: 147–60.

Dion, Michelle. 2000. "Understanding Social Policy-Making: The Origins of Mexican Social Security Policy." Paper prepared for delivery at the meeting of the Latin American Studies Association, Miami, Fla., Mar.

Dix, Robert H. 1989. "Cleavage Structures and Party Systems in Latin America." *Comparative Politics* (Oct.): 23–37.

Dolowitz, David P., and David Marsh. 2000. "Learning from Abroad: The Role of Policy Transfer in Contemporary Policy-Making." *Governance* 13, no. 1 (Jan.): 5–24.

Domínguez, Jorge, ed. 1997. *Technopols: Freeing Politics and Markets in Latin America in the 1990s*. University Park: Pennsylvania State University Press.

Draibe, Sônia Miriam, and Milko Matijascic. 1999. "The Market Orientation of Social Security: The Brazilian Case." Universidade Estadual de Campinas—UNICAMP—Núcleo de Estudos de Políticas Públicas, Caderno 44 (Dec.).

Drazen, Allen, and Vittorio Grilli. 1993. "The Benefit of Crises for Economic Reforms." *American Economic Review* 83 (June): 598–607.

Durán, Viviana. 1993. "La evasión en el sistema de seguridad social de Argentina." In *Serie política fiscal* 50. Santiago de Chile: CEPAL.

Eckstein, Harry. 1975. "Case Study and Theory in Political Science." In *The Hand-*

book of Political Science, ed. Fred I. Greenstein and Nelson W. Polsby, vol. 7. Menlo Park, Calif.: Addison-Wesley.

Edwards, Sebastian. 1995. *Crisis and Reform in Latin America: From Despair to Hope.* New York: Oxford University Press.

Ensignia, Jaime. 1996. "El debate sobre la seguridad social en América Latina: La posición del sindicalismo en la región." Fundación Friedrich Ebert, Santiago de Chile, Nov.

Ensignia, Jaime, and Rolando Díaz, eds. 1997. *La Seguridad Social en América Latina: Reforma o Liquidación?* Caracas: Editorial Nueva Sociedad.

"Entre las conductas políticas renovadas y la influencia de los grupos organizados." 1995. *Cuadernos del CLAEH* 2, no. 20: 9–41.

Epstein, Edward. 1989. "Labor Populism and Hegemonic Crisis in Argentina." In *Labor Autonomy and the State in Latin America*, ed. Edward Epstein. Boston: Unwin Hyman.

Erro, Davide G. 1993. *Resolving the Argentine Paradox: Politics and Development, 1960–1992.* Boulder, Colo.: Lynne Rienner.

Esping-Andersen, Gøsta. 1985. *States Against Markets.* Princeton, N.J.: Princeton University Press.

———. 1990. *The Three Worlds of Welfare Capitalism.* Princeton, N.J.: Princeton University Press.

Etchemendy, Sebastián. 1995. "Límites al decisionismo? El poder ejecutivo y la formulación de la legislación laboral (1983–1994)." In *Política y Sociedad en los Años del Menemismo*, ed. Ricardo Sidicaro and Jorge Meyer. Buenos Aires: University of Buenos Aires Press.

Europa Publications. Various years. *The Europa World Year Book.* London: Unwin Brothers Ltd.

Evelin, Guilherme. 1996. "Vicentinho em apuros." *Istoé*, Jan. 31.

"Exposición de motivos: Ley del sistema de ahorro para pensiones." 1997. San Salvador: Instituto Salvadoreño del Seguro Social. URL: http://www.spensiones .gob.sv/Documentos/Motivos.html

Federación Internacional de Administradoras de Fondos de Pensiones (FIAP). 2002. URL: http://www.fiap.cl/

Feldman, Jorge, Laura Golbert, and Ernesto A. Isuani. 1988. *Maduración y Crisis del Sistema Previsional Argentino.* Buenos Aires: Centro Editor de América Latina.

Feldstein, Martin. 1999. "Public Policies and Private Saving in Mexico." *National Bureau of Economic Research Working Paper* 6930. Cambridge, Mass.: NBER.

Fennell, Lee C. 1974. "Reasons for Roll Calls: An Exploratory Analysis with Argentine Data." *American Journal of Political Science* 18, no. 2: 395–403.

Ferge, Zsuzsa. 1999. "The Politics of the Hungarian Pension Reform." In *Transformation of Social Security Pensions in Central-Eastern Europe*, ed. Katharina Müller, Andreas Ryll, and Hans-Jurgen Wagener. Heidelberg, Germany: Physica-Verlag.

Ferreira Rubio, Delia, and Matteo Goretti. 1998. "When the President Governs Alone: The Decretazo in Argentina, 1989–93." In *Executive Decree Authority*, ed. John M. Carey and Matthew Soberg Shugart. Cambridge: Cambridge University Press.

"FF.AA. escuchan pero no aceptan imposiciones." 1996. *Presencía* (Sección de economía), Nov. 13.

"Fidelidade do PFL garantiu aprovação." 1998. *O Globo*, Feb. 12.

FIEL. 1995. *El Sistema de Seguridad Social*. Buenos Aires: Consejo Empresarial Argentino.

Figueiredo, Argelina, and Fernando Limongi. 1995. "Partidos políticos na câmara dos deputados: 1989–1994." *Dados* 38, no. 3: 497–524.

———. 1998. "Reforma da previdência e instituições políticas." *Novos Estudos CEBRAP* 51 (June): 63–90.

———. 2000. "Presidential Power, Legislative Organization, and Party Behavior in Brazil." *Comparative Politics* (Jan.): 151–70.

Filgueira, Fernando, and Juan Andrés Moraes. 1999. "Political Environments, Sector Specific Configurations, and Strategic Devices: Understanding Institutional Reform in Uruguay." *Inter-American Development Bank, Office of the Chief Economist, Latin American Research Network, Working Paper R-351.*

Finnemore, Martha. 1990. "International Organizations as Teachers of Norms: UNESCO and Science Policy." Ph.D. dissertation, Stanford University.

Finnemore, Martha, and Kathryn Sikkink. 1998. "International Norm Dynamics and Political Change." *International Organization* 52, no. 4 (fall): 887–917.

"First Defeat Suffered." 1995. *Gazeta Mercantil* (New York ed.), Mar. 20.

"Foi dando que FHC recebeu." 1996. *Veja*, Mar. 27.

Força Sindical. n.d. *Um Projeto para o Brasil: A Proposta da Força Sindical*. São Paulo: Editorial Geração.

Franco Agudelo, Saúl. 1994. "La nueva ley de seguridad social." In *Síntesis '94: Anuario social, político y económico de Colombia*, ed. Luis Alberto Restrepo. Santa Fe de Bogotá: T/M editores.

Frías Santillán, Amalia. 1995. "Urgen reformas en seguridad social para que se genere ahorro interno." *La Jornada*, Nov. 29.

"Fuga de capitales: El largo camino a casa." 1990. *Mercado*, May 31.

Furman, Rubén, and Guillermo Alfieri. 1992. "El gran acuerdo." *Página 12*, July 18.

Gaceta de Economía. 1997. 2, no. 4 (spring).

Garduño Espinosa, Roberto, and Raúl Llanos Samaniego. 1996. "No hay impedimento para crear una afore en el IMSS." *La Jornada*, Apr. 21.

Garrett, Geoffrey. 1995. "Capital Mobility, Trade and the Domestic Politics of Economic Policy." *International Organization* 49, no. 4 (fall): 657–87.

———. 1998. *Partisan Politics in the Global Economy*. Cambridge: Cambridge University Press.

Garrido, Luis Javier. 1993. *La ruptura: La corriente democrática del PRI*. Mexico City: Editorial Grijalba.

Gastil, Raymond. Various years. *Freedom in the World*. New York: Freedom House.

Geddes, Barbara. 1990. "How the Cases You Choose Affect the Answers You Get: Selection Bias in Comparative Politics." In *Political Analysis*, vol. 2, ed. James A. Stimson. Ann Arbor: University of Michigan Press.

———. 1995. "The Politics of Economic Liberalization." *Latin American Research Review* 30, no. 2: 195–214.

George, Alexander L. 1982. "Case Studies and Theory Development." A paper delivered at the Second Annual Symposium on Information Processing in Organizations, Carnegie Mellon University, Oct.

Gerchunoff, Pablo, and Juan Carlos Torre. 1996. "La política de liberalización económica en la administración de Menem." *Desarrollo Económico* 36, no. 143 (Oct.–Dec.): 733–68.

Gibson, Edward. 1990. "Democracy and the New Electoral Right in Argentina." *Journal of Interamerican Studies and World Affairs* 32, no. 3 (fall): 177–228.

Gillion, Colin. 2000. "The Development and Reform of Social Security Pensions: The Approach of the International Labour Office." *International Social Security Review* 53, no. 1: 35–63.

Goldstein, Judith, and Robert O. Keohane, eds. 1993. *Ideas and Foreign Policy: Beliefs, Institutions and Political Change.* Ithaca, N.Y.: Cornell University Press.

Golinowska, Stanislawa. 1999. "Political Actors and Reform Paradigms in Old-Age Security in Poland." In *Transformation of Social Security Pensions in Central-Eastern Europe,* ed. Katharina Müller, Andreas Ryll, and Hans-Jurgen Wagener. Heidelberg, Germany: Physica-Verlag.

Golob, Stephanie R. 1997. "'Making Possible What is Necessary': Pedro Aspe, the Salinas Team and the Next Mexican 'Miracle.'" In *Technopols,* ed. Jorge Domínguez. University Park: Pennsylvania State University Press.

"Goni: Ley de pensiones fue copiada de Chile." 1996. *Presencia* (Sección de Economía), Nov. 13.

González Rossetti, Alejandra, and Olivia Mogollon. 2000. "Enhancing the Political Feasibility of Health Reform: The Mexico Case." Latin America and Caribbean Health Sector Reform Initiative, Harvard School of Public Health. Document 41.

González Rossetti, Alejandra, and Patricia Ramírez. 2000. "Enhancing the Political Feasibility of Health Reform: The Colombian Case." Latin America and Caribbean Health Sector Reform Initiative, Harvard School of Public Health. Document 39.

Goodman, John B., and Louis W. Pauly. 1993. "The Obsolescence of Capital Controls? Economic Management in an Age of Global Markets." *World Politics* 46, no. 1 (Oct.): 50–82.

"Government Faces Defeat." 1996. *Gazeta Mercantil* (New York ed.). Mar. 11.

"Gradual Extension of Social Insurance Schemes in Latin American Countries." 1958. *International Labour Review* 78, no. 3 (Sept.): 257–83.

Graham, Carol. 1999. *Improving the Odds: Political Strategies for Institutional Reform in Latin America.* Washington, D.C.: Inter-American Development Bank.

Gray-Molina, George, Ernesto Pérez de Rada, and Ernesto Yañez. 1999. "La economía política de reformas institucionales en Bolivia." *Inter-American Development Bank, Office of the Chief Economist, Latin American Research Network, Working Paper* R-350, Mar.

Greenway, Gregory, and John Tuman. 1996. "Restructuring State-Labor Relations in Contemporary Mexico: Implications for Democratization in the Era of Neoliberalism." Paper prepared for delivery at the Comparative Democratization Seminar, Stanford University, Stanford, Calif., Nov.

"El gremialismo atempera sus críticas al decreto." 1993. *La Nación*, Jan. 9.

Grindle, Merilee. 1991. *Public Choices and Policy Change: The Political Economy of Reform in Developing Countries*. Baltimore, Md.: Johns Hopkins University Press.

———. 1996. *Challenging the State*. Cambridge: Cambridge University Press.

Gurría, José Angel. 1995. "Capital Flows: The Mexican Case." In *Coping with Capital Surges: The Return of Finance to Latin America*, ed. Ricardo French-Davis and Stephany Griffith-Jones. Boulder, Colo.: Lynne Rienner.

Haas, Peter M. 1992. "Introduction: Epistemic Communities and International Policy Coordination." *International Organization* 46, no. 1 (winter): 1–35.

Haggard, Stephan, and Robert R. Kaufman, eds. 1992. *The Politics of Economic Adjustment*. Princeton, N.J.: Princeton University Press.

———. 1995. *The Political Economy of Democratic Transitions*. Princeton, N.J.: Princeton University Press.

Haindl, Erik. 1997. "The Chilean Pension Fund Reform and Its Impact on Saving." In *Generating Savings for Latin American Development*, ed. Robert Grosse. Coral Gables, Fla.: North-South Center Press.

Hall, Peter, ed. 1989. *The Political Power of Economic Ideas: Keynesianism Across Nations*. Princeton, N.J.: Princeton University Press.

Harberger, Arnold C. 1993. "Secrets of Success: A Handful of Heroes." *American Economic Review* 83, no. 2: 343–50.

———. 1997. "Good Economics Comes to Latin America, 1955–1995." In *The Post-1945 Internationalization of Economics*, ed. A. W. Coats. Durham, N.C.: Duke University Press.

Hausner, Jerzy. 2001. "Security Through Diversity: Conditions for Successful Reform of the Pension System in Poland." In *Reforming the State*, ed. János Kornai, Stephan Haggard, and Robert R. Kaufman. Cambridge: Cambridge University Press.

Hazas, Alejandro. 1995. "Propuesta que presenta la comisión nacional de seguridad social de la COPARMEX para la solución de la problemática ante el IMSS." In Cámara de Diputados, *Foro: Beneficios, Costos y Financiamento de la Seguridad Social*. Mexico City: Cámara de Diputados, July.

Heclo, Hugh. 1974. *Modern Social Politics in Britain and Sweden*. New Haven, Conn.: Yale University Press.

Hellman, Joel S. 1998. "Winners Take All: The Politics of Partial Reform in Postcommunist Transitions." *World Politics* 50, 2: 203–34.

Herrera, Berlioth. 1999. "Aprueban ley de protección al trabajador: Sí a cambios en cesantía." *La Nación*, Dec. 14.

Hicks, Alexander. 1999. *Social Democracy and Welfare Capitalism: A Century of Income Security Politics*. Ithaca, N.Y.: Cornell University Press.

Hinrichs, Karl. 2001. "Elephants on the Move: Patterns of Public Pension Reform in OECD Countries." In *Welfare State Futures*, ed. Stephen Leibfried. Cambridge: Cambridge University Press.

Hira, Anil. 1998. *Ideas and Economic Policy in Latin America*. Westport, Conn.: Praeger Publishers.

Hochman, Gilberto. 1988. "Aprendizado e difusão na constituição de políticas: A previdência social e seus técnicos." *Revista Brasileira de Ciências Sociais* 3, no. 7: 84–98.

Hojman, David E. 1994. "The Political Economy of Recent Conversions to Market Economics in Latin America." *Journal of Latin American Studies* 26: 191–219.

Holt, Stanley. 1991. "Private Pension Plans: Whose Security?" *Business Mexico*, June.

Holzmann, Robert. 1996. "Pension Reform, Financial Market Development, and Economic Growth: Preliminary Evidence from Chile." *IMF Working Paper* WP/96/94. Aug.

———. 1997. "Pension Reform in Central and Eastern Europe: Necessity, Approaches and Open Questions." United Nations Economic Commission for Latin America, *Serie Financiamento del Desarrollo* 45.

———. 1998. "A World Bank Perspective on Pension Reform." *Social Protection Discussion Paper Series* 9807. Washington, D.C.: World Bank.

———. 2000. "The World Bank Approach to Pension Reform." *International Social Security Review* 53, no. 1: 11–34.

Holzmann, Robert, et al. 2001. "Comments on Rethinking Pension Reform: Ten Myths about Social Security Systems." In *New Ideas about Old Age Security*, ed. Robert Holzmann and Joseph E. Stiglitz. Washington, D.C.: World Bank.

Hommes, Rudolf. 1995. "Colombia: Social Security Reforms—A Case Study of Political and Financial Viability." Paper presented at the Second Hemispheric Conference on Social Security, Pension Reforms and Capital Markets Development, Washington, D.C., June.

Horowitz, Joel. 1995. "When Argentine Employers and Workers Agreed: Opposition to a Government Pension Plan in 1923 and 1924." Paper prepared for the XIX International Congress of the Latin American Studies Association, Washington, D.C., Sept.

Huber, Evelyne. 1996. "Options for Social Policy in Latin America: Neoliberal versus Social Democratic Models." In *Welfare States in Transition: National Adaptations in Global Economies*, ed. Gosta Esping-Andersen. London: Sage Publications.

Huber, Evelyne, and Sergio Berensztein. 1995. "The Politics of Social Policy in Chile, Costa Rica, and Mexico: Crisis and Response." Paper prepared for the XIX International Congress of the Latin American Studies Association, Washington, D.C., Sept.

Huber, Evelyne, Charles Ragin, and John Stephens. 1993. "Social Democracy, Constitutional Structure and the Welfare State." *American Journal of Sociology* 99, no. 3: 711–49.

Huber, Evelyne, and John D. Stephens. 2000. "The Political Economy of Pension Reform: Latin America in Comparative Perspective." Paper prepared for the meeting of the Latin American Studies Association, Hyatt Regency, Miami, Fla., Mar.

———. 2001. *Political Choice in Global Markets: Development and Crisis of Advanced Welfare States*. Chicago: University of Chicago Press.

Huneeus, Carlos. 1997. "Technocrats and Politicians in the Democratic Politics of Argentina (1983–95)." In *The Politics of Expertise in Latin America*, ed. Miguel A. Centeno and Patrico Silva. New York: St. Martin's Press.

Immergut, Ellen M. 1992. "The Rules of the Game: The Logic of Health Policy-

Making in France, Switzerland, and Sweden." In *Structuring Politics: Historical Institutionalism in Comparative Analysis*, ed. Sven Steinmo, Kathleen Thelen, and Frank Longstreth. Cambridge: Cambridge University Press.

Informe de Previdência Social. 1997a. 9, no. 1 (Jan.).

———. 1997b. 9, no. 2 (Feb.).

Inglot, Tomasz. 1995. "The Politics of Social Policy Reform in Post-Communist Poland." *Communist and Post-Communist Studies* 28, no. 3: 361–73.

Instituto Mexicano de la Seguridad Social (IMSS). 1952. *Mexico y la Seguridad Social.* Mexico City: IMSS.

———. 1995. *Diagnóstico.* Mexico City: IMSS.

———. 1996. *Aportaciones al Debate: La Seguridad Social ante el Futuro.* Mexico City: IMSS.

Instituto Nacional de Estadísticas Geográficas y Información (INEGI). 1996. *Anuario Estadístico de los Estados Unidos Mexicanos.* Mexico City: INEGI.

Instituto Nicaragüense de Seguridad Social. 2000. "Sobre la reforma de pensiones: Las razones que la justifican." URL: http://www.inss.org.ni/CREPEN.htm

"Intensas gestiones para evitar el paro." 1992. *La Nación*, July 15.

Inter-American Development Bank (IADB). 1996a. *Economic and Social Progress in Latin America—1996 Report.* Baltimore, Md.: Johns Hopkins University Press.

———. 1996b. "Project Abstract—Mexico—Contractual Savings Development." Project no. ME-0197, Oct. 30.

———. 1997. *Latin America after a Decade of Reforms—Economic and Social Progress in Latin America.* Washington, D.C.: Inter-American Development Bank.

International Labour Office (ILO). 1997. *World Labour Report 1997–98: Industrial Relations, Democracy and Social Stability.* Geneva: ILO.

———. Various years. *The Cost of Social Security.* Geneva: ILO.

International Monetary Fund (IMF). Various years. *Exchange Arrangements and Exchange Restrictions.* Washington, D.C.: IMF.

International Social Security Review. 1996. 49, no. 2.

International Social Security Association (ISSA). 1998. "The Future of Social Security—The Stockholm Conference." Stockholm, June–July.

Isuani, Ernesto A. 1985. *Los Orígenes Conflictivos de la Seguridad Social Argentina.* Buenos Aires: Centro Editor de América Latina.

Isuani, Ernesto A., and Jorge San Martino. 1993. *La Reforma Previsional Argentina: Opciones y Riesgos.* Buenos Aires: Mino y Davila Editores.

———. 1995. "El nuevo sistema previsional Argentino." *Boletín Informativo Techint* 282 (Apr.–June): 43–67.

James, Estelle. 1996. "Protecting the Old and Promoting Growth: A Defense of *Averting the Old Age Crisis*." *World Bank Policy Research Working Paper* 1570. Washington, D.C.: World Bank.

———. 1997a. "New Systems for Old Age Security: Theory, Practice and Empirical Evidence." *World Bank Policy Research Working Paper* 1766. Washington, D.C.: World Bank.

———. 1997b. "Pension Reform: Is There a Tradeoff Between Efficiency and Equity?" *World Bank Policy Research Working Paper* 1767. Washington, D.C.: World Bank.

James, Estelle, and Sarah Brooks. 2001. "The Political Economy of Structural Pension Reform." In *New Ideas about Old Age Security*, ed. Robert Holzmann and Joseph E. Stiglitz. Washington, D.C.: World Bank.

Jáuregui, Marcela. 1994. *Crisis y Reformulación del Régimen Previsional Argentino*. Cuaderno 15. Buenos Aires: Instituto de Estudios sobre Estado y Participación.

Jiménez, Ronulfo. 2000. "El Proceso de la Aprobación de la Ley de Protección al Trabajador." In *Los Retos Políticos de la Reforma Económica en Costa Rica*, ed. Ronulfo Jiménez. San Jose: Academia de Centroamérica.

Jones, Mark. 1998. "Explaining the High Level of Party Discipline in the Argentine Congress." A paper delivered at the meeting of the Latin American Studies Association, Chicago, Ill., Sept.

Jubilados. 1996. Organo de la Mesa Coordinadora de Jubilados y Pensionados de la República Argentina, Buenos Aires (Mar).

Kahler, Miles. 1990. "Orthodoxy and Its Alternatives: Explaining Approaches to Stabilization and Adjustment." In *Economic Crisis and Policy Choice*, ed. Joan M. Nelson. Princeton, N.J.: Princeton University Press.

———. 1992. "External Influence, Conditionality, and the Politics of Adjustment." In *The Politics of Economic Adjustment*, ed. Stephan Haggard and Robert R. Kaufman. Princeton, N.J.: Princeton University Press.

Kane, Cheik, and Robert Palacios. 1996. "The Implicit Pension Debt." *Finance and Development* 33, no. 2 (June): 38–41.

Kaufman, Robert R. 1986. "Democratic and Authoritarian Responses to the Debt Issue: Brazil and Mexico." In *The Politics of International Debt*, ed. Miles Kahler. Ithaca, N.Y.: Cornell University Press.

———. 1999. "Approaches to the Study of State Reform in Latin American and Postsocialist Countries." *Comparative Politics* (Apr.): 357–75.

Kay, Stephen. 1998. "Politics and Social Security Reform in the Southern Cone and Brazil." Ph.D. dissertation, University of California at Los Angeles.

———. 1999. "Unexpected Privatizations: Politics and Social Security Reform in the Southern Cone." *Comparative Politics* (July): 403–22.

Kepp, Michael. 1995. "Reform Effort Stalls in Brazil." *Pensions and Investments*, Dec. 25.

"Key Reforms Approved." 1998. *Latin American Weekly Report*, Feb. 17.

King, Gary, Robert O. Keohane, and Sidney Verba. 1994. *Designing Social Inquiry*. Princeton, N.J.: Princeton University Press.

Knoke, David. 1990. *Political Networks: The Structural Perspective*. New York: Cambridge University Press.

Korpi, Walter. 1983. *The Democratic Class Struggle*. London: Routledge and Kegan Paul.

Kuhnle, Stein. 1981. "The Growth of Social Insurance Programs in Scandinavia: Outside Influences and Internal Forces." In *The Development of Welfare States in Europe and America*, ed. Peter Flora and Arnold Heidenheimer. New Brunswick, N.J.: Transaction Books.

Kurczyn, Sergio. 1996. "Reforma del sistema de pensiones Mexicano: Principales aspectos macroeconómicos." *Comercio Exterior* 46, no. 9 (Sept.): 741–54.

La Botz, Dan. 1992. *Mask of Democracy*. Boston: South End Press.

Laborda, Fernando. 1993. "Retrocede el poder sindical en diputados." *La Nación,* Oct. 6.

Lacey, Robert. 1996. "La reforma de la jubilación en América Latina: Los retos y el papel del Banco Mundial." *Comercio Exterior* 46, no. 9 (Sept.): 683–91.

Lago, Rudolfo. 1998. "Governo joga tudo pela previdência." *O Globo,* Feb. 12.

Lamadrid, Alejandro, and Alvaro Orsatti. 1991. "Una revisión de las medidas sobre la tasa de sindicalización en Argentina." *Estudios de Trabajo* 2 (July–Dec.): 135–59.

Lamounier, Bolívar, and Amaury de Souza. 1995. *O Congreso Nacional frente aos Desafíos da Reforma do Estado.* São Paulo: FIESP/CIESP.

Lange, Peter, and Geoffrey Garrett. 1985. "The Politics of Growth: Strategic Interaction and Economic Performance in the Advanced Industrial Democracies." *Journal of Politics* 47, no. 3 (Aug.): 792–827.

Langston, Joy. 1996. "Why Rules Matter: The Formal Rules of Candidate Selection and Leadership Section in the PRI, 1978–1996." *Documento de Trabajo* 58. Mexico City: División de Estudios Políticos, Centro de Investigación y Docencia Económica.

Laurell, Asa Cristina. 1995. "La reforma de los sistemas de salud y de seguridad social: Concepciones y propuestas de los distintos actores sociales." *Documento de Trabajo* 47. Mexico City: Fundación Friedrich Ebert.

Leite, Paulo Moreira, and Tales Alvarenga. 1996. "O Brasil está com rumo." *Veja,* Jan. 17.

Levitsky, Steven, and Lucan A. Way. 1998. "Between a Shock and a Hard Place: The Dynamics of Labor-Backed Adjustment in Poland and Argentina." *Comparative Politics* (Jan.): 171–92.

Ley 24.241: Sistema Integrado de Jubilaciones y Pensiones. 1993. Buenos Aires: YPF.

Lima, Maria, and Cristiane Jungblut. 1998. "Governo tentará salvar reforma." *O Globo,* May 8.

Lindeman, David, Michal Rutkowski, and Oleksiy Sluchynsky. 2001. "The Evolution of Pension Systems in Eastern Europe and Central Asia." A paper presented at the Private Pensions Conference, Ministry of Labour and Social Policy of Bulgaria, Apr.

Lipjhart, Arend. 1971. "Comparative Politics and the Comparative Method." *American Political Science Review* 65 (Sept.): 682–93.

———. 1975. "The Comparable-Cases Strategy in Comparative Research." *Comparative Political Studies* 8, no. 2 (July): 158–77.

López Angel, Carlos. 1996. "ISSSTE: La Reforma Pendiente." *El Cotidiano* (Sept.): 63–72.

López Villegas, Virginia. 1990. "En el periodo de la unidad nacional y de la segunda guerra mundial, 1940–1946." In *Historia de la CTM: 1936–1990,* vol. 1, ed. J. Aguilar García. Mexico City: UNAM.

Lora, Eduardo, and Carmen Pagés. 1996. "La legislación laboral en el proceso de reformas estructurales de América Latina y el Caribe." Washington, D.C.: Banco InterAmericano de Desarrollo—Oficina del Economista Jefe. (Dec.)

———. 2000. "Hacia un envejecimiento responsable: Las reformas de los sistemas pensionales en América Latina." *Working Paper* 433. Washington, D.C.: Banco InterAmericano de Desarrollo. (Oct.)

Loureiro, Maria Rita. 1997. "The Professional and Political Impacts of the Internationalization of Economics in Brazil." In *The Post-1945 Internationalization of Economics*, ed. A. W. Coats. Durham, N.C.: Duke University Press.

Lozano, Claudio. 1995. *Los niveles de sindicalización y la propuesta del CTA*. Buenos Aires: Instituto de Estudios sobre Estado y Participación.

Lustig, Nora. 1992. *Mexico: The Remaking of an Economy*. Washington, D.C.: Brookings Institution.

Madrid, Raúl L. 1997. "The Politics of Social Security Privatization." A paper delivered at the meeting of the Latin American Studies Association, Guadalajara, Mexico, Apr.

———. 1998. "The Determinants of Pension Reform around the World, 1992–97." A paper delivered at the meeting of the American Political Science Association, Boston, Mass., Sept.

———. 1999. "The New Logic of Social Security Reform: Politics and Pension Privatization in Latin America." Ph.D. dissertation, Stanford University.

———. 2002. "The Politics (and Economics) of Pension Privatization in Latin America." *Latin American Research Review* 37, no. 2: 159–82.

———. 2003. "Labouring Against Neoliberalism: Unions and Patterns of Reform in Latin America." *Journal of Latin American Studies* 35, no. 1: 53–88.

Mainwaring, Scott. 1991. "Politicians, Parties and Electoral Systems: Brazil in Comparative Perspective." *Comparative Politics* (Oct.): 21–43.

———. 1995. "Brazil: Weak Parties, Feckless Democracy." In *Building Democratic Institutions: Party Systems in Latin America*, ed. Scott Mainwaring and Timothy R. Scully. Stanford, Calif.: Stanford University Press.

———. 1997. "Multipartism, Robust Federalism and Presidentialism in Brazil." In *Presidentialism and Democracy in South America*, ed. Scott Mainwaring and Matthew Soberg Shugart. Cambridge: Cambridge University Press.

———. 1999. *Rethinking Party Systems in the Third Wave of Democratization: The Case of Brazil*. Stanford, Calif.: Stanford University Press.

Mainwaring, Scott, and Aníbal Pérez Liñán. 1996. "Party Discipline in Multiparty Systems: A Methodological Note and an Analysis of the Brazilian Constitutional Congress." Paper delivered at the annual meeting of the American Political Science Association, San Francisco, Calif., Aug.–Sept.

Mainwaring, Scott, and Timothy R. Scully, eds. 1995. *Building Democratic Institutions: Party Systems in Latin America*. Stanford, Calif.: Stanford University Press.

Mainwaring, Scott, and Matthew Soberg Shugart. 1997. "Conclusion: Presidentialism and the Party System." In *Presidentialism and Democracy in Latin America*, ed. Scott Mainwaring and Matthew Soberg Shugart. Cambridge: Cambridge University Press.

———, eds. 1997. *Presidentialism and Democracy in Latin America*. Cambridge: Cambridge University Press.

Mallet, Alfredo. 1970. "Diversification or Standardisation: Two Trends in Latin American Social Security." *International Labour Review* 101 (Jan.): 49–83.

Malloy, James. 1979. *The Politics of Social Security in Brazil*. Pittsburgh, Pa.: University of Pittsburgh Press.

———. 1985. "Statecraft and Social Security Policy in Crisis: A Comparison of

Latin America and the United States." In *The Crisis of Social Security and Health Care*, ed. Carmelo Mesa-Lago. Pittsburgh, Pa.: University of Pittsburgh Press.

————. 1989. "Policy Analysts, Public Policy and Regime Structure in Latin America." *Governance* 2: 315–38.

Manzetti, Luigi. 1999. *Privatization South American Style*. Oxford: Oxford University Press.

Marcussen, Martin. 2000. *Ideas and Elites: The Social Construction of the Economic and Monetary Union*. Aalborg, Denmark: Aalborg University Press.

Mares, Isabel. 1997. "Is Unemployment Insurable? Employers and the Introduction of Unemployment Insurance." *Journal of Public Policy* 17, no. 3: 299–327.

Markoff, John, and Verónica Montecinos. 1993. "The Ubiquitous Rise of Economists." *Journal of Public Policy* 13, no. 1: 37–68.

Maxfield, Sylvia. 1990. *Governing Capital*. Ithaca, N.Y.: Cornell University Press.

Maxfield, Sylvia, and Ricardo Anzaldúa, eds. 1987. *Government and Private Sector in Contemporary Mexico*. La Jolla, Calif.: Center for U.S.-Mexican Studies (University of California at San Diego).

McGreevey, William. 1990. "Social Security in Latin America: Issues and Options for the World Bank." *World Bank Discussion Paper* 110. Washington, D.C.: World Bank.

McGuire, James W. 1996. "Union Strength and Human Development in East Asia and Latin America." A paper delivered at the 92nd Annual Meeting of the American Political Science Association, San Francisco, Calif., Aug.–Sept.

————. 1997. *Peronism Without Perón: Unions, Parties and Democracy in Argentina*. Stanford, Calif.: Stanford University Press.

————. 1998. "Labor Strength and Human Development in Ninety-Three Countries." A paper prepared for delivery at the annual meeting of the American Political Science Association, Boston, Mass., Sept.

McNamara, Kathleen. 1998. *The Currency of Ideas: Monetary Politics in the European Union*. Ithaca, N.Y.: Cornell University Press.

Meireles, Andrei, and Sônia Filgueiras. 1996. "Os vilões do Real." *Istoé* 1391 (May 29).

Melo, Marcus André. 1997a. "O jogo das regras: A política da reforma constitucional de 1993/96." *Revista Brasileira das Ciências Sociais* 33, no. 12 (Feb.): 63–85.

————. 1997b. "Reformando a reforma: Interesses, atores e instituiçoes da seguridade social no Brasil." *São Paulo em Perspectiva* 11, no. 2.

————. 1998. "When Institutions Matter: The Politics of Administrative, Social Security, and Tax Reforms in Brazil." A paper delivered at the meeting of the Latin American Studies Association, Chicago, Ill., Sept.

Meneguello, Rachel. 1997. "Tendências políticas e eleitorais no Brasil: O papel dos partidos no período pós-85." A paper delivered at the meeting of the Latin American Studies Association, Guadalajara, Mexico, Apr. 17–19.

Mercado Lora, Marcelo. 1998. "La reforma del sistema de pensiones de la seguridad social." In *Las Reformas Estructurales en Bolivia*, ed. Juan Carlos Chávez Corrales. La Paz, Bolivia: Fundación Milenio.

Mesa del Diálogo Político. 1992. Buenos Aires. Mimeo.

Mesa-Lago, Carmelo. 1978. *Social Security in Latin America*. Pittsburgh, Pa.: University of Pittsburgh Press.

―――. 1989. *Ascent to Bankruptcy: Financing Social Security in Latin America.* Pittsburgh, Pa.: University of Pittsburgh Press.

―――. 1991a. "Portfolio Performance of Selected Social Security Institutes in Latin America." *World Bank Discussion Paper* 139. Washington, D.C.: World Bank.

―――. 1991b. "Social Security and Prospects for Equity in Latin America." *World Bank Discussion Paper* 140. Washington, D.C.: World Bank.

―――. 1994. *Changing Social Security in Latin America.* Boulder, Colo.: Lynne Rienner.

―――. 1996a. "Las reformas de pensiones de seguridad social en América Latina: Sistemas publicos, privados, mixtos y paralelos." *Estudios de la Seguridad Social* 80: 58–85.

―――. 1996b. "Las reformas de las pensiones en América Latina y la posición de los organismos internacionales." *Revista de la CEPAL* 60 (Dec.): 73–94.

―――. 1997a. "Análisis comparativo de reformas de pensiones estructurales en ocho países Latinoamericanos: Descripción, evaluación y lecciones." In *Capitalización: La Reforma Económica y Social de Bolivia,* ed. Margaret H. Pierce. La Paz: Ministerio de Capitalización de Bolivia.

―――. 1997b. "Social Welfare Reform in the Context of Economic-Political Liberalization: Latin American Cases." *World Development* 25, no. 4: 497–517.

―――. 1999. "Política y reforma de la seguridad social en América Latina." *Nueva Sociedad* 160: 133–50.

―――. 2000. "Estudio comparativo de los costos fiscales en la transición de ocho reformas de pensiones en América Latina." *Serie Financiamento del Desarrollo* 93. Santiago de Chile: CEPAL. (Mar.)

―――. 2001. "Structural Reform of Social Security Pensions in Latin America: Models, Characteristics, Results and Conclusions." *International Social Security Review* 54, no. 4: 67–92.

Mesa-Lago, Carmelo, and Alberto Arenas de Mesa. 1998. "The Chilean Pension System: Evaluation, Lessons and Challenges." In *Do Options Exist? The Reform of Pension and Health Care in Latin America,* ed. María Amparo Cruz-Saco and Carmelo Mesa-Lago. Pittsburgh, Pa.: University of Pittsburgh Press.

Mesa-Lago, Carmelo, and Fabio Bertranou. 1998. *Manual de Economía de la Seguridad Social.* Montevideo, Uruguay: Centro Latinoamericano de la Economía Humana.

Mesa-Lago, Carmelo, and Katharina Müller. 2002. "The Politics of Pension Reform in Latin America." *Journal of Latin American Studies* 34 (Aug.): 687–715.

Meyer, John. 1994. "The Changing Cultural Content of the Nation-State: A World Society Perspective." Dept. of Sociology, Stanford University. Mimeo.

Meyer, John, Francisco Ramírez, and Yasemin Soysal. 1992. "World Expansion of Mass Education, 1870–1980." *Sociology of Education* 65, no. 2: 128–49.

Middlebrook, Kevin J. 1991. "State-Labor Relations in Mexico." In *Unions, Workers, and the State in Mexico,* ed. Middlebrook. La Jolla, Calif.: Center for U.S.-Mexican Studies (University of California at San Diego).

―――. 1995. *The Paradox of Revolution.* Baltimore, Md.: Johns Hopkins University Press.

Millán, René. 1988. *Los Empresarios Mexicanos ante el Estado y la Sociedad.* Mexico City: UNAM.

Ministério da Previdência e Assistência Social (MPAS). 1997. *Livro Branco da Previdência Social: Versão Simplificada.* Brasília: MPAS.
Ministerio de Economía y Obras Públicas de la República Argentina. 1992. "Acuerdo de facilidades ampliadas República Argentina—Fondo monetario internacional: memoranda de política económica." Buenos Aires: Ministerio de Economía. (Mar.)
———. 1993. *Argentina: A Growing Nation.* Buenos Aires: Ministerio de Economía.
———. 1994. *Argentina: A Country for Investment and Growth.* Buenos Aires: Ministerio de Economía.
"Ministérios não renderam votos." 1996. *Veja,* May 29.
"El ministro de trabajo dijo que la reforma previsional es prioritaria." 1993. *La Nación,* Jan. 29.
Mintrom, Michael, and Sandra Vergari. 1998. "Policy Networks and Innovation Diffusion: The Case of State Education Reforms." *The Journal of Politics* 60, no. 1 (Feb.): 126–48.
Montecinos, Verónica. 1988. "Economics and Power: Chilean Economists in Government, 1958–1985." Ph.D. Dissertation, University of Pittsburgh.
Montesinos, Rafael. 1992. "Empresarios en el nuevo orden estatal." *El Cotidiano* 50 (Sept.–Oct.): 108–14.
Mooney, Christopher. 2001. "Modeling Regional Effects on State Policy Diffusion." *Political Research Quarterly* 54, no. 1 (Mar.): 103–24.
Mora y Araujo, Manuel. 1991. "El cuadro político y electoral Argentino." In *Reforma Institucional y Cambio Político,* ed. Dieter Nohlen and Liliana de Riz. Buenos Aires: Editorial Legasa/CEDES.
Mora y Araujo, Noguera, et al. 1994. "Informe mensual de opinion publica: Indicadores cuantitativos." June.
Morandé, F. 1996. "Savings in Chile: What Went Right?" *Inter-American Development Bank Working Paper Series* 322. Washington, D.C.: Inter-American Development Bank.
Mosley, Paul, Jane Harrigan, and John Toye. 1991. *Aid and Power: The World Bank and Policy-based Lending.* London: Routledge.
"Movilización contra la reforma previsional." 1993. *La Nación.* Mar. 11.
Movimento Unificador Nacional de Jubilados y Pensionados (MUNJP). 1995. "Por la defensa y desarrollo de la seguridad social mexicana." In Cámara de Diputados, *Foro: Beneficios, Costos y Financiamento de la Seguridad Social.* Mexico City: Cámara de Diputados. (July.)
Müller, Katharina. 1999. *The Political Economy of Pension Reform in Central-Eastern Europe.* Northampton, Mass.: Edward Elgar.
———. 2002. "Privatising Old-Age Security: Latin America and Eastern Europe Compared." Research Report. Frankfurt Institute for Transformation Studies, Frankfurt, Germany. Mar.
Muñoz, Nefer. 2000. "Economy-Costa Rica: Mixed Pensions System to Invigorate Economy." Interpress Service, Feb. 14.
Murillo, M. Victoria. 2000. "From Populism to Neoliberalism: Labor Unions and Market Reforms in Latin America." *World Politics* 52, no. 2 (Jan.): 135–74.

————. 2001. *Labor Unions, Partisan Coalitions and Market Reforms in Latin America.* Cambridge: Cambridge University Press.

Mustapic, Ana María, and Matteo Goretti. 1992. "Gobierno y oposición en el congreso: La práctica de la cohabitación durante la presidencia de Alfonsín (1983–1989)." *Desarrollo Económico* 32: 251–69.

Myles, John, and Paul Pierson. 2001. "The Comparative Political Economy of Pension Reform." In *The New Politics of the Welfare State*, ed. Paul Pierson. Oxford: Oxford University Press.

Nacif, Benito. 1996. "Political Careers, Political Ambitions and Career Goals." *Documento de Trabajo* 51. Mexico City: División de Estudios Políticos, Centro de Investigación y Docencia Económicas.

Nacional Financiera. 1995. *La Economía Mexicana en Cifras.* Mexico: Nacional Financiera.

Naím, Moisés. 1995. "Latin America: The Second Stage of Reform." In *Economic Reform and Democracy*, ed. Larry Diamond and Marc F. Plattner. Baltimore, Md.: Johns Hopkins University Press.

Nelson, Joan M. 1994. *Intricate Links: Democratization and Market Reforms in Latin America and Eastern Europe.* New Brunswick, N.J.: Transaction Books.

————. 1995. "Linkages Between Politics and Economics." In *Economic Reform and Democracy*, ed. Larry Diamond and Marc F. Plattner. Baltimore, Md.: Johns Hopkins University Press.

————. 1998. "The Political Economy of Colombia's Health Reforms of 1993." Washington, D.C.: Overseas Development Council. Mimeo. (June 26.)

————. 2001. "The Politics of Pension and Health Care Reforms in Hungary and Poland." In *Reforming the State*, ed. János Kornai, Stephan Haggard, and Robert R. Kaufman. Cambridge: Cambridge University Press.

Nelson, Joan M., ed. 1990. *Economic Crisis and Policy Choice: The Politics of Adjustment in the Third World.* Princeton, N.J.: Princeton University Press.

Neto, Octavio Amorim, and Fabiano G. M. Santos. 1997. "The Executive Connection: Explaining the Puzzles of Party Cohesion in Brazil." A paper prepared for delivery at the meeting of the Latin American Studies Association, Guadalajara, Mexico, Apr.

Neves, Javier. 1994. "El Fondo de la Cuestión." *Quehacer* 89 (May–June): 16–19.

Nicolau, Jairo Marconi. 1996. *Multipartidarismo e democracia: Um estudo sobre o sistema partidário brasileiro (1985–94).* Rio de Janeiro: Fundação Getulio Vargas.

Noriega, Carlos. 1997. "Ahorro doméstico y la reforma al sistema de pensiones en México." *Gaceta de Economía* 2, no. 4 (spring): 125–42.

Nun, José. 1994. "Populismo, representación y menemismo." *Sociedad* no. 5 (Oct.): 93–121.

O'Donnell, Guillermo. 1973. *Modernization and Bureaucratic Authoritarianism.* Berkeley: Institute for International Studies, University of California at Berkeley.

————. 1994. "Delegative Democracy." *Journal of Democracy* 5, no. 1 (Jan.): 55–69.

Olcott, Martha Brill. 1997. "Kazakhstan: Nursultan Nazarbaev as Strong President." In *Post-Communist Presidents*, ed. Ray Taras. Cambridge: Cambridge University Press.

"The Oldest, Biggest Private System." 1997. *Latin America Special Report*, June.

Oliveira, Franciso Barreto de, Kaizô Iwakami Beltrão, and André Cezar Medici. 1994. "Financing Social Security in Brazil." In *Social Security Systems in Latin America*, ed. Oliveira. Washington, D.C.: Inter-American Development Bank.

"Opinión contraria de diputados opositores." 1992. *La Nación*, June 20.

Orenstein, Mitchell A. 1999. "How Politics and Institutions Affect Pension Reform in Three Post-Communist Countries." *World Bank Policy Research Working Paper*. Washington, D.C.: World Bank.

Organization for Economic Cooperation and Development (OECD). 1996. *International Capital Markets Statistics, 1950–1995*. Paris: OECD.

Orszag, Peter R., and Joseph E. Stiglitz. 2001. "Rethinking Pension Reform: Ten Myths About Social Security Systems." In *New Ideas about Old Age Security*, ed. Robert Holzmann and Joseph E. Stiglitz. Washington, D.C.: World Bank.

Ortiz de Zevallos, Gabriel, Hugo Eyzaguirre, Rosa María Palacios, and Pierina Pollarolo. 1999. "La economía política de las reformas institucionales en el Peru: Los casos de educación, salud y pensiones." *Inter-American Development Bank, Office of the Chief Economist, Latin American Research Network, Working Paper R-348*, Mar.

Otaegui, Javier. 1993. "La mayoria quiere elegir." *Fondos de Pension*, July.

"Otra denuncia de soborno en Diputados." 1993. *Página 12*, Apr. 14.

Packenham, Robert. 1992. "The Politics of Economic Liberalization: Argentina and Brazil in Comparative Perspective." A paper delivered at the annual meeting of the American Political Science Association, Chicago, Ill., Sept.

Palacios, Robert, and Montserrat Pallarès-Miralles. 2000. "International Patterns of Pension Provision." Washington, D.C.: World Bank. Mimeo. URL: http://www.worldbank.org/pensions.

Palacios, Robert, and Roberto Rocha. 1998. "The Hungarian Pension System in Transition." *World Bank Social Protection Discussion Paper 9805*. Washington, D.C.: World Bank. (Mar.)

Papadópulos, Jorge. 1992. *Seguridad Social y Política en el Uruguay*. Montevideo, Uruguay: CIESU.

"Para el gobierno, la decisión cegetista es un adelanto político." 1992. *La Nación*, July 18.

Pei, Minxin. 1995. "The Puzzle of East Asian Exceptionalism." In *Economic Reform and Democracy*, ed. Larry Diamond and Marc F. Plattner. Baltimore, Md.: Johns Hopkins University Press.

"Peligro de crisis recurrente, si no se fortalece el ahorro interno: Zedillo." 1996. *La Jornada*, Apr. 10.

"Pensions Privatization Is Rushed Through—But Critics Object." 1997. *El Salvador—Economist Intelligence Unit Country Report*. 1st quarter.

Pérez, Martín. 2000. "Circuito político de una política pública: Reforma al sistema de pensiones en Bolivia." Centro Boliviano de Estudios Multidisciplinarios, La Paz, Bolivia. Mimeo. URL: http://www.cebem.com/centdocum/ensayos/ma-circuito.htm

Pierson, Paul. 1994. *Dismantling the Welfare State?* New York: Cambridge University Press.

———. 1996. "The New Politics of the Welfare State." *World Politics* 48 (Jan.): 143–79.

———. 2000. "Three Worlds of Welfare State Research." *Comparative Political Studies* 33, nos. 6–7 (Aug.–Sept.): 791–821.

———. 2001. "Post-Industrial Pressures on the Mature Welfare States." In *The New Politics of the Welfare State*, ed. Paul Pierson. Oxford: Oxford University Press.

Piñera Echenique, José. 1991. *El Cascabel al Gato: La Batalla por la Reforma Previsional.* Santiago de Chile: Zig-Zag.

Pinheiro, Liliana. 1997. "Força Sindical vai propor sistema misto de previdência." *O Estado de São Paulo*, Mar. 7.

Pinheiro, Vinícius C. 2000. "A Política da Reforma da Previdência no Brasil." Paper delivered at the Woodrow Wilson Center Conference on Learning from Foreign Models in Latin American Policy Reform, Washington, D.C. Sept. Forthcoming in *Learning from Foreign Models in Latin American Policy Reform*, ed. Kurt Weyland. Washington, D.C.: Woodrow Wilson Center, Johns Hopkins University Press.

Plenario Permanente de Organizaciones de Jubilados. 1992. "Criticas al proyecto de ley del poder ejecutive nacional." Buenos Aires. Mimeo.

Posadas, Laura. 1994. "El nuevo sistema de jubilaciones y pensiones y el deficit previsional publico." *Estudios* (Jan.–Mar.): 41–59.

Pozas Horcasitas, Ricardo. 1990. "De lo duro a lo seguro: La fundación del seguro social mexicano." In *Entre la Guerra y la Estabilidad Política*, ed. R. Loyola, 109–35. Mexico City: Grijalbo.

"O presidente riu por último." 1996. *Istoé* 1382, Mar. 27.

"Problemas pessoais influíram na derrota na votação do redutor." 1998. *O Globo*, June 19.

"Projeto é inaceitável, diz CUT." 1996. *Folha de São Paulo*, Mar. 8.

"Proposición de la Cámara de Comercio de Caracas." 1989. Rpt., *El Universal*, Feb. 12, 1995.

"Propuesta obrero-empresarial de alianza para el fortalecimiento y modernización de la seguridad social." 1995. *Proceso* 992, Nov. 6.

Proyecto Aguila. 1995. Apr. 25.

"Un proyecto consensuado va camino del congreso." 1992. *La Nación*, Nov. 27.

Proyecto de Ley—"Ley de Proteccion al Trabajador"—Exposición de Motivos. 1999. Gobierno de Costa Rica. Aug. URL: http://www.nacion.co.cr/ln_ee/Especiales/pensiones/leypro1.html

Przeworski, Adam, and Fernando Limongi. 1993. "Political Regimes and Economic Growth." *Journal of Economic Perspectives* 7, no. 3: 51–69.

———. 1997. "Modernization: Theories and Facts." *World Politics* 49 (Jan.): 155–83.

Puga, Cristina. 1993. *Mexico: Empresarios y Poder.* Mexico City: UNAM.

"Qué se dijo." 1992. *Expansión.* Feb. 5.

Queisser, Monika. 1998. "The Second-Generation Pension Reforms in Latin America." *Working Paper* AWP 5.4. Paris: OECD.

———. 2000. "Pension Reform and International Organizations: From Conflict to Convergence." *International Social Security Review* 53, no. 2: 31–45.

"Reforma da previdência social: Nota oficial conjunta." 1996. Brasília, Jan. 18. Mimeo.

"La reforma de la seguridad social quedó aprobada en el parlamento." 1995. *El País*. Aug. 24.

Remmer, Karen L. 1986. "The Politics of Economic Stabilization: IMF Standby Programs in Latin America." *Comparative Politics* (Oct.).

————. 1990. "Democracy and Economic Crisis: The Latin American Experience." *World Politics* 42, no. 3 (Apr.): 315–35.

————. 1998. "The Politics of Neoliberal Economic Reform in South America, 1980–1994." *Studies in Comparative International Development* 33, no. 2 (summer): 3–29.

"Reparos legislativos a la reforma previsional." 1992. *La Nación*, June 6.

Reyes del Campillo, Juan. 1990. "El movimiento obrero en la cámara de diputados (1979–1988)." *Revista Mexicana de Sociología* (Mar.): 139–60.

Rhodes, Martin. 2001. "The Political Economy of Social Pacts: 'Competitive Corporatism' and European Welfare Reform." In *The New Politics of the Welfare State*, ed. Paul Pierson. Oxford: Oxford University Press.

Rivera Ríos, Miguel. 1992. "La práctica del liberalismo social." *Economía Informa* (July): 22–24.

Roberts, Kenneth M., and Erik Wibbels. 2000. "The Politics of Economic Crisis and Policy Change in Latin America." Paper prepared for delivery at the annual meeting of the American Political Science Association, Washington, D.C., Aug.–Sept.

Rock, David. 1987. *Argentina, 1516–1987*. Berkeley and Los Angeles: University of California Press.

Rodrik, Dani. 1996. "Understanding Economic Policy Reform." *The Journal of Economic Literature* 34 (Mar.): 9–41.

Rofman, Rafael, and Hugo Bertín. 1996. "Lessons from Pension Reform: The Argentine Case." A paper delivered at the World Bank Conference "Pension Systems: From Crisis to Reform," Washington, D.C., Nov.

Rogers, Everett M. 1995. *The Diffusion of Innovations*. 4th ed. New York: The Free Press.

Roggero, Mario. 1993. *Escoja Usted*. Lima.

————. 1997. "Peru." In *La Revolución LatinoAmericano de las Pensiones*, ed. José Piñera. Santiago de Chile: International Center for Pension Privatization. Mimeo.

Romero, Ismael, and Elena Gallegos. 1995. "La iniciativa de reformas a la ley del IMSS divide a diputados." *La Jornada*, Nov. 23.

Rosenberg, Mark B. 1979. "Social Security Policymaking in Costa Rica: A Research Report." *Latin American Research Review* 14, no. 1: 116–34.

Rosenberg, Mark B., and James M. Malloy. 1978. "Indirect Participation versus Social Equity in the Evolution of Latin American Social Security Policy." In *Political Participation in Latin America: Citizen and State*, ed. John Booth and Mitchell Seligson. New York: Holmes and Meier.

Ross, Stanford G. 2000. "Doctrine and Practice in Social Security Pension Reform." *International Social Security Review* 53, no. 2: 3–29.

Sáenz Garza, Miguel Angel. 1996. "La reforma a la seguridad social mexicana, cambios a la iniciativa presidencial." *El Cotidiano* (Sept.): 53–62.

Sales, Carlos, Fernando Solís, and Alejandro Villagómez. 1998. "Pension System Reform: The Mexican Case." In *Privatizing Social Security*, ed. Martin Feldstein. Chicago: University of Chicago Press.

Samstad, James G. 1995. "Labor and Corporatism under Mexican Neoliberalism." Paper delivered at the meeting of the Latin American Studies Association, Washington, D.C., Sept.

Samuels, David J. 1996. "Legislative Lilliputians? Towards a Theory of Party Cohesion in the Brazilian Chamber of Deputies." Paper delivered at the annual meeting of the American Political Science Association, San Francisco, Calif., Aug.–Sept.

———. 1998. "Careerism and its Consequences: Federalism, Elections, and Policymaking in Brazil." Ph.D. dissertation. University of California at San Diego.

Sánchez Vargas, Gustavo. 1963. *Orígenes y Evolución de la Seguridad Social en México.* Mexico City: UNAM.

Santamaría, Marco. 1992. "Privatizing Social Security: The Chilean Case." *Columbia Journal of World Business* (spring): 39–51.

Santos, Juan Manuel. 1997. "Colombia." In *La Revolución Latinoamericana de las Pensiones*, ed. José Piñera. Santiago de Chile: International Center for Pension Privatization. Mimeo.

Sartori, Giovanni. 1970. "Concept Misformation in Comparative Politics." *American Political Science Review* 64, no. 4: 1033–53.

Scherman, K. G. 2000. "A New Social Security Reform Consensus? The ISSA's Stockholm Initiative." *International Social Security Review* 53, no. 1: 65–82.

Schmidt-Hebbel, Klaus. 1995. "Colombia's Pension Reform: Fiscal and Macroeconomic Effects." *World Bank Discussion Papers* 314. Washington, D.C.: World Bank.

Schneider, Ben Ross. 1998a. "The Material Bases of Technocracy: Investor Confidence and Neoliberalism in Latin America." In *The Politics of Expertise in Latin America*, ed. Miguel A. Centeno and Patricio Silva. New York: St. Martin's Press.

———. 1998b. "The State and Collective Action: Business Politics in Latin America." Paper prepared for delivery at the annual meeting of the Latin American Studies Association, Chicago, Ill. Sept.

Schulthess, Walter. 1990. *Sistema Nacional de Previsión Social: Su Evolución y Situación a fines de la Década del Ochenta.* Buenos Aires: Programa Nacional de Asistencia Técnica para la Administración de los Servicios Sociales en la Argentina (PRONATASS).

———. 1991. "El sistema previsional en la Argentina." Speech delivered to the 7th convention of the Association of Argentine Banks (ADEBA). Document 10, Buenos Aires: Asociación de Bancos Argentinos (ADEBA). (Aug.)

———. 1992. "El sistema de seguridad social en la Argentina." Speech delivered to the Fundación Omega Seguros, Buenos Aires, Oct. 17, 1991. Rpt., *Conferencias.* Buenos Aires: Fundación Omega Seguros.

———. 1994a. "Antecedentes y fundamentos del anteproyecto de ley de solidaridad previsional." *Previsión Social* 16 (Oct.–Dec.): 1–22.

———. 1994b. "El desafío del Siglo XXI: Innovar y adaptar los sistemas de seguridad social a los cambios económicos sociales y demográficos en las Américas." In *Innovar y Adaptar la Seguridad Social en las Américas.* Geneva: Asociación de la Seguridad Social.

Schulthess, Walter, and Gustavo Demarco. 1993. *Argentina: Evolución del Sistema Nacional de Previsión Social y Propuesta de Reforma.* Santiago de Chile: CEPAL/PNUD.

Schwarz, Anita M., and Asli Demirgüç-Kunt. 1999. "Taking Stock of Pension Reforms around the World—An Update." Washington, D.C.: World Bank. Mimeo. URL: http://www.worldbank.org/pensions

"Se eliminó la supergarantía del Banco Nación." 1994. *La Nación,* May 4.

Secretaría de Estado de Trabajo. 2001. "Ley no. 87–01 que crea el sistema dominicano de seguridad social." Santo Domingo: Secretaría de Estado de Trabajo. (May 9.)

Secretaría de la Honorable Cámara de Diputados de la Nación. 1993. *Cámara de Diputados de la Nación: Su Composición y Comisiones.* Buenos Aires: Cámara de Diputados.

Senado (Mexico). 1995. *Diario de los Debates* 30, no. 12 (Dec.).

"Senado votó en general reform previsional." 1995. *El País,* Aug. 4.

"Las 62 se alejan del gobierno." 1993. *La Nación,* Mar. 6.

Shalev, Michael. 1983. "The Social Democratic Model and Beyond." *Comparative Social Research* 6: 315–51.

Sheahan, John. 1980. "Market Oriented Economic Policies and Political Repression in Latin America." *Economic Development and Cultural Change* 28, no. 2: 267–91.

Sheridan, Mary Beth. 1996. "Mexico Completes Sweeping Overhaul of Social Security." *Los Angeles Times,* Apr. 26.

Siegel, Richard L., and Leonard B. Weinberg. 1977. *Comparing Public Policy: United States, Soviet Union and Europe.* Homewood, Ill.: Dorsey Press.

Sikkink, Kathryn. 1991. *Ideas and Institutions: Developmentalism in Brazil and Argentina.* Ithaca, N.Y.: Cornell University Press.

Silva, Patricio. 1991. "Technocrats and Politics in Chile: From the Chicago Boys to the CIEPLAN Monks." *Journal of Latin American Studies* 23, no. 2: 385–410.

Simmons, Beth, and Zachary Elkins. 2001. "Globalization and Policy Diffusion: Explaining Three Decades of Liberalization." Paper delivered at the meeting of the American Political Science Association, San Francisco, Calif., Aug.–Sept.

Smith, William C. 1990. "Democracy, Distributional Conflicts and Macroeconomic Policymaking in Argentina." *Journal of Interamerican Studies and World Affairs* 32, no. 2 (summer) 1990: 1–42.

———. 1991. *Authoritarianism and the Crisis of the Argentine Political Economy.* Stanford, Calif.: Stanford University Press.

Smith, William C., Carlos H. Acuña, and Eduardo A. Gamarra, eds. 1994. *Latin American Political Economy in the Age of Neoliberal Reform.* New Brunswick, N.J.: Transaction Publishers.

Soares, Lucila. 1999. "É tudo ou nada." *Veja,* Oct. 20.

Solís, Fernando, and Alejandro Villagómez. 1996. "Domestic Savings in Mexico and Pension Reform." *Documento de Trabajo* 66. División de Economía, Centro de Investigación y Docencia Económicas. Mexico City.

———. 1999. "Las pensiones." In *La Seguridad Social en México,* ed. Fernando Solís and Alejandro Villagómez. Mexico City: CIDE.

Soto, Carlos Jorge. 1992. "El sistema mexicano de pensiones." In *Sistema de Pensiones en América Latina*, vol. 2, ed. Andras Uthoff and Raquel Szalachman. Santiago de Chile: CEPAL.

Spalding, Rose J. 1980. "Welfare Policymaking: Theoretical Implications of a Mexican Case Study." *Comparative Politics* (July): 419–38.

Srinivas, P. S., E. Whitehouse, and J. Yermo. 2000. "Regulating Private Pension Funds, Structure, Performance and Investments: Cross-country Evidence." *Social Protection Discussion Paper*. Washington, D.C.: World Bank. URL: http://www .worldbank.org/pensions

Stallings, Barbara. 1992. "International Influence on Economic Policy: Debt, Stabilization, and Structural Reform." In *The Politics of Economic Adjustment*, ed. Stephan Haggard and Robert R. Kaufman. Princeton, N.J.: Princeton University Press.

"Stephanes tentou substituir membros do PFL na Comissão." 1995. *Jornal do Aposentado*, Oct. 1–15.

Stephens, John D. 1979. *The Transition from Capitalism to Socialism*. Champaign-Urbana: University of Illinois Press.

Story, Dale. 1986. *The Mexican Ruling Party: Stability and Authority*. New York: Praeger Publishers.

Strang, David, and Patricia Mei Yin Chang. 1993. "The International Labor Organization and the Welfare State: Institutional Effects on National Welfare Spending 1960–80." *International Organization* 47, no. 2 (spring): 235–62.

Suárez Dávila, Francisco. 1996. "La reforma mexicana de los sistemas de ahorro para el retiro: Perspectiva de un legislador." *Comercio Exterior* 46, no. 9 (Sept.): 725–29.

Suassuna, Luciano, and Eumano Silva. 1995. "Sai dessa, Presidente." *Istoé* 1330, Mar. 29.

"Susto na largada." 1995. *Veja*, Mar. 29.

Tarrow, Sidney. 1995. "Bridging the Quantitative-Qualitative Divide in Political Science." *American Political Science Review* 89, no. 2: 471–74.

Teichman, Judith. 1995. *Privatization and Political Change in Mexico*. Pittsburgh, Pa.: University of Pittsburgh Press.

———. 2001. *The Politics of Freeing Markets in Latin America: Chile, Argentina, and Mexico*. Chapel Hill: University of North Carolina Press.

Thacker, Strom. 2000. *Big Business, the State, and Free Trade*. Cambridge: Cambridge University Press.

Thompson, Lawrence. 1998. *Older and Wiser: The Economics of Public Pensions*. Washington, D.C.: Urban Institute.

Thullen, Peter. 1985. "The Financing of Social Security Pensions: Principles, Current Issues and Trends." In *The Crisis of Social Security and Health Care*, ed. Carmelo Mesa-Lago. Pittsburgh, Pa.: University of Pittsburgh Press.

Tirado, Ricardo, and Matilde Luna. 1995. "El consejo coordinador empresarial de México. De la unidad contra el reformismo a la unidad para el TLC (1975–1993)." *Revista Mexicana de Sociología* 4: 27–59.

Tommasi, Mariano, and Andrés Velasco. 1995. "Where Are We in the Political Economy of Reform?" A paper presented at the Conference on Economic Reform in Developing and Transitional Economies, Columbia University, May.

Torre, Juan Carlos, and Pablo Gerchunoff. 1999. "La economía política de las reformas institucionales en Argentina." Inter-American Development Bank, Office of the Chief Economist, Latin American Research Network. *Working Paper* R-349. Mar.

"Los trabajadores elegirán libremente su obra social." 1993. *La Nación*, Jan. 8.

Tsebelis, George. 1995. "Decision Making in Political Systems: Comparison of Presidentialism, Parliamentarism, Multicameralism, and Multipartism." *British Journal of Political Science* 25, no. 3 (July): 289–325.

Ulloa Padilla, Odilia. 1996a. "Enfoque liberal de la seguridad social en México." *Economía Informa* 245 (Mar.): 37–46.

———. 1996b. "Nueva ley del seguro social: La reforma previsional de fin de siglo." *El Cotidiano* 78 (Sept.): 27–52.

Unión Cívica Radical (UCR). 1992. *Documento de la Comisión de Previsión Social del Comité Nacional de la Unión Cívica Radical.* Buenos Aires: UCR. (Apr.)

Unión Industrial Argentina. 1990. "Comentario al proyecto de reforma al sistema previsional elaborado por la subsecretaria de seguridad social." Mimeo.

———. 1992. *Propuesta de Régimen Jubilatorio.* Mimeo.

United Nations (UN). 1995. *World Population Prospects—1994.* New York: UN.

United Nations—Economic Commission for Latin America and the Caribbean (UN-ECLAC). 1968. *Economic Bulletin for Latin America* 13, no. 2 (Nov.).

———. 1994. *Economic Survey of Latin America and the Caribbean 1994.* Santiago de Chile: UN-ECLAC.

———. 1995. *La Inversión Extranjera en América Latina y el Caribe.* Santiago de Chile: UN-ECLAC.

Uribe Vélez, Alvaro. 1993. "Solidaridad . . . es seguridad." *Estrategia* (Aug.).

Usui, Chikako. 1987. "The Origin and the Development of Modern Welfare States: A Study of Societal Forces and World Influences on the Adoption of Social Insurance Policies Among Sixty-three Countries, 1880–1976." Ph.D. dissertation, Stanford University.

———. 1994. "Welfare State Development in a World System Context." In *The Comparative Political Economy of the Welfare State*, ed. Thomas Janoski and Alexander M. Hicks. Cambridge: Cambridge University Press.

Valdés, Juan Gabriel. 1995. *Pinochet's Economists.* Cambridge: Cambridge University Press.

Valdés Ugalde, Franciso. 1994. "From Bank Nationalization to State Reform: Business and the New Mexican Order." In *The Politics of Economic Restructuring: State-Society Relations and Regime Change in Mexico*, ed. María Lorena Cook et al. La Jolla, Calif.: Center for U.S.-Mexican Studies (University of California at San Diego).

Veja. 1996. Jan. 3.

"La verdad sobre una renuncia." 1991. *Jubilados* 58 (Feb.).

Walker, Jack L. 1969. "The Diffusion of Innovations Among the American States." *American Political Science Review* 63 (Sept.): 880–99.

———. 1981. "The Diffusion of Knowledge, Policy Communities and Agenda Setting: The Relationship of Knowledge and Power." In *New Strategic Perspectives on Social Policy*, ed. John E. Tropman et al. New York: Pergamon Press.

Waterbury, John. 1992. "The Heart of the Matter? Public Enterprise and the Adjustment Process." In *The Politics of Economic Adjustment*, ed. Stephan Haggard and Robert R. Kaufman. Princeton, N.J.: Princeton University Press.

Weldon, Jeffrey. 1997. "Political Sources of Presidencialismo en Mexico." In *Presidentialism and Democracy in Latin America*, ed. Scott Mainwaring and Matthew Soberg Shugart. Cambridge: Cambridge University Press.

Weyland, Kurt. 1996a. *Democracy Without Equity: Failures of Reform in Brazil*. Pittsburgh, Pa.: University of Pittsburgh Press.

————. 1996b. "How Much Political Power do Economic Forces Have? Conflicts Over Social Insurance Reform in Brazil." *Journal of Public Policy* 16, no. 1: 59–84.

————. 1998. "The Fate of Market-Oriented Reform in Latin America, Africa, and Eastern Europe." *International Studies Quarterly* 42, no. 4 (Dec.): 645–74.

————. 2001. "Learning from Foreign Models in Latin American Policy Reform." Paper delivered at the Southern Political Science Association Meeting, Atlanta, Ga., Nov.

————. 2002. *The Politics of Market Reform in Fragile Democracies: Argentina, Brazil, Peru, and Venezuela*. Princeton, N.J.: Princeton University Press.

Wilensky, Harold. 1975. *The Welfare State and Equality: Structural and Ideological Roots of Public Expenditures*. Berkeley and Los Angeles: University of California Press.

Williamson, John B. 1990. *The Progress of Policy Reform in Latin America*. Washington, D.C.: Institute for International Economics.

————, ed. 1994. *The Political Economy of Policy Reform*. Washington, D.C.: Institute for International Economics.

Williamson, John B., and Stephan Haggard. 1994. "The Political Conditions for Economic Reform." In *The Political Economy of Policy Reform*, ed. John Williamson. Washington, D.C.: Institute for International Economics.

Williamson, John B., and Fred C. Pampel. 1993. *Old-Age Security in Comparative Perspective*. New York: Oxford University Press.

Wood, Stewart. 2001. "Labour Market Regimes under Threat? Sources of Continuity in Germany, Britain, and Sweden." In *The New Politics of the Welfare State*, ed. Paul Pierson. Oxford: Oxford University Press.

World Bank. 1989. *World Debt Tables*. Washington, D.C.: World Bank.

————. 1990. *Mexico: Contractual Savings Report*. Washington, D.C.: World Bank.

————. 1993. *Argentina: from Insolvency to Growth*. Washington, D.C.: World Bank.

————. 1994a. *Argentina Capital Markets Study*, Report 12963–AR. Washington, D.C.: World Bank.

————. 1994b. *Averting the Old Age Crisis*. New York: Oxford University Press.

————. 1995a. *Brazil: Social Insurance and Private Pensions*. Report 12336-BR. Washington, D.C.: World Bank.

————. 1995b. "Technical Annex—Bolivia—Financial Markets and Pension Reform Technical Assistance Project." Report number: T-6412-BO. Washington, D.C.: World Bank.

————. 1995c. *World Tables*. Washington, D.C.: World Bank.

————. 1997. *World Development Indicators*. Washington, D.C.: World Bank.

————. 2000. *World Development Indicators*. Washington, D.C.: World Bank.

"World Bank Research in the Marketplace of Ideas." 1996. *World Bank Policy and Research Bulletin* (Jan.–Mar.): 1–4.

Zapata, Francisco. 1995. *El Sindicalismo Mexicano Frente a la Restructuración.* Mexico City: El Colegio de México.

Zazueta, César, and Ricardo de la Peña. 1984. *La Estructura del Congreso del Trabajo.* Mexico City: Fondo de Cultura Económica.

Zertuche Muñoz, Fernando, ed. 1980. *Historia del Instituto Mexicano del Seguro Social: Los Primeros Años, 1943–1944.* Mexico City: IMSS.